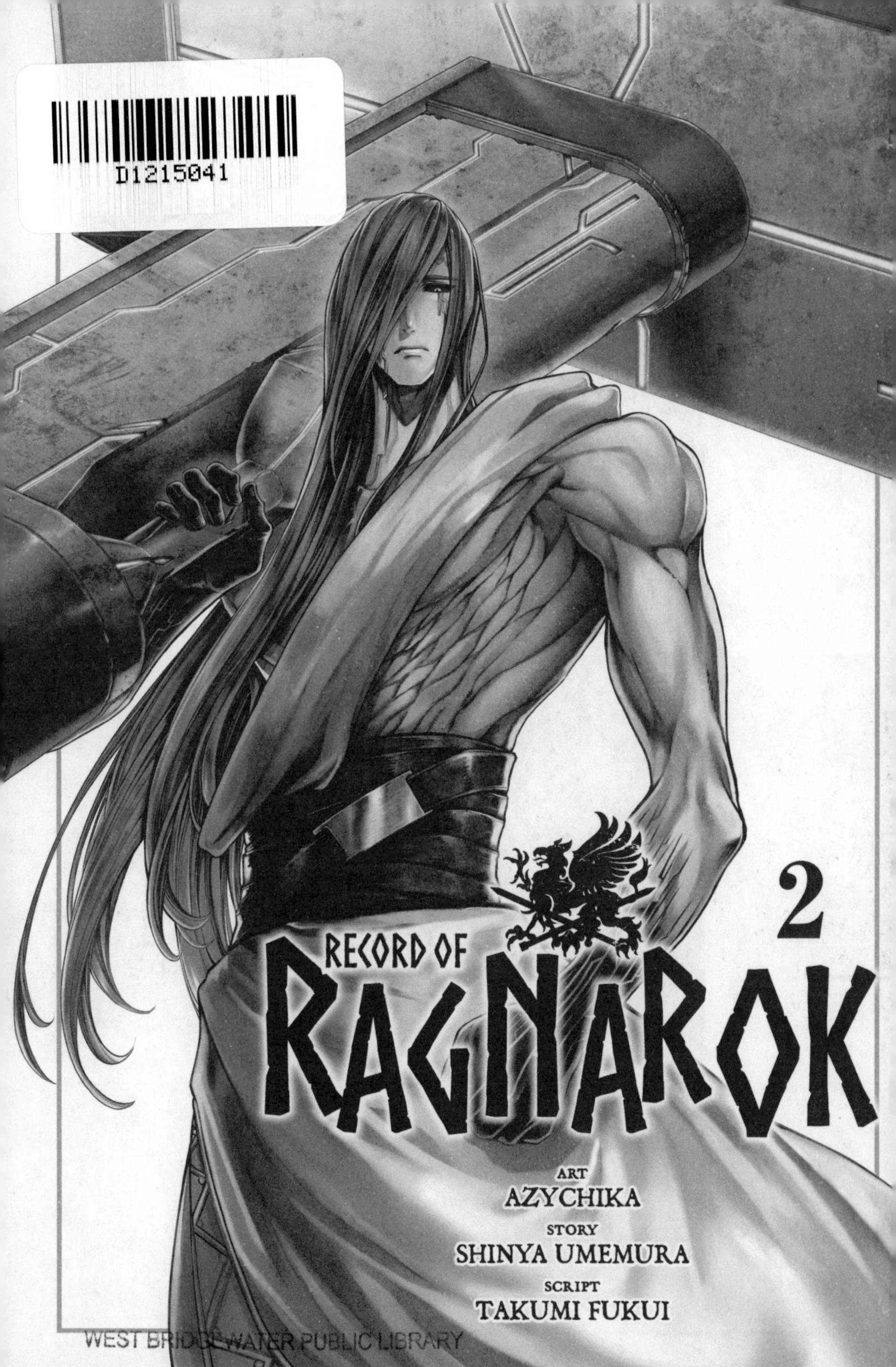
2
RECORD OF
RAGNAROK
ART
AZYCHIKA
STORY
SHINYA UMEMURA
SCRIPT
TAKUMI FUKUI

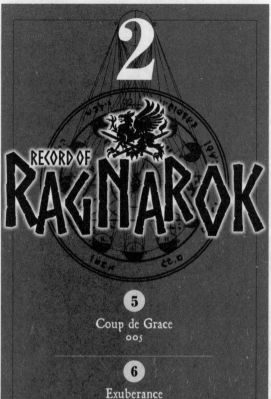

2

RECORD OF RAGNAROK

5

Coup de Grace
005

6

Exuberance
037

7

File No. 00000000001
073

8

Unexpected
109

9

Impeccable Imitation
149

THE STORY SO FAR...

Once every millennium, in a realm beyond time and space, the gods hold the Human Extinction Conference, where they determine whether or not to end humanity. This time, it seems like extinction is imminent, until the Valkyrie Brunhilde convinces them to let the decision be made by Ragnarok, a 13-round, winner-take-all fighting tournament between the gods and humanity.

In round one, the ultimate Norse god Thor squares off with the ultimate Three Kingdoms warrior Lü Bu. Flying in the face of the widely held expectation of an overwhelming victory for the gods, both fighters seem to be equally matched.

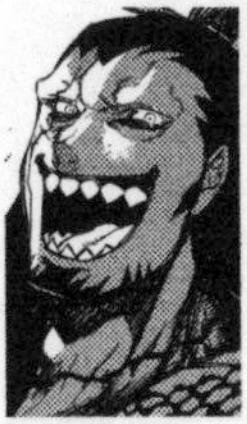

Lü Bu
CHINA

Fighting for humanity in round one. The most powerful general of the Three Kingdoms.

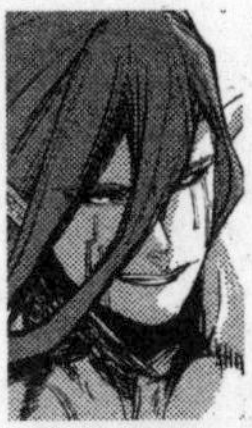

Thor
NORSE PANTHEON

Fighting for the gods in round one. The Norse pantheon's ultimate warrior, he wields the Divine Instrument Mjölnir.

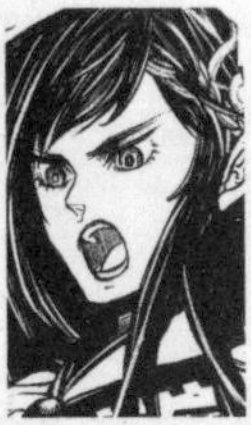

Brunhilde
NORSE PANTHEON

The eldest of the 13 Valkyrie sisters. Proposed Ragnarok to the gods as they prepared to end humanity.

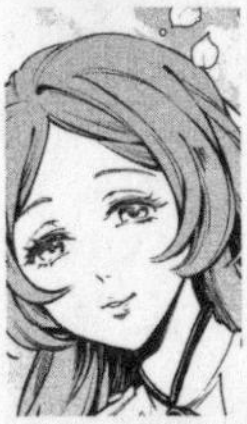

Randgrid
NORSE PANTHEON

Fourth oldest of the 13 Valkyrie sisters. Her name means "shield-destroyer." She became Lü Bu's weapon through the process of Volund.

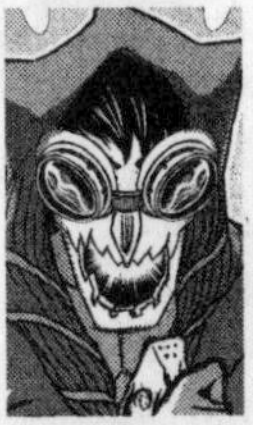

Heimdall
NORSE PANTHEON

He signaled the start of Ragnarok. Called the "Watchman of the Apocalypse," he serves as the commentator of Ragnarok.

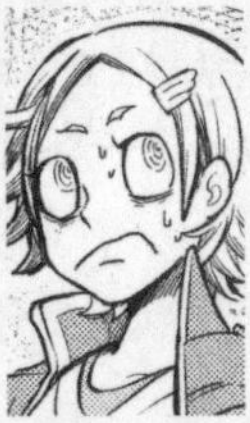

Geir
NORSE PANTHEON

The youngest of the 13 Valkyrie sisters. She admires Brunhilde, but is uncertain about her intentions and methods.

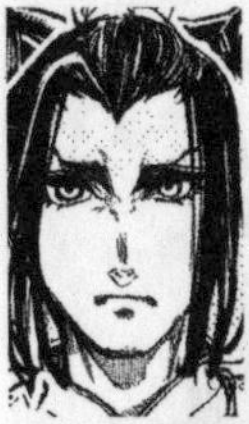

Chen Gong
CHINA

Lü Bu's military adviser. In life he left Cáo Cao, another powerful warlord, in order to serve Lü Bu until his death.

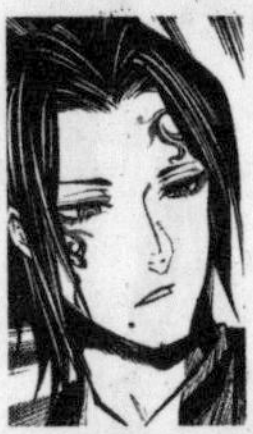

Hermes
GREEK PANTHEON

One of the 12 Olympians. Eloquent and shrewd, as the herald of the gods he is a close aide to Zeus.

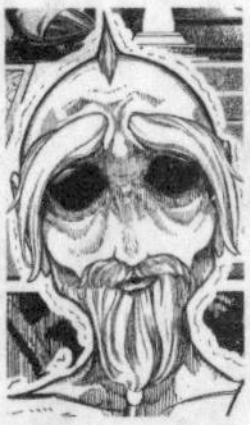

Zeus
GREEK PANTHEON

The all-knowing, all-powerful king of the gods in Greek mythology. He's a fervent fan of battles and war.

Record of Ragnarok

HUMANITY

QIN SHI HUANG
KING LEONIDAS
NIKOLA TESLA
KOJIRO SASAKI
JACK THE RIPPER
ADAM
RAIDEN TAMEEMON
SOJI OKITA
GRIGORI RASPUTIN
NOSTRADAMUS
LÜ BU
SIMO HÄYHÄ
KINTOKI SAKATA

THE GODS

ZEUS
BUDDHA
LOKI
APOLLO
POSEIDON
SUSANOO-NO-MIKOTO
HERACLES
THOR
BISHAMON
ANUBIS
ODIN
BEELZEBUB
SHIVA

RECORD OF RAGNAROK

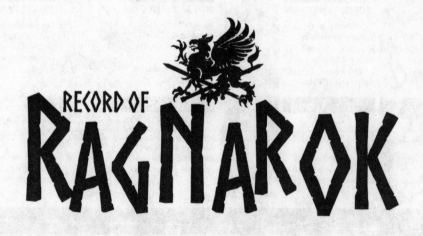

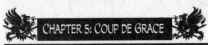

Chapter 5: Coup de Grace

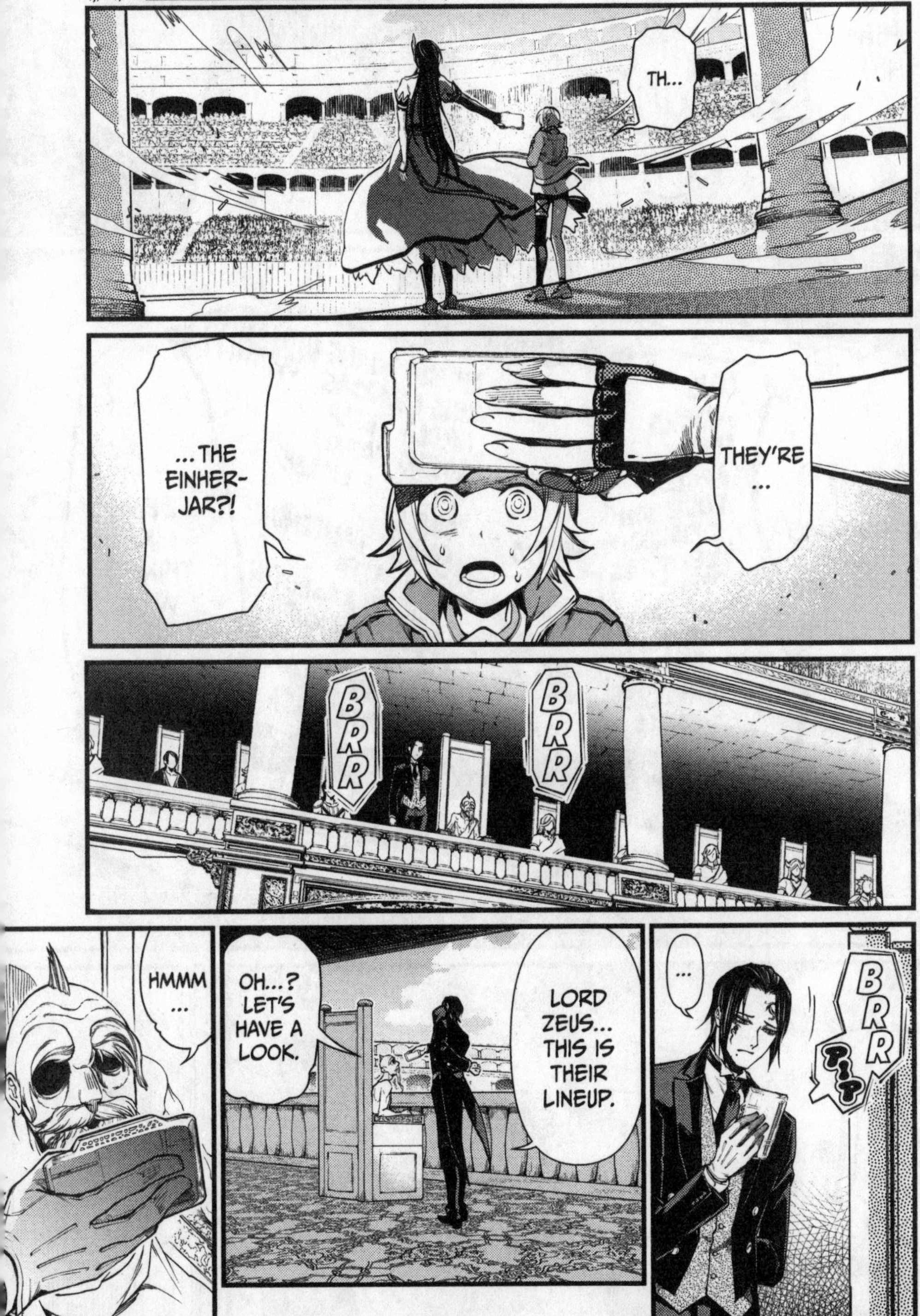
TH...
THEY'RE ...
... THE EINHER-JAR?!
BRR
BRR
BRR
PIP
...
LORD ZEUS... THIS IS THEIR LINEUP.
OH...? LET'S HAVE A LOOK.
HMMM ...

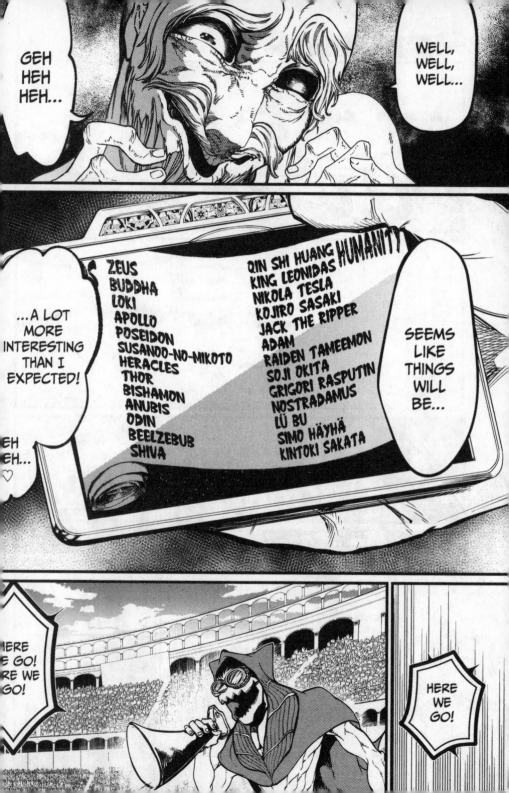

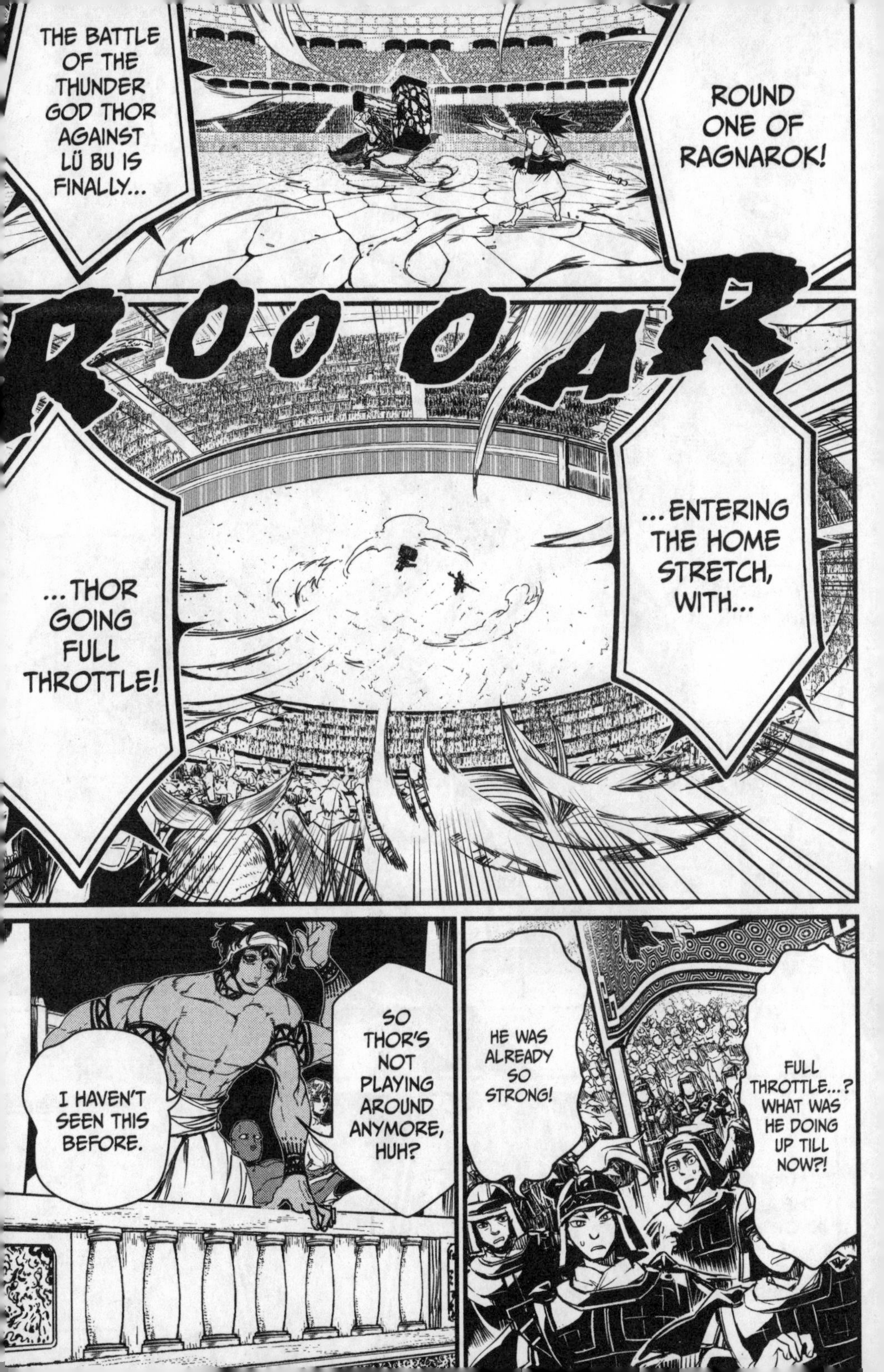
ROUND ONE OF RAGNAROK!
THE BATTLE OF THE THUNDER GOD THOR AGAINST LÜ BU IS FINALLY...
ROOOAR
...ENTERING THE HOME STRETCH, WITH...
...THOR GOING FULL THROTTLE!
FULL THROTTLE...? WHAT WAS HE DOING UP TILL NOW?!
HE WAS ALREADY SO STRONG!
SO THOR'S NOT PLAYING AROUND ANYMORE, HUH?
I HAVEN'T SEEN THIS BEFORE.

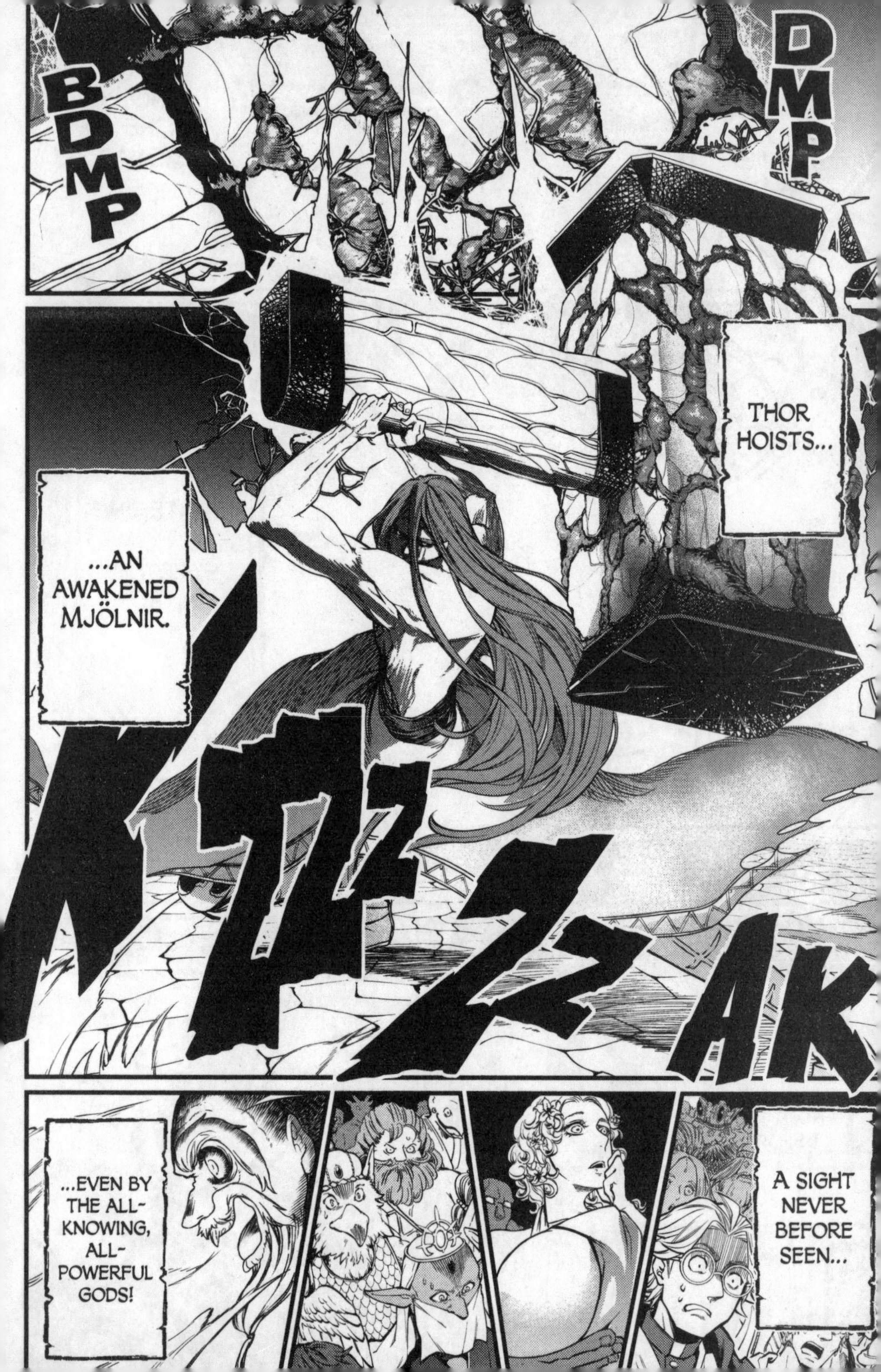
DMP
BDMP
THOR HOISTS...
...AN AWAKENED MJÖLNIR.
A SIGHT NEVER BEFORE SEEN...
...EVEN BY THE ALL-KNOWING, ALL-POWERFUL GODS!

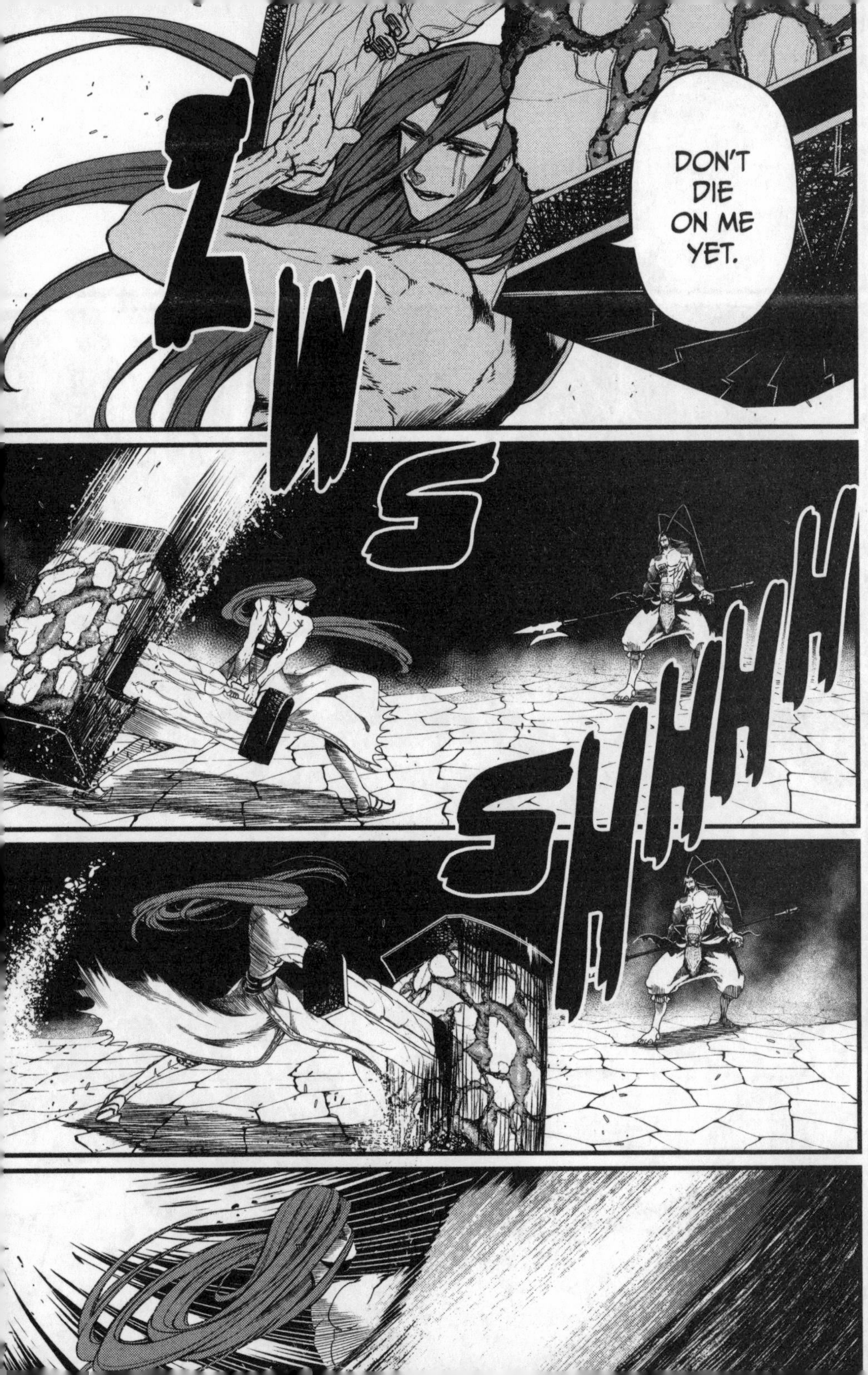
DON'T DIE ON ME YET.
SWSHHHH

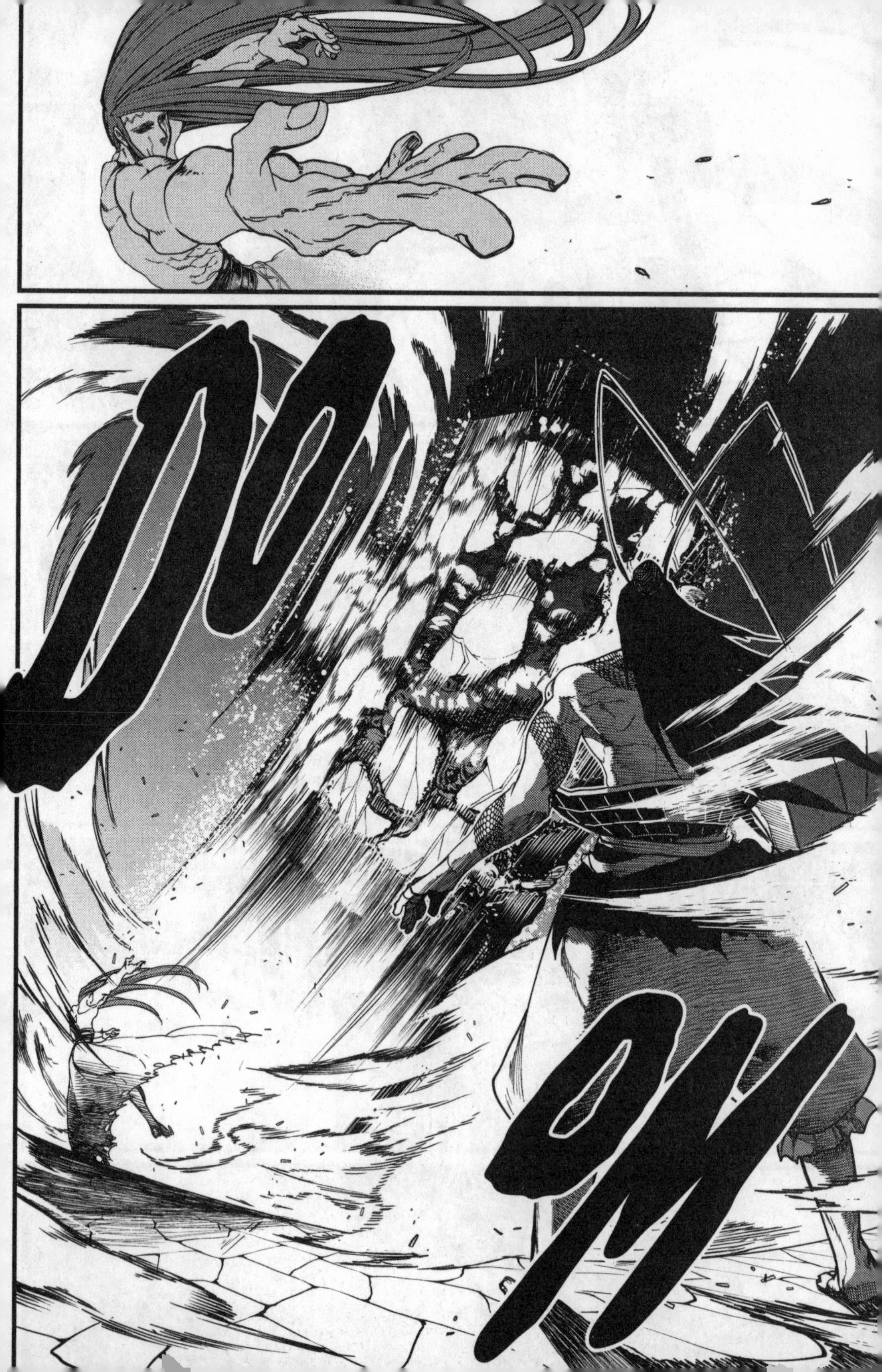

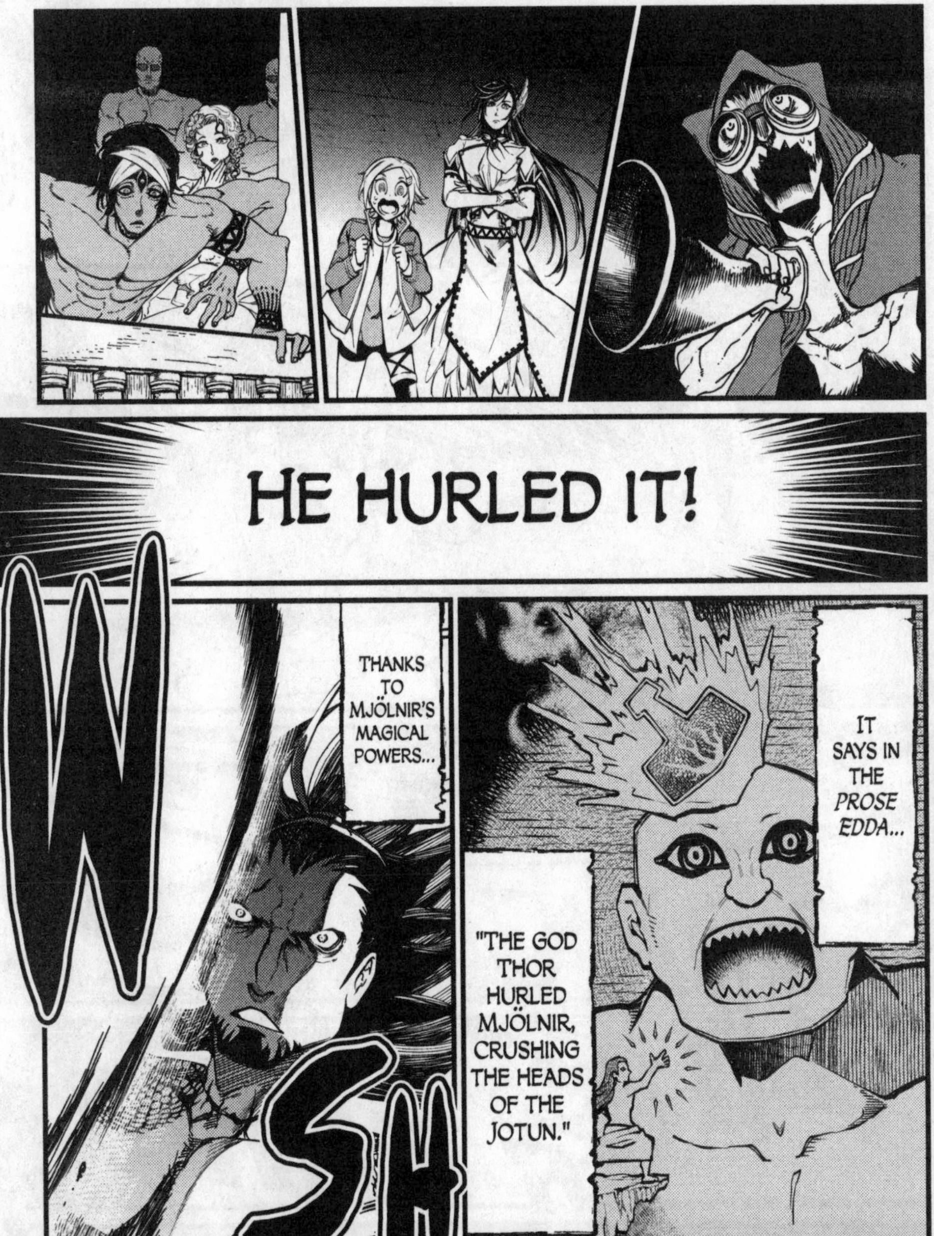
HE HURLED IT!
IT SAYS IN THE *PROSE EDDA*...
"THE GOD THOR HURLED MJÖLNIR, CRUSHING THE HEADS OF THE JOTUN."
THANKS TO MJÖLNIR'S MAGICAL POWERS...
W
SH

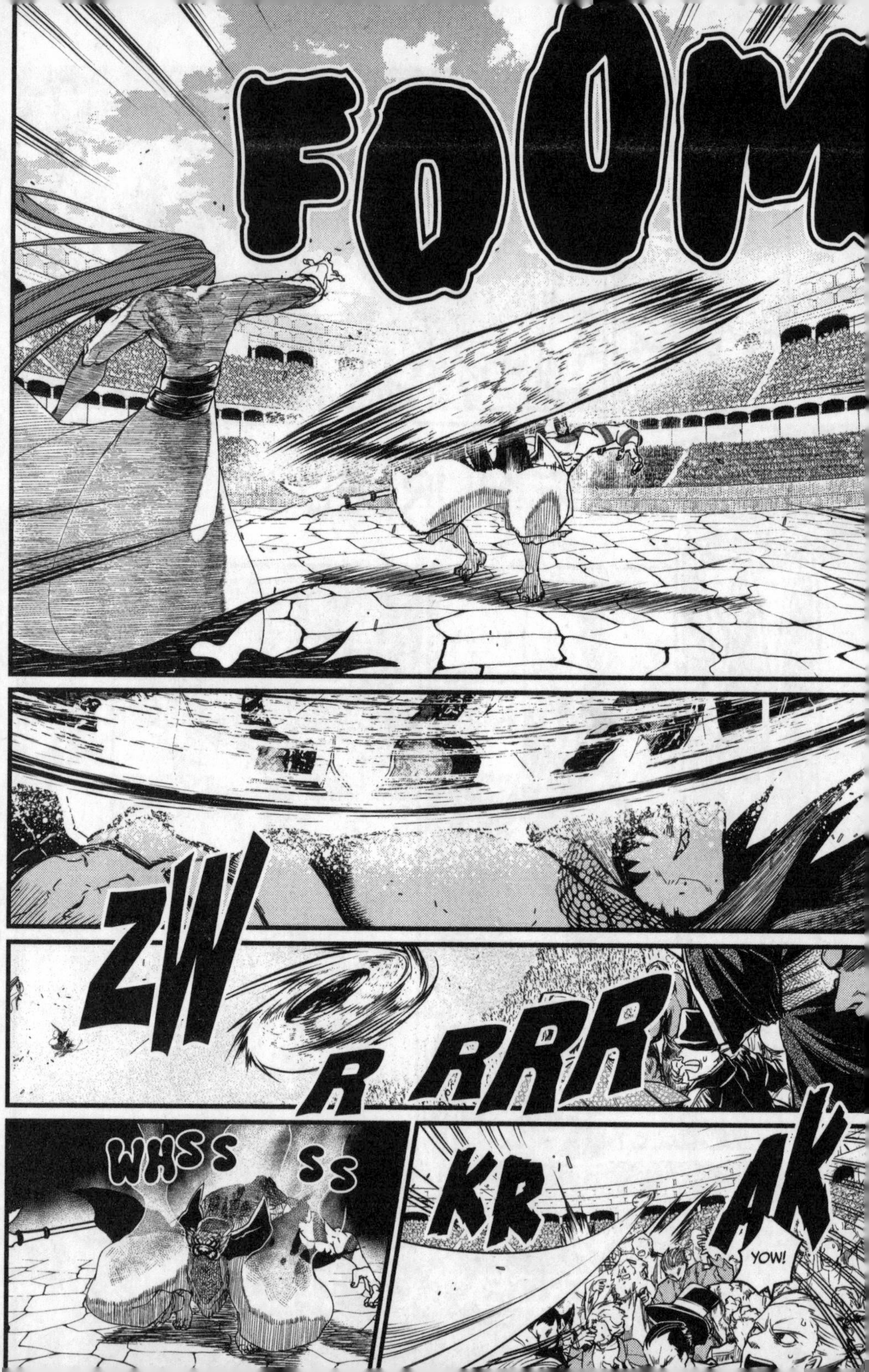
FOOM
ZW R RRR
KRAK
YOW!
WHSS S SS

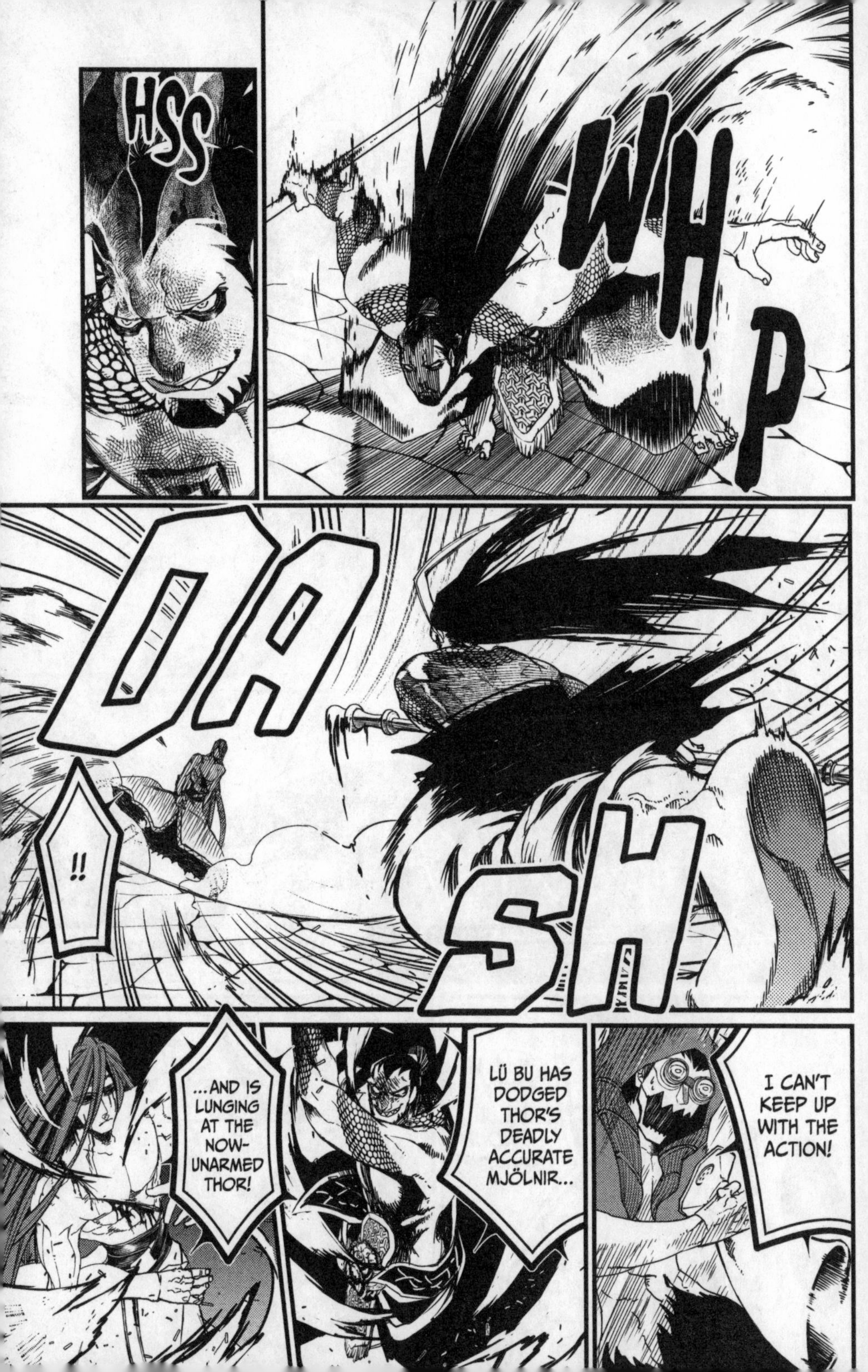
WHIP
HSS
DASH
!!
I CAN'T KEEP UP WITH THE ACTION!
LÜ BU HAS DODGED THOR'S DEADLY ACCURATE MJÖLNIR...
...AND IS LUNGING AT THE NOW-UNARMED THOR!

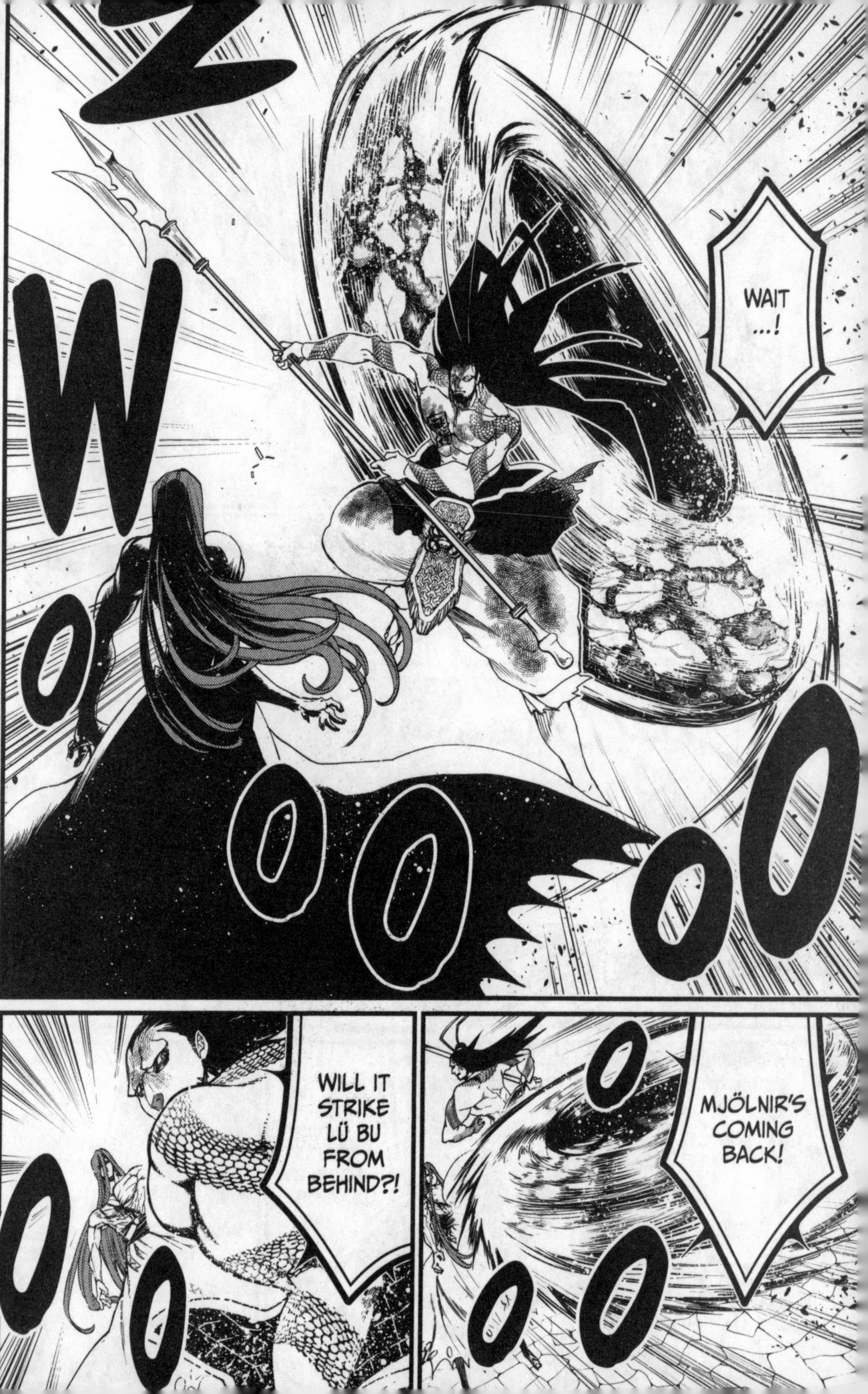
WOOOOOOO
WAIT ...!
MJÖLNIR'S COMING BACK!
WILL IT STRIKE LÜ BU FROM BEHIND?!
OOOO
OOO

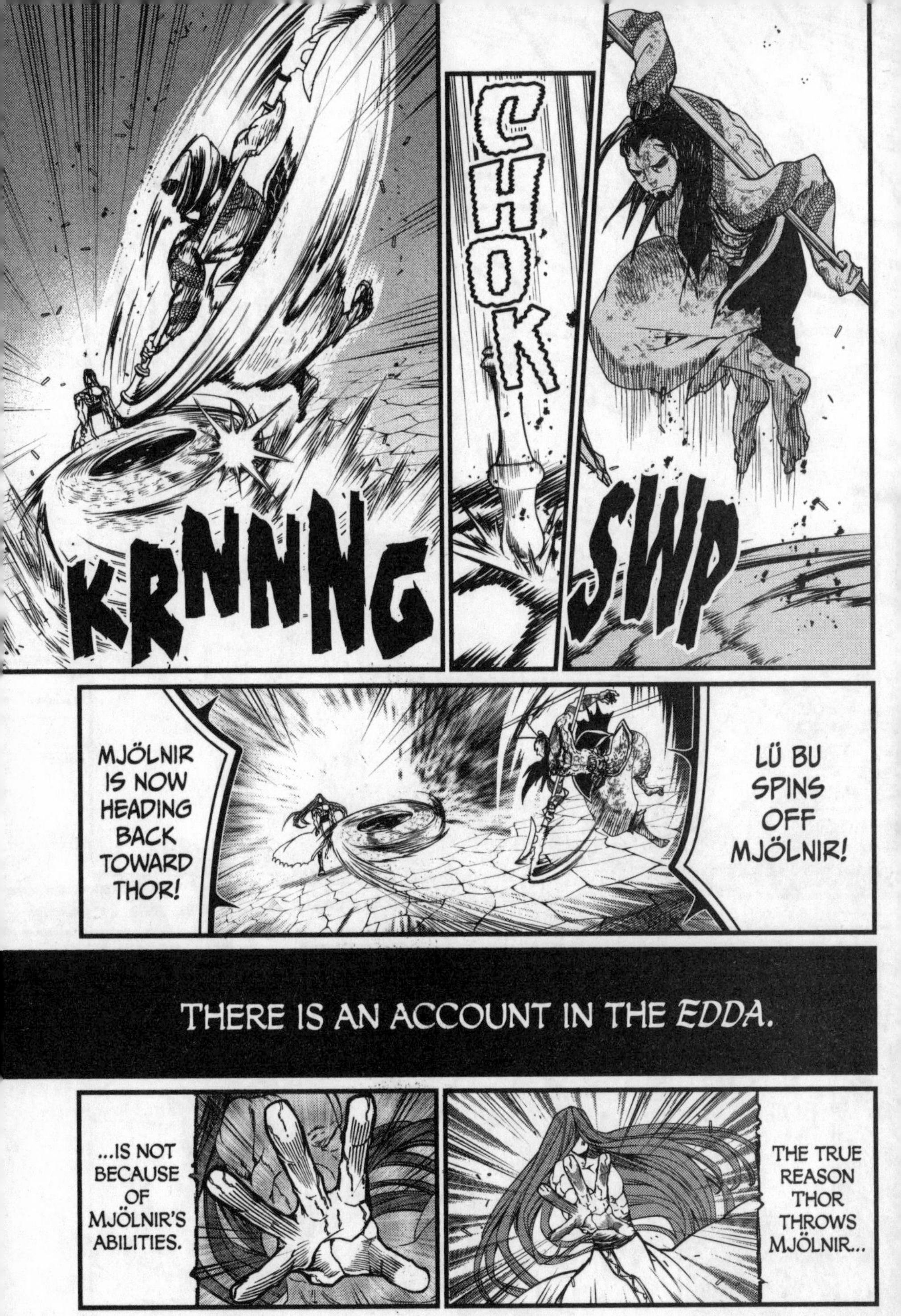
SWP
CHOK
KRNNNG
LÜ BU SPINS OFF MJÖLNIR!
MJÖLNIR IS NOW HEADING BACK TOWARD THOR!
THERE IS AN ACCOUNT IN THE *EDDA*.
THE TRUE REASON THOR THROWS MJÖLNIR...
...IS NOT BECAUSE OF MJÖLNIR'S ABILITIES.

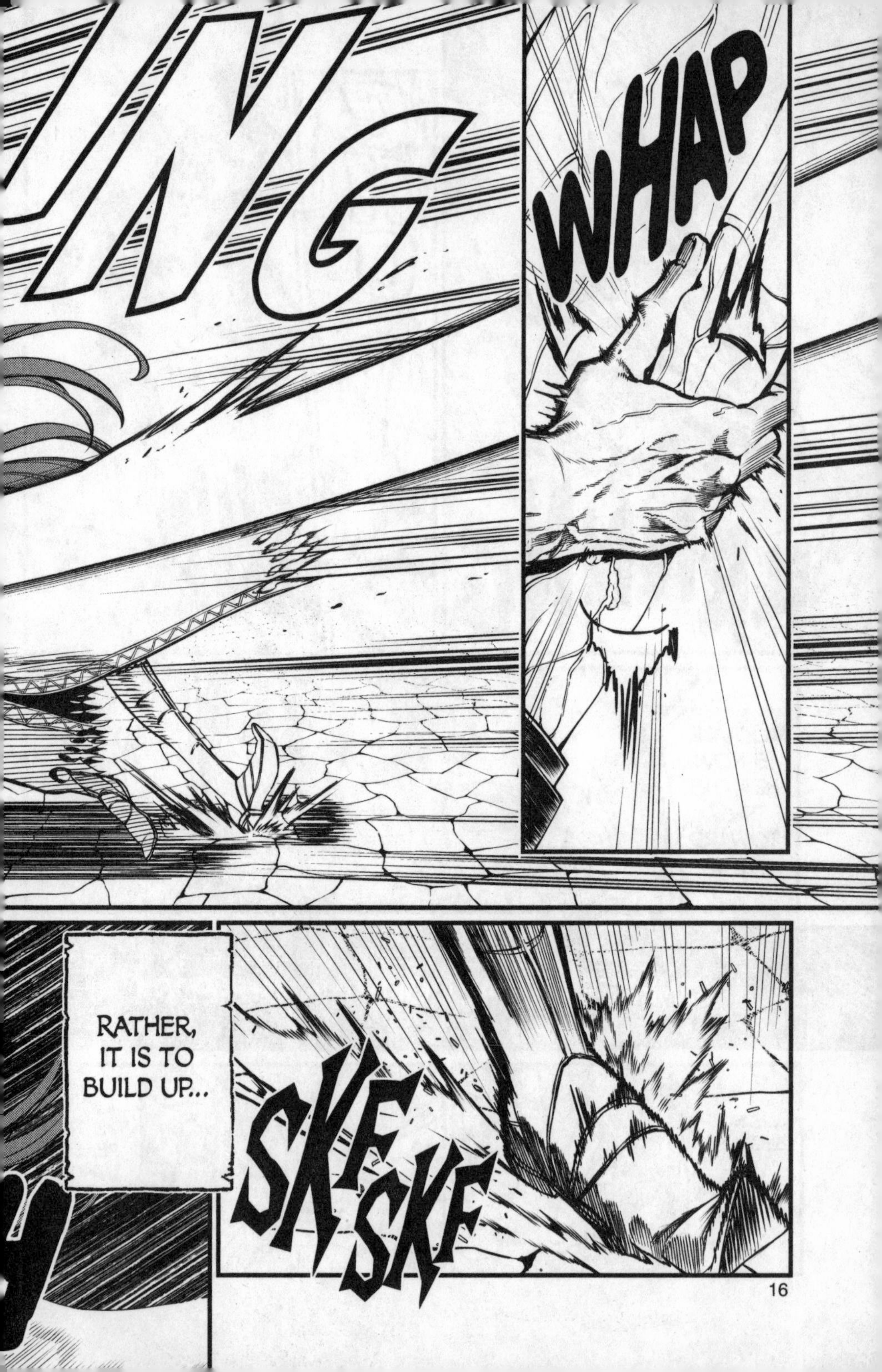
WHAP
SKF
SKF
RATHER, IT IS TO BUILD UP...

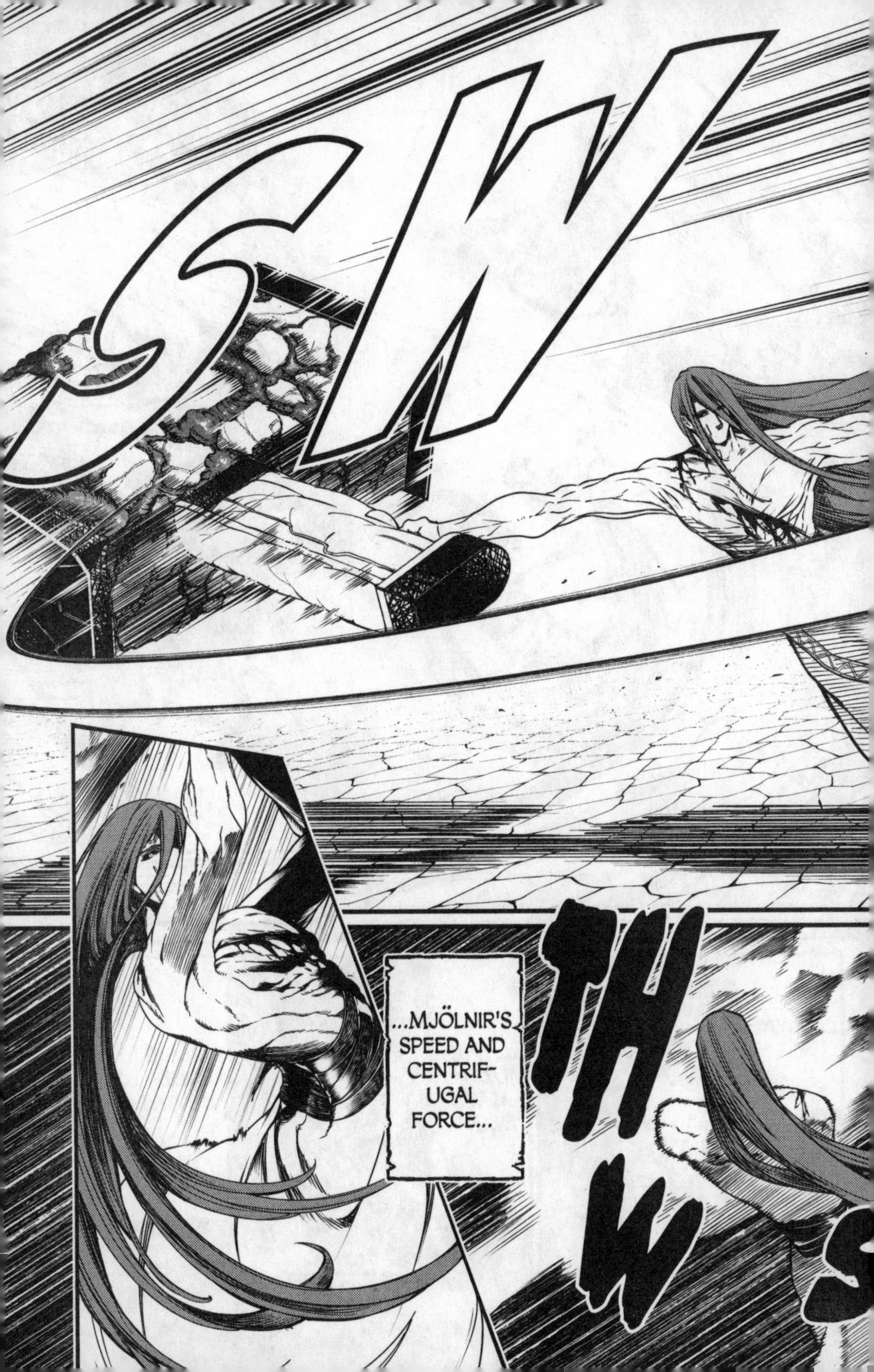
SW
TH
W
S
...MJÖLNIR'S SPEED AND CENTRIF-UGAL FORCE...

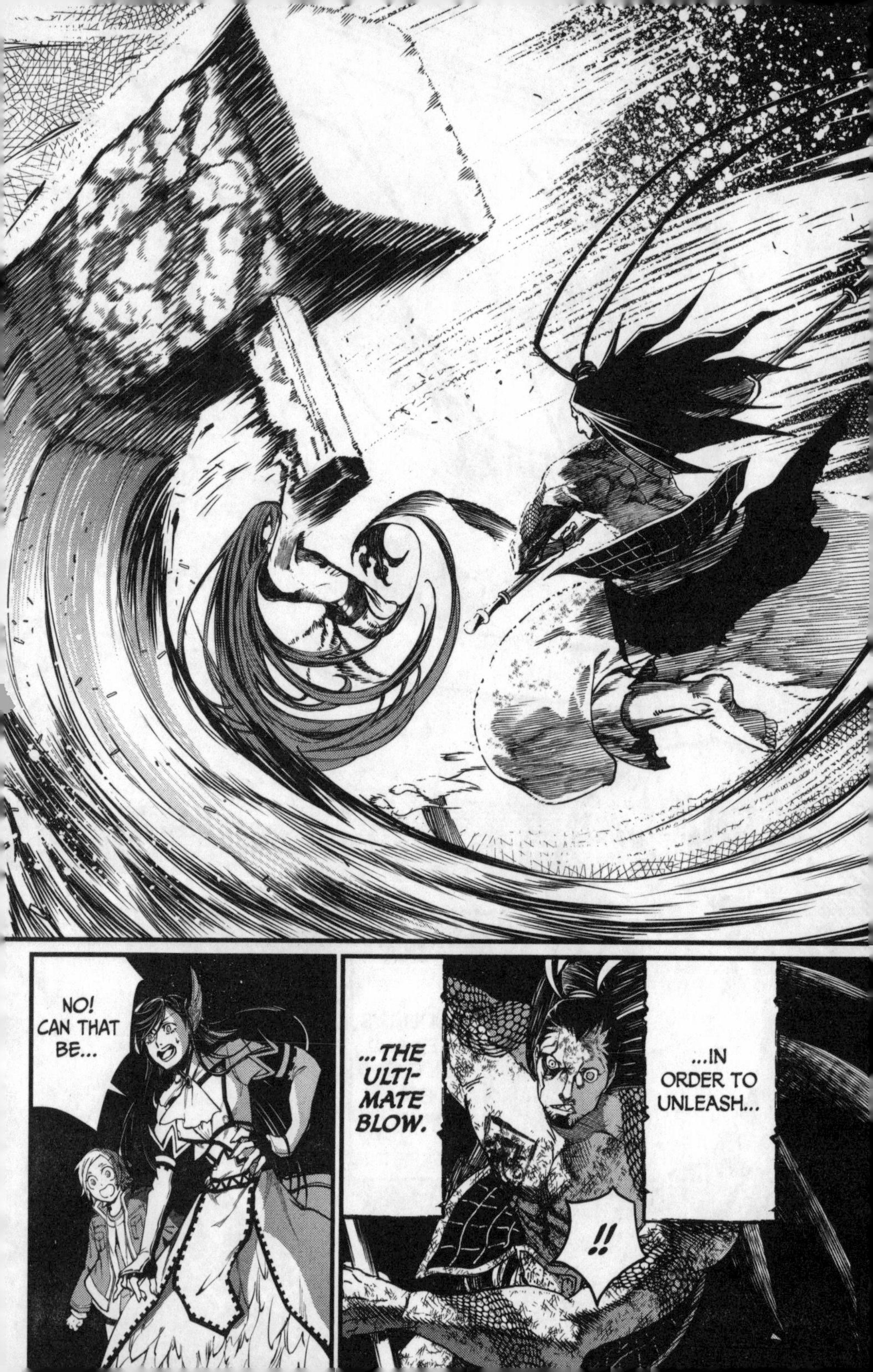
...IN ORDER TO UNLEASH...
...THE ULTI-MATE BLOW.
!!
NO! CAN THAT BE...

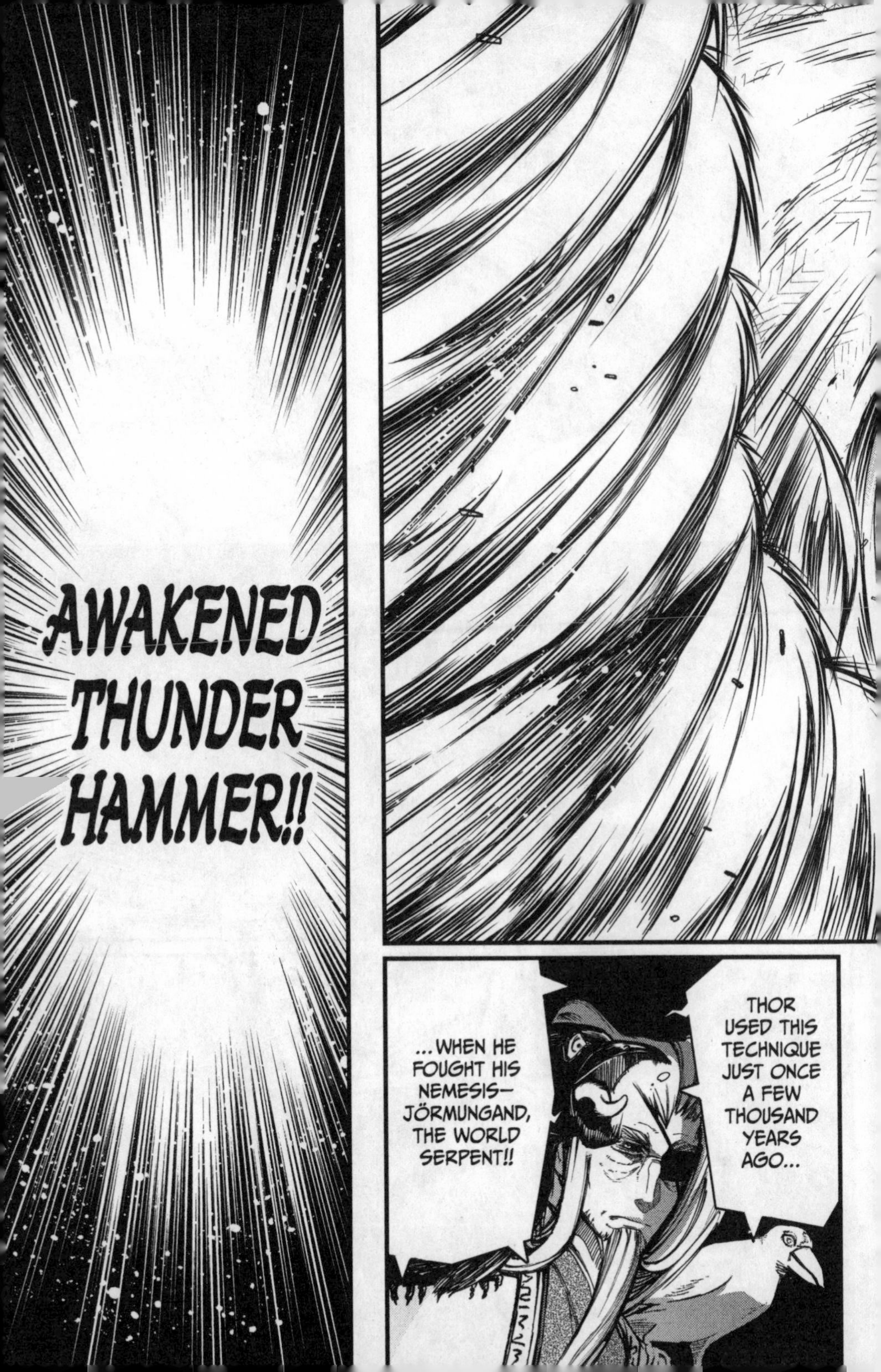
THOR USED THIS TECHNIQUE JUST ONCE A FEW THOUSAND YEARS AGO...
...WHEN HE FOUGHT HIS NEMESIS— JÖRMUNGAND, THE WORLD SERPENT!!
AWAKENED THUNDER HAMMER!!

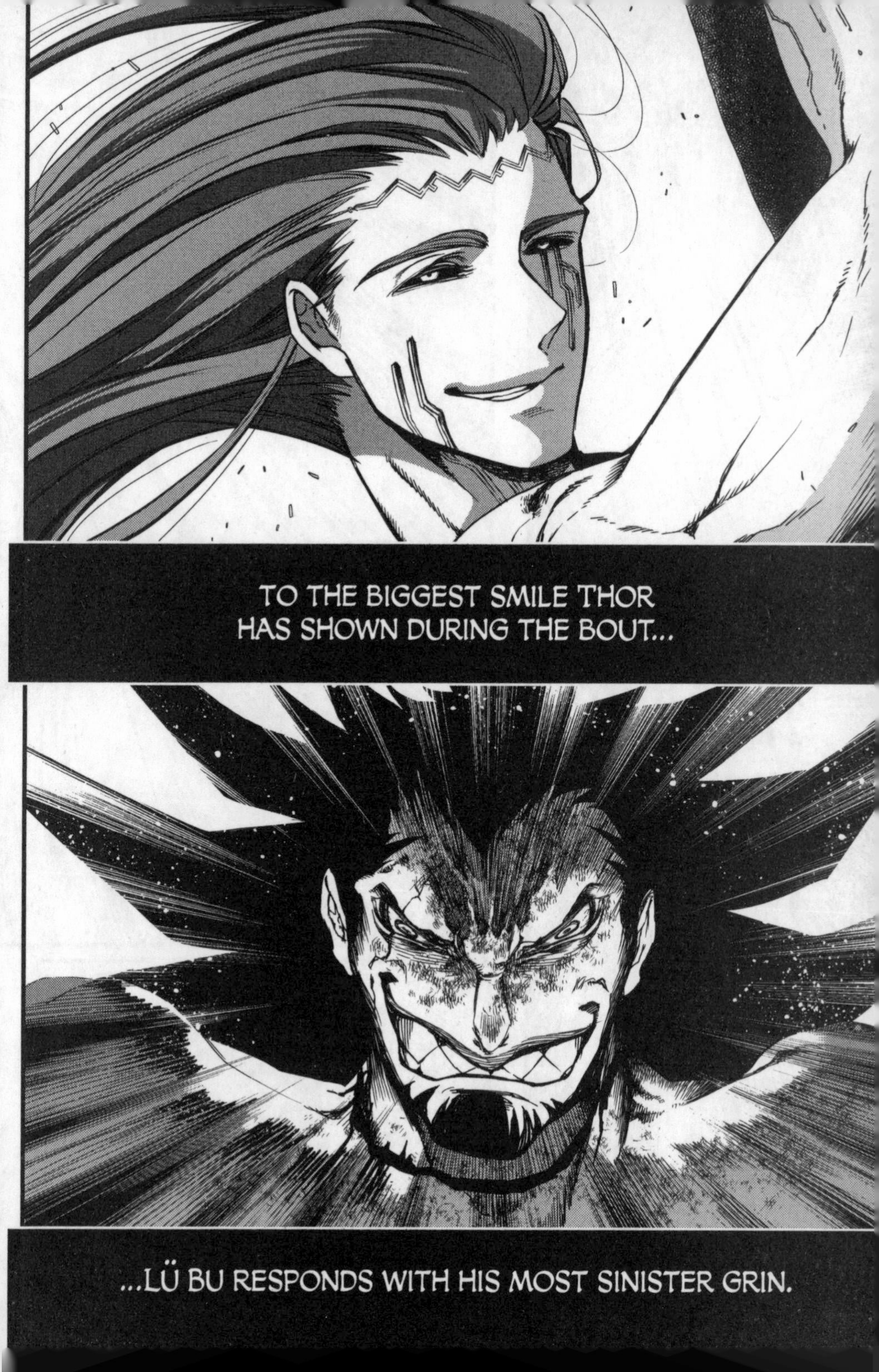
TO THE BIGGEST SMILE THOR HAS SHOWN DURING THE BOUT...
...LÜ BU RESPONDS WITH HIS MOST SINISTER GRIN.

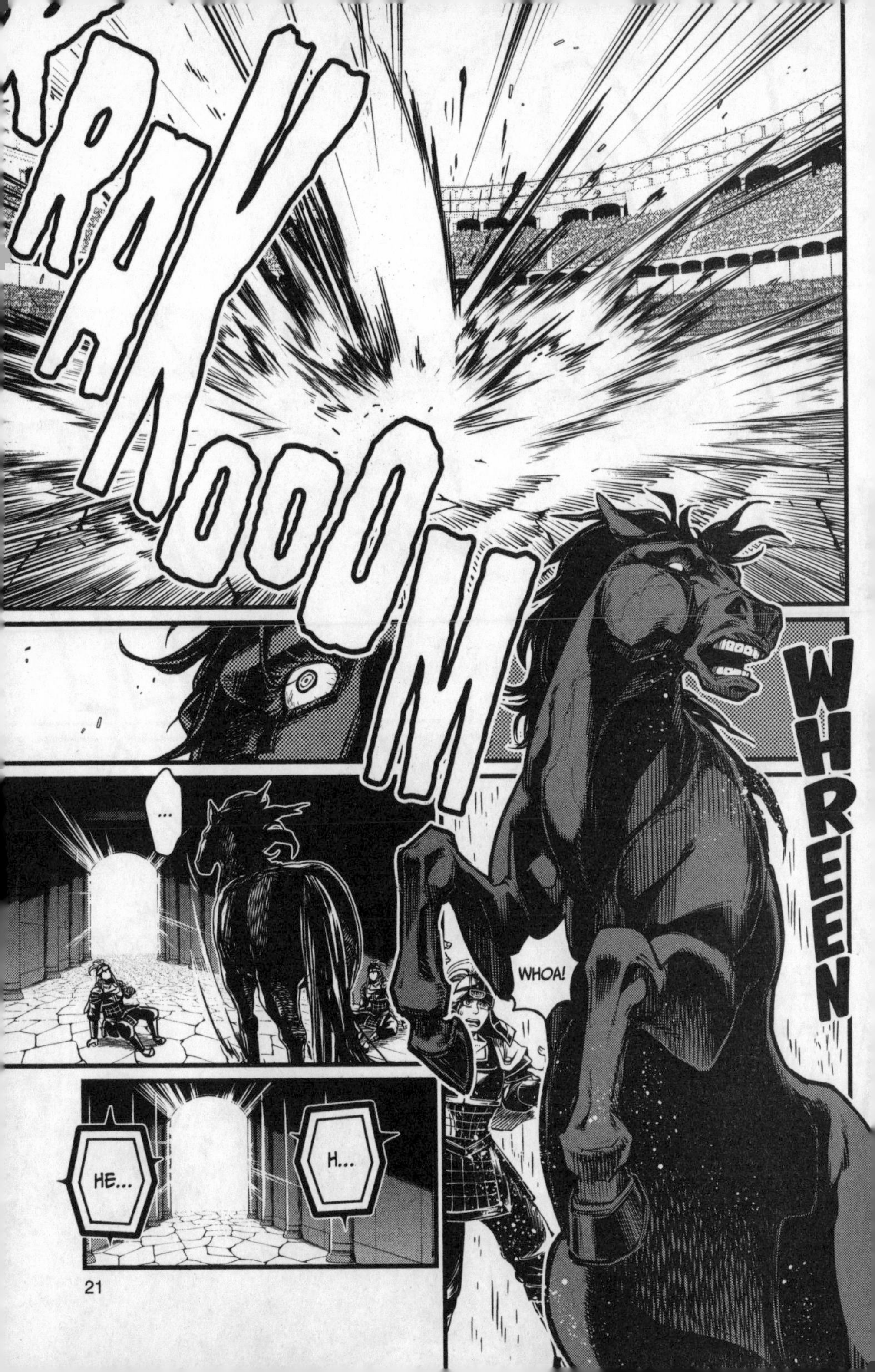
RAKOOOM
WHREEN
WHOA!
...
H...
HE...

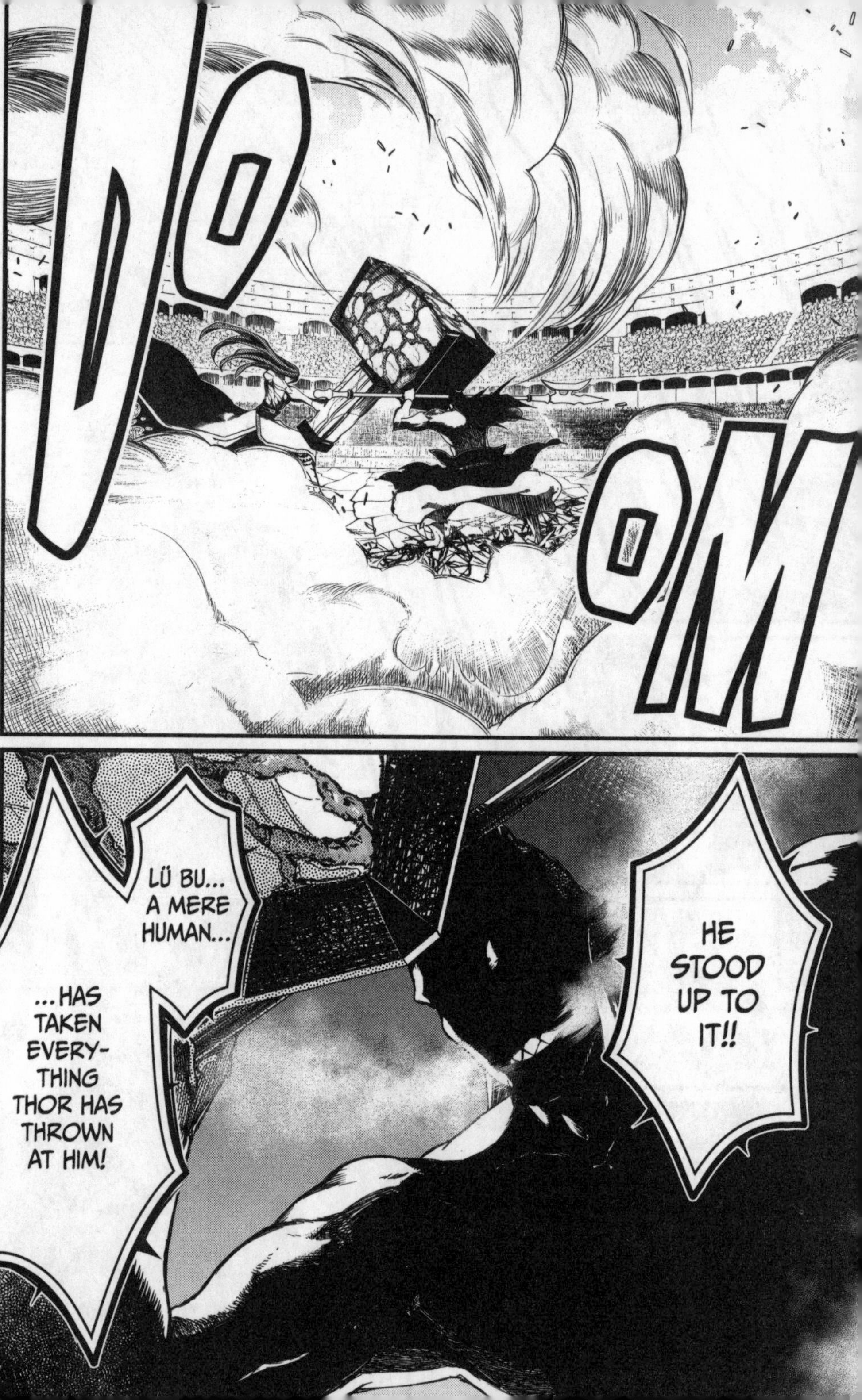
DOOM
LÜ BU... A MERE HUMAN...
...HAS TAKEN EVERY-THING THOR HAS THROWN AT HIM!
HE STOOD UP TO IT!!

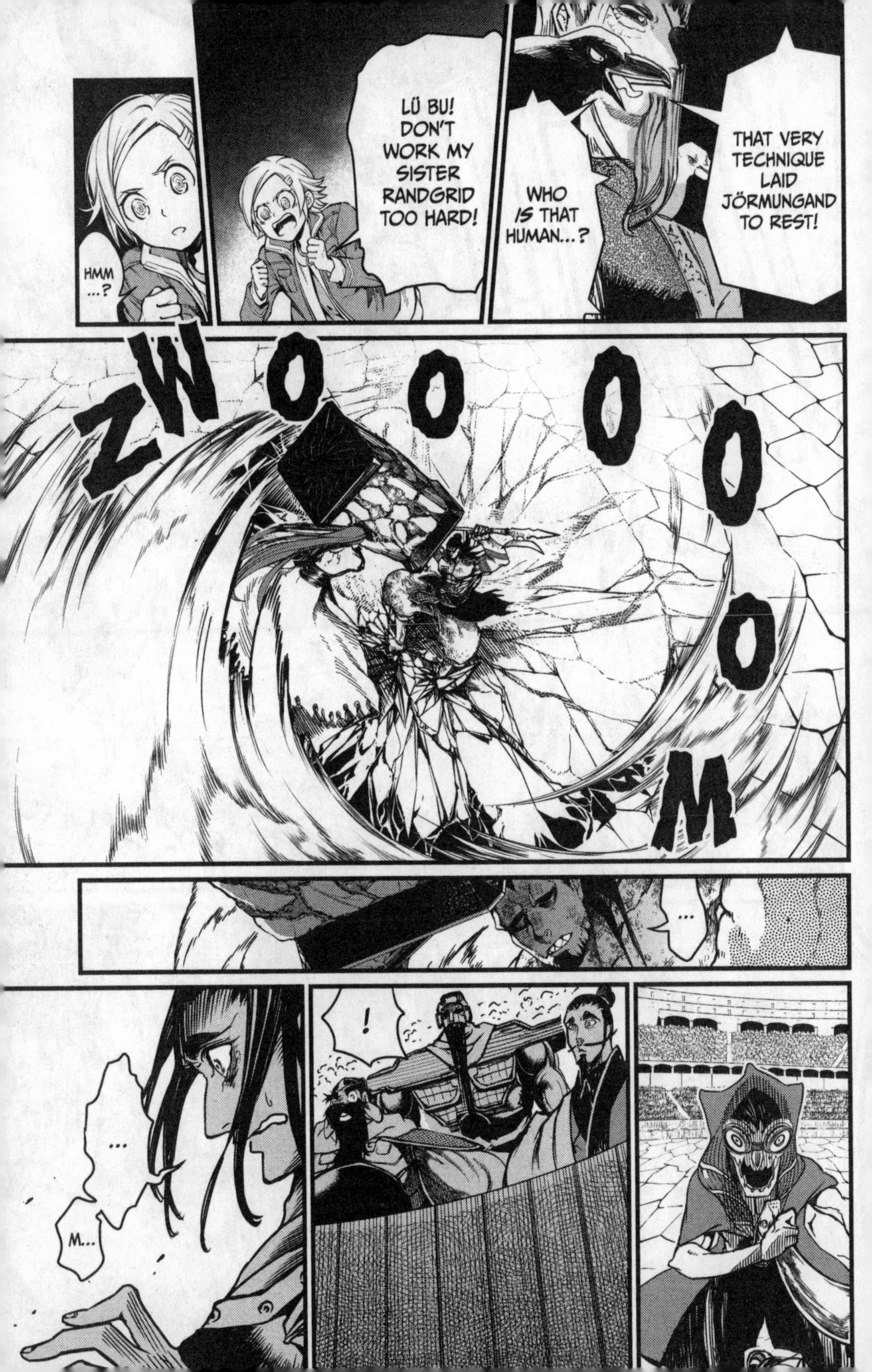
THAT VERY TECHNIQUE LAID JÖRMUNGAND TO REST!
WHO *IS* THAT HUMAN...?
LÜ BU! DON'T WORK MY SISTER RANDGRID TOO HARD!
HMM ...?
ZWOOOOOM
...
!
...
M...

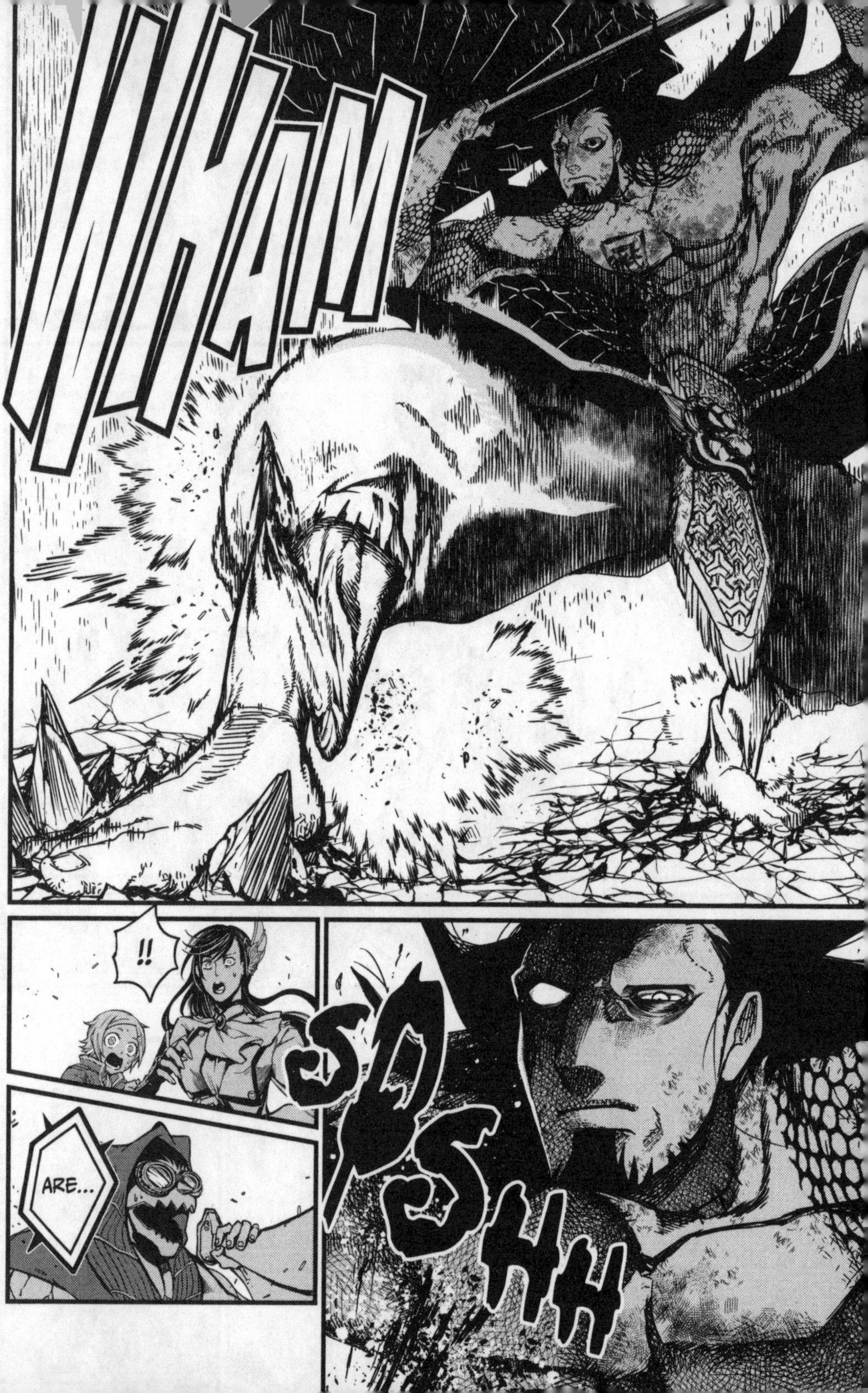
WHAM
!!
ARE...

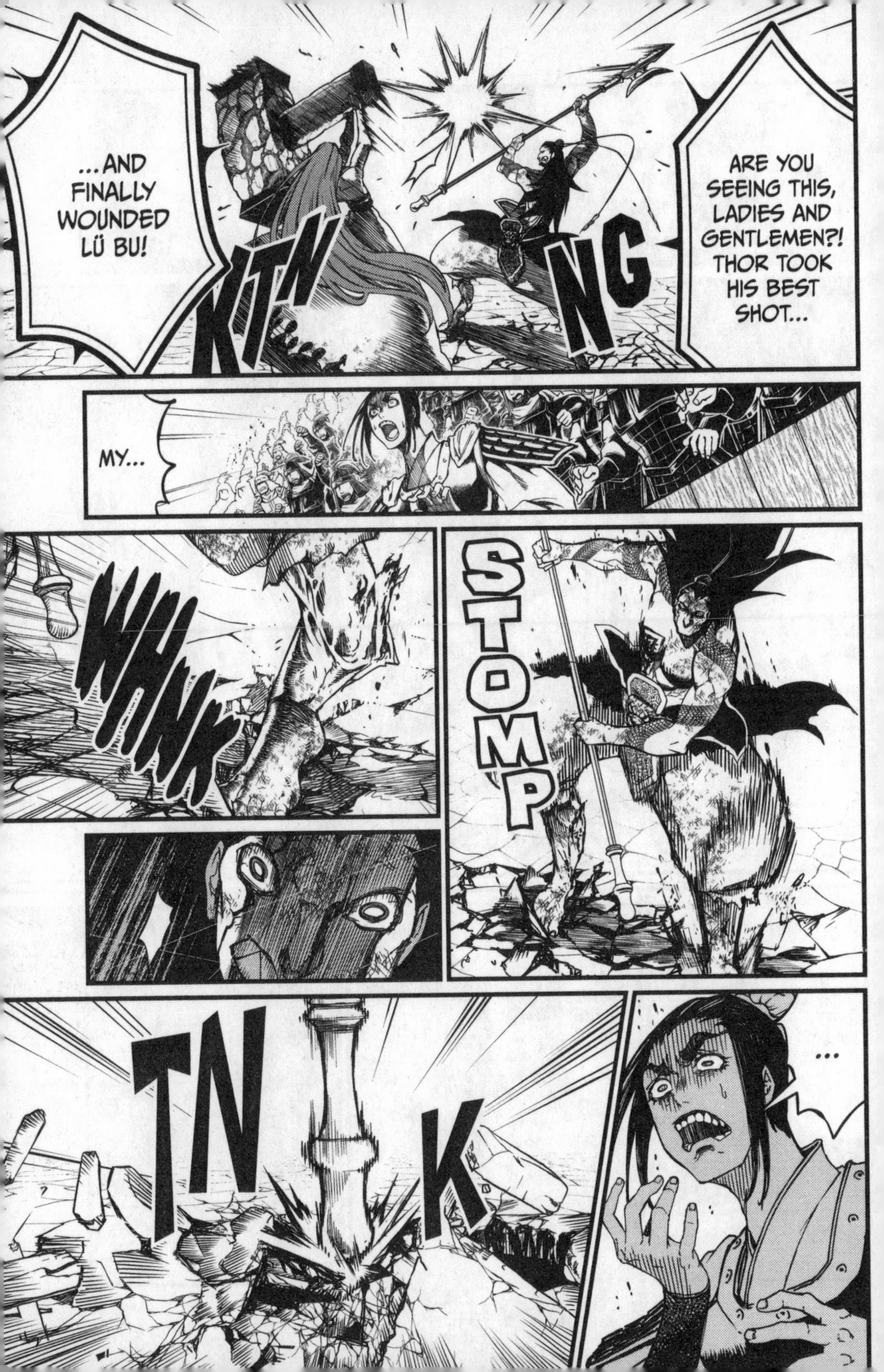
ARE YOU SEEING THIS, LADIES AND GENTLEMEN?! THOR TOOK HIS BEST SHOT...
KTN NG
...AND FINALLY WOUNDED LÜ BU!
MY...
STOMP
WHUNK
...
TNK

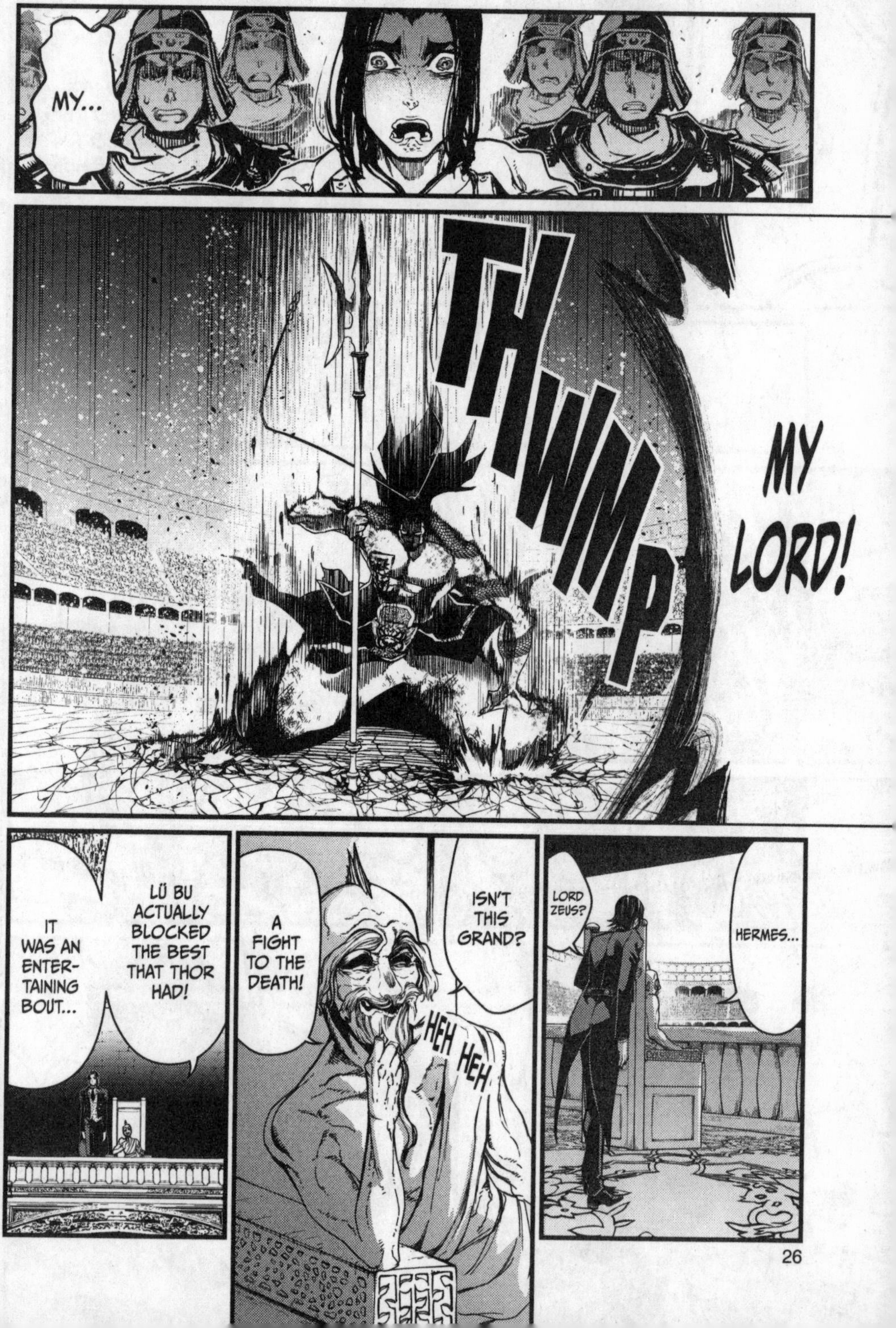
MY...
MY LORD!
THWMP
HERMES...
LORD ZEUS?
ISN'T THIS GRAND?
A FIGHT TO THE DEATH!
HEH HEH
LŪ BU ACTUALLY BLOCKED THE BEST THAT THOR HAD!
IT WAS AN ENTER-TAINING BOUT...

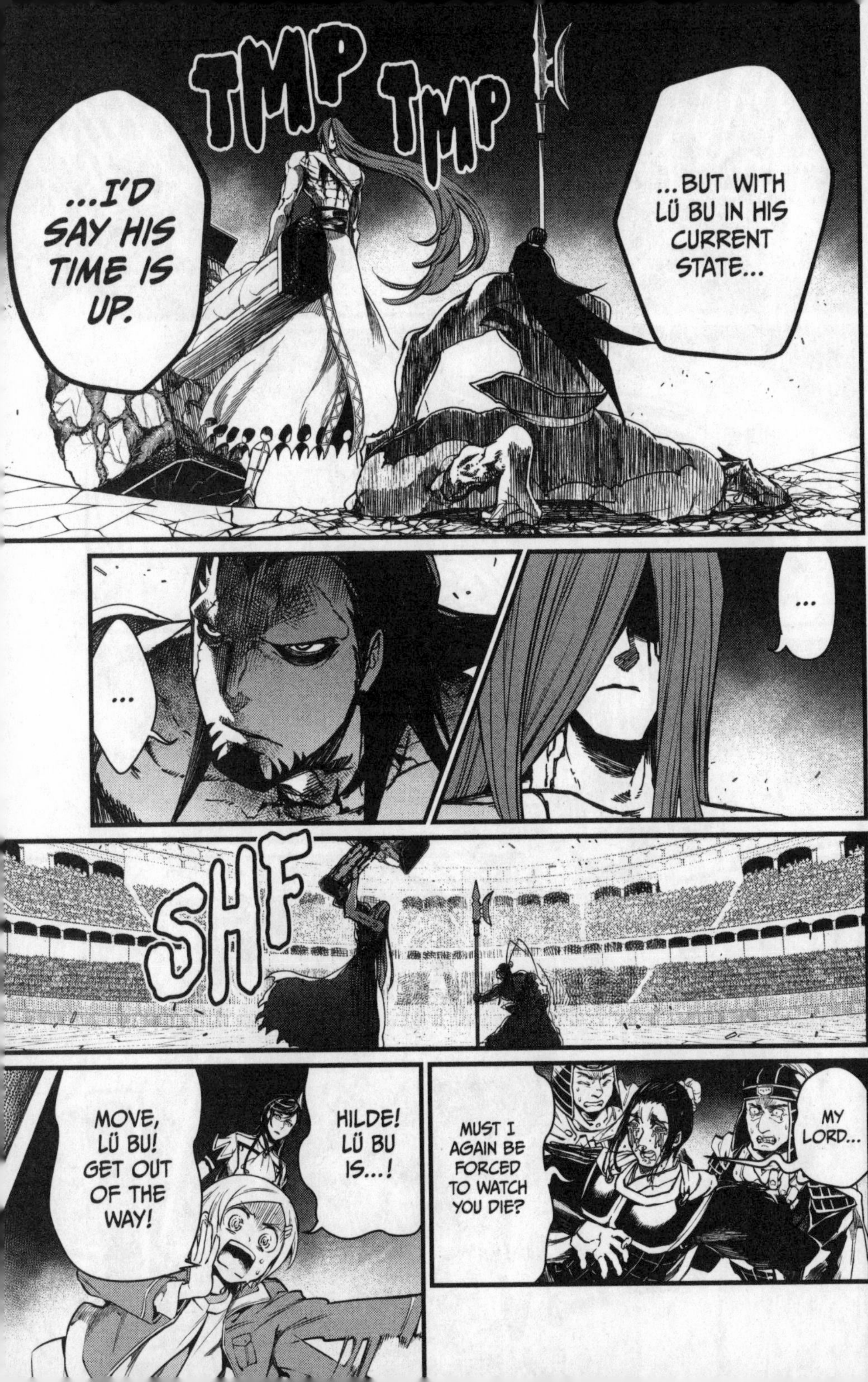
TMP TMP
...BUT WITH LÜ BU IN HIS CURRENT STATE...
...I'D SAY HIS TIME IS UP.
...
...
SHF
MY LORD...
MUST I AGAIN BE FORCED TO WATCH YOU DIE?
HILDE! LÜ BU IS...!
MOVE, LÜ BU! GET OUT OF THE WAY!

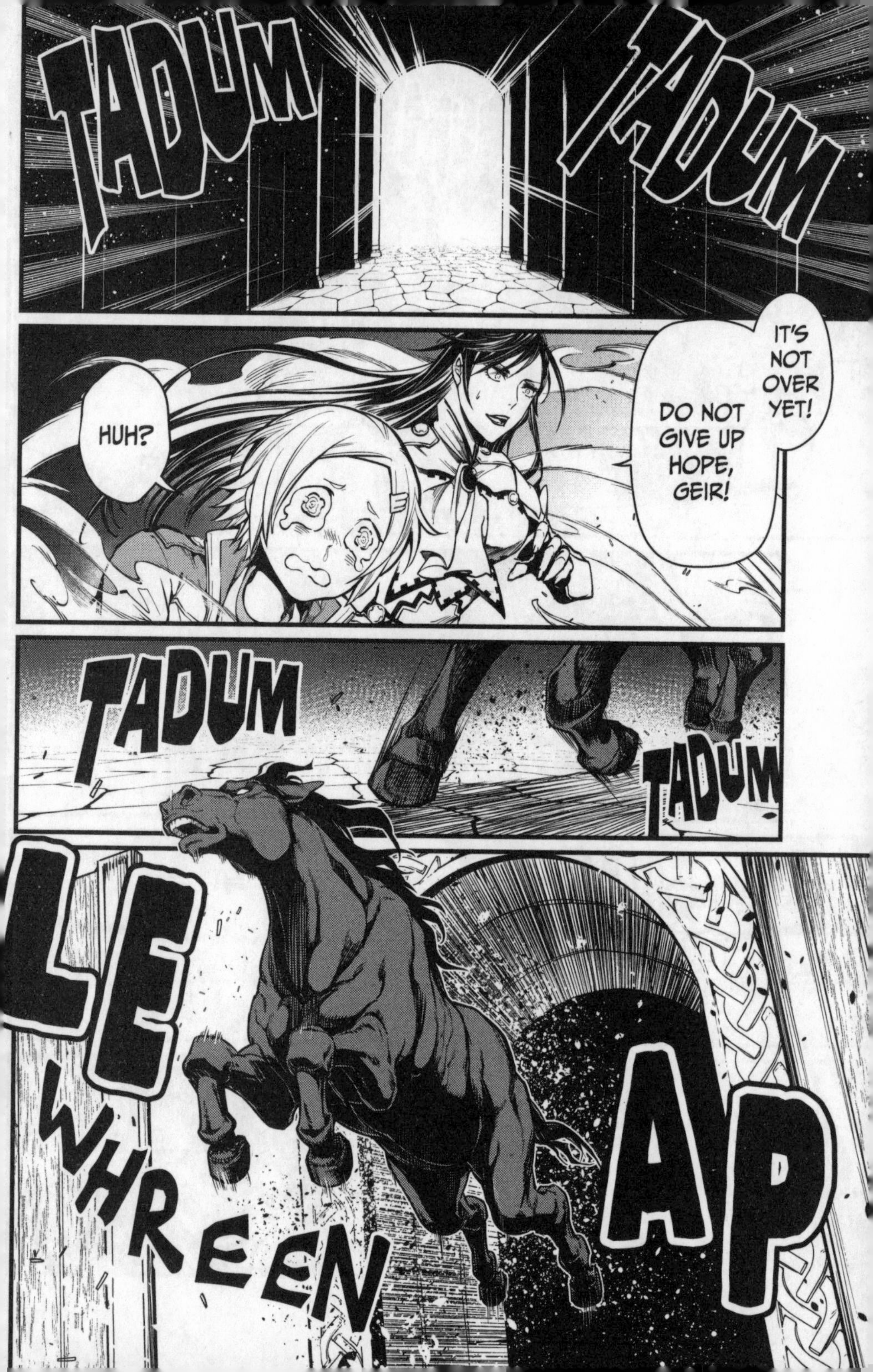
TADUM
TADUM
IT'S NOT OVER YET!
DO NOT GIVE UP HOPE, GEIR!
HUH?
TADUM
TADUM
LEAP
WHREEN

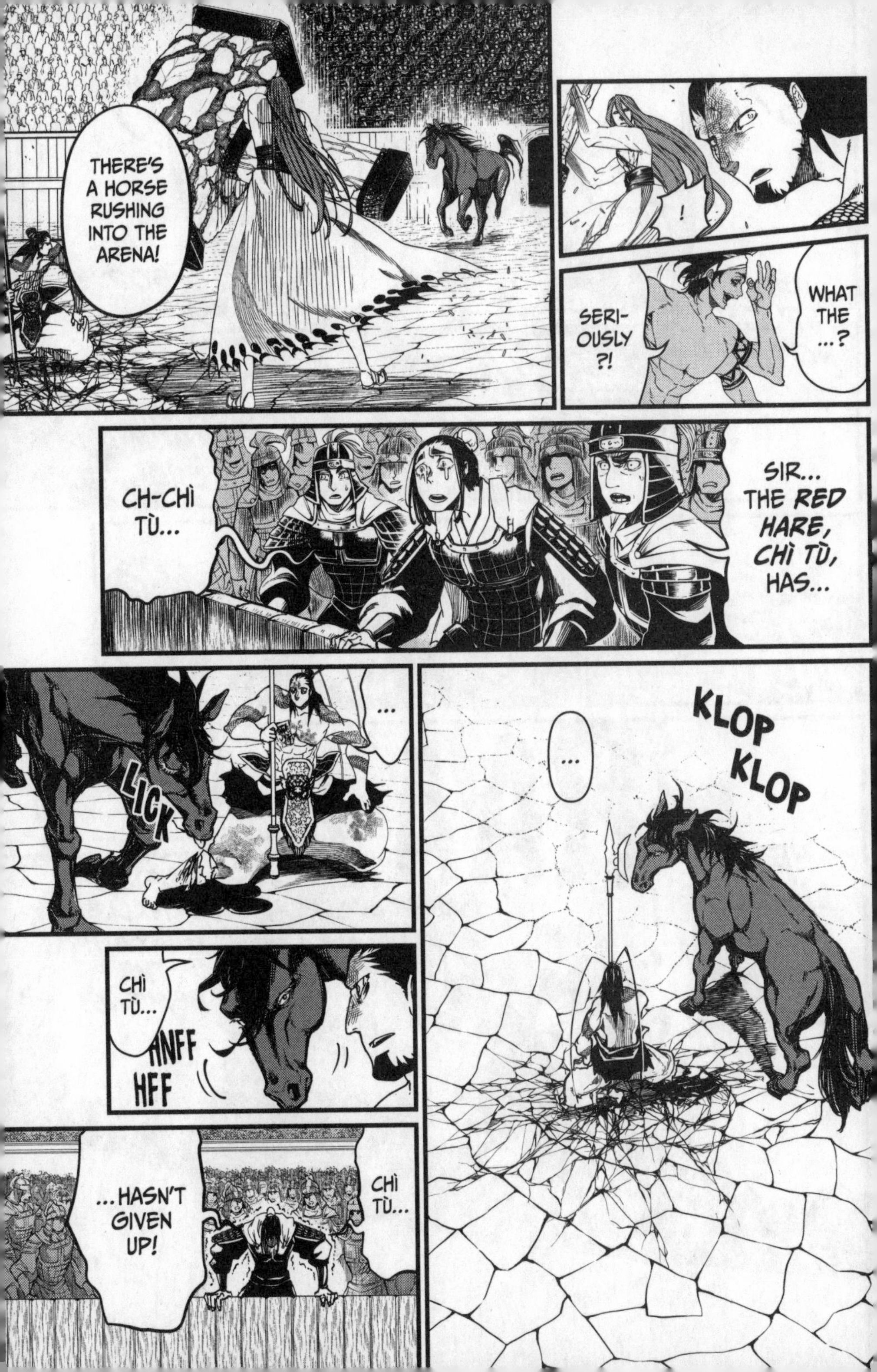
!
WHAT THE ...?
SERI-OUSLY ?!
THERE'S A HORSE RUSHING INTO THE ARENA!
SIR... THE RED HARE, CHÌ TÙ, HAS...
CH-CHÌ TÙ...
KLOP KLOP
...
...
LICK
CHÌ TÙ...
HNFF HFF
CHÌ TÙ...
...HASN'T GIVEN UP!

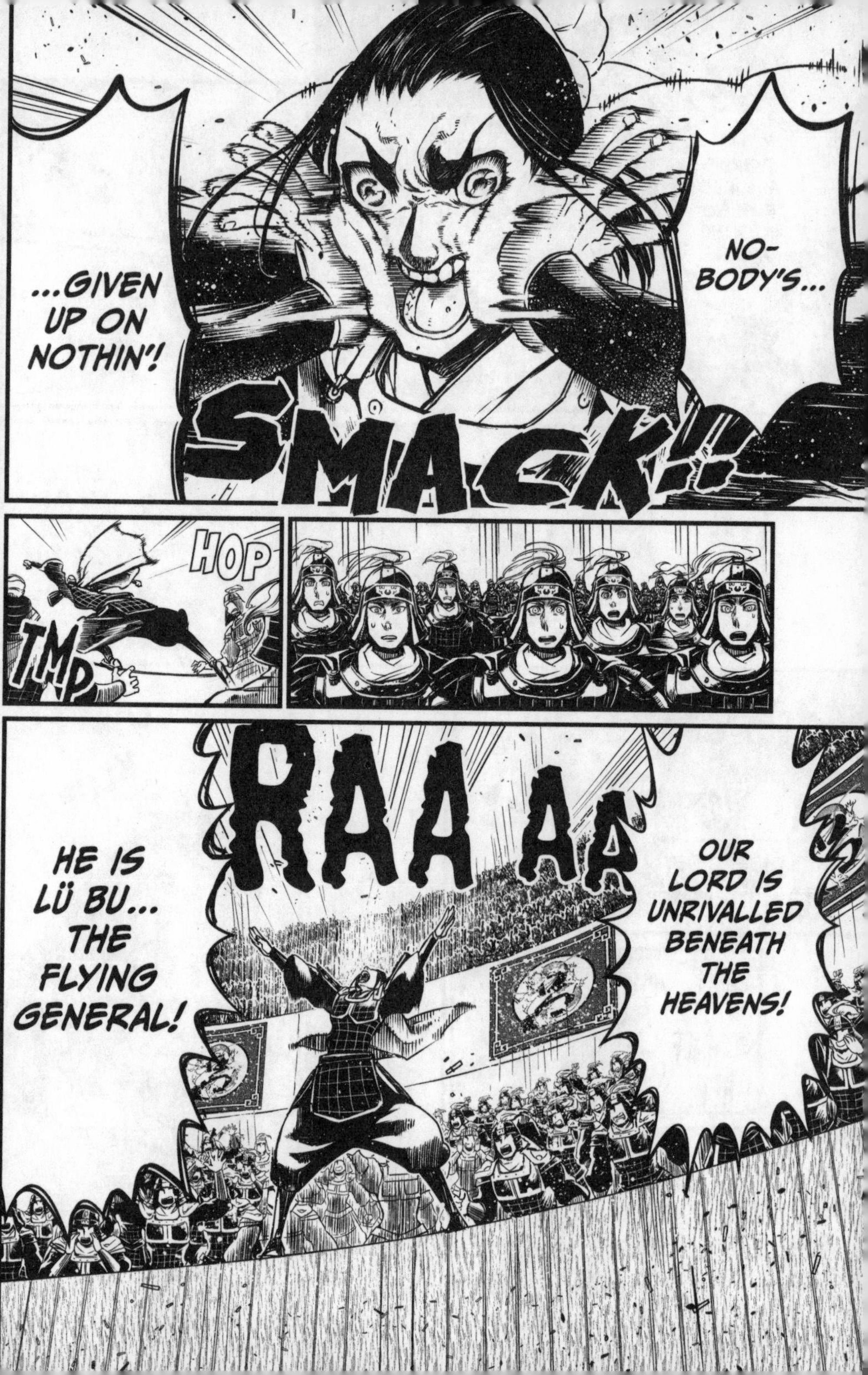
NO-BODY'S...
...GIVEN UP ON NOTHIN'!
SMACK!!
HOP
TMP
RAAAA
OUR LORD IS UNRIVALLED BENEATH THE HEAVENS!
HE IS LÜ BU... THE FLYING GENERAL!

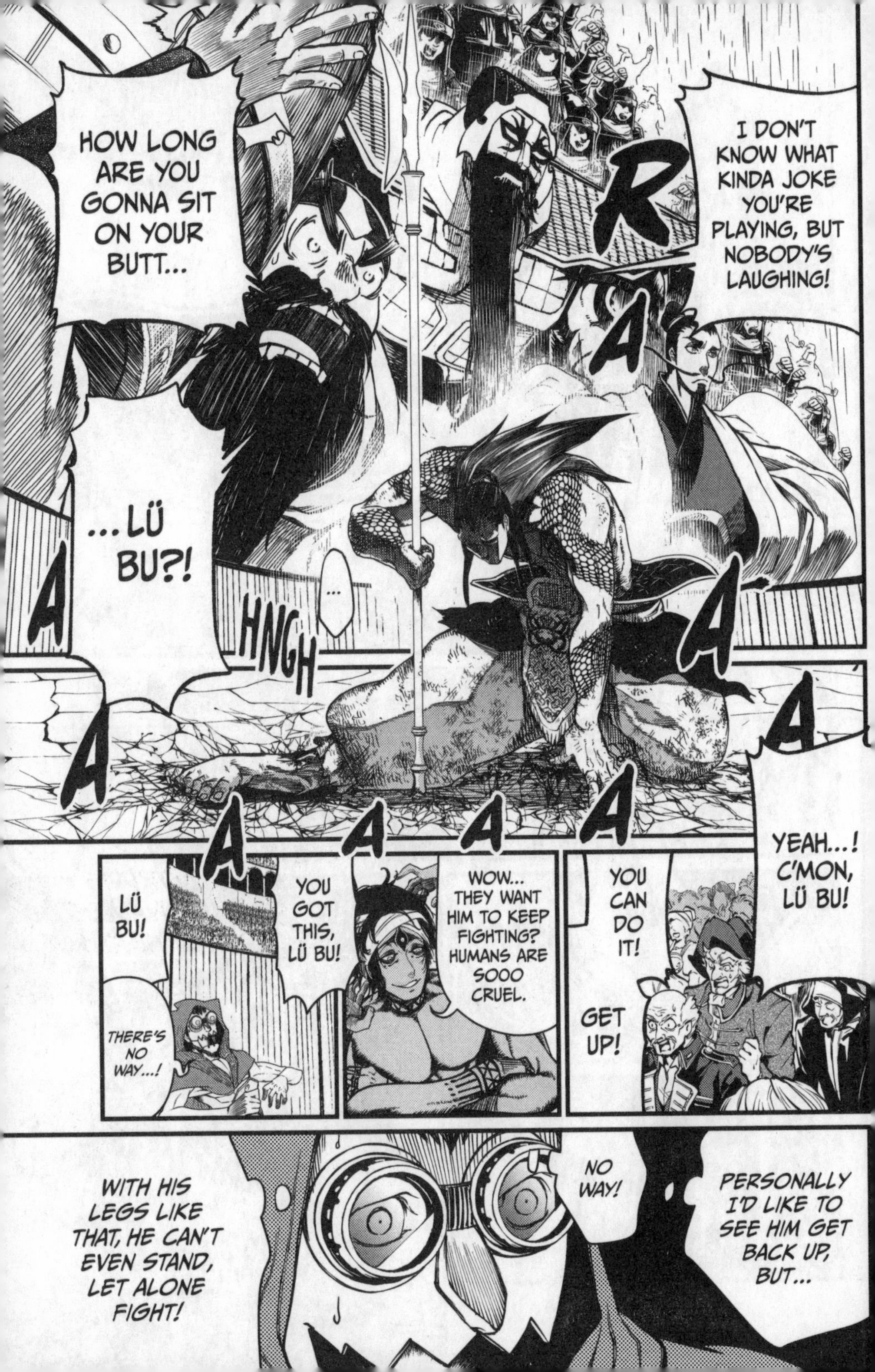
I DON'T KNOW WHAT KINDA JOKE YOU'RE PLAYING, BUT NOBODY'S LAUGHING!
HOW LONG ARE YOU GONNA SIT ON YOUR BUTT...
RAAAAAAAAA
...LÜ BU?!
...
HNGH
YEAH...! C'MON, LÜ BU!
YOU CAN DO IT!
GET UP!
WOW... THEY WANT HIM TO KEEP FIGHTING? HUMANS ARE SOOO CRUEL.
YOU GOT THIS, LÜ BU!
LÜ BU!
THERE'S NO WAY...!
PERSONALLY I'D LIKE TO SEE HIM GET BACK UP, BUT...
NO WAY!
WITH HIS LEGS LIKE THAT, HE CAN'T EVEN STAND, LET ALONE FIGHT!

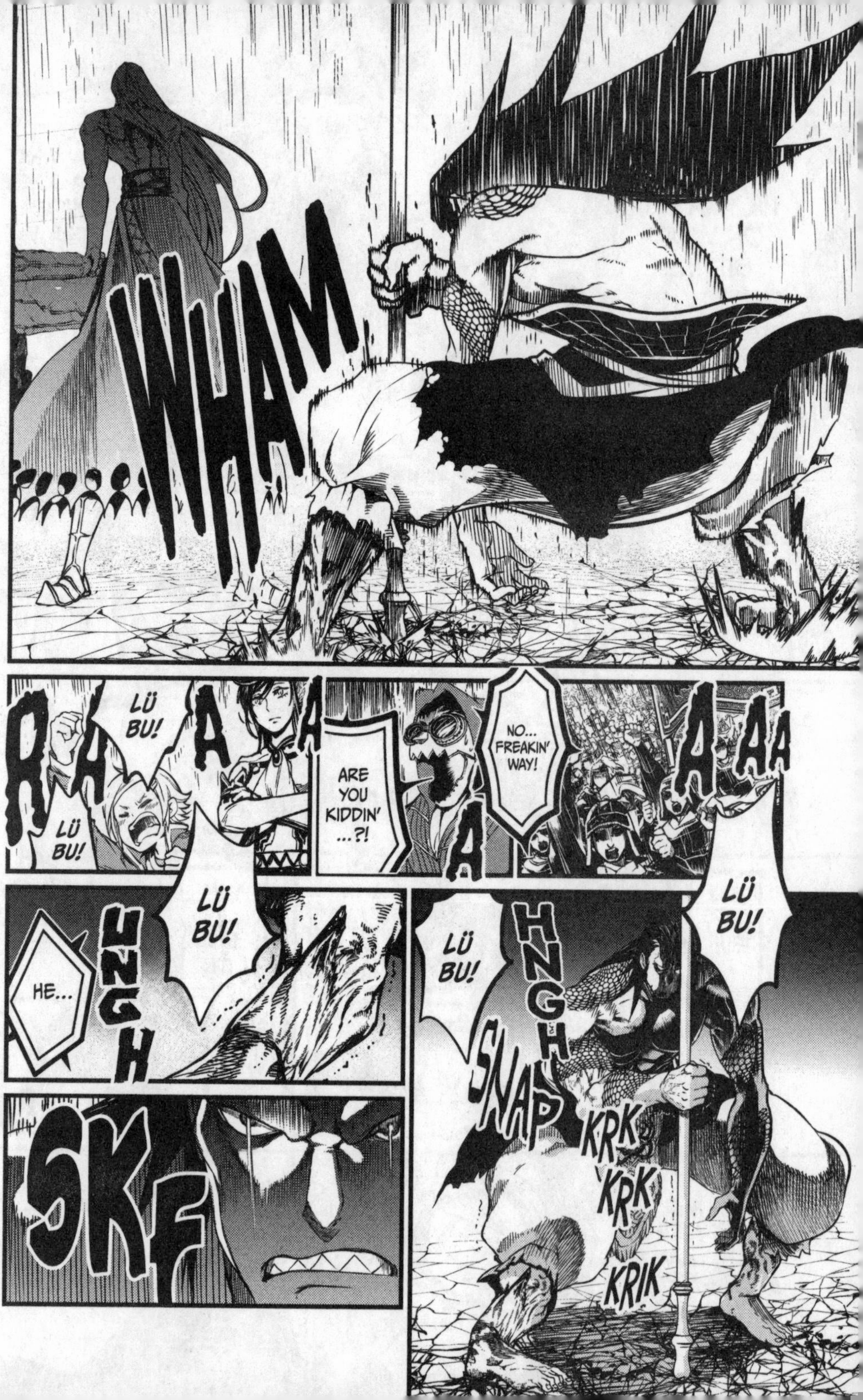
WHAM
RAAAAAAAAA
NO... FREAKIN' WAY!
ARE YOU KIDDIN' ...?!
LÜ BU!
LÜ BU!
LÜ BU!
LÜ BU!
HNGH
HNGH
SNAP
KRK
KRK
KRIK
LÜ BU!
HE...
UNGH
SKF

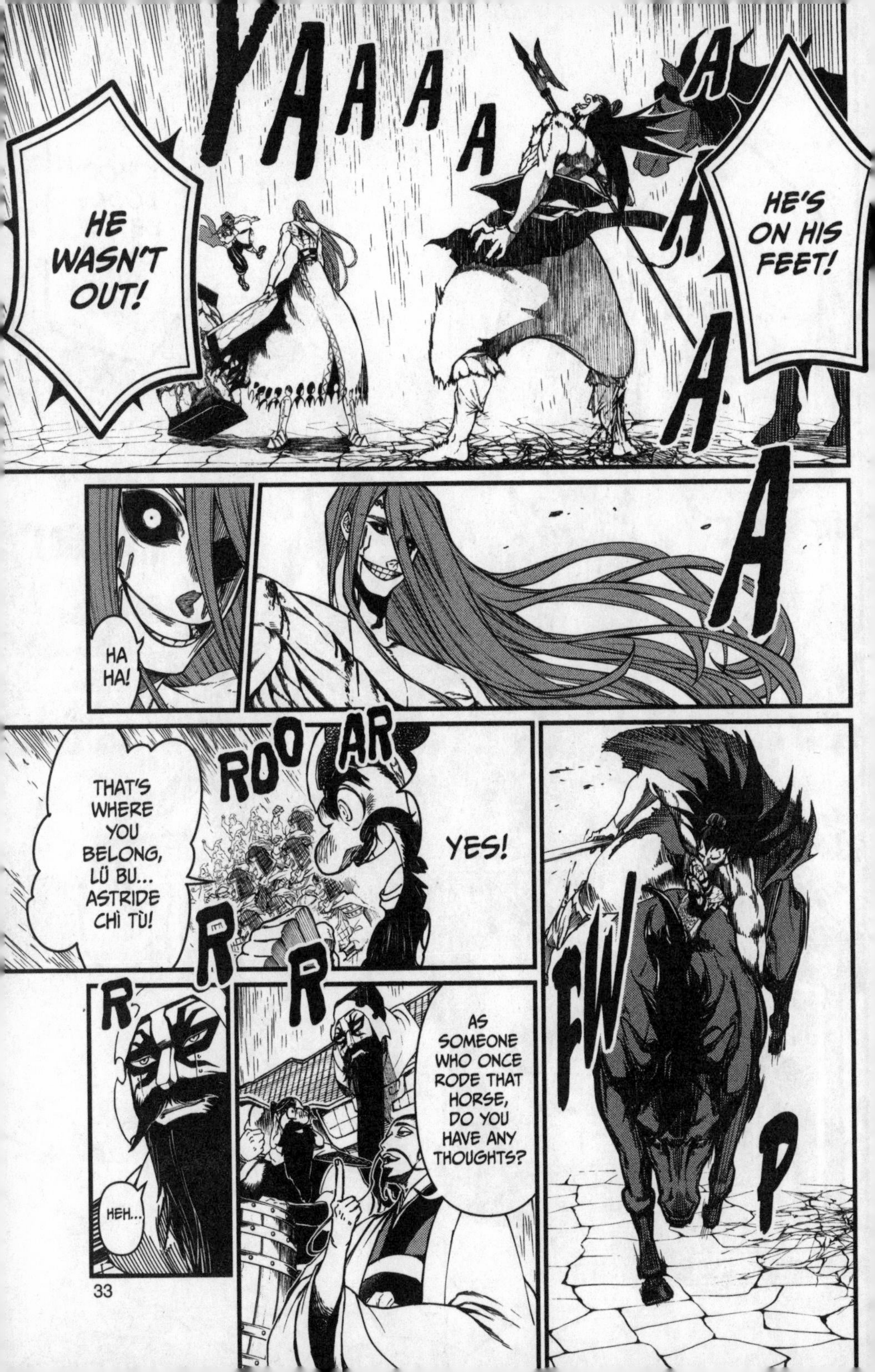
YAAAAAAAAAA
HE'S ON HIS FEET!
HE WASN'T OUT!
HA HA!
FWP
ROOARRRR
YES!
THAT'S WHERE YOU BELONG, LÜ BU... ASTRIDE CHÌ TÙ!
AS SOMEONE WHO ONCE RODE THAT HORSE, DO YOU HAVE ANY THOUGHTS?
HEH...

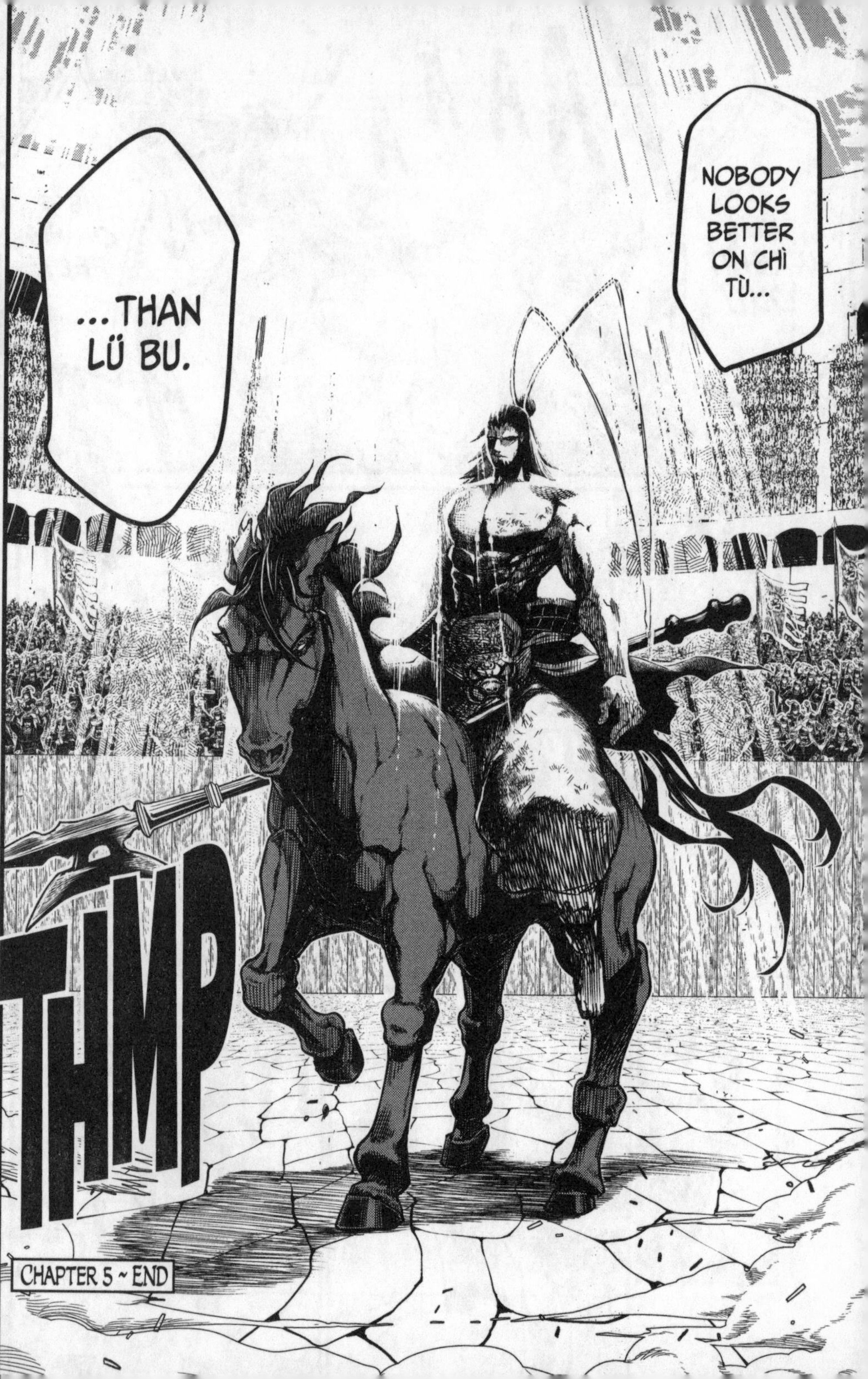
NOBODY LOOKS BETTER ON CHÌ TÙ...
...THAN LÜ BU.
THMP
CHAPTER 5 ~ END

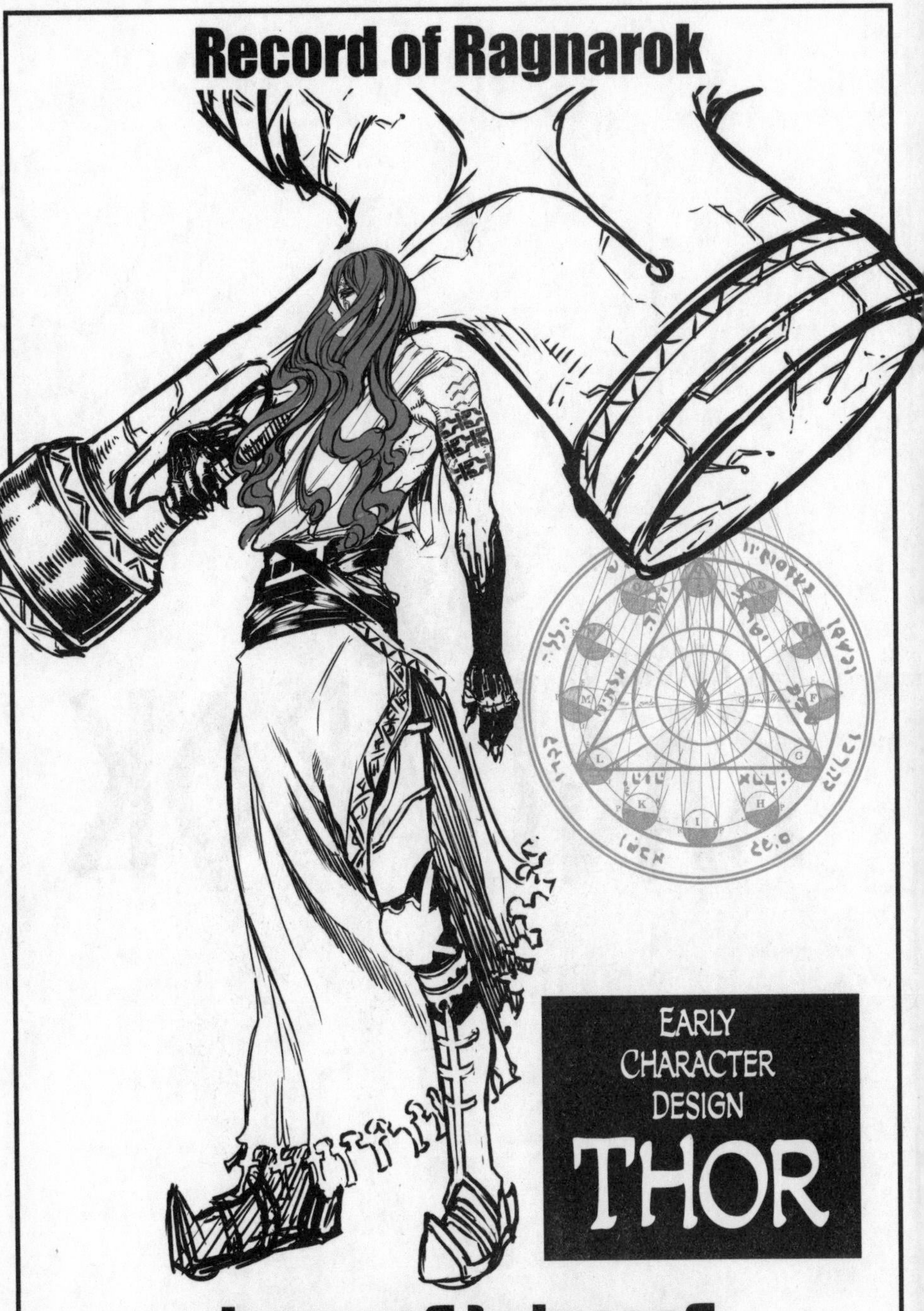
Record of Ragnarok
EARLY
CHARACTER
DESIGN
THOR
Record of Ragnarok

RECORD OF
RAGNAROK

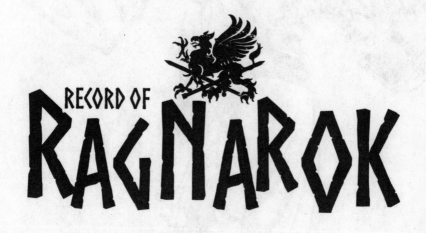

CHAPTER 6: EXUBERANCE

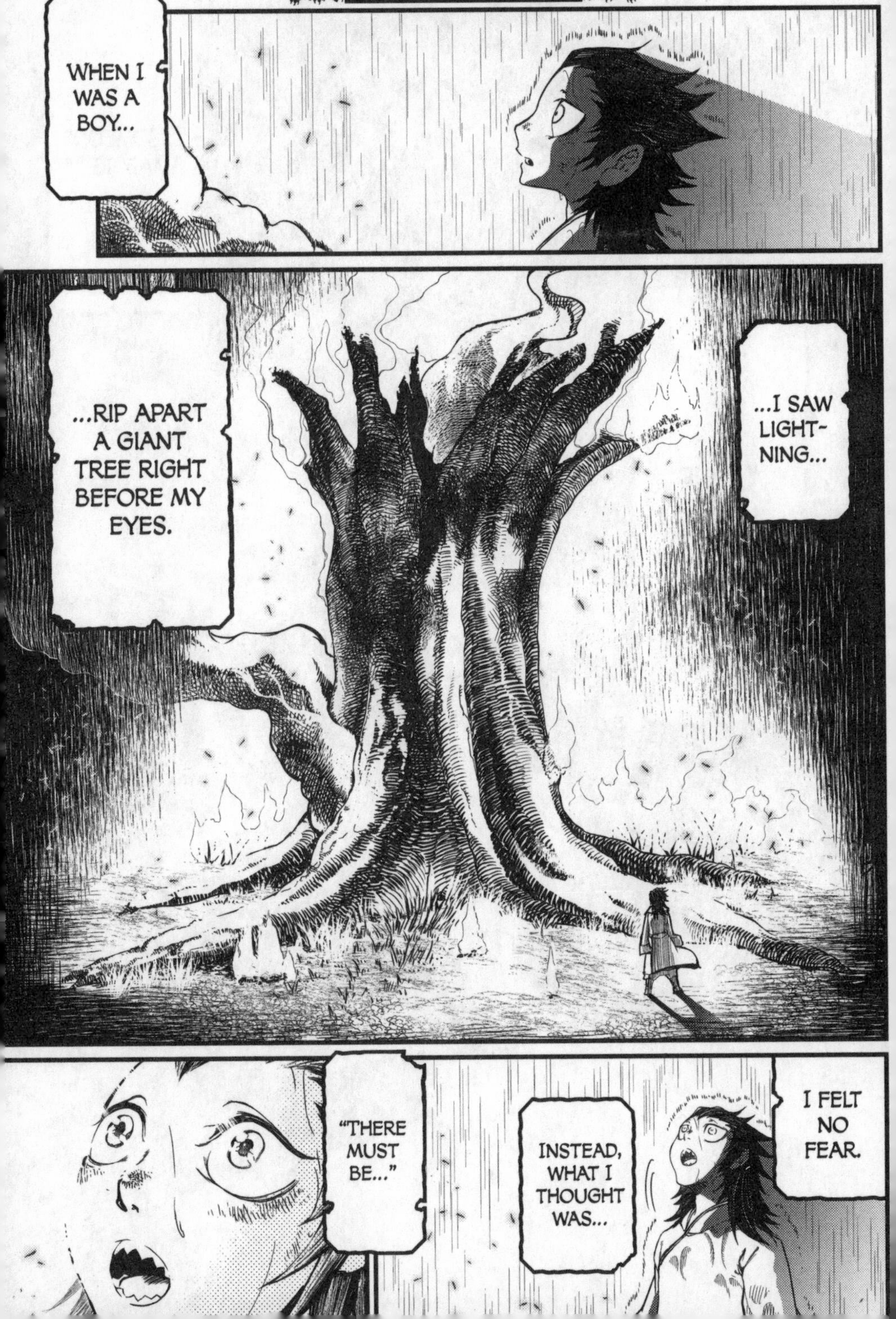
WHEN I WAS A BOY...
...I SAW LIGHT-NING...
...RIP APART A GIANT TREE RIGHT BEFORE MY EYES.
I FELT NO FEAR.
INSTEAD, WHAT I THOUGHT WAS...
"THERE MUST BE..."

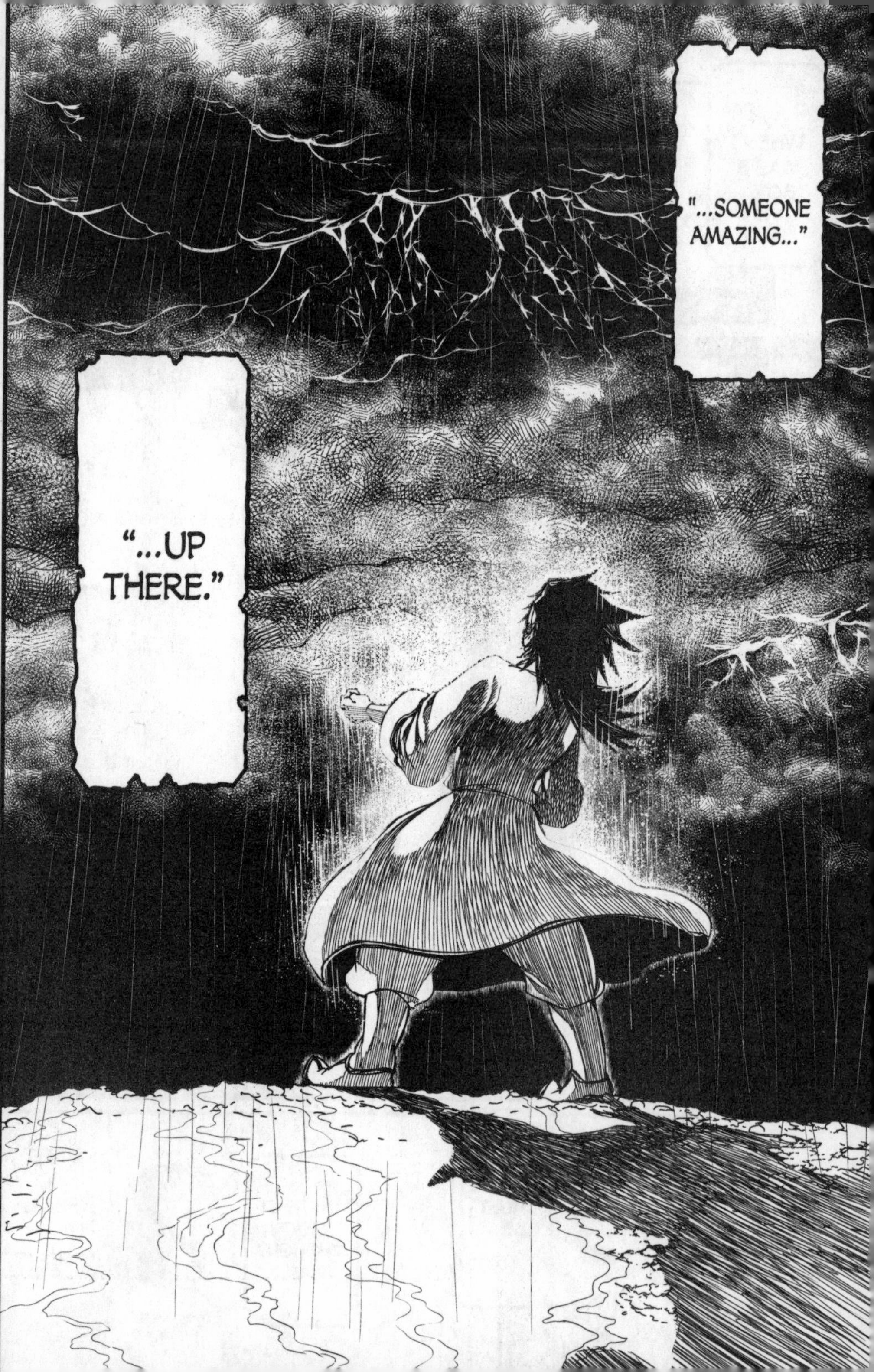
"...SOMEONE AMAZING..."
"...UP THERE."

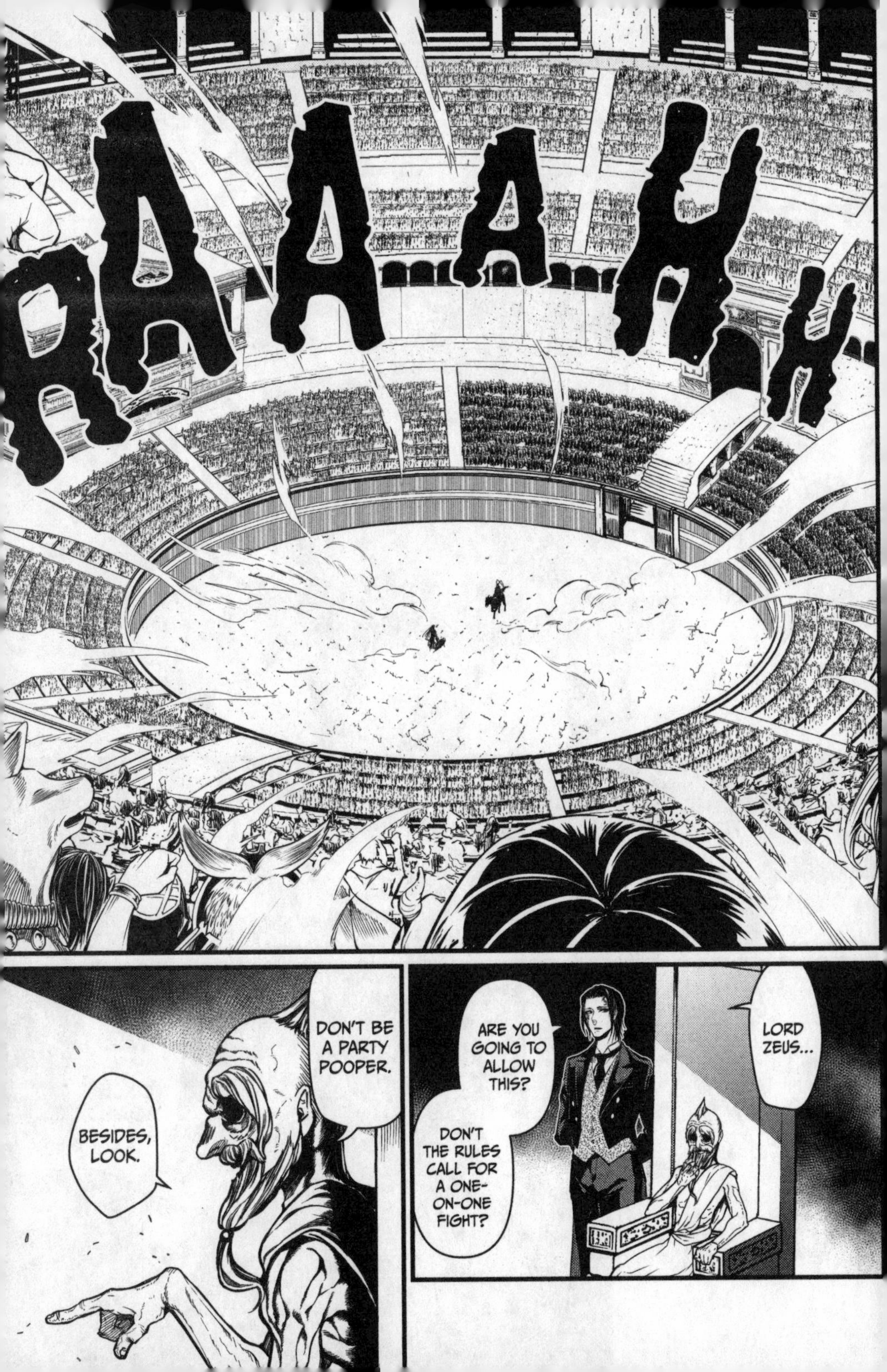
RAAAHH
LORD ZEUS...
ARE YOU GOING TO ALLOW THIS?
DON'T THE RULES CALL FOR A ONE-ON-ONE FIGHT?
DON'T BE A PARTY POOPER.
BESIDES, LOOK.

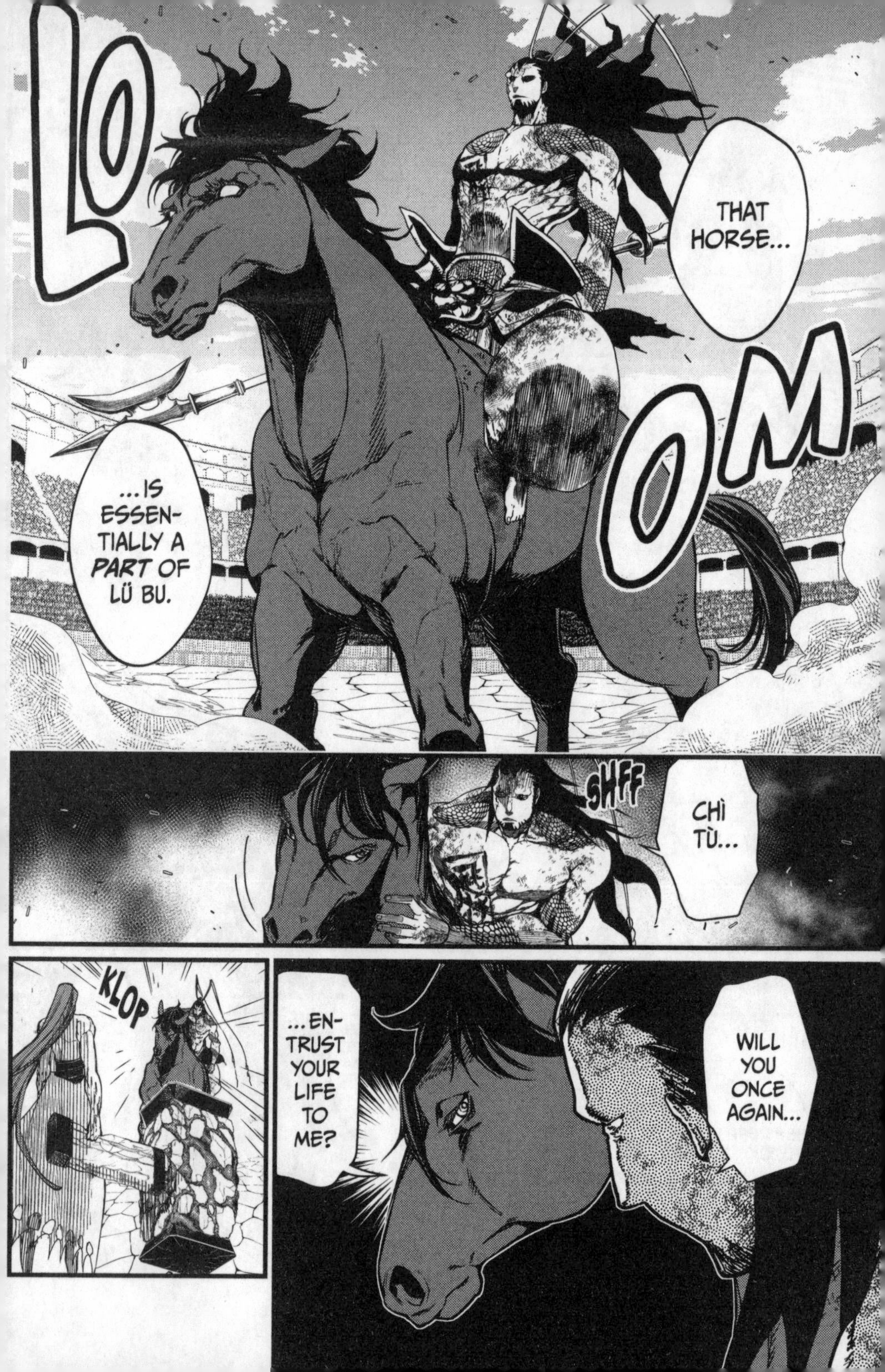
LOOM
THAT HORSE...
...IS ESSENTIALLY A *PART* OF LÜ BU.
SHFF
CHÌ TÙ...
WILL YOU ONCE AGAIN...
...ENTRUST YOUR LIFE TO ME?
KLOP

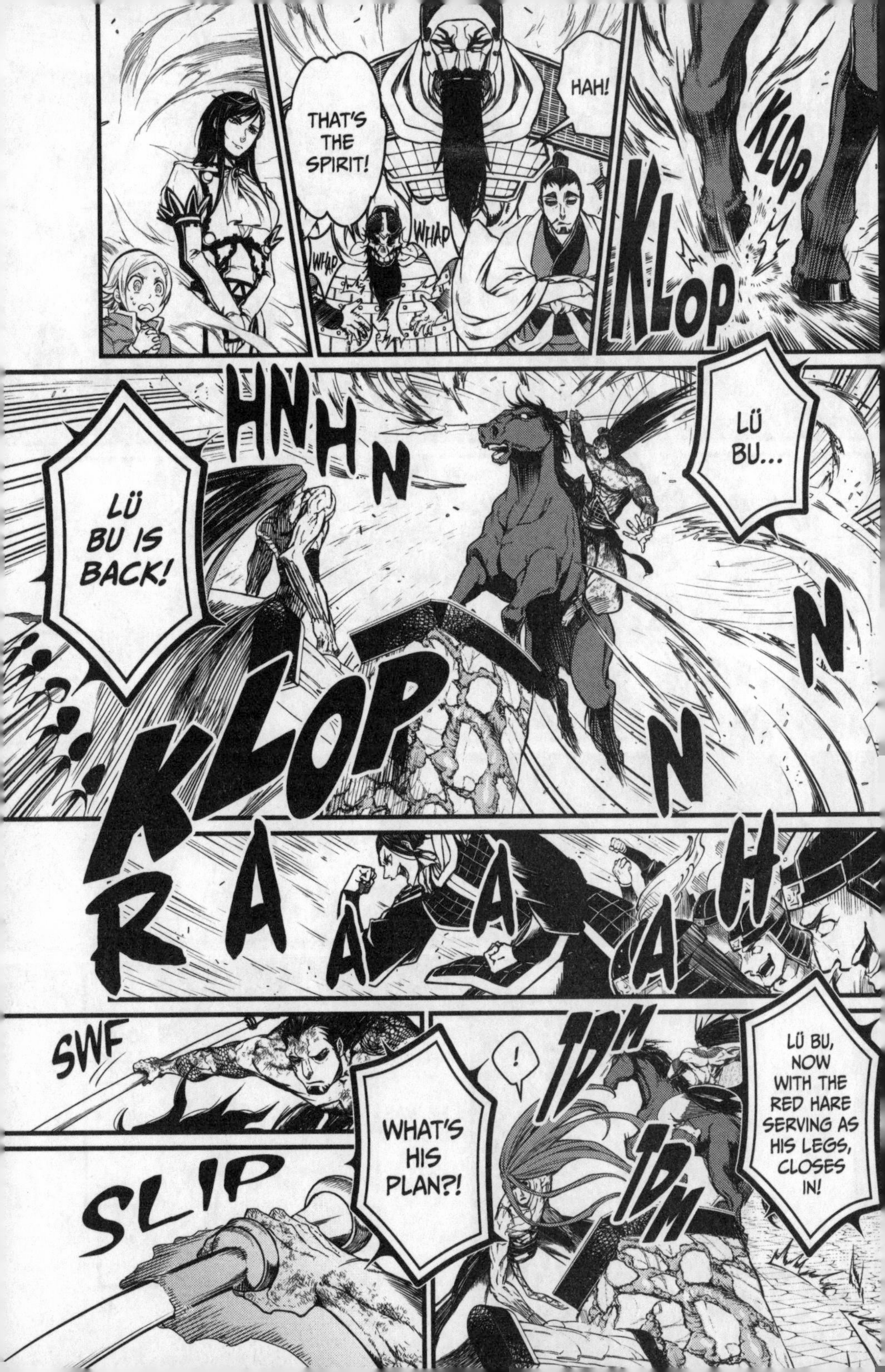
KLOP
KLOP
HAH!
THAT'S THE SPIRIT!
WHAP
WHAP
LÜ BU...
HNHHN
NNN
LÜ BU IS BACK!
KLOP
RAAAAAH
LÜ BU, NOW WITH THE RED HARE SERVING AS HIS LEGS, CLOSES IN!
TDM
TDM
!
WHAT'S HIS PLAN?!
SWF
SLIP

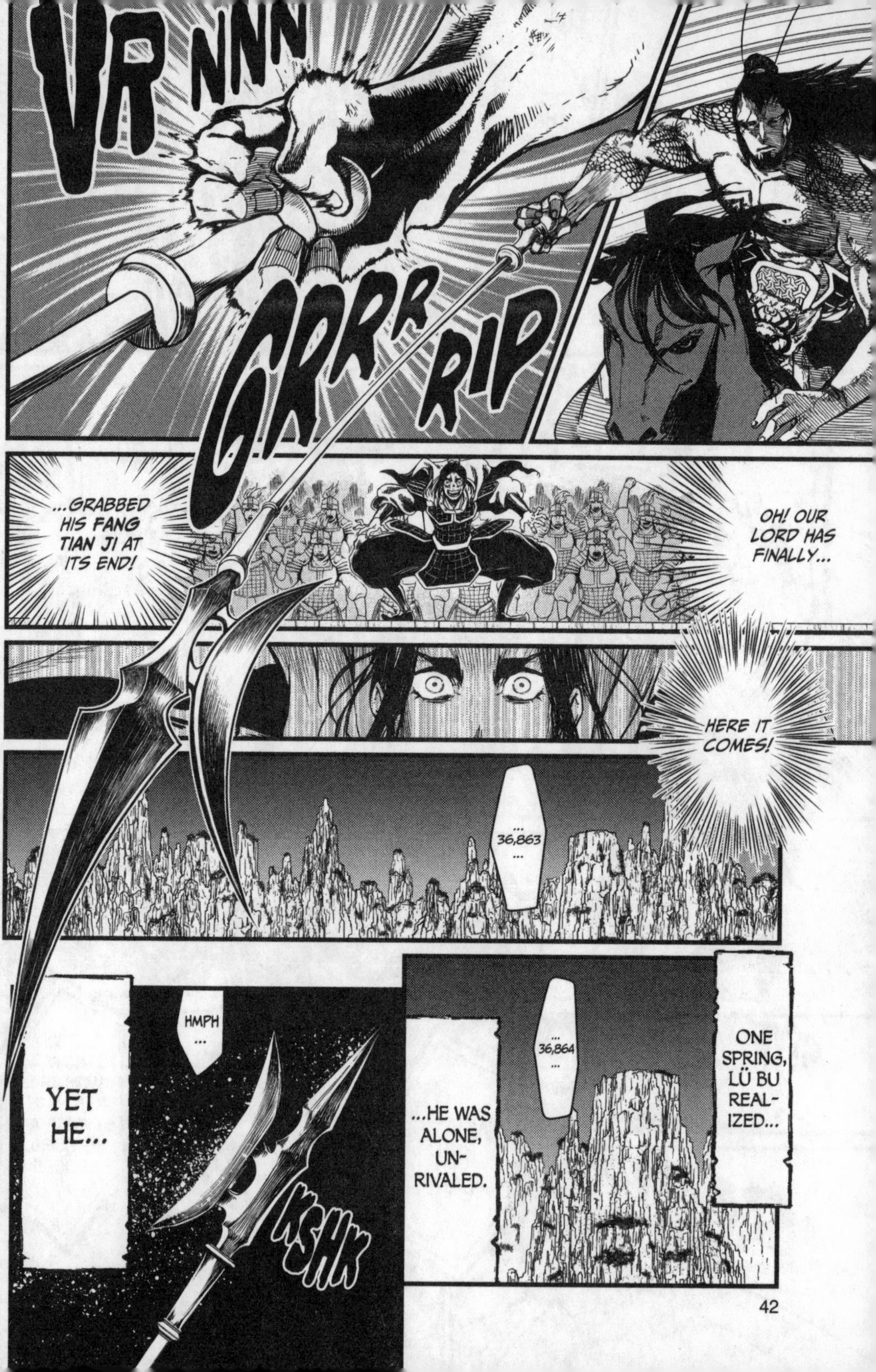
VRNNN
GRRR RIP
OH! OUR LORD HAS FINALLY...
...GRABBED HIS FANG TIAN JI AT ITS END!
HERE IT COMES!
...36,863...
ONE SPRING, LÜ BU REAL-IZED...
...36,864...
...HE WAS ALONE, UN-RIVALED.
HMPH...
YET HE...
KSHK

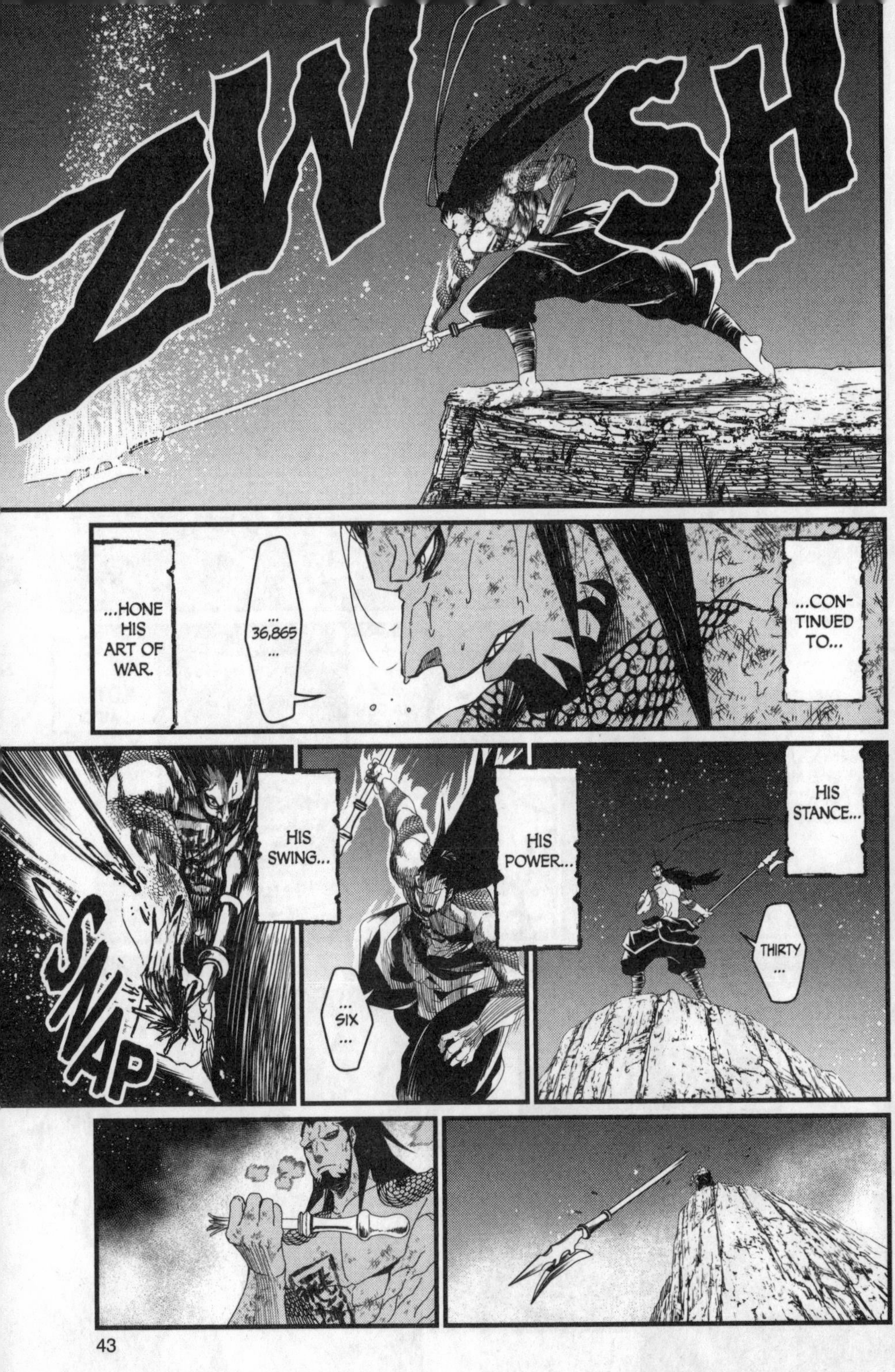
ZWSH
...CON-TINUED TO...
... 36,865 ...
...HONE HIS ART OF WAR.
HIS STANCE...
THIRTY ...
HIS POWER...
... SIX ...
HIS SWING...
SNAP

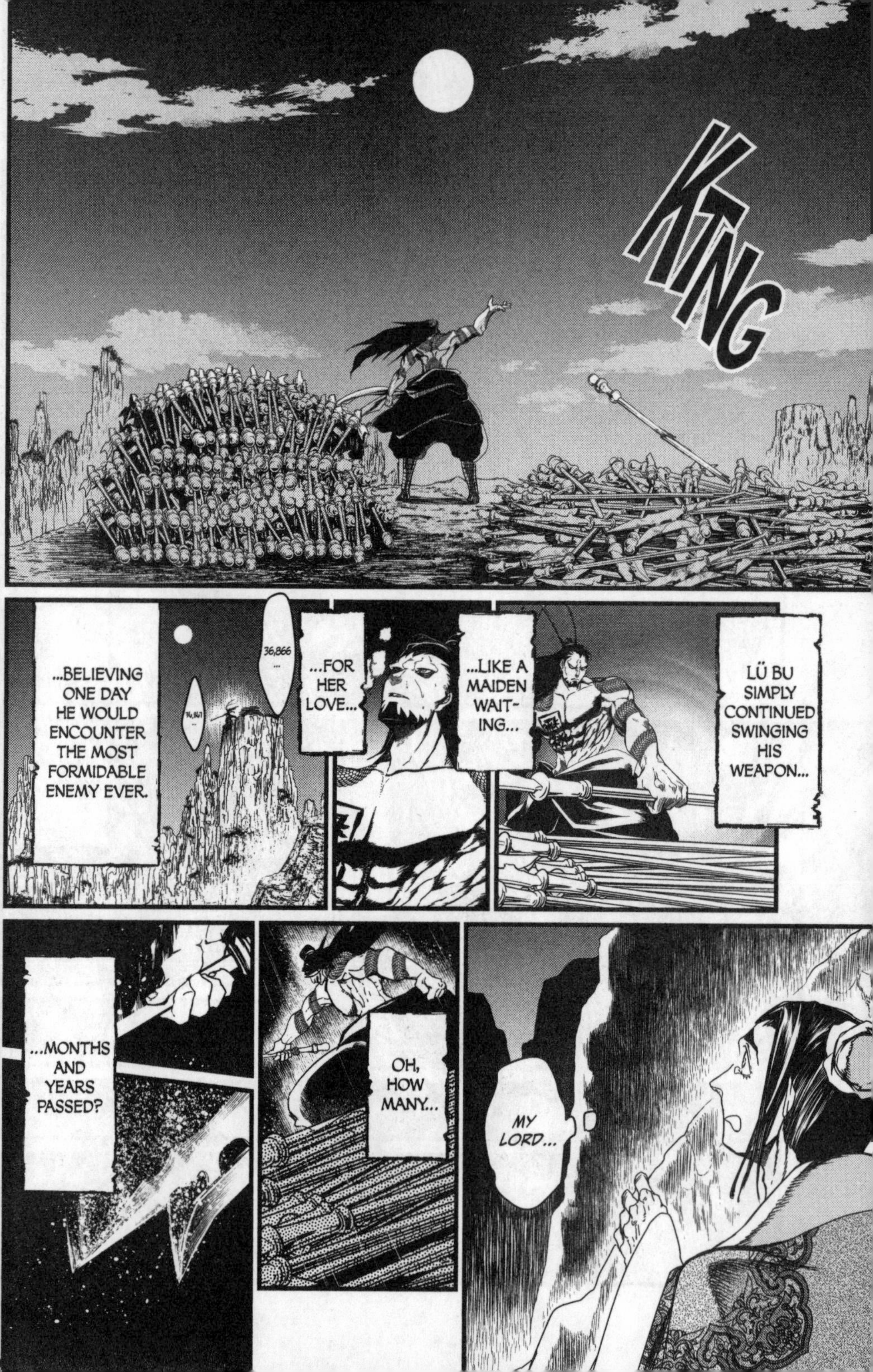
KING
LÜ BU SIMPLY CONTINUED SWINGING HIS WEAPON...
...LIKE A MAIDEN WAITING...
...FOR HER LOVE...
36,866...
36,867...
...BELIEVING ONE DAY HE WOULD ENCOUNTER THE MOST FORMIDABLE ENEMY EVER.
MY LORD...
OH, HOW MANY...
...MONTHS AND YEARS PASSED?

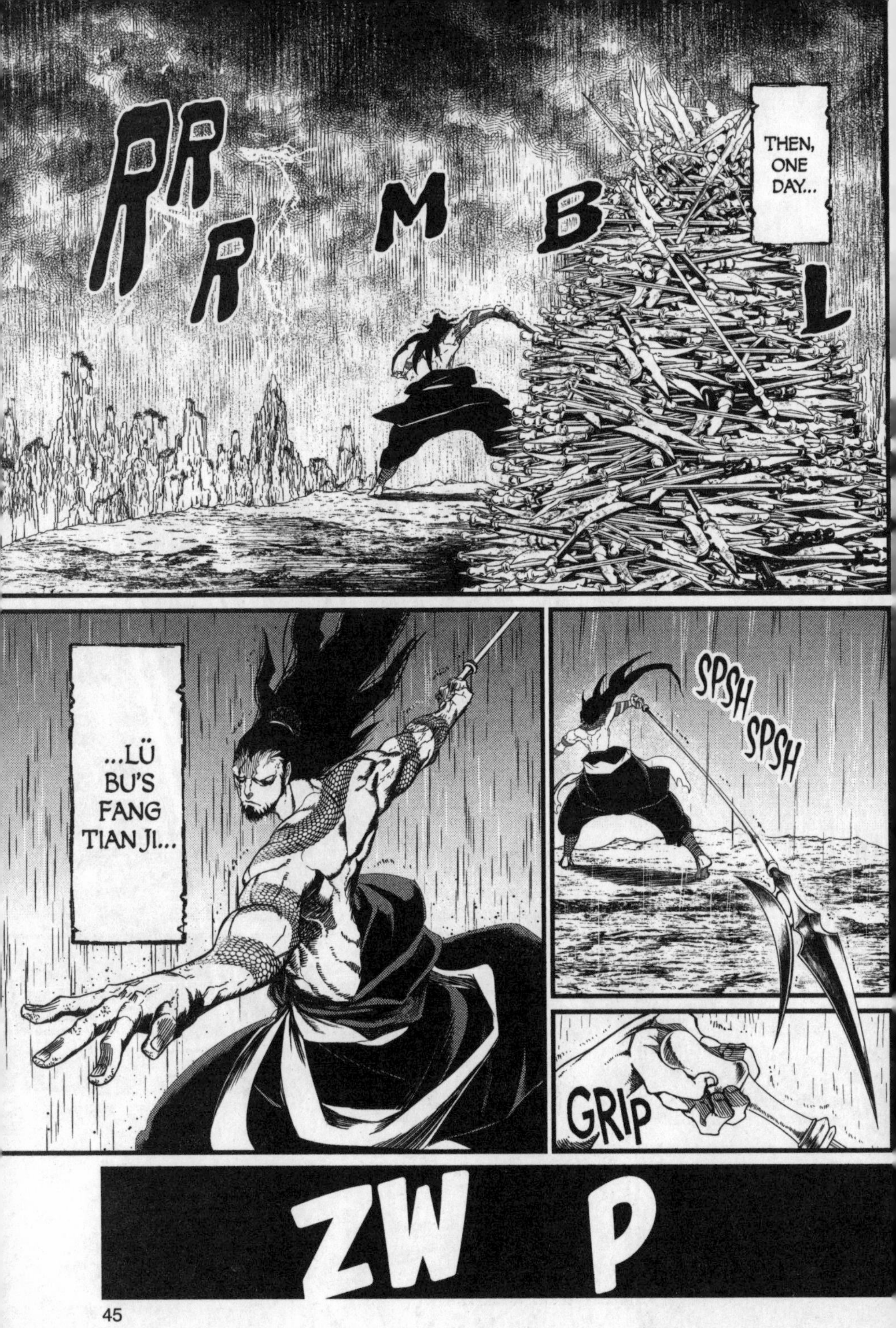
THEN, ONE DAY...
RRRMBL
SPSH SPSH
GRIP
...LÜ BU'S FANG TIAN JI...
ZW P

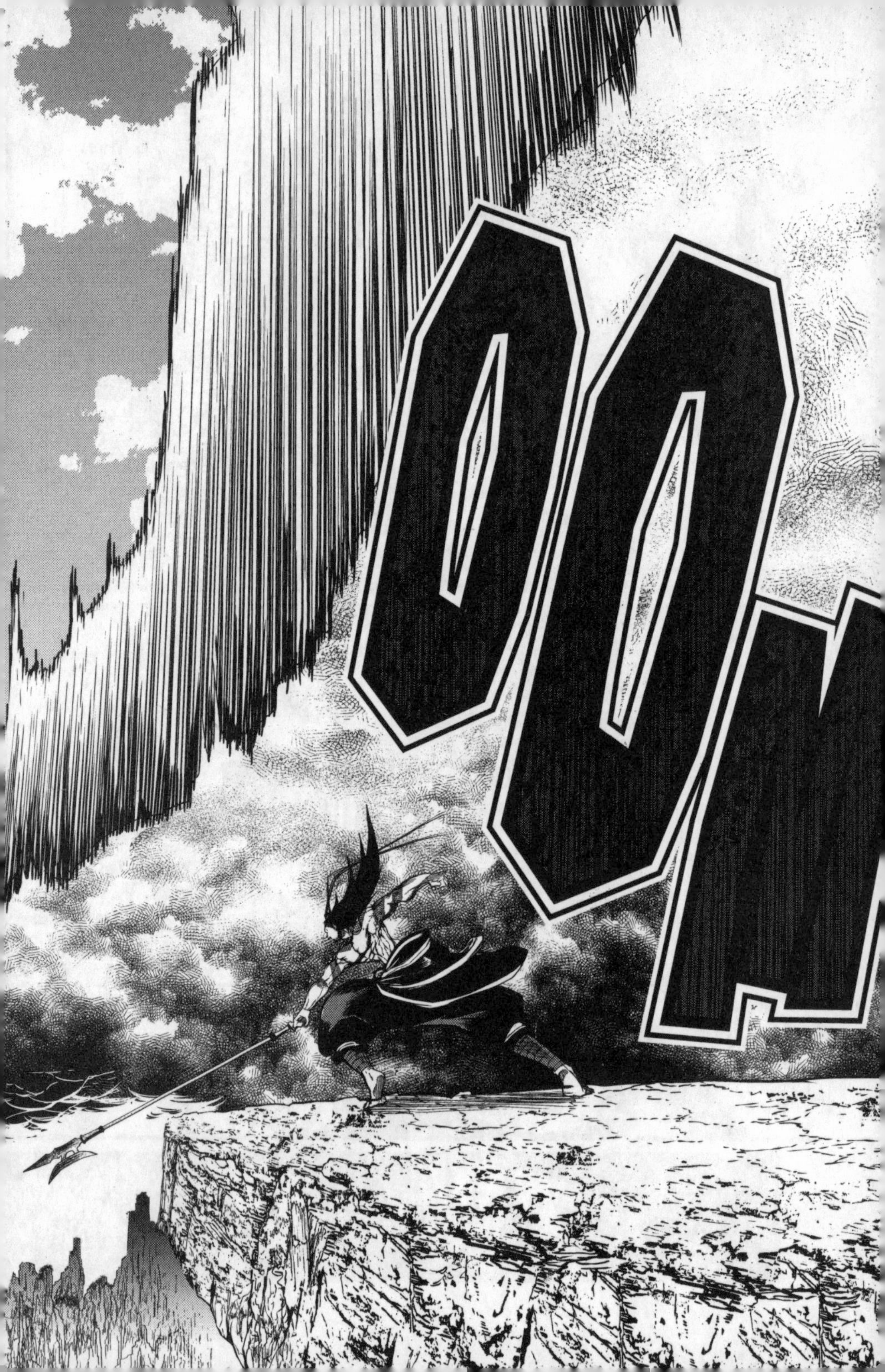
OO

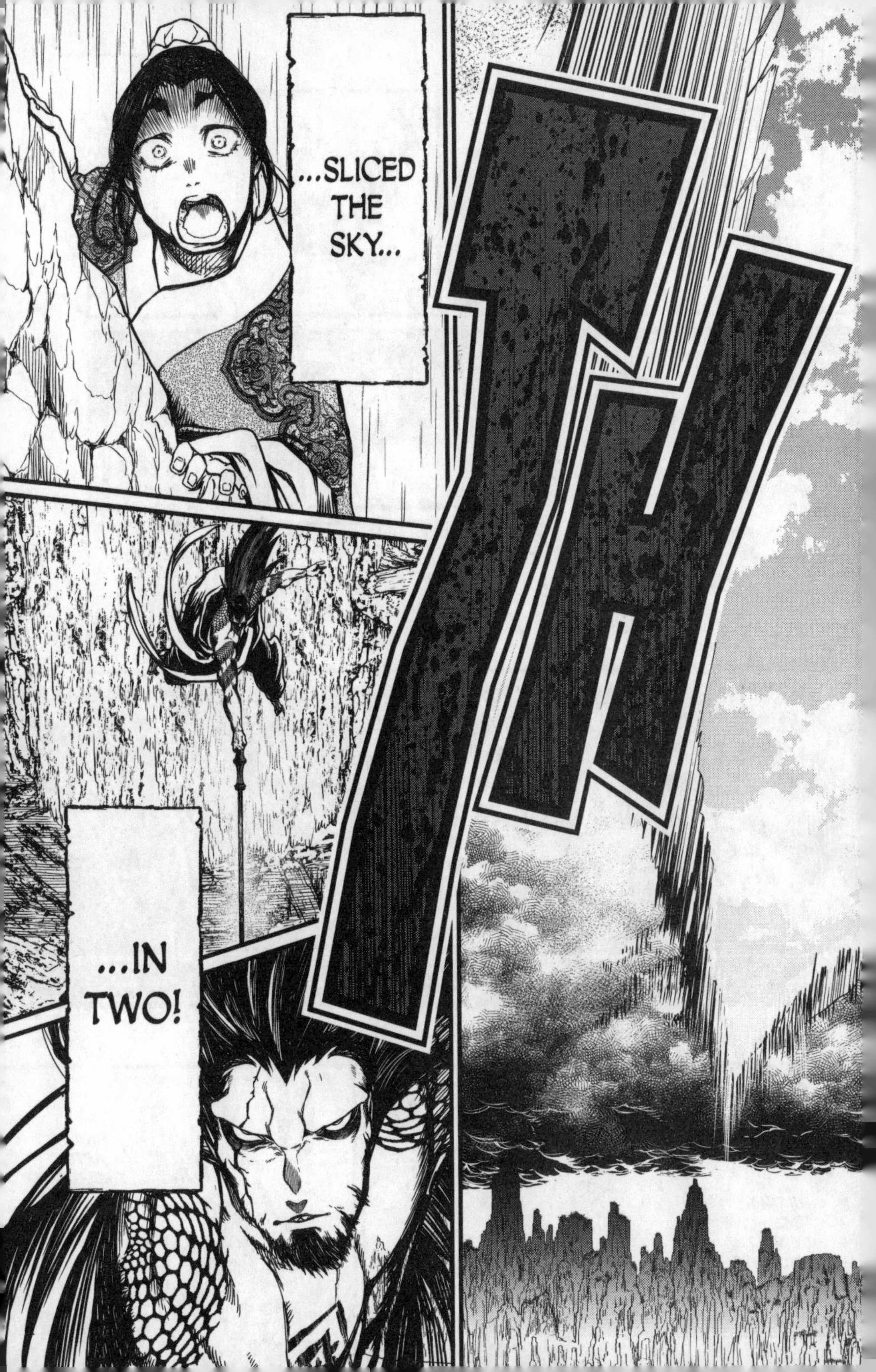
...SLICED THE SKY...
...IN TWO!

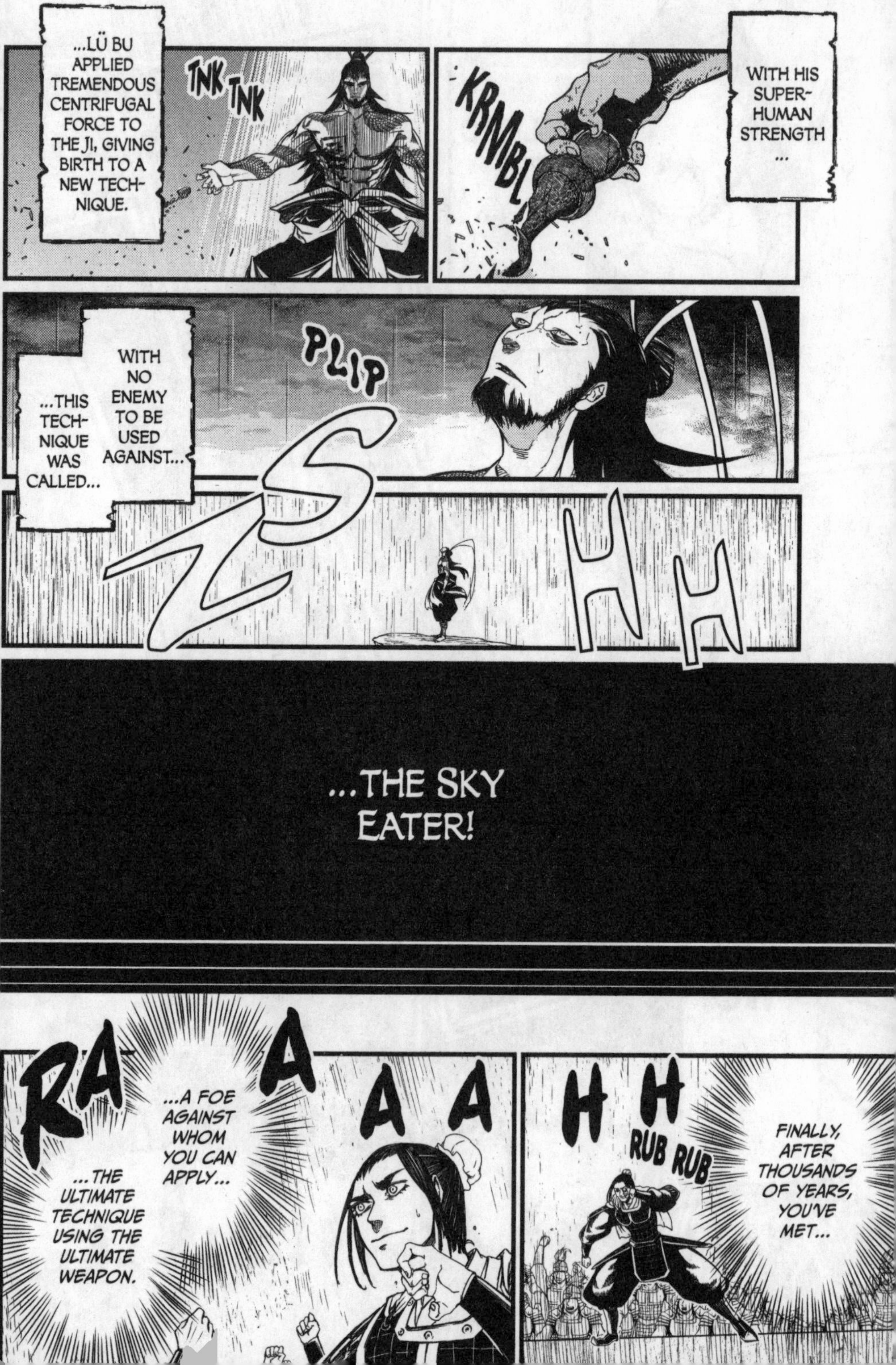
WITH HIS SUPER-HUMAN STRENGTH ...
KRMBL
...LÜ BU APPLIED TREMENDOUS CENTRIFUGAL FORCE TO THE JI, GIVING BIRTH TO A NEW TECH-NIQUE.
TNK TNK
PLIP
WITH NO ENEMY TO BE USED AGAINST...
...THIS TECH-NIQUE WAS CALLED...
ZSHH
...THE SKY EATER!
RAAAAHH
FINALLY, AFTER THOUSANDS OF YEARS, YOU'VE MET...
RUB RUB
...A FOE AGAINST WHOM YOU CAN APPLY...
...THE ULTIMATE TECHNIQUE USING THE ULTIMATE WEAPON.

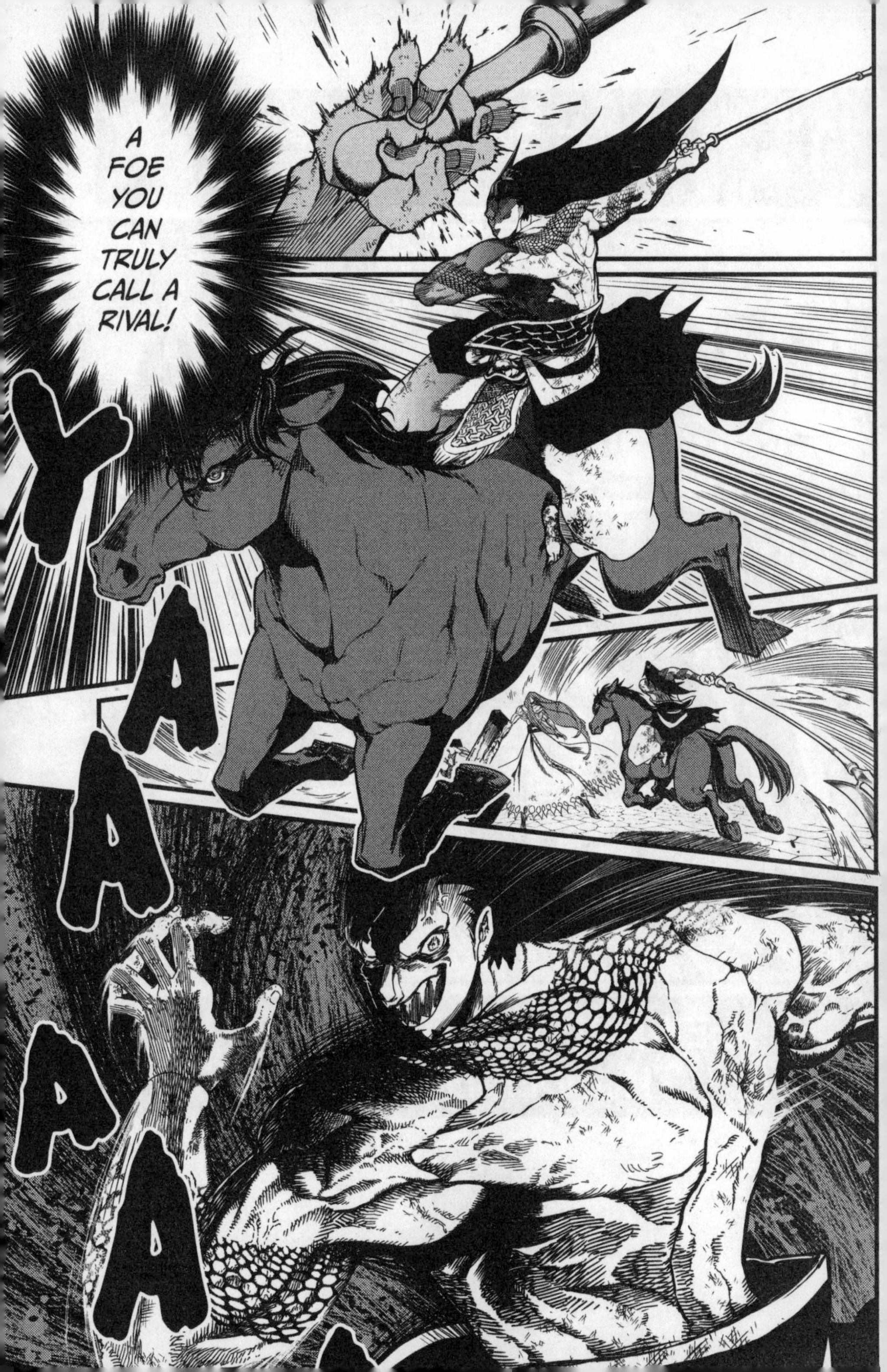
A FOE YOU CAN TRULY CALL A RIVAL!
YAAAAA

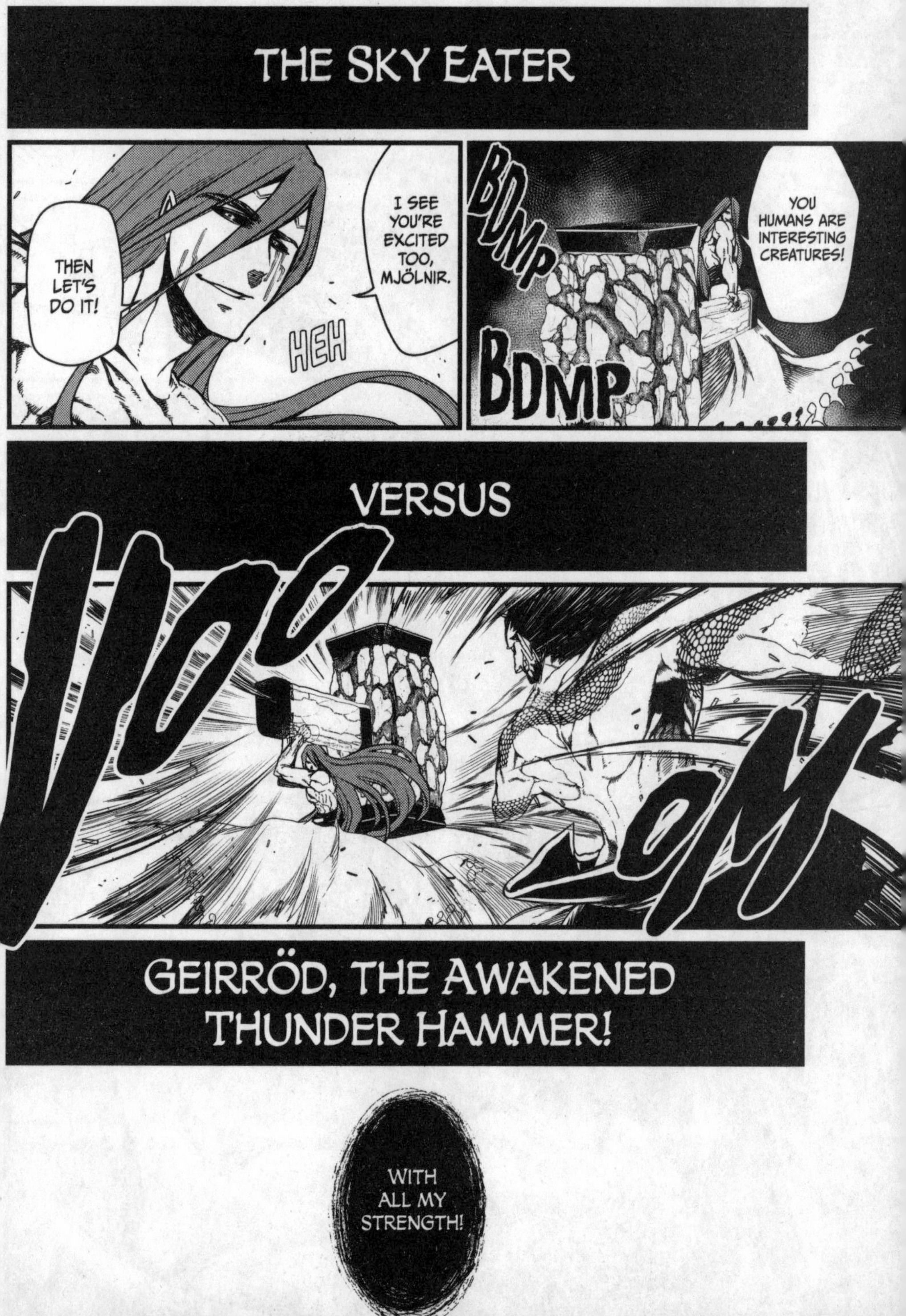
THE SKY EATER
YOU HUMANS ARE INTERESTING CREATURES!
BDMP
BDMP
I SEE YOU'RE EXCITED TOO, MJÖLNIR.
HEH
THEN LET'S DO IT!
VERSUS
GEIRRÖD, THE AWAKENED THUNDER HAMMER!
WITH ALL MY STRENGTH!

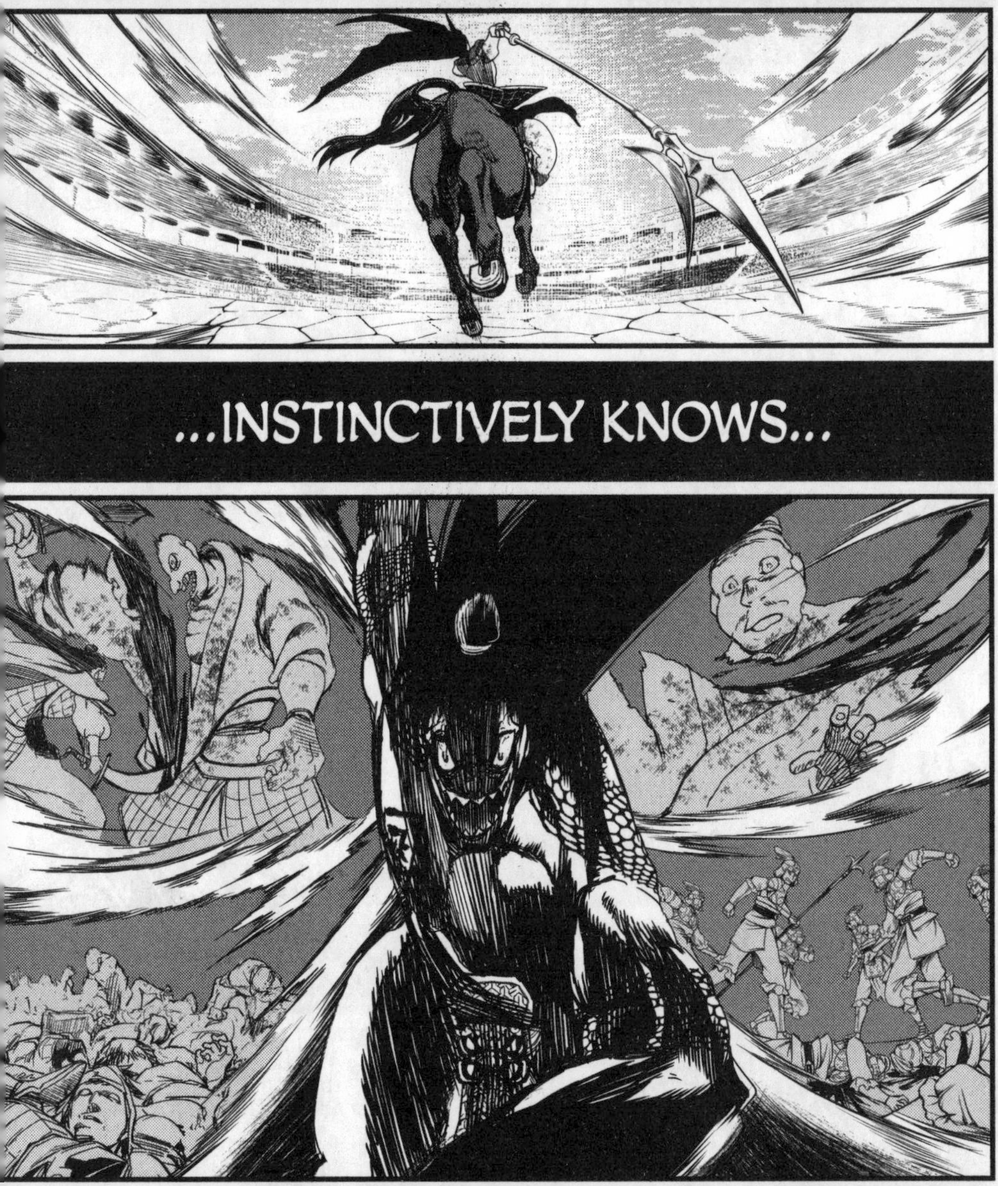
...INSTINCTIVELY KNOWS...

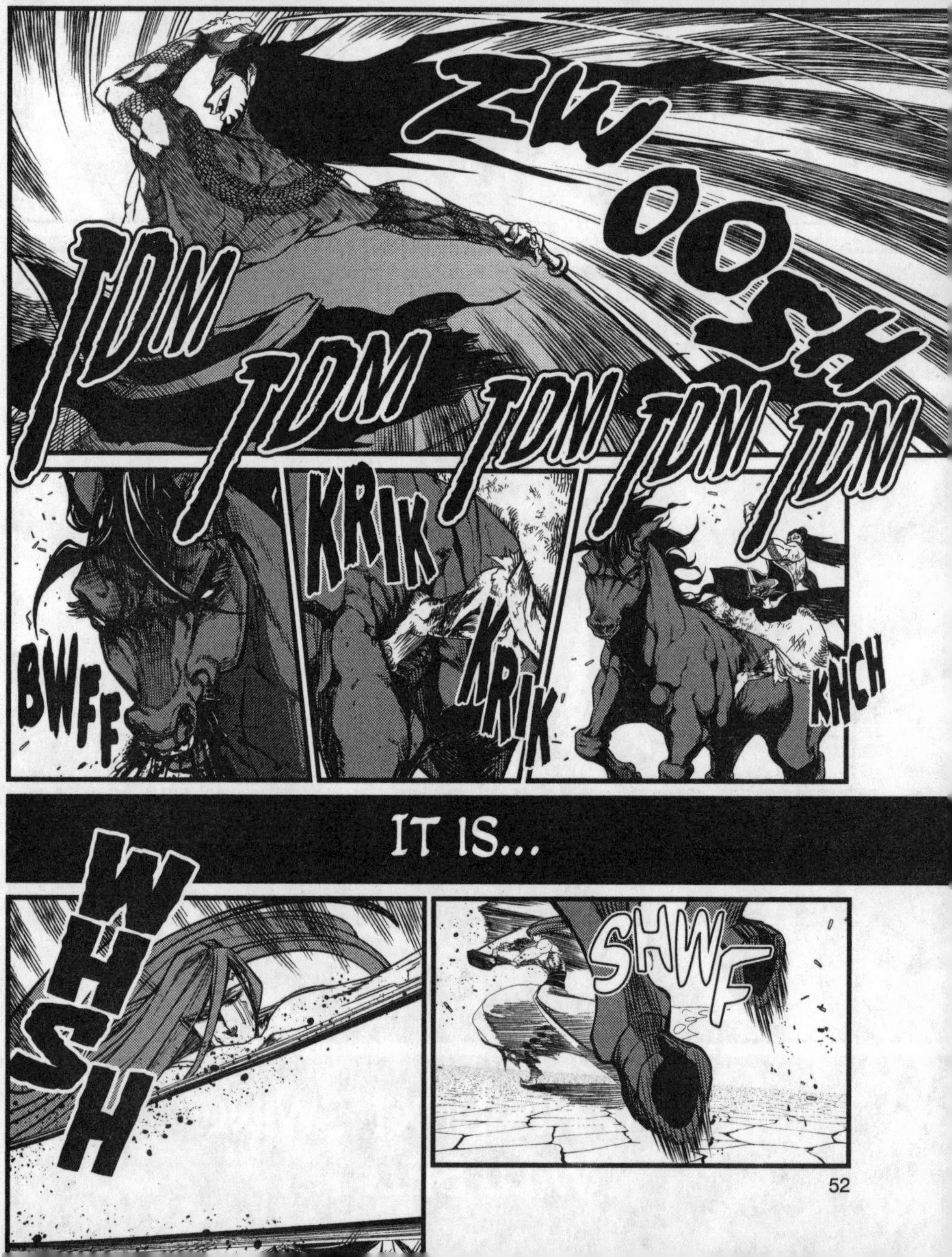
ZWOOSH
TDM
TDM
TDM
TDM
TDM
KNCH
KRIK
KRIK
BWFF
IT IS...
SHWF
WHSH

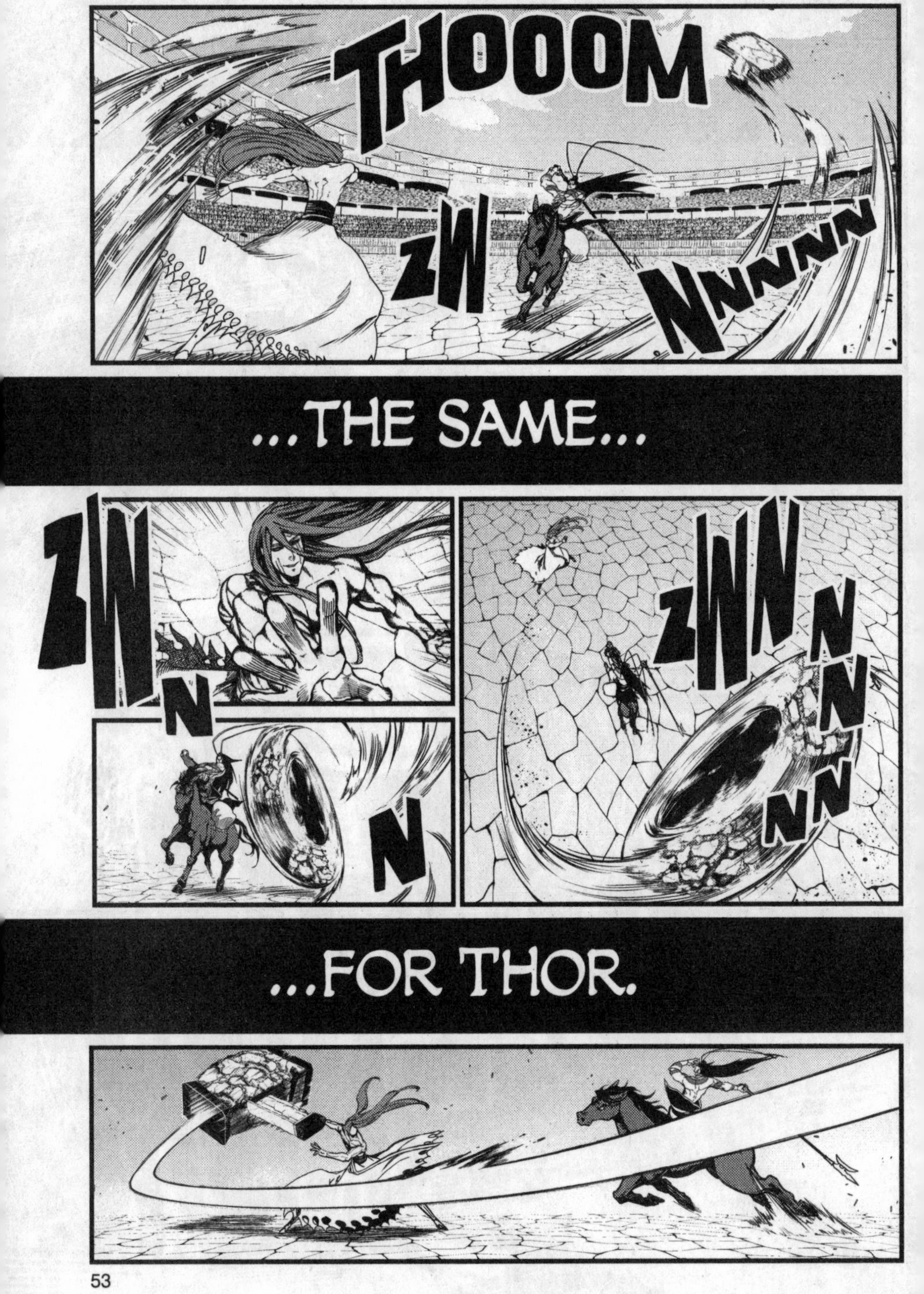
THOOOM
ZW
NNNNNN
...THE SAME...
ZWNN
N
N
N
NN
ZWN
N
N
...FOR THOR.

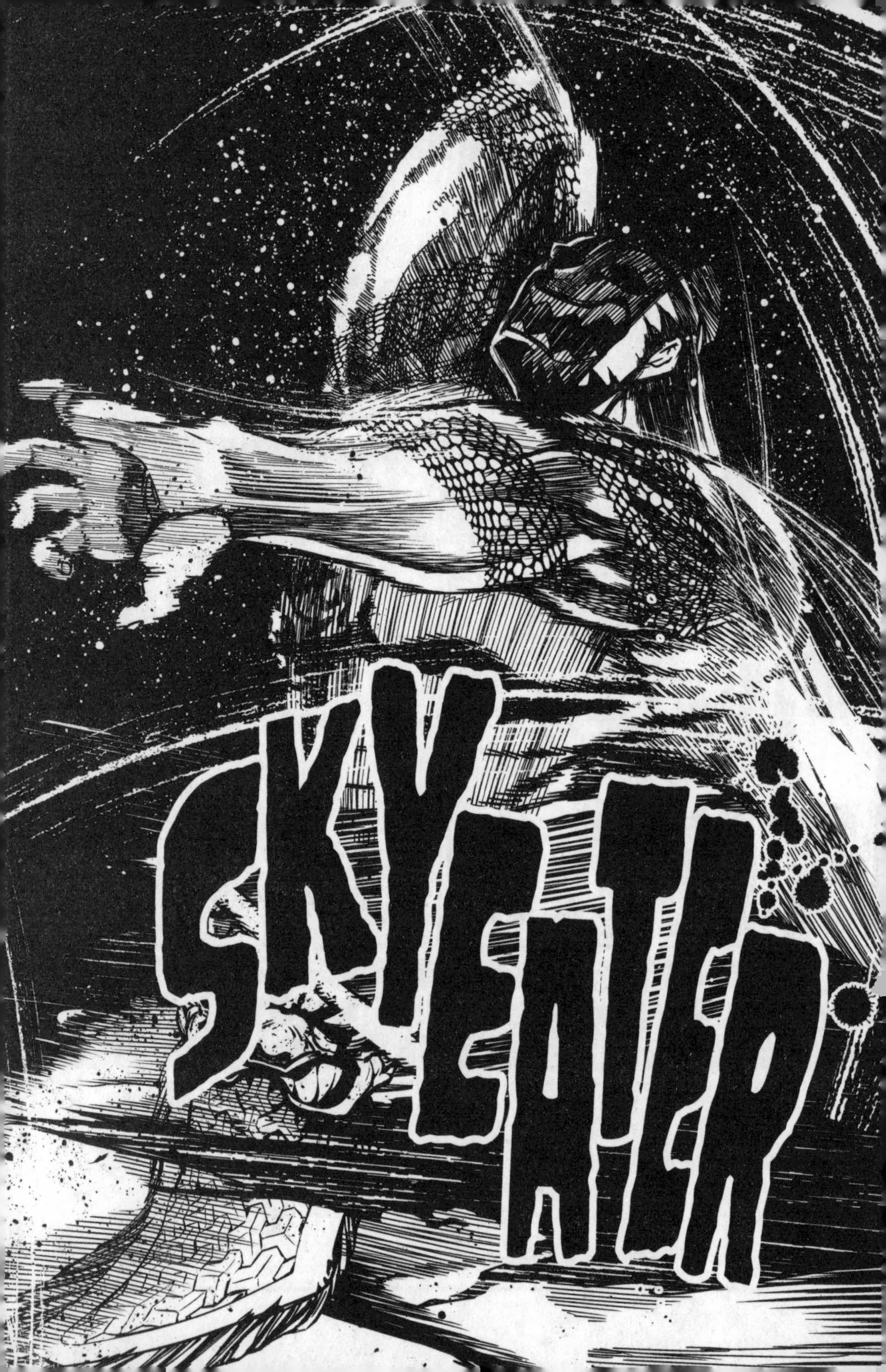
SKYEATER

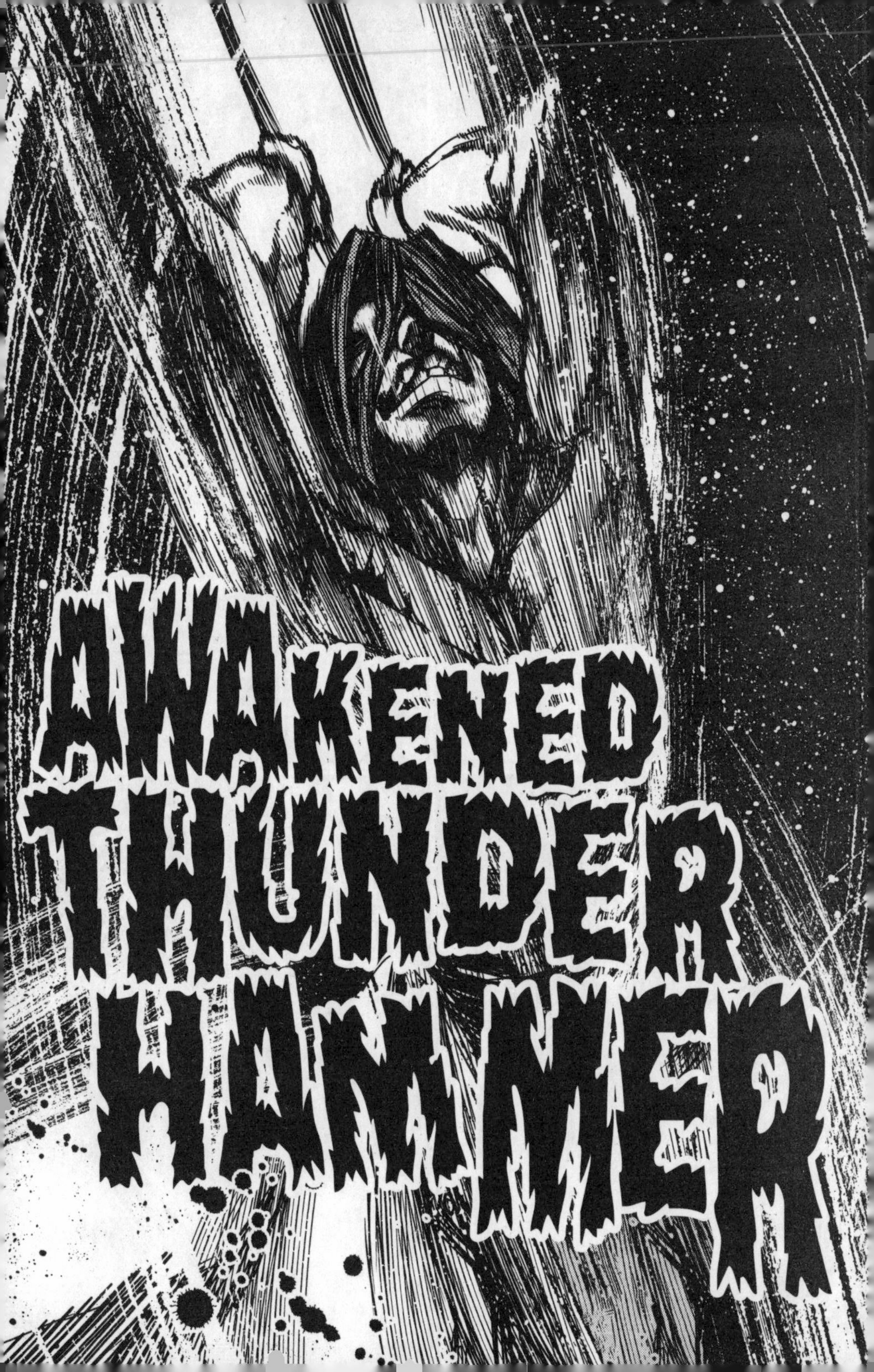
AWAKENED
THUNDER
HAMMER

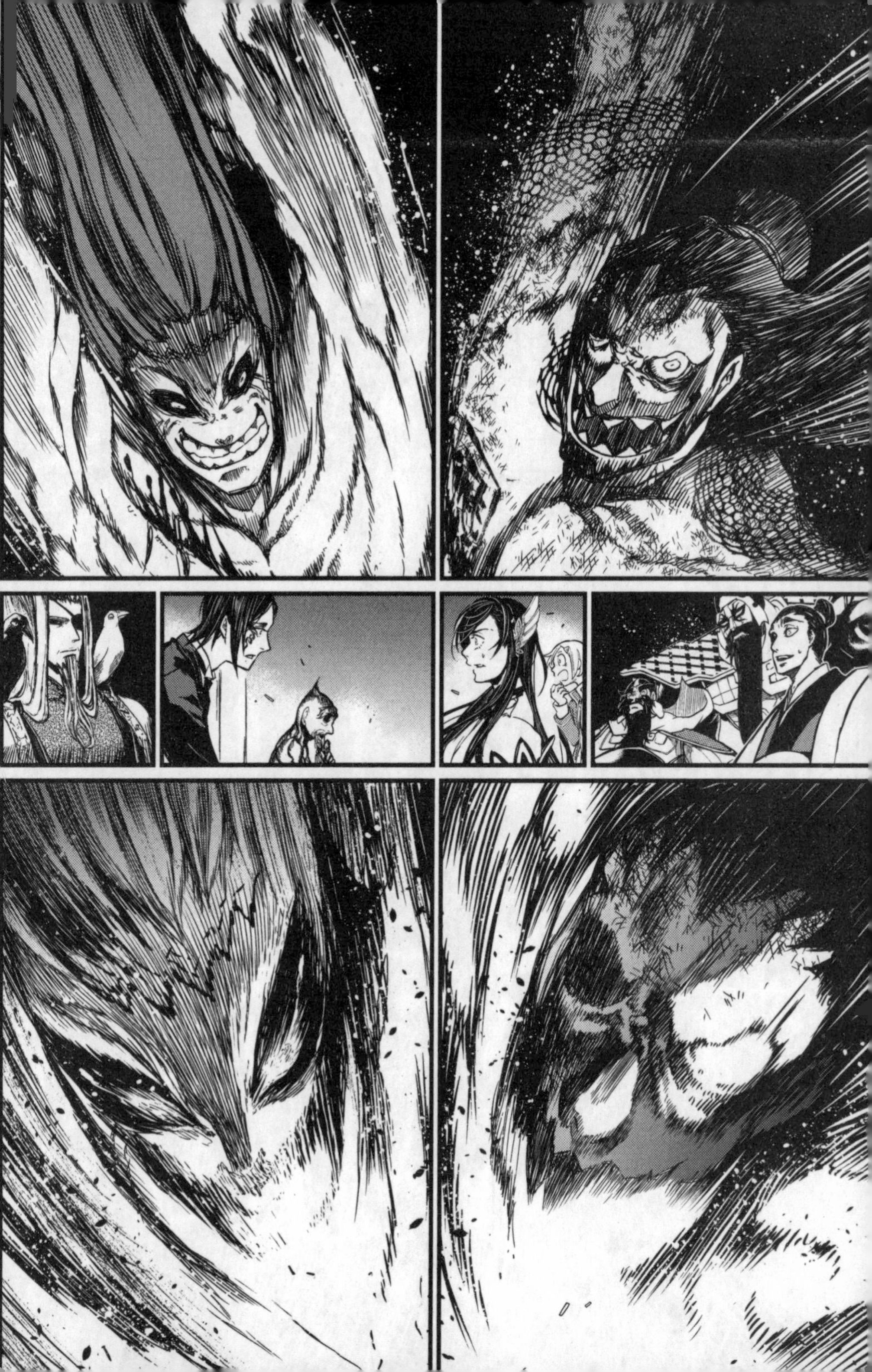

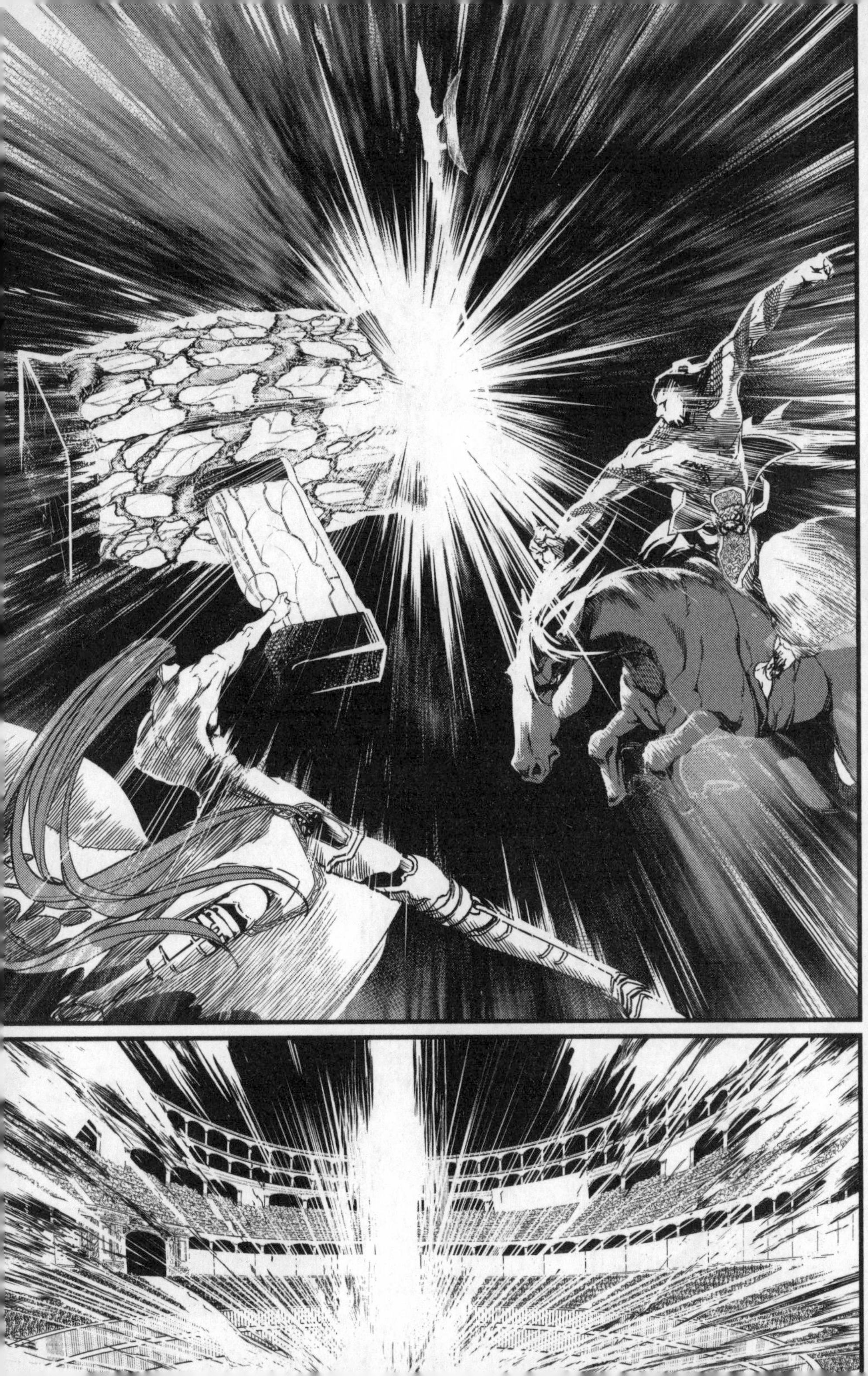

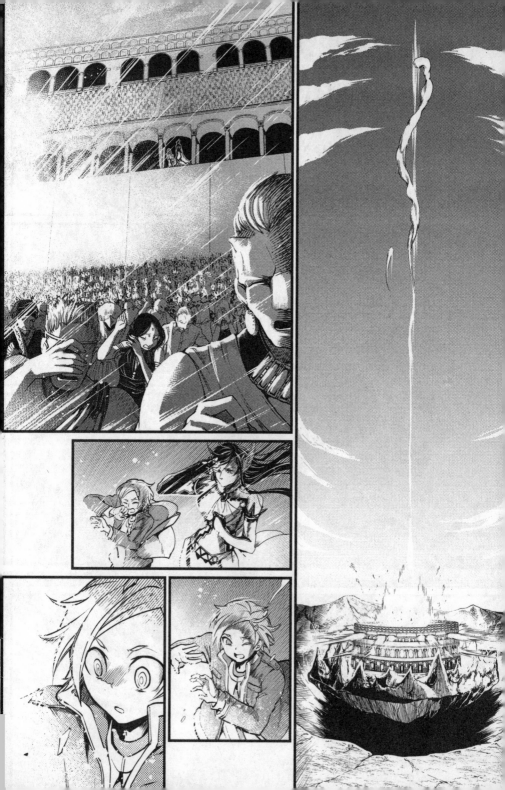

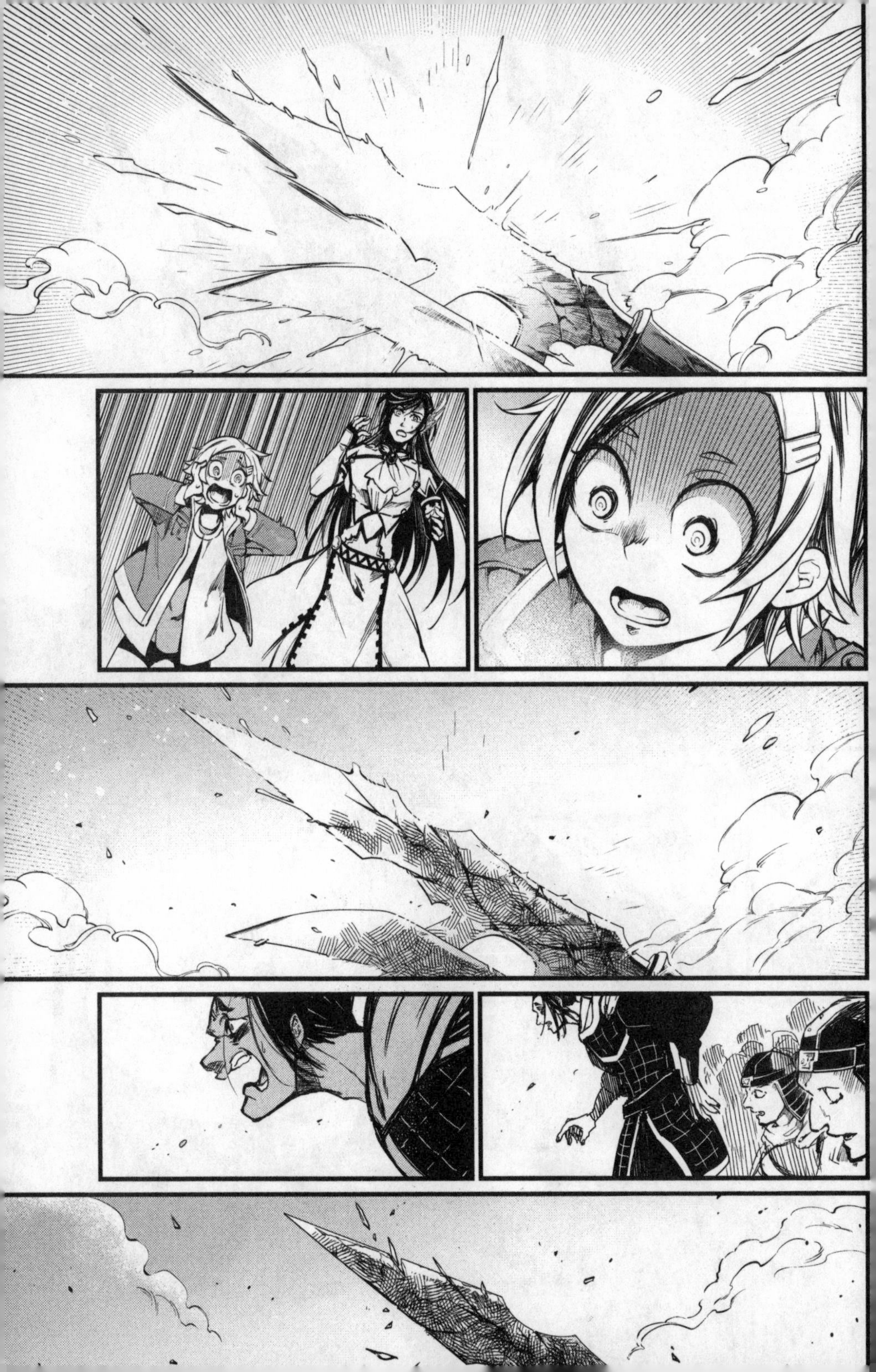

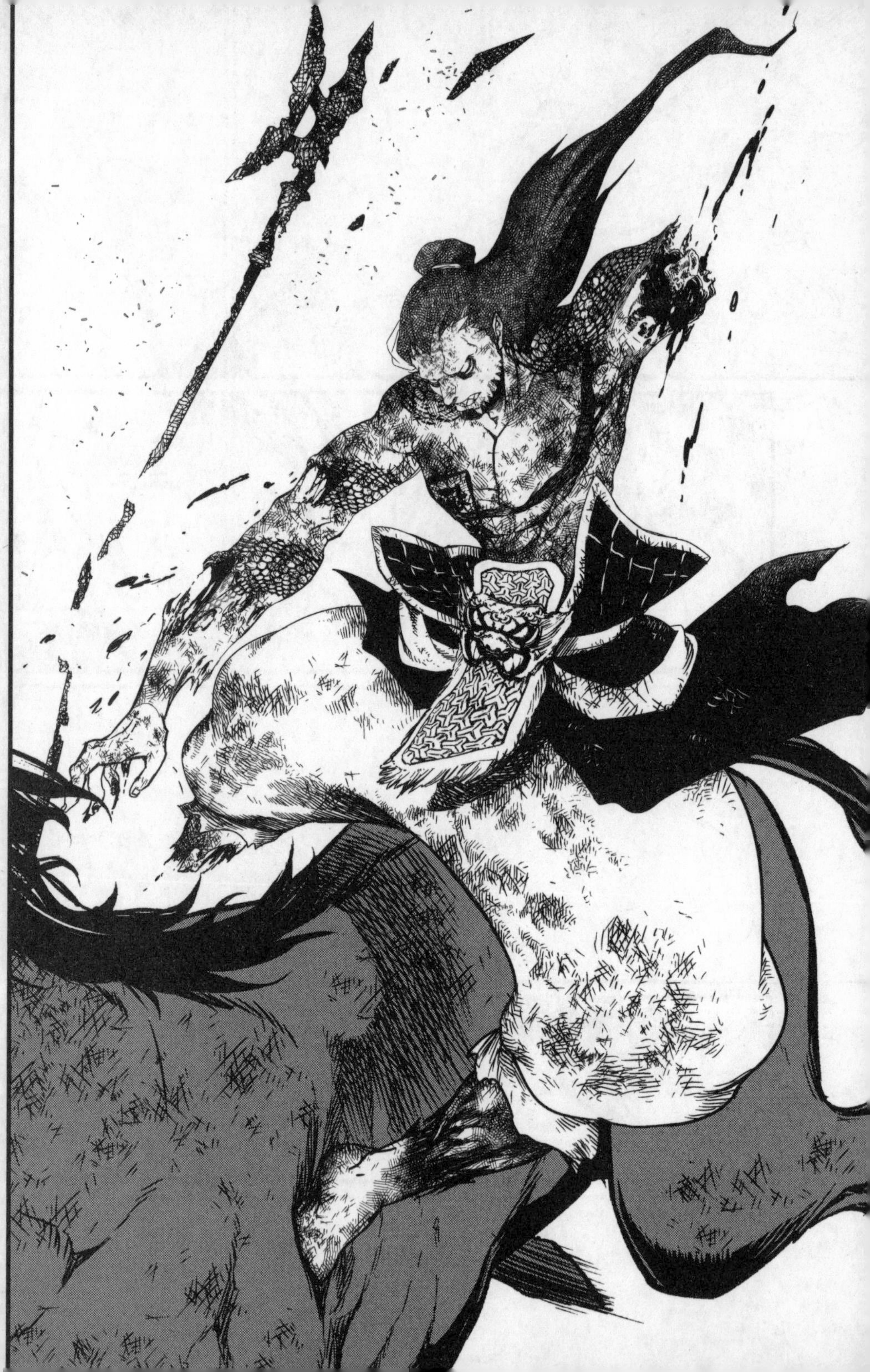

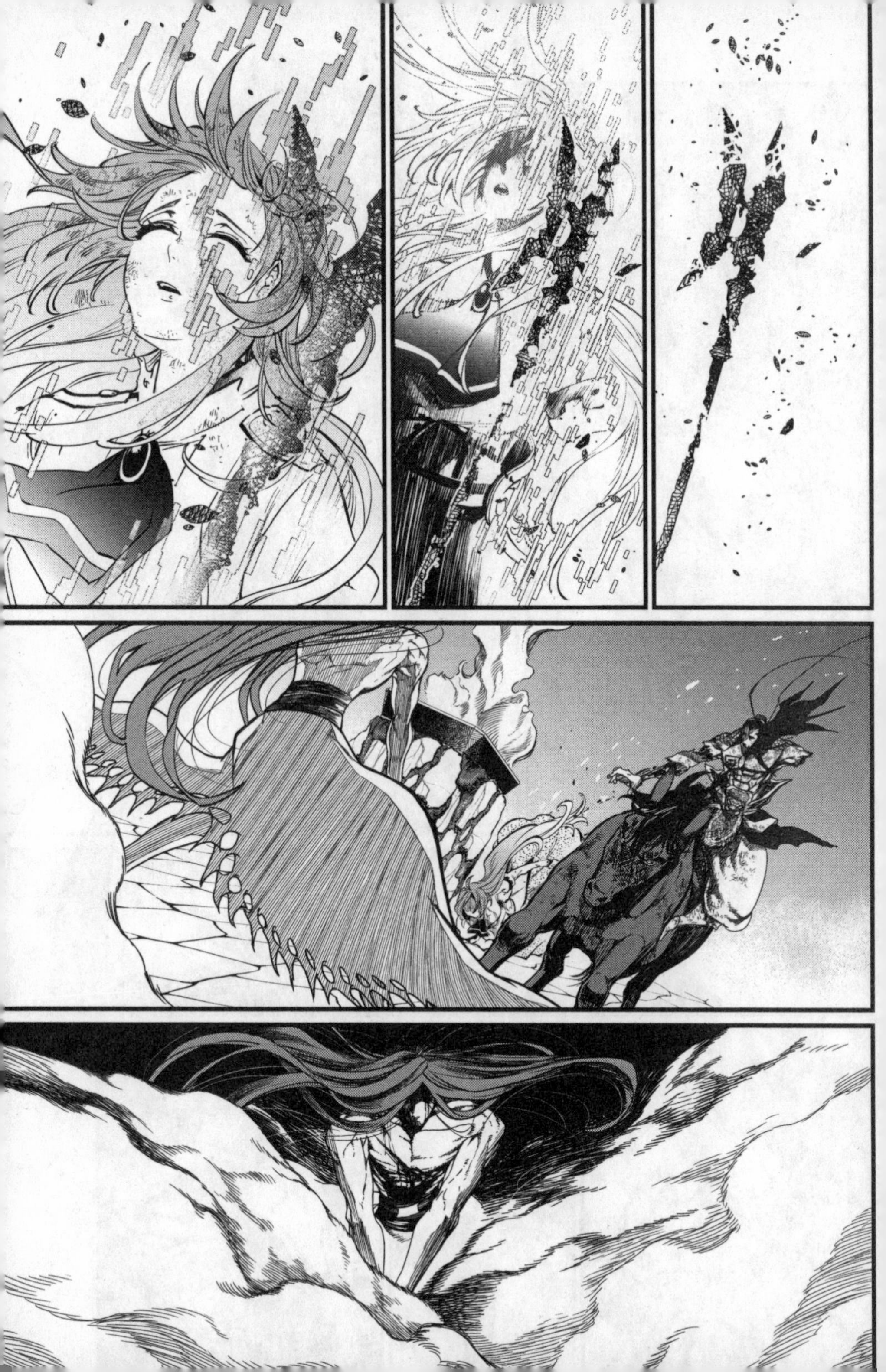

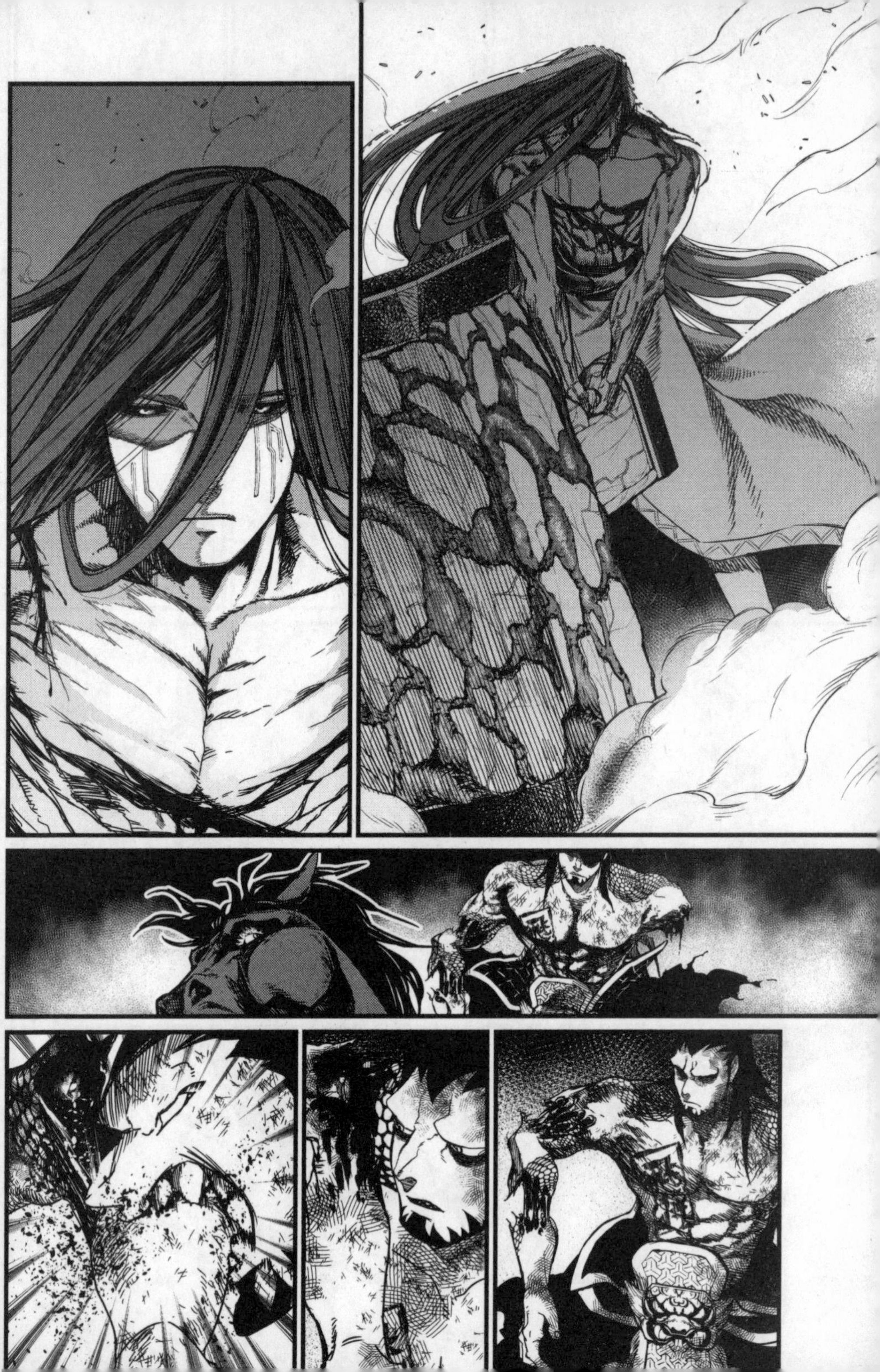

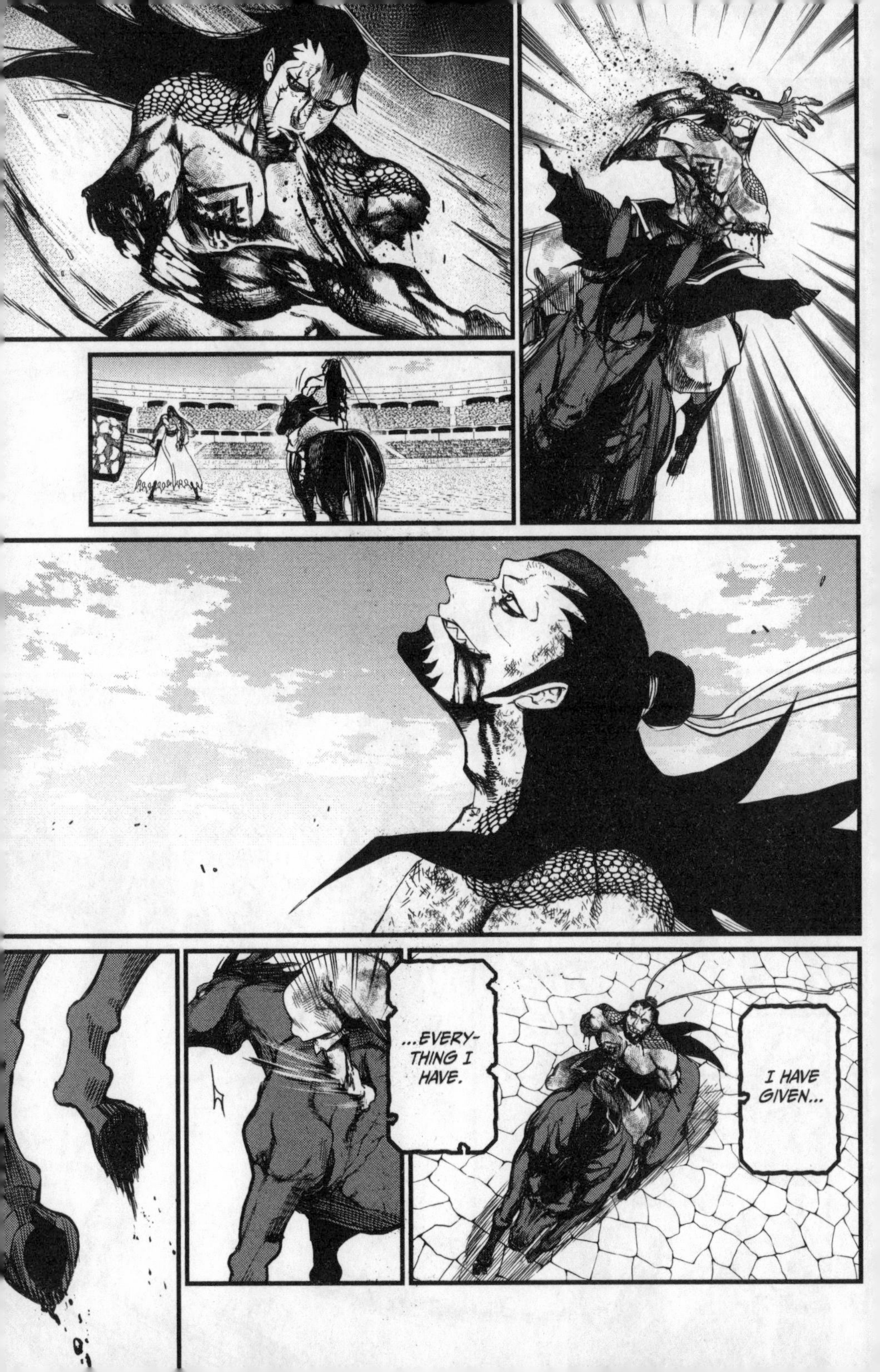
I HAVE GIVEN...
...EVERY-THING I HAVE.

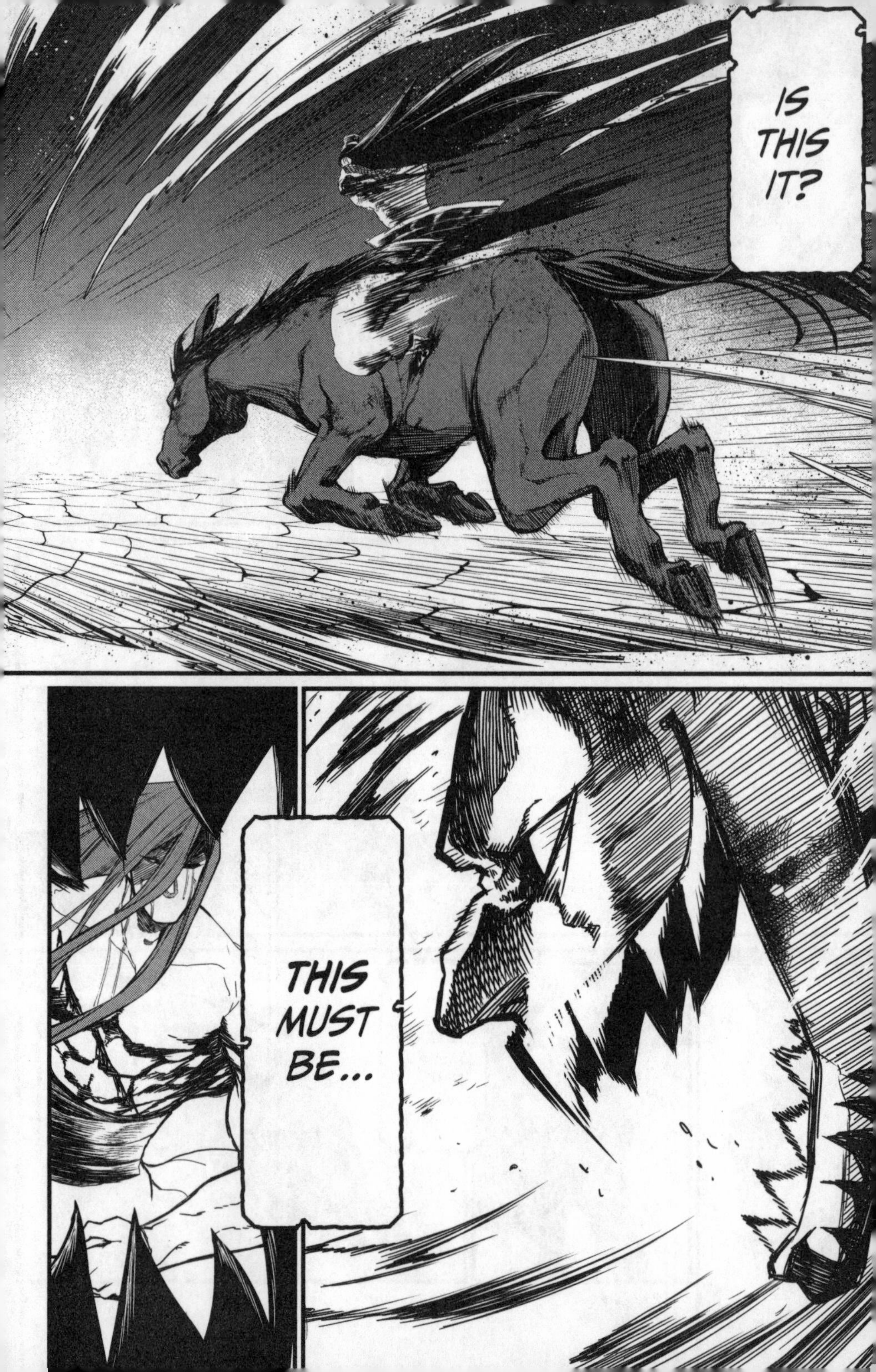
IS THIS IT?
THIS MUST BE...

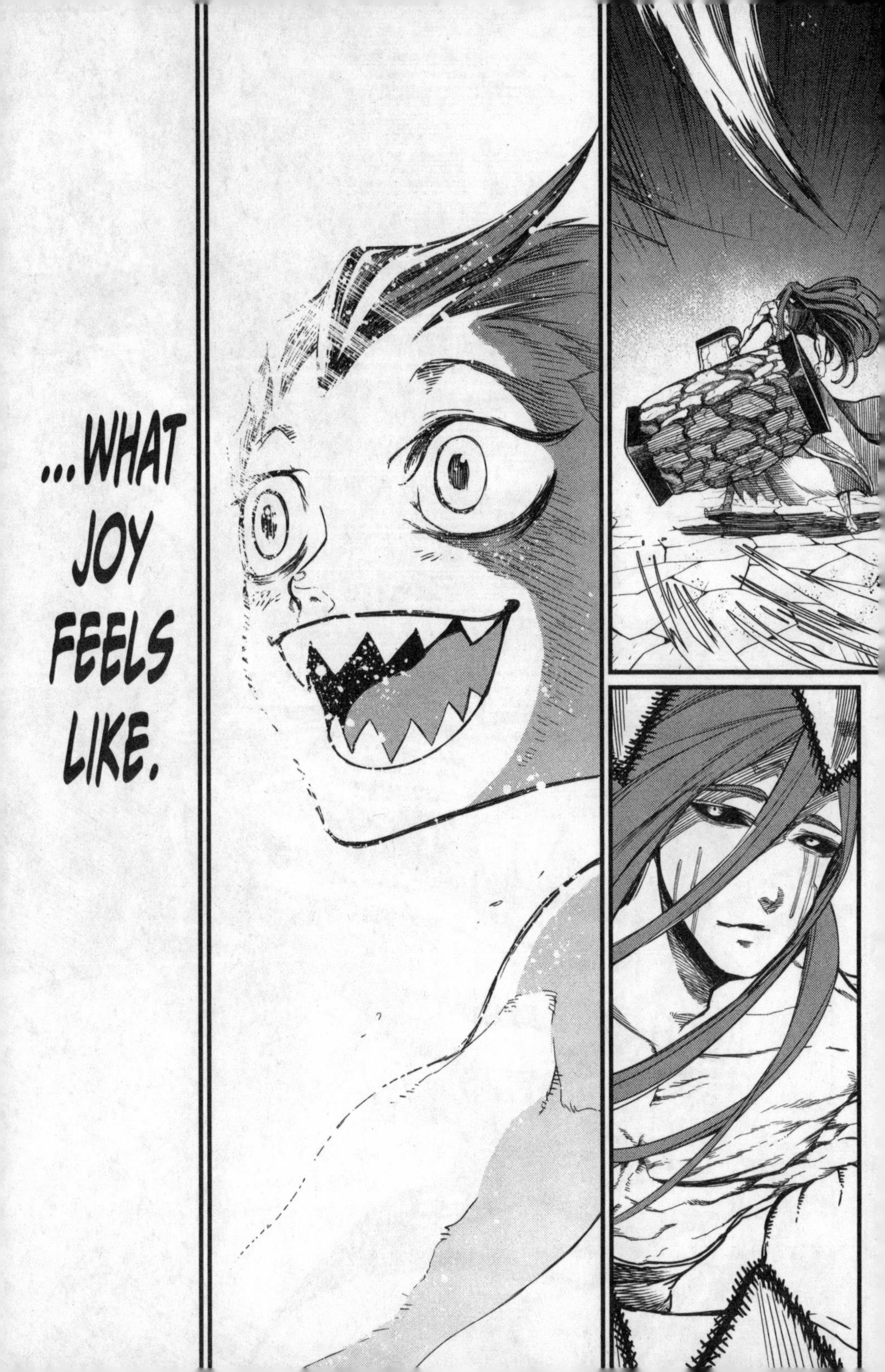
...WHAT JOY FEELS LIKE.

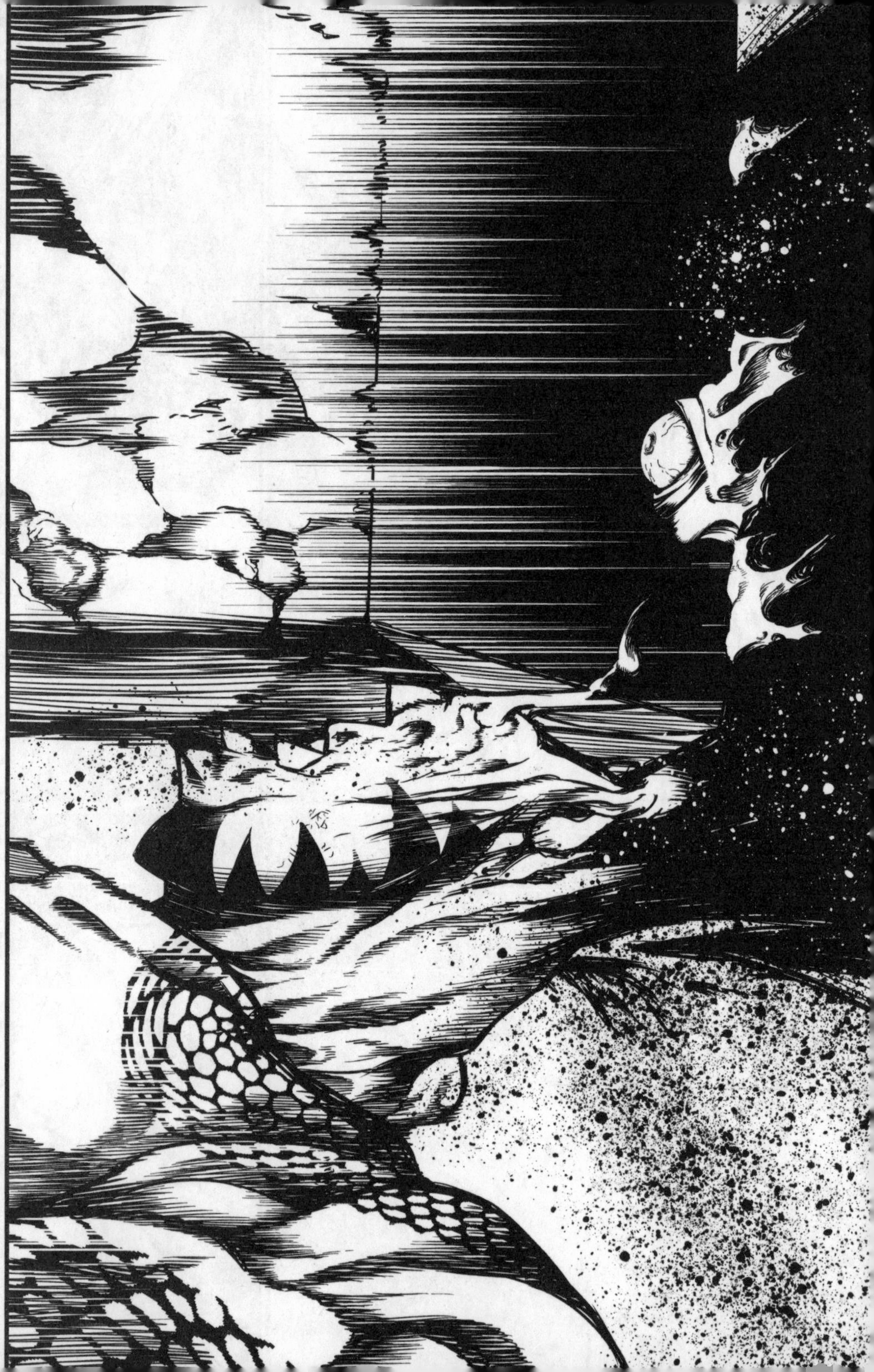

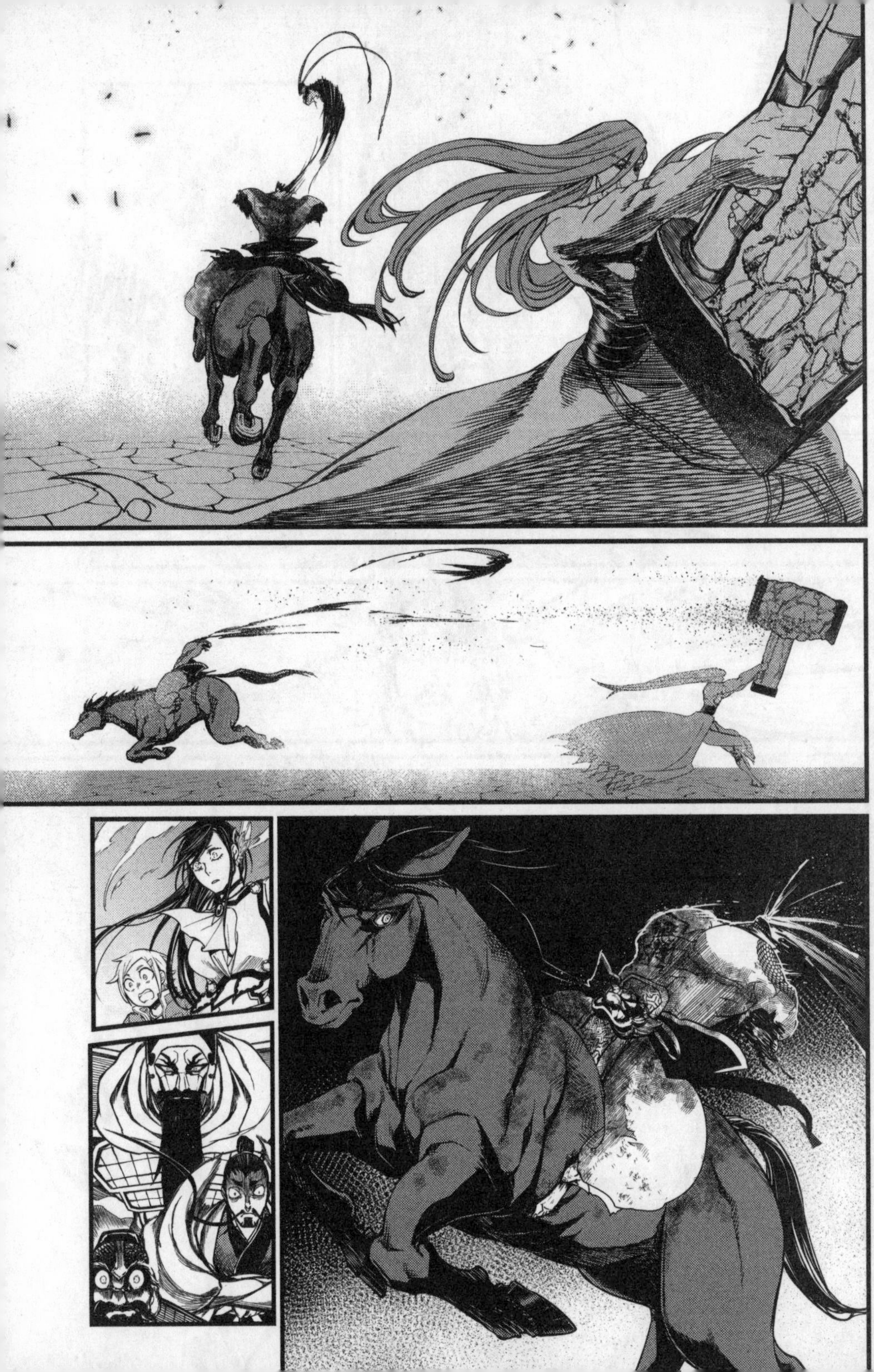

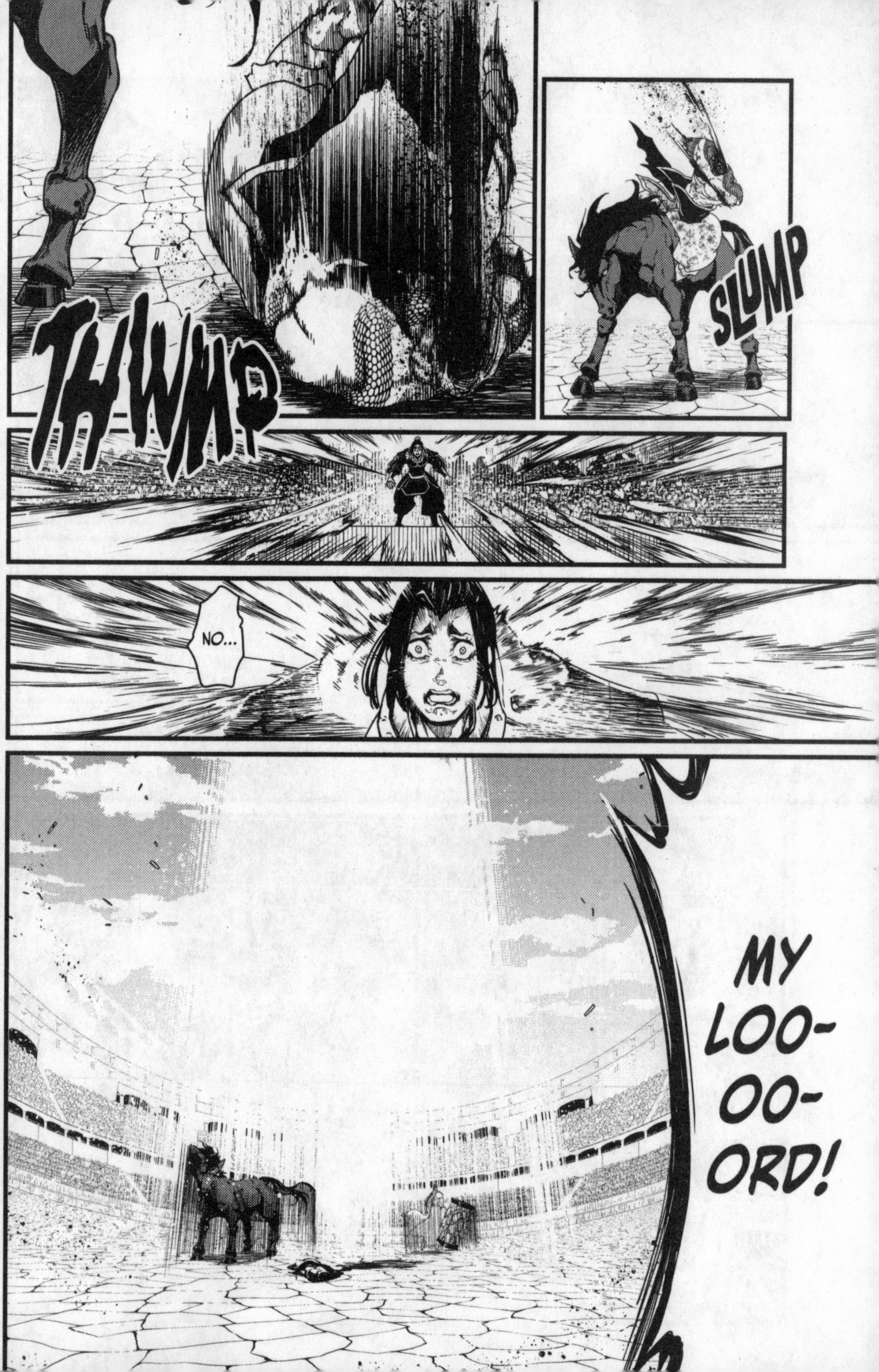
SLUMP
THWMP
NO...
MY LOO-OO-ORD!

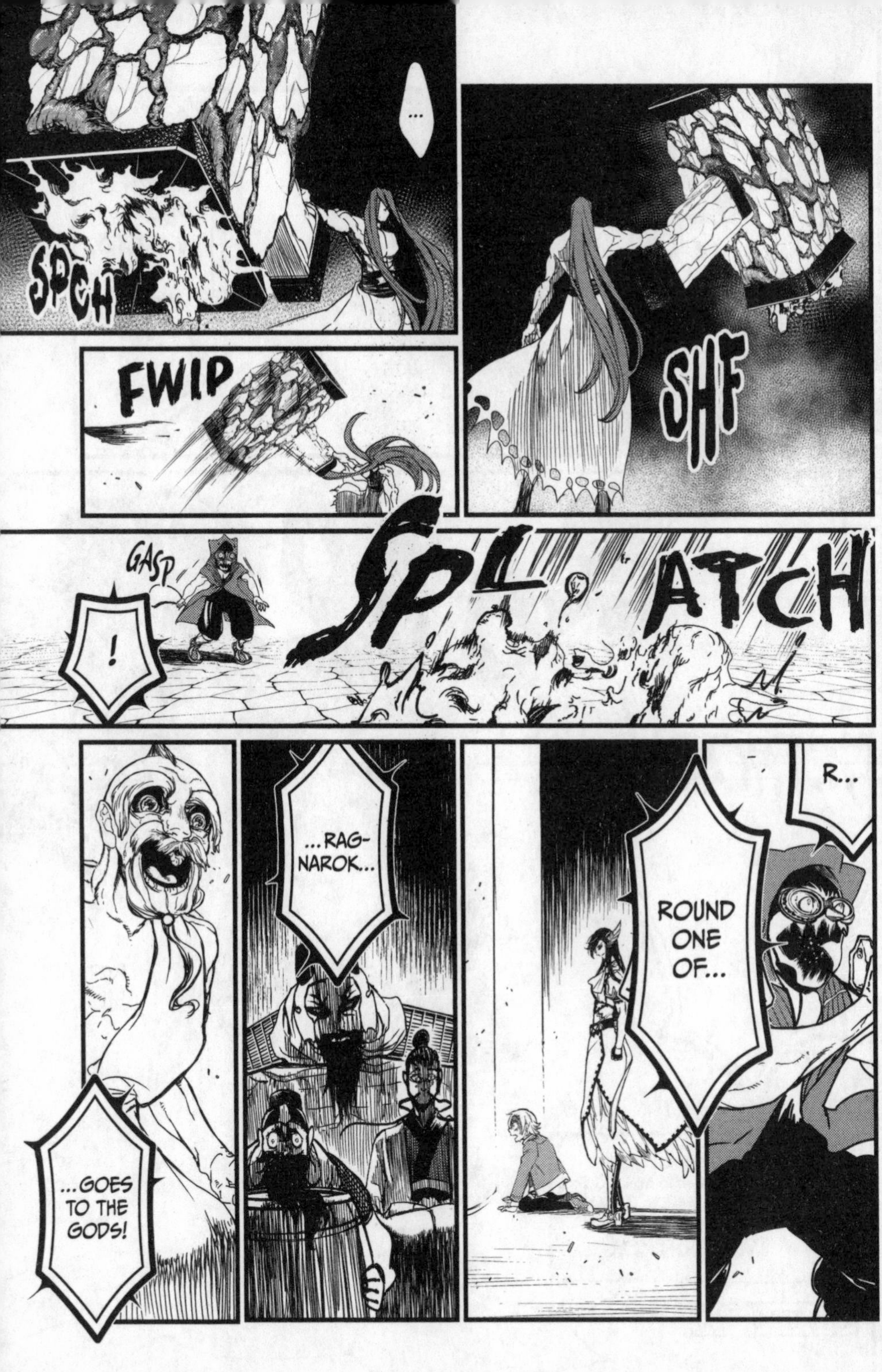
SHF
...
SPCH
FWIP
SPLATCH
GASP
!
R...
ROUND ONE OF...
...RAG-NAROK...
...GOES TO THE GODS!

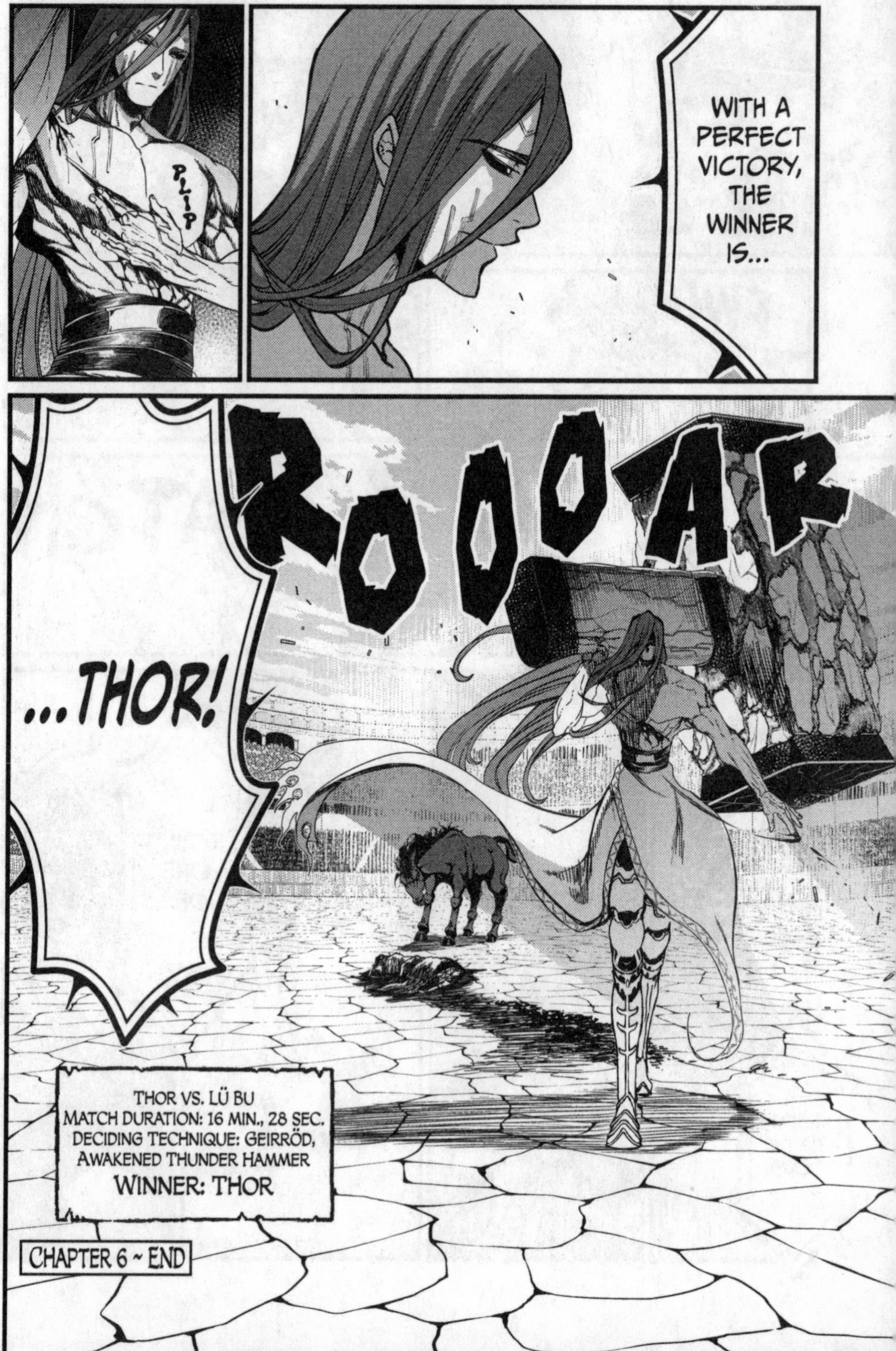

WITH A PERFECT VICTORY, THE WINNER IS...
PLIP
...THOR!
ROOOAR
THOR VS. LŪ BU
MATCH DURATION: 16 MIN., 28 SEC.
DECIDING TECHNIQUE: GEIRRÖD, AWAKENED THUNDER HAMMER
WINNER: THOR
CHAPTER 6 ~ END

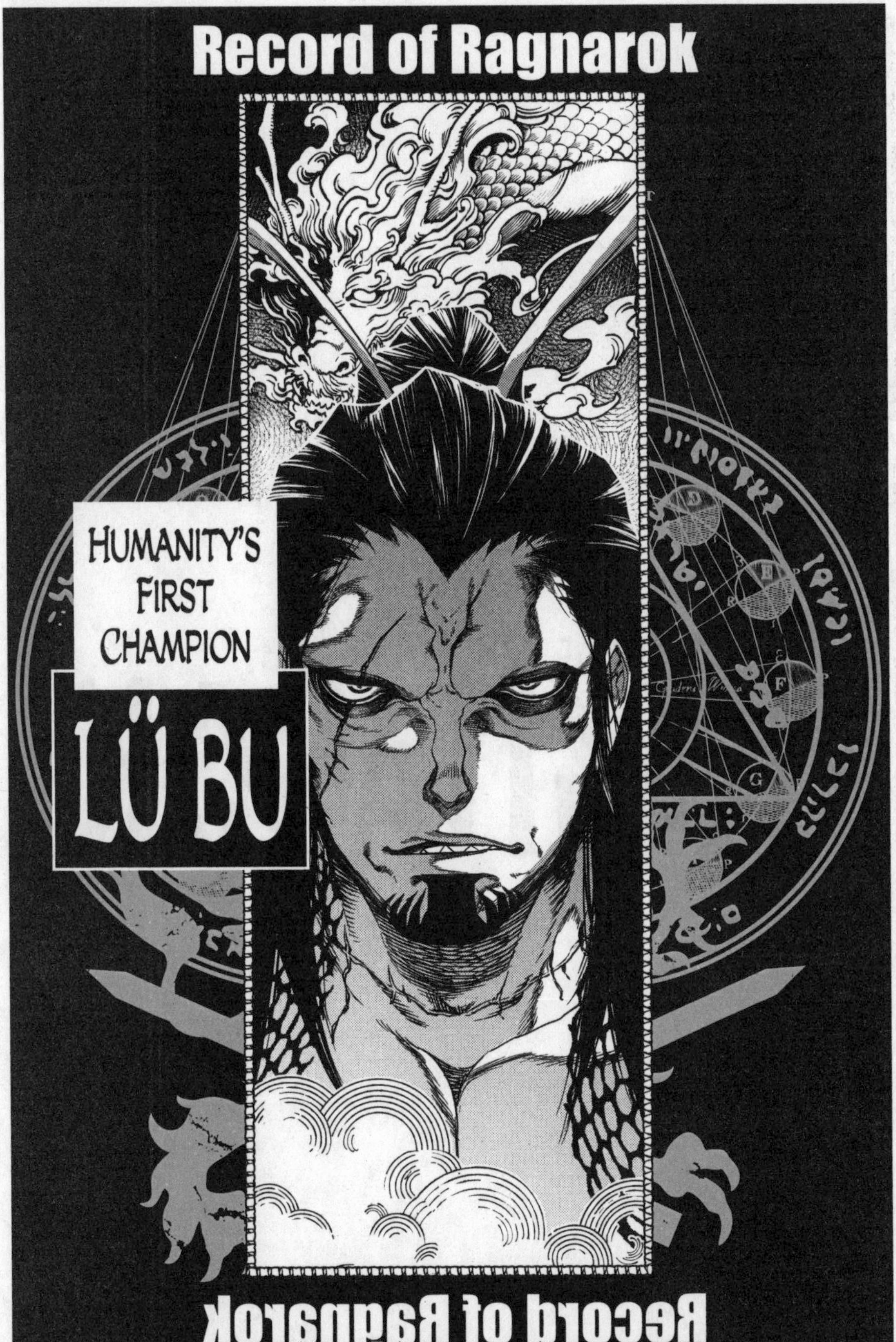
Record of Ragnarok
HUMANITY'S FIRST CHAMPION
LÜ BU
Record of Ragnarok

RECORD OF

RAGNAROK

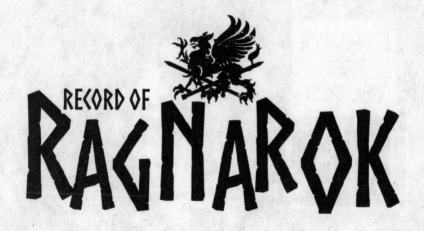

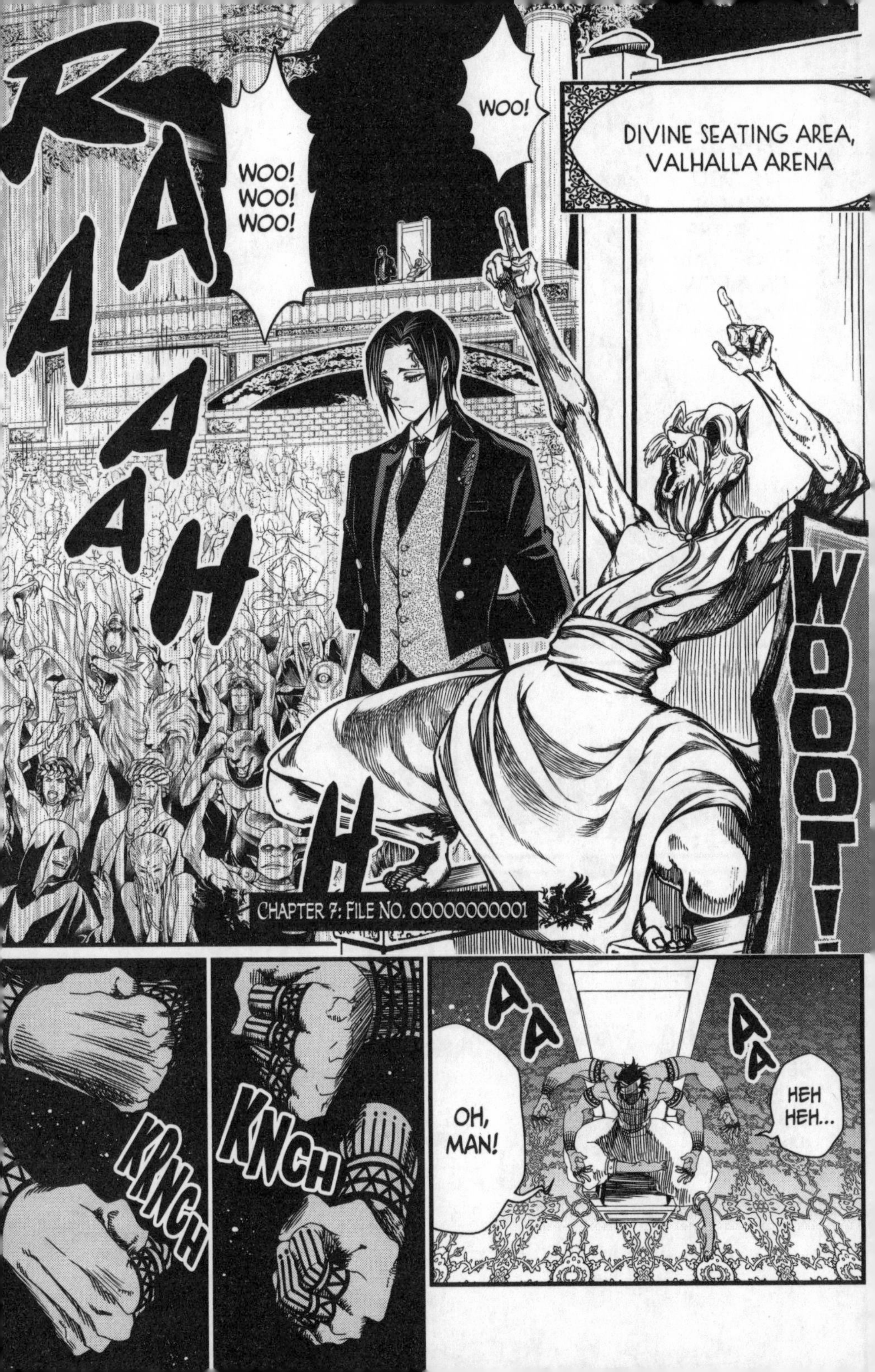
DIVINE SEATING AREA, VALHALLA ARENA
WOO!
WOO! WOO! WOO!
RAAAAHH
WOOOT!
CHAPTER 7: FILE NO. 00000000001
AA
AA
HEH HEH...
OH, MAN!
KNCH
KNCH

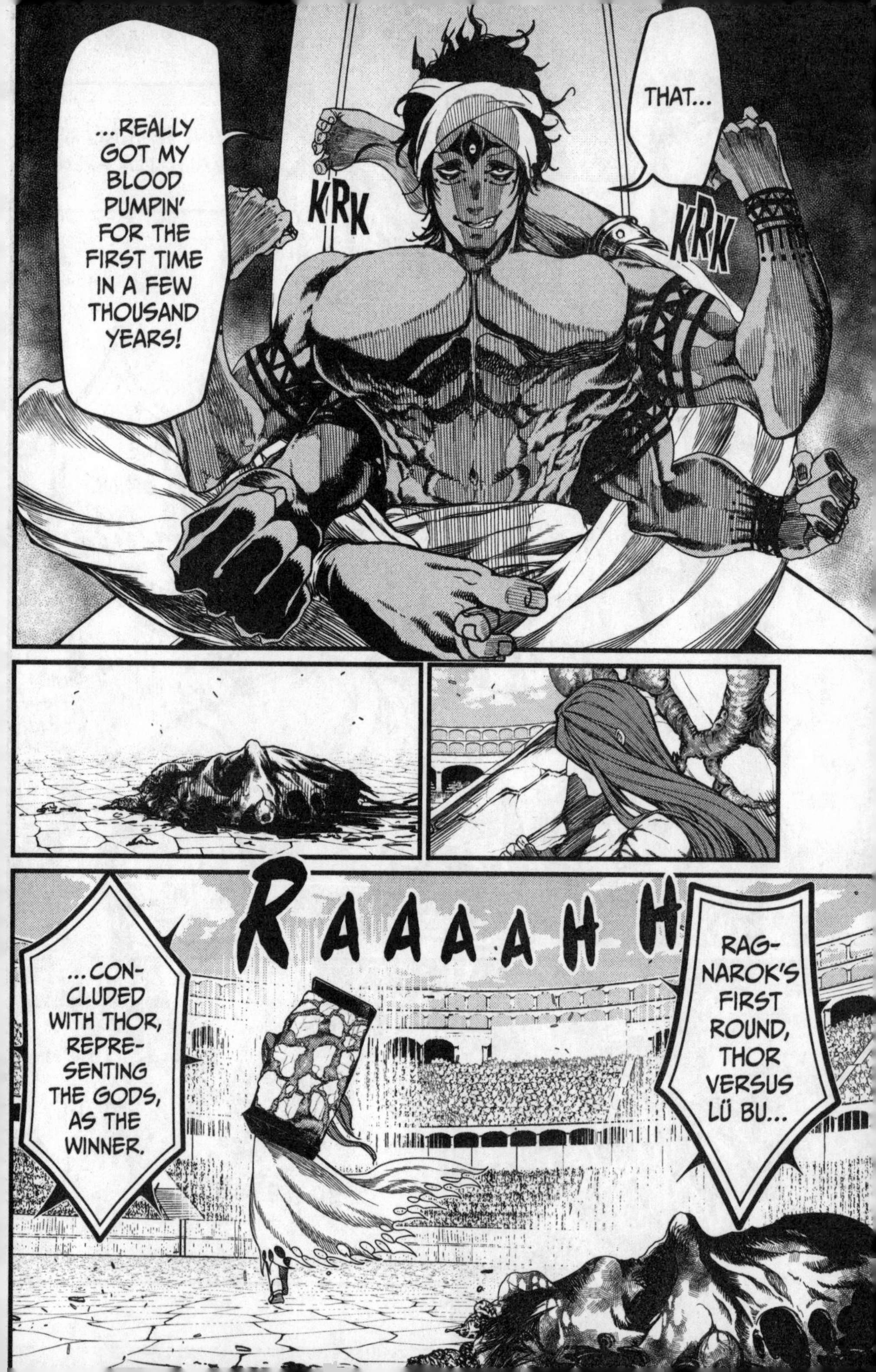
THAT...
...REALLY GOT MY BLOOD PUMPIN' FOR THE FIRST TIME IN A FEW THOUSAND YEARS!
KRK
KRK
RAAAAH
RAG-NAROK'S FIRST ROUND, THOR VERSUS LÜ BU...
...CON-CLUDED WITH THOR, REPRE-SENTING THE GODS, AS THE WINNER.

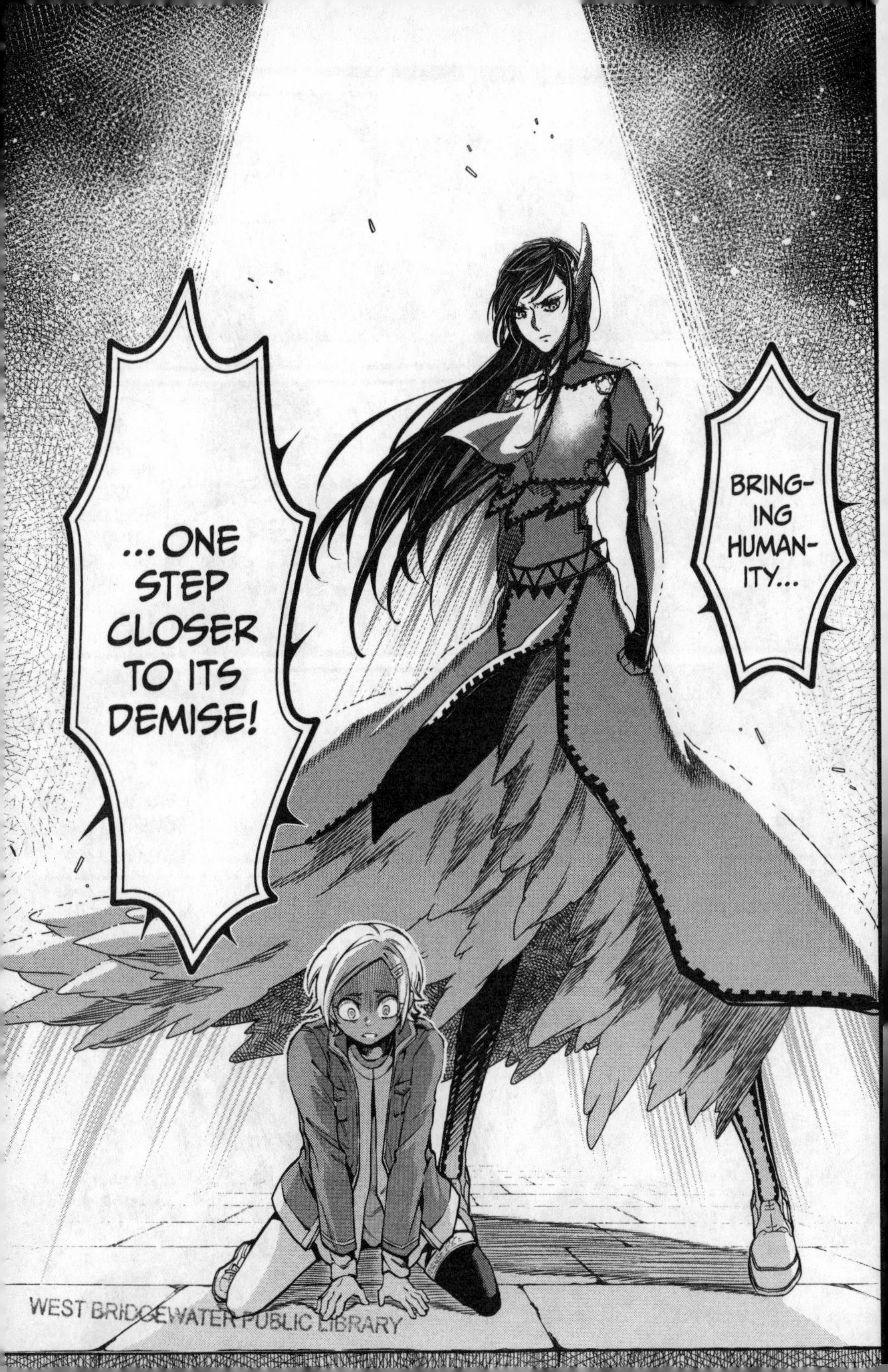
BRING-ING HUMAN-ITY...
...ONE STEP CLOSER TO ITS DEMISE!

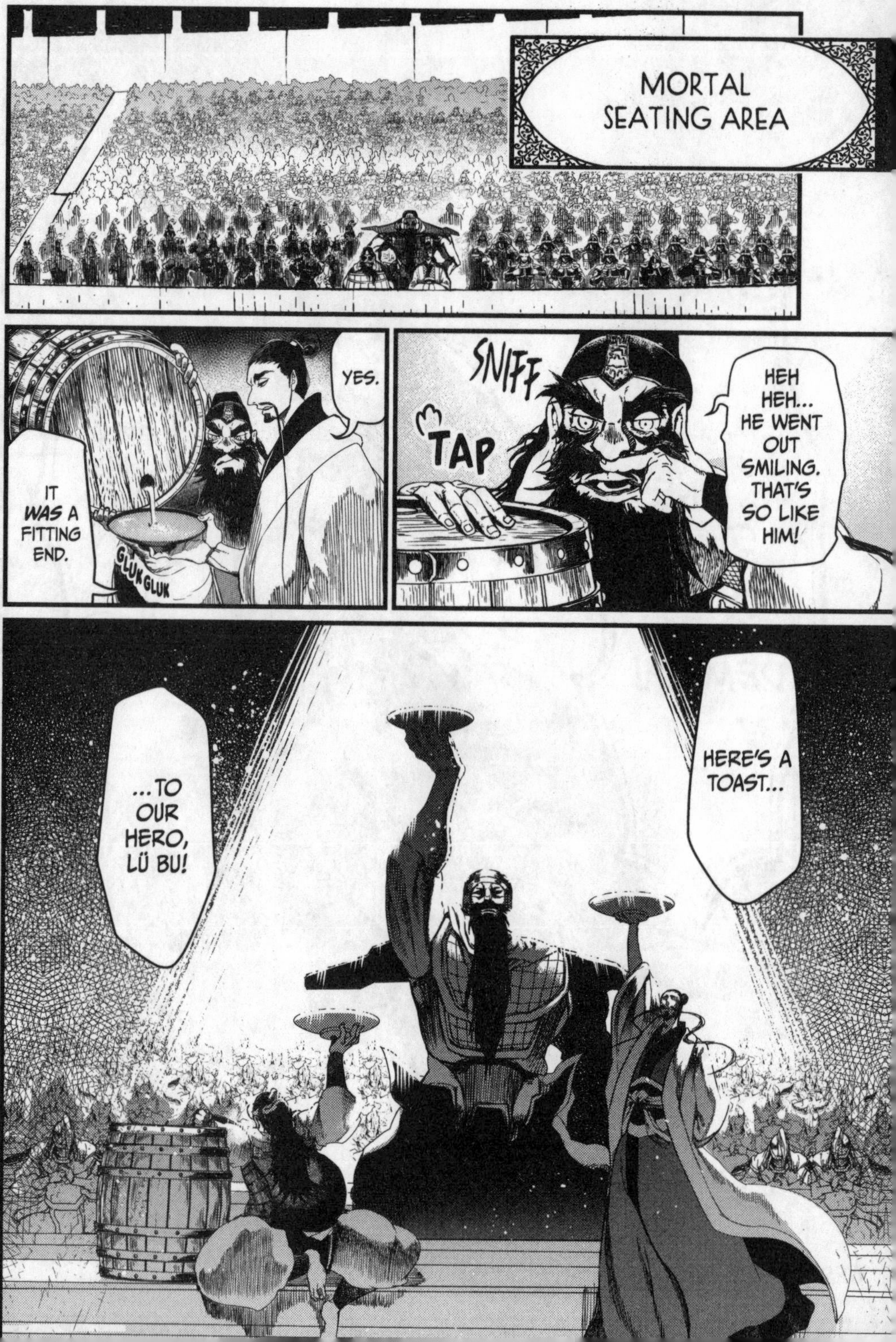
MORTAL SEATING AREA
SNIFF
TAP
HEH HEH... HE WENT OUT SMILING. THAT'S SO LIKE HIM!
YES.
IT *WAS* A FITTING END.
GLUK GLUK
HERE'S A TOAST...
...TO OUR HERO, LÜ BU!

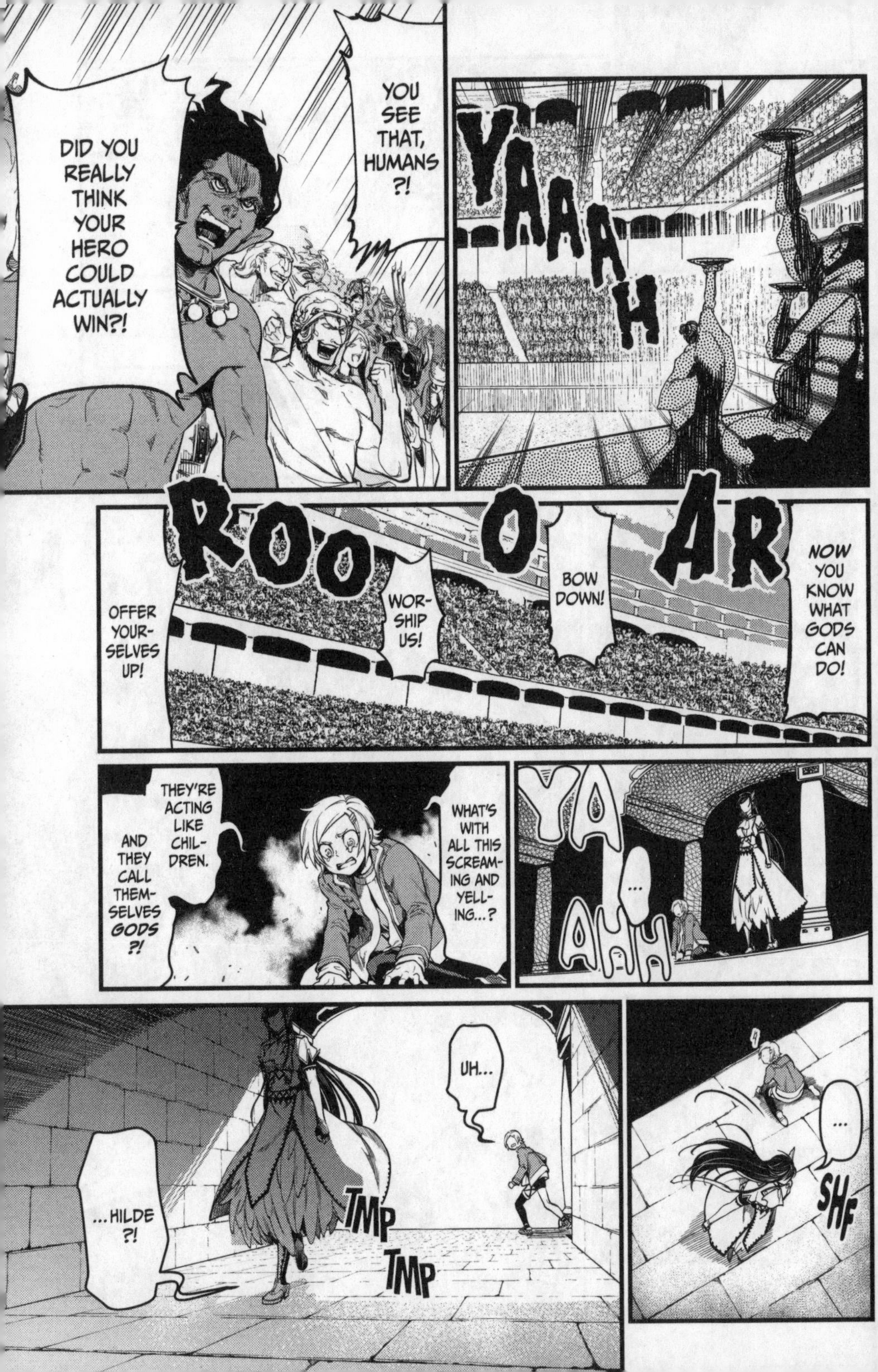
YAAAH
YOU SEE THAT, HUMANS?!
DID YOU REALLY THINK YOUR HERO COULD ACTUALLY WIN?!
ROOOAR
NOW YOU KNOW WHAT GODS CAN DO!
BOW DOWN!
WOR-SHIP US!
OFFER YOUR-SELVES UP!
YAAHH
...
WHAT'S WITH ALL THIS SCREAM-ING AND YELL-ING...?
THEY'RE ACTING LIKE CHIL-DREN.
AND THEY CALL THEM-SELVES GODS?!
...
SHF
UH...
TMP
TMP
...HILDE?!

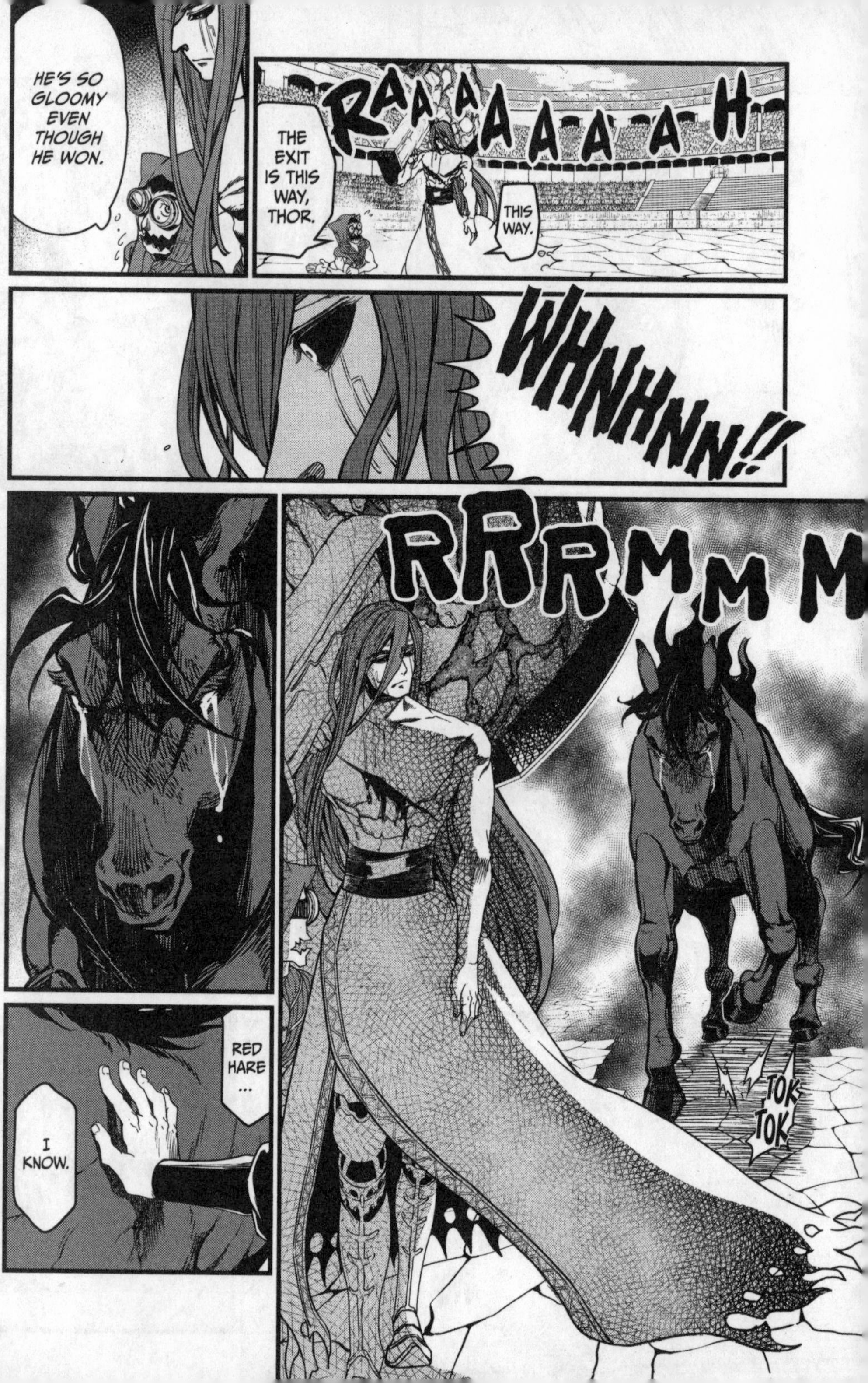
RAAAAAAAH
THE EXIT IS THIS WAY, THOR.
THIS WAY.
HE'S SO GLOOMY EVEN THOUGH HE WON.
WHNHNNN!!
RRRMMM
TOK TOK
RED HARE ...
I KNOW.

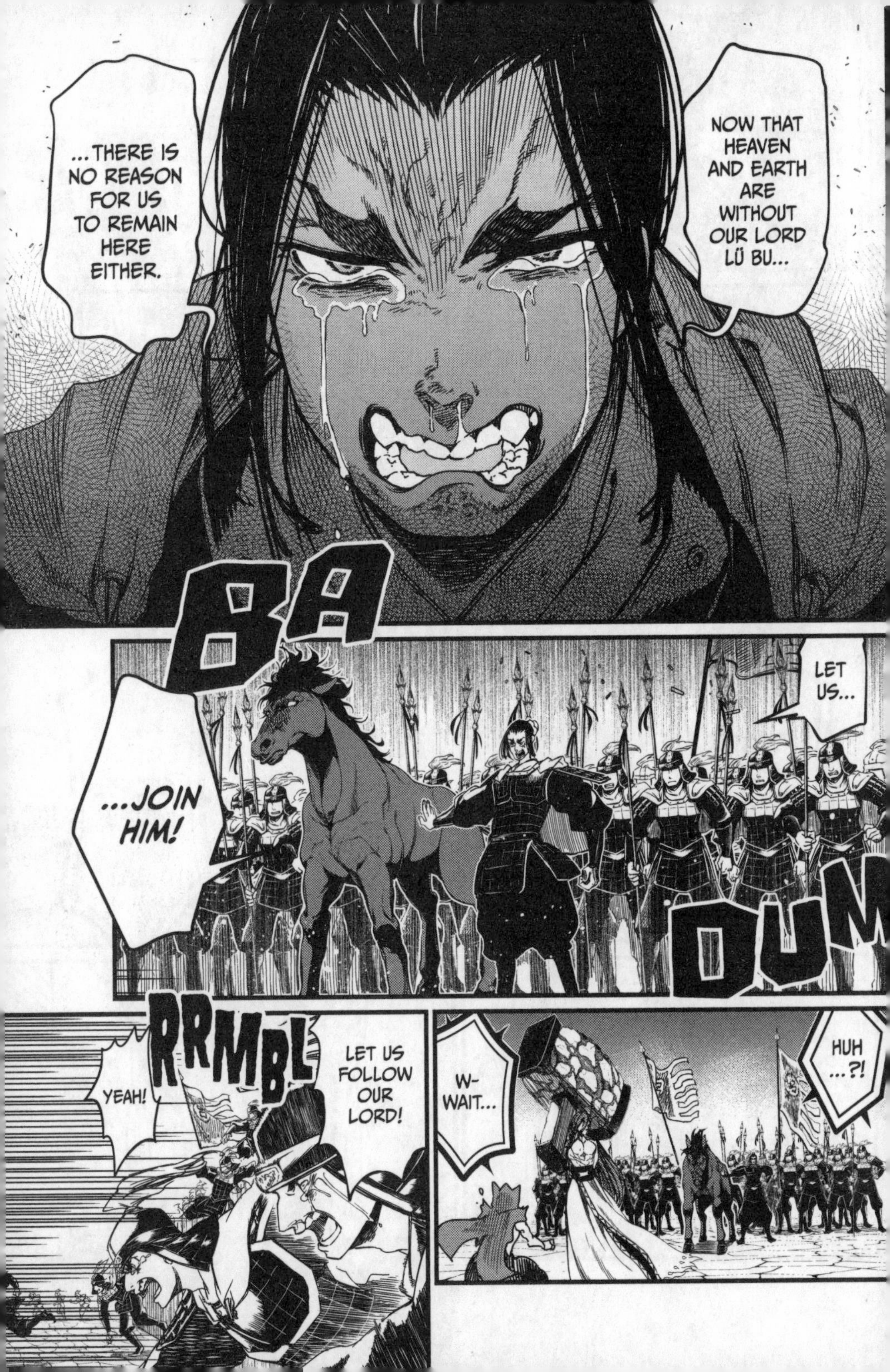
NOW THAT HEAVEN AND EARTH ARE WITHOUT OUR LORD LÜ BU...
...THERE IS NO REASON FOR US TO REMAIN HERE EITHER.
BA
LET US...
...JOIN HIM!
DUM
HUH ...?!
W-WAIT...
RRMBL
LET US FOLLOW OUR LORD!
YEAH!

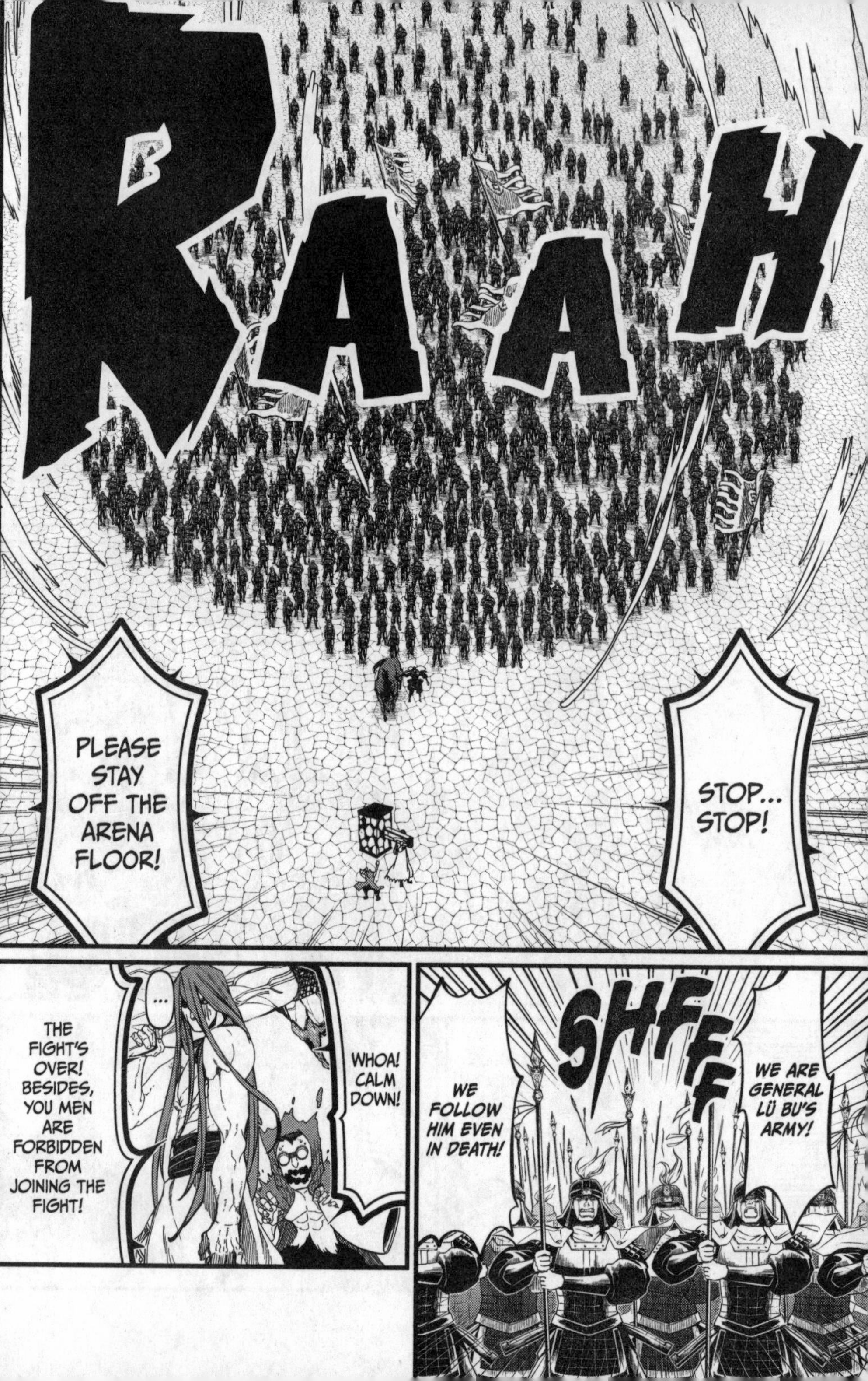
RAAH
STOP... STOP!
PLEASE STAY OFF THE ARENA FLOOR!
WE ARE GENERAL LÜ BU'S ARMY!
SHFF
WE FOLLOW HIM EVEN IN DEATH!
WHOA! CALM DOWN!
...
THE FIGHT'S OVER! BESIDES, YOU MEN ARE FORBIDDEN FROM JOINING THE FIGHT!

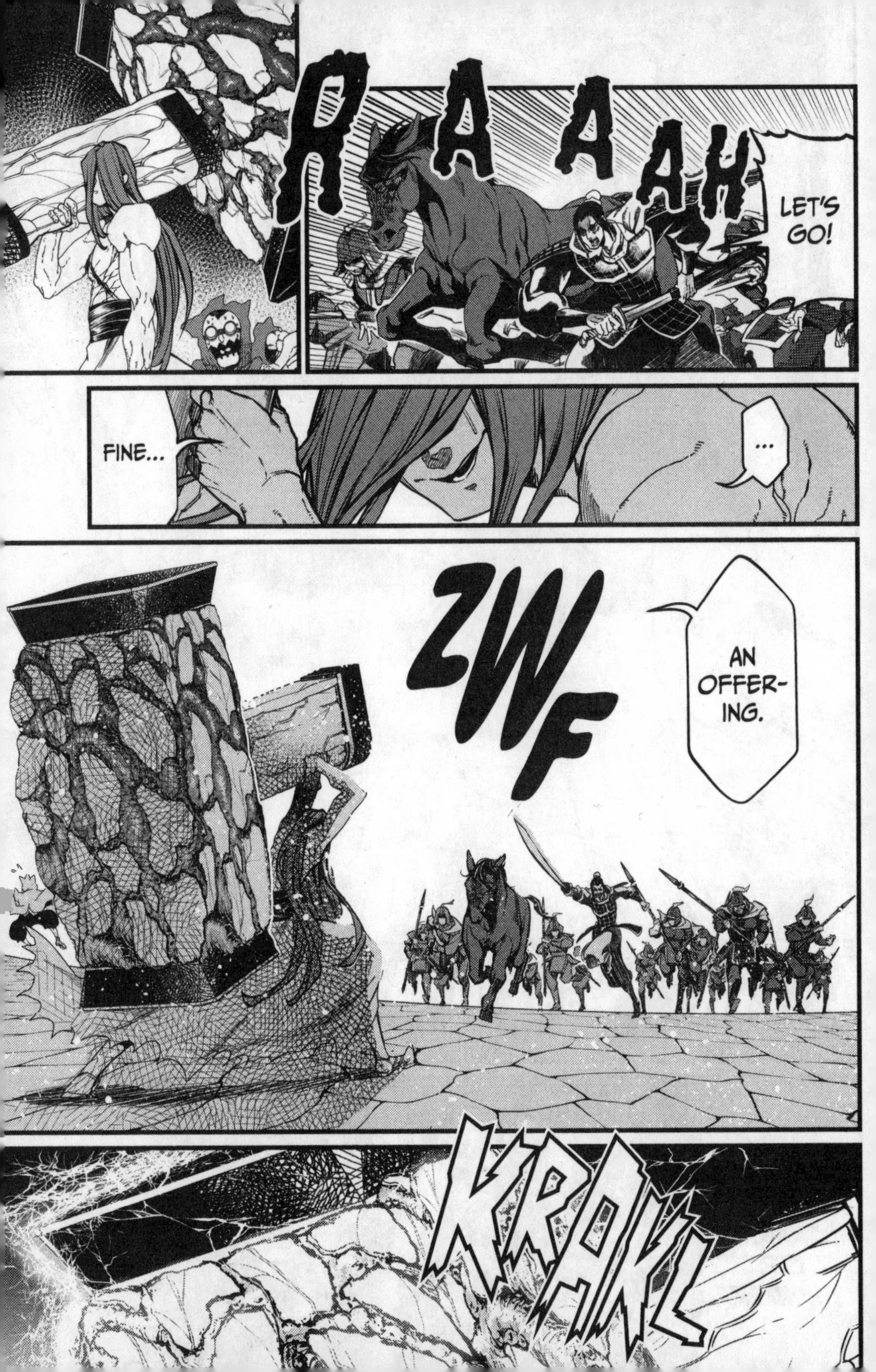
RAAAH
LET'S GO!
...
FINE...
ZWF
AN OFFERING.
KRAKL

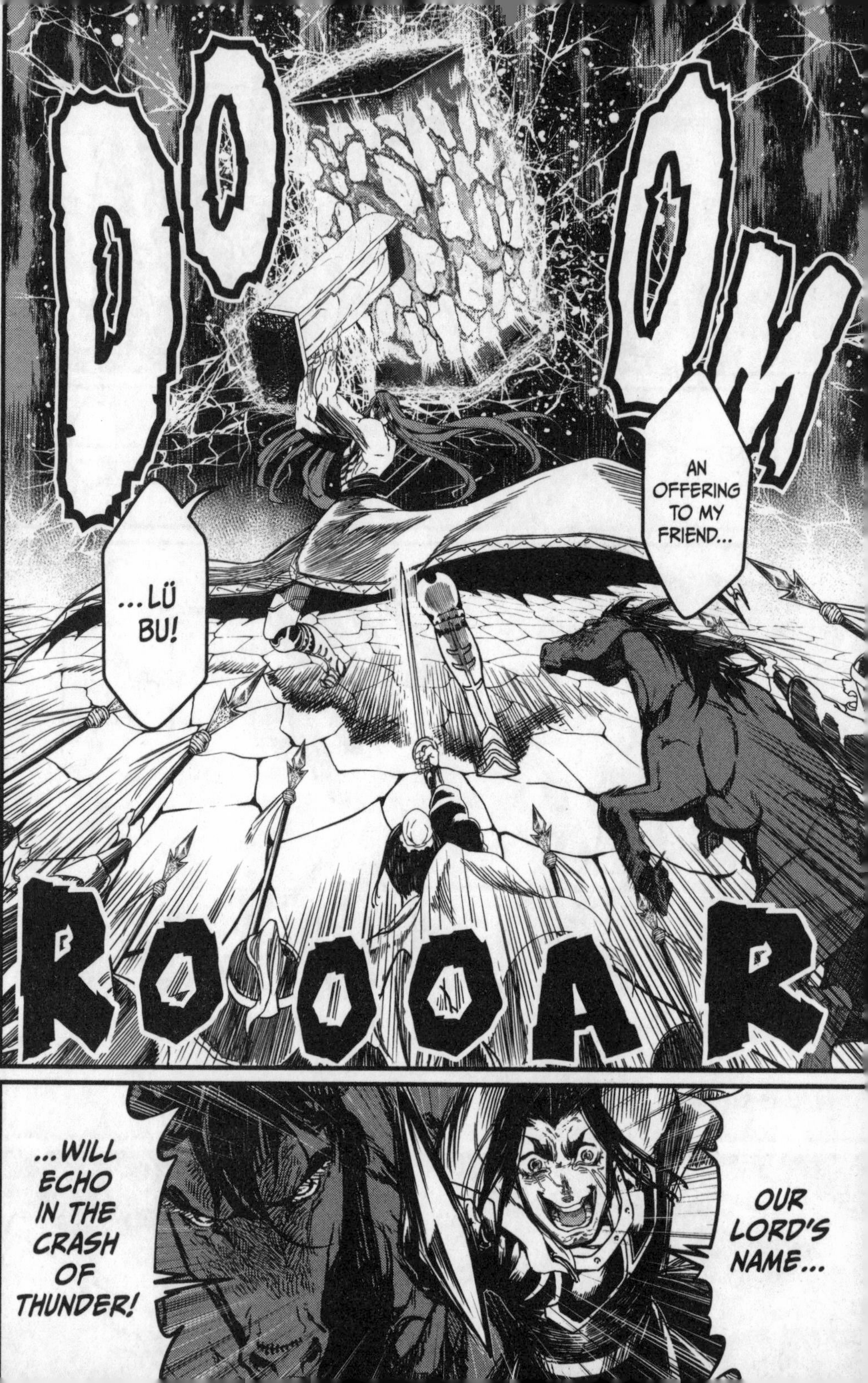
DOOM
AN OFFERING TO MY FRIEND...
...LÜ BU!
ROOOAR
OUR LORD'S NAME...
...WILL ECHO IN THE CRASH OF THUNDER!

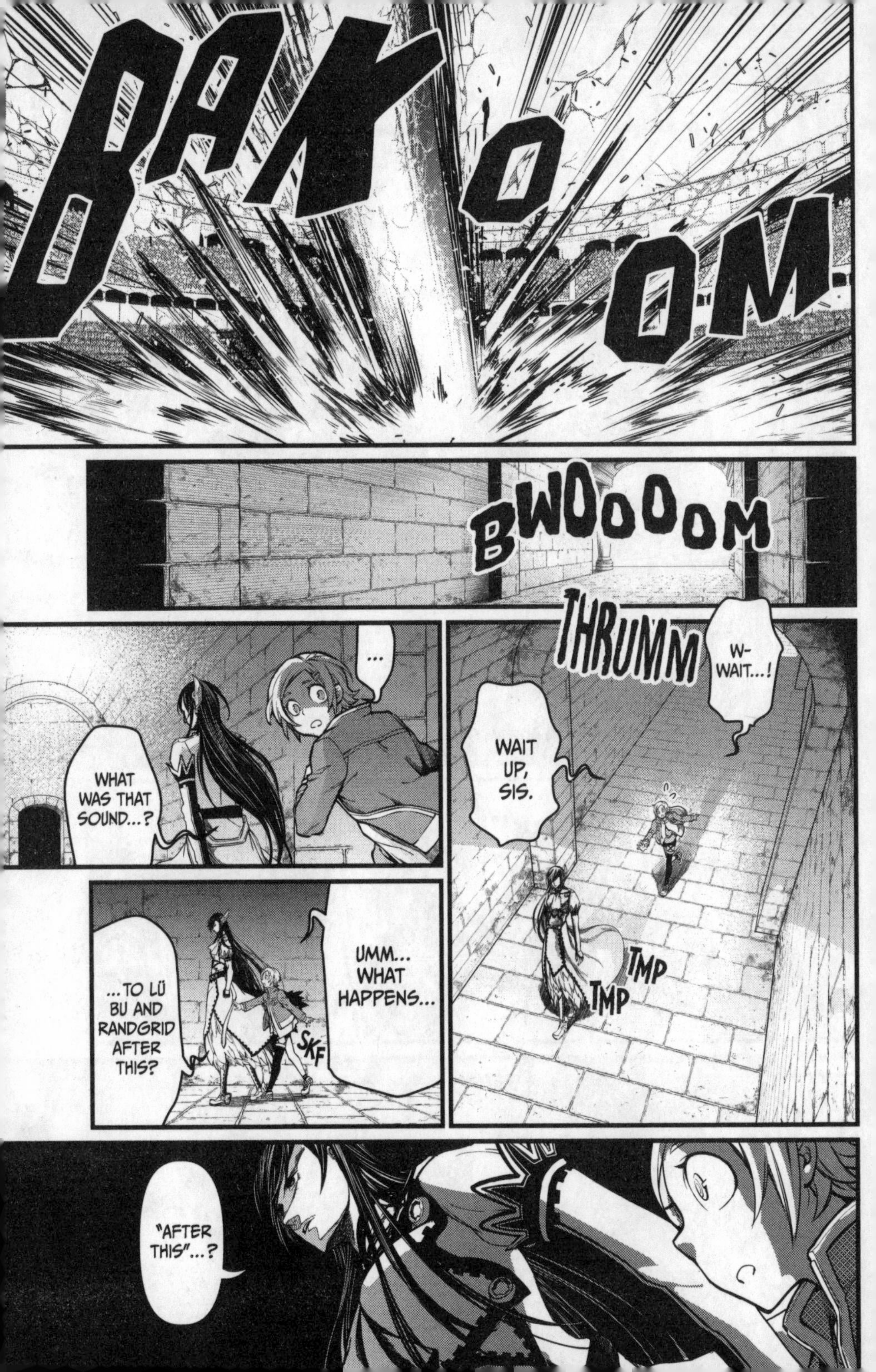
BAKOOM
BWOOOOM
THRUMM
W- WAIT...!
WAIT UP, SIS.
TMP
TMP
...
WHAT WAS THAT SOUND...?
UMM... WHAT HAPPENS...
SKF
...TO LÜ BU AND RANDGRID AFTER THIS?
"AFTER THIS"...?

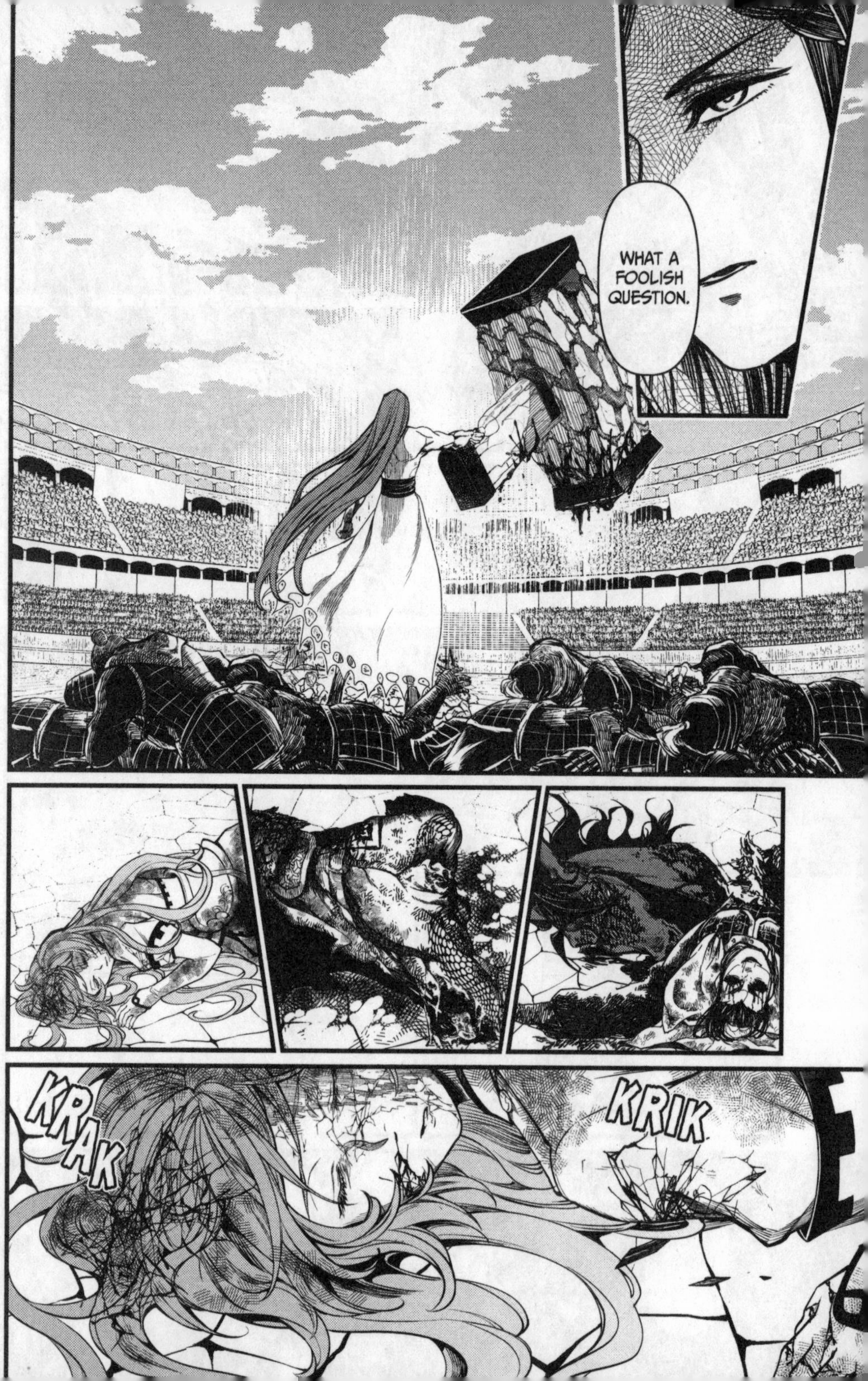
WHAT A FOOLISH QUESTION.
KRIK
KRAK

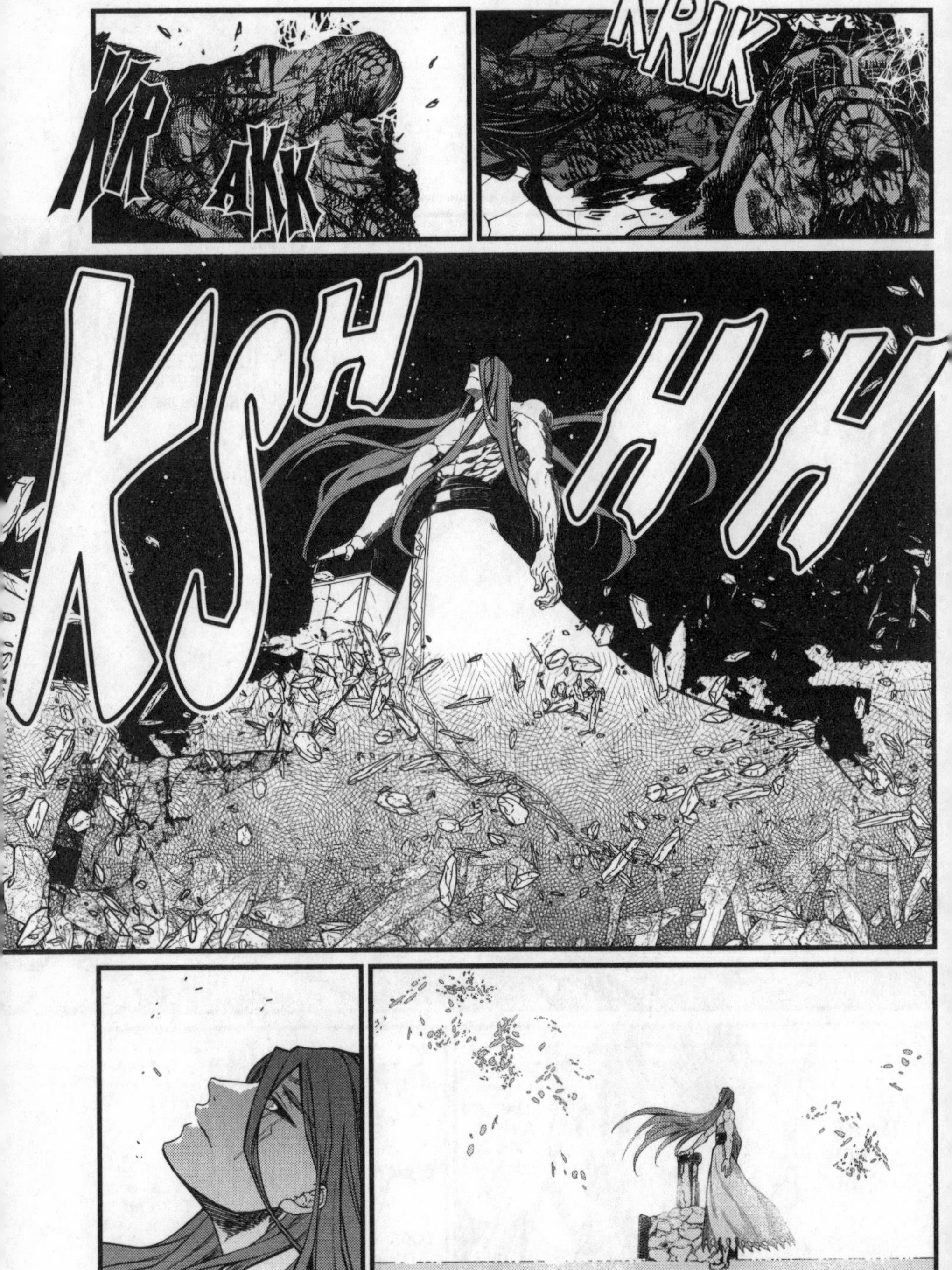
KRIK
KRAKK
KSHHHH

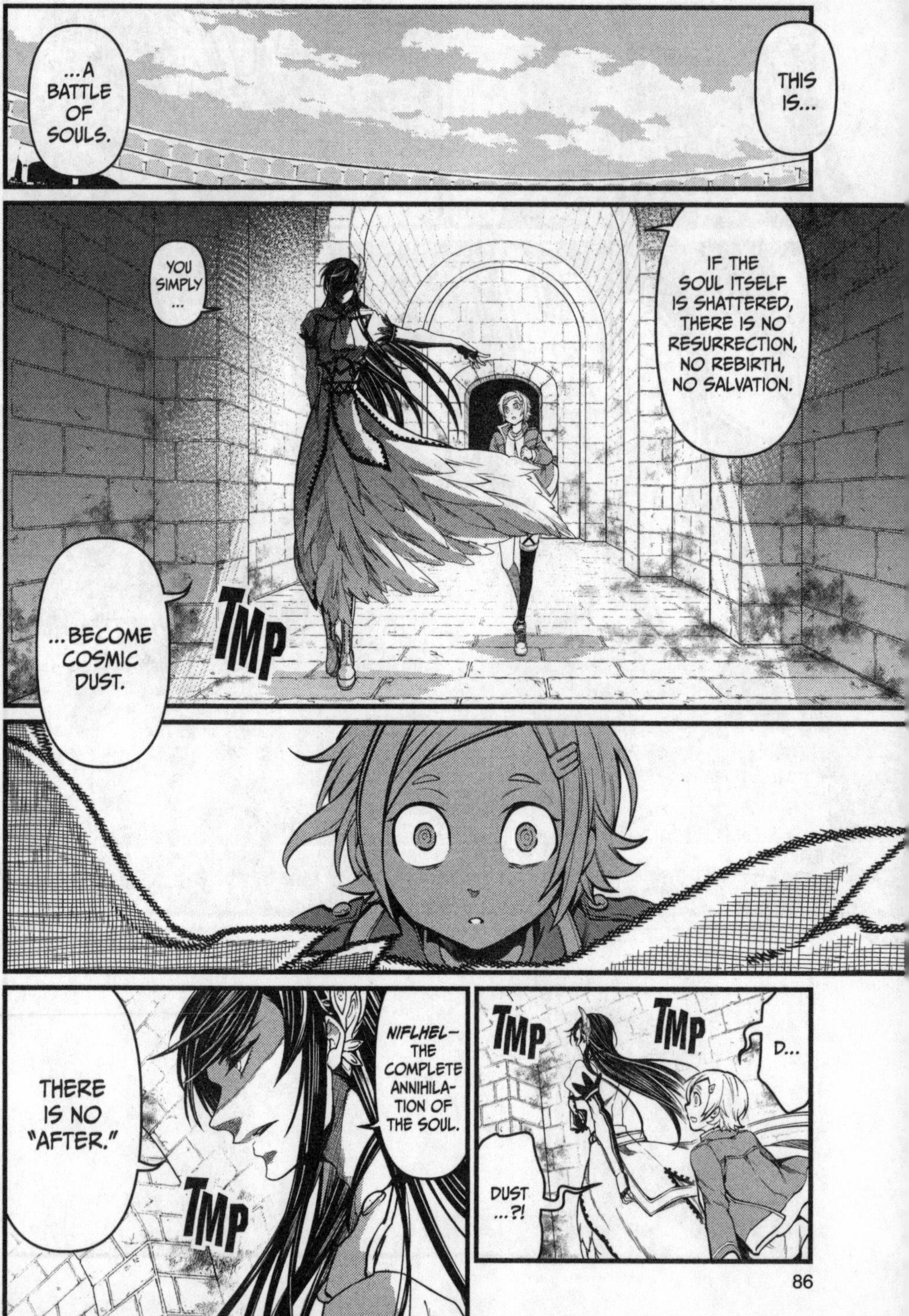
THIS IS...
...A BATTLE OF SOULS.
IF THE SOUL ITSELF IS SHATTERED, THERE IS NO RESURRECTION, NO REBIRTH, NO SALVATION.
YOU SIMPLY ...
TMP
...BECOME COSMIC DUST.
D...
TMP
TMP
DUST ...?!
NIFLHEL— THE COMPLETE ANNIHILATION OF THE SOUL.
THERE IS NO "AFTER."
TMP

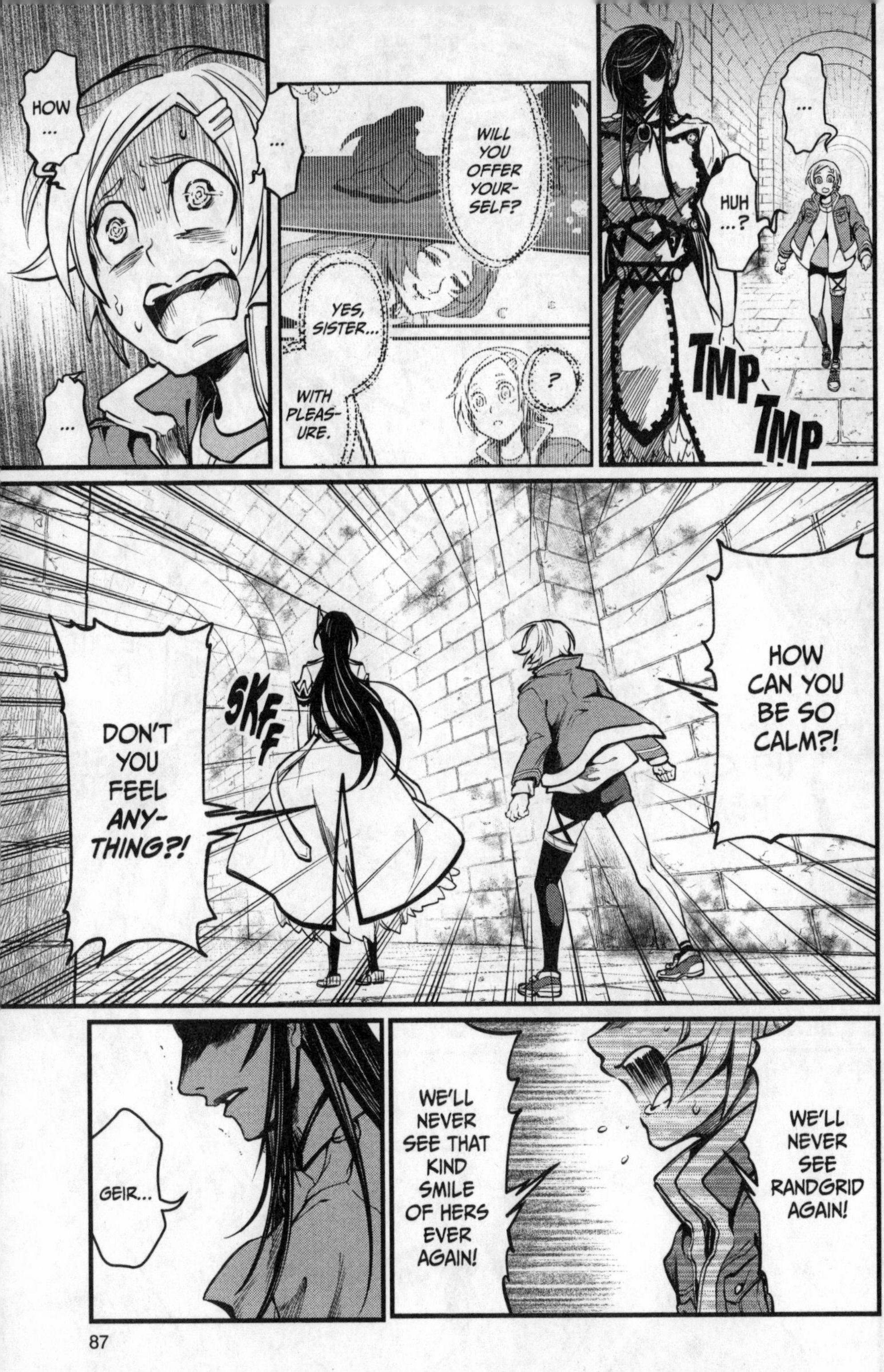
...
HUH ...?
TMP TMP
WILL YOU OFFER YOURSELF?
YES, SISTER...
WITH PLEASURE.
?
...
HOW ...
...
HOW CAN YOU BE SO CALM?!
SKFF
DON'T YOU FEEL ANYTHING?!
WE'LL NEVER SEE RANDGRID AGAIN!
WE'LL NEVER SEE THAT KIND SMILE OF HERS EVER AGAIN!
GEIR...

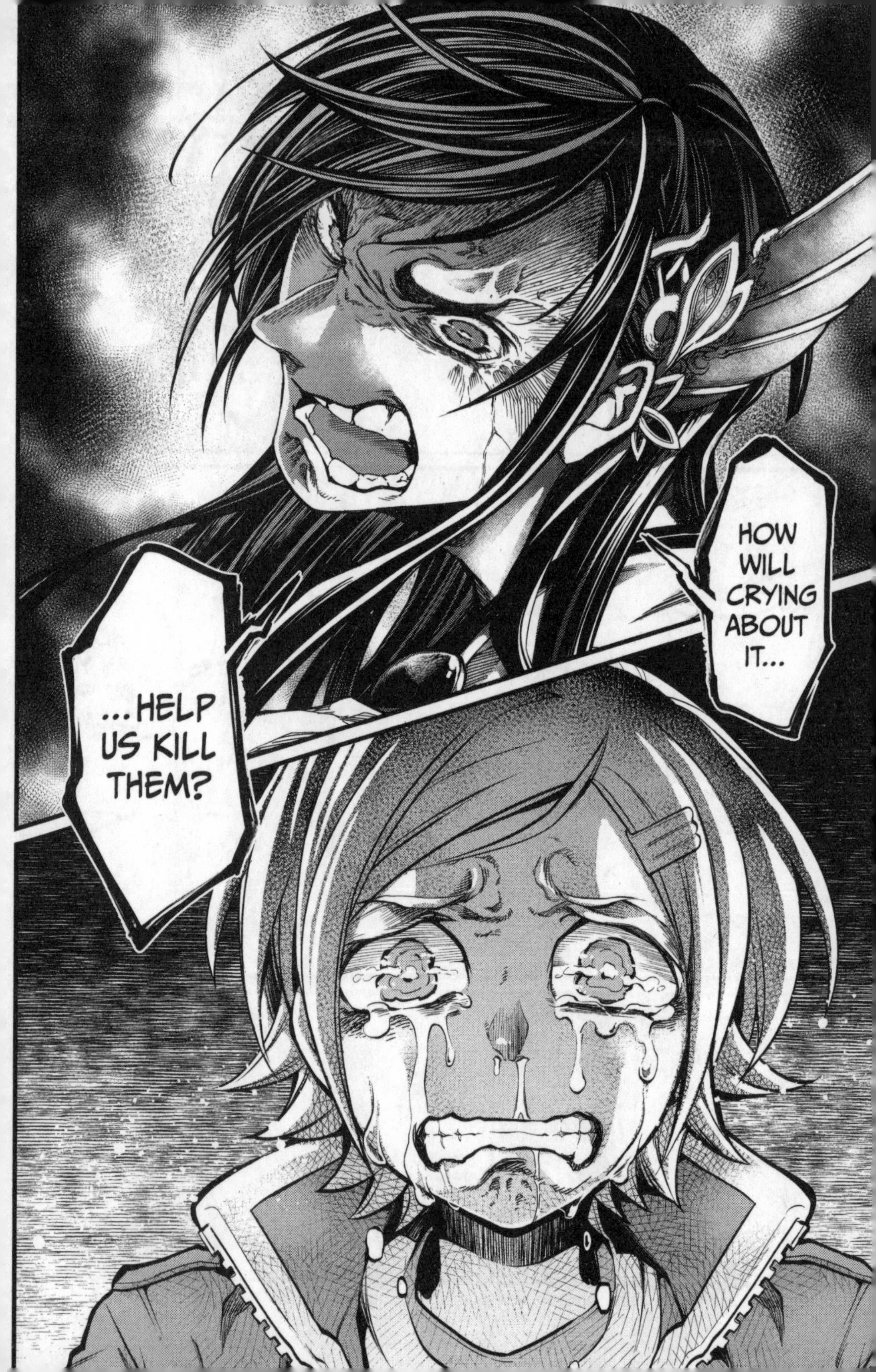
HOW WILL CRYING ABOUT IT...
...HELP US KILL THEM?

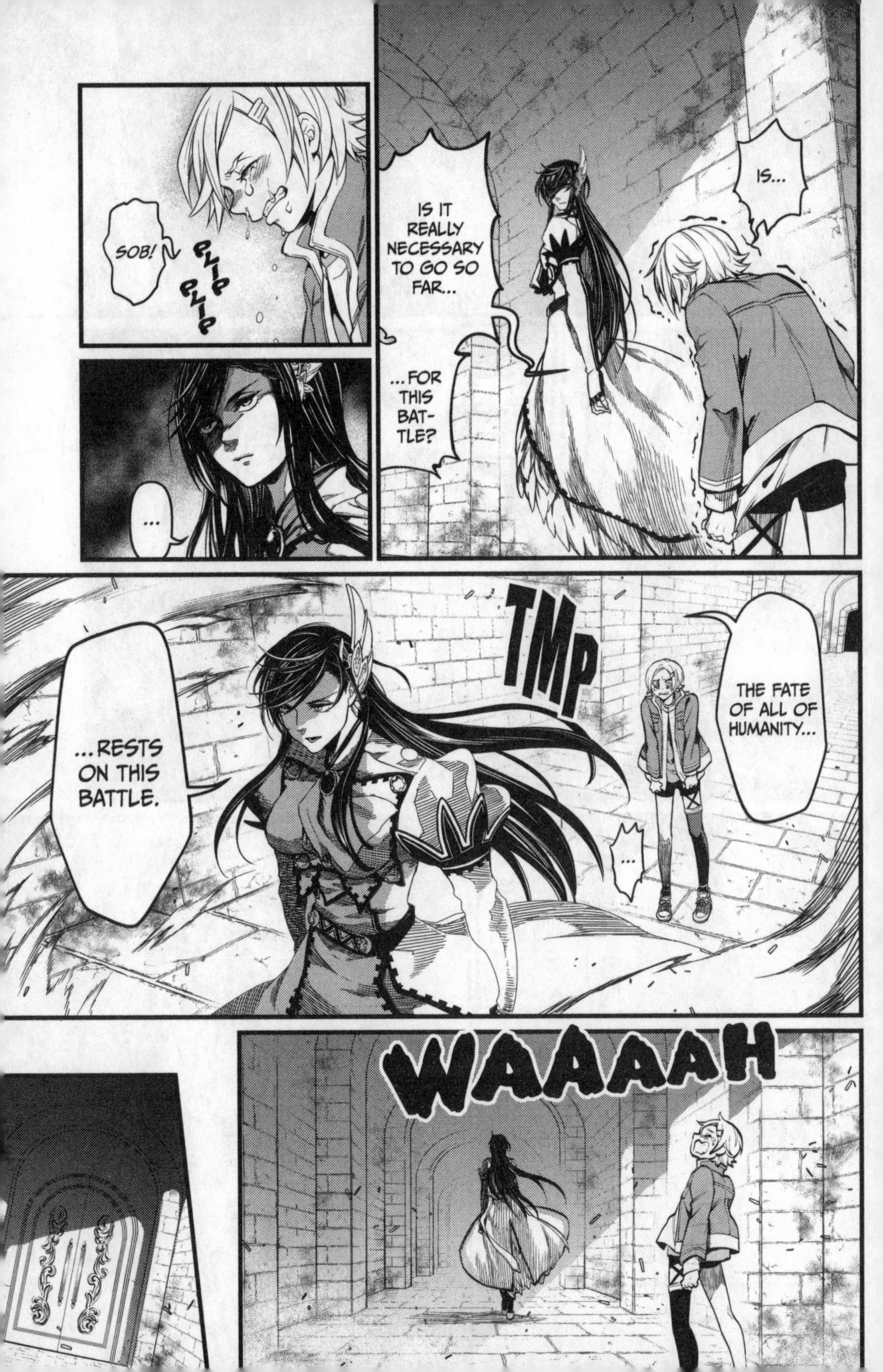
IS...
IS IT REALLY NECESSARY TO GO SO FAR...
...FOR THIS BATTLE?
SOB!
PLIP PLIP
...
THE FATE OF ALL OF HUMANITY...
TMP
...
...RESTS ON THIS BATTLE.
WAAAAH

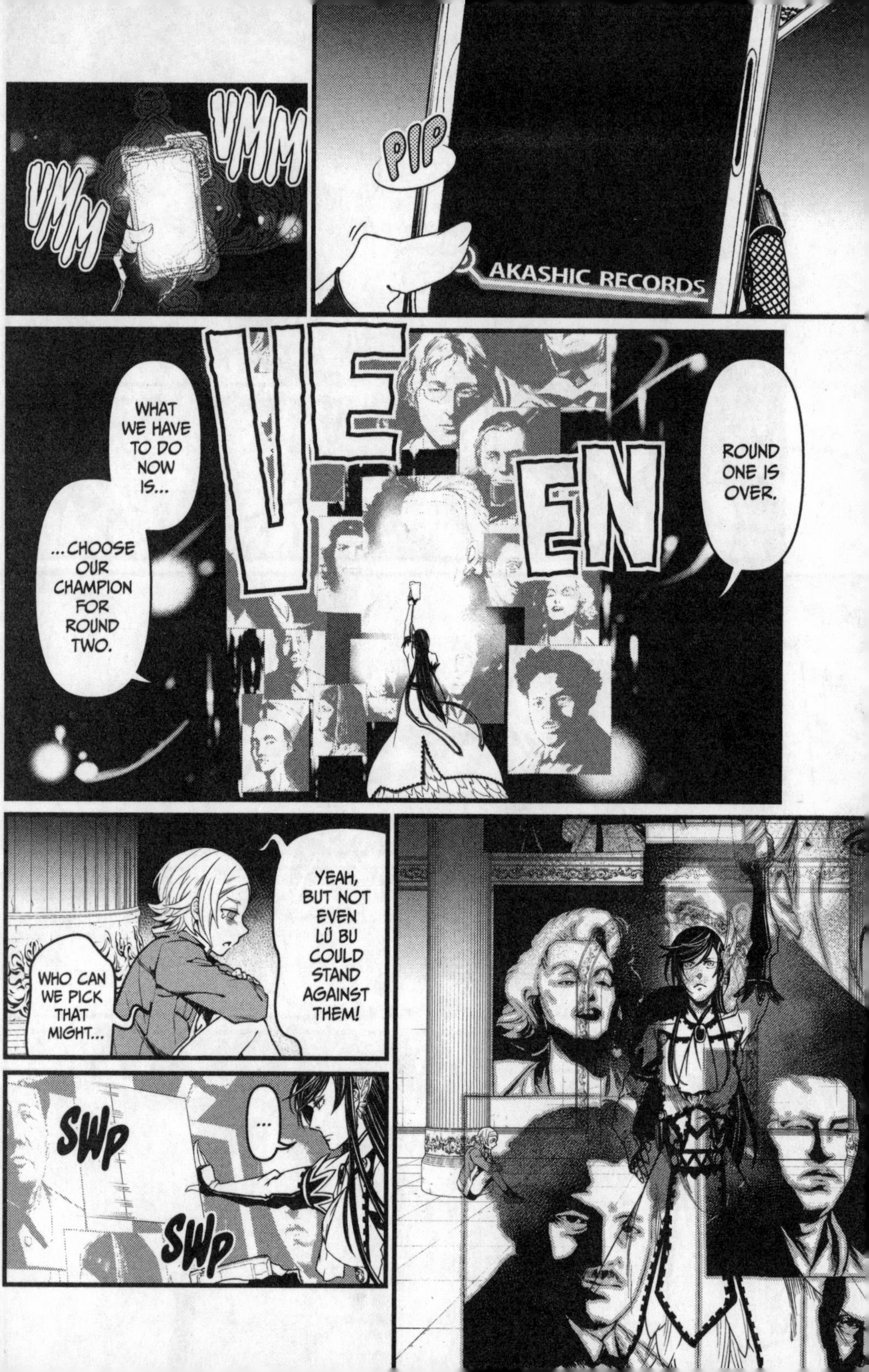
PIP
AKASHIC RECORDS
VMM
VMM
ROUND ONE IS OVER.
VE
EN
WHAT WE HAVE TO DO NOW IS...
...CHOOSE OUR CHAMPION FOR ROUND TWO.
YEAH, BUT NOT EVEN LÜ BU COULD STAND AGAINST THEM!
WHO CAN WE PICK THAT MIGHT...
...
SWP
SWP

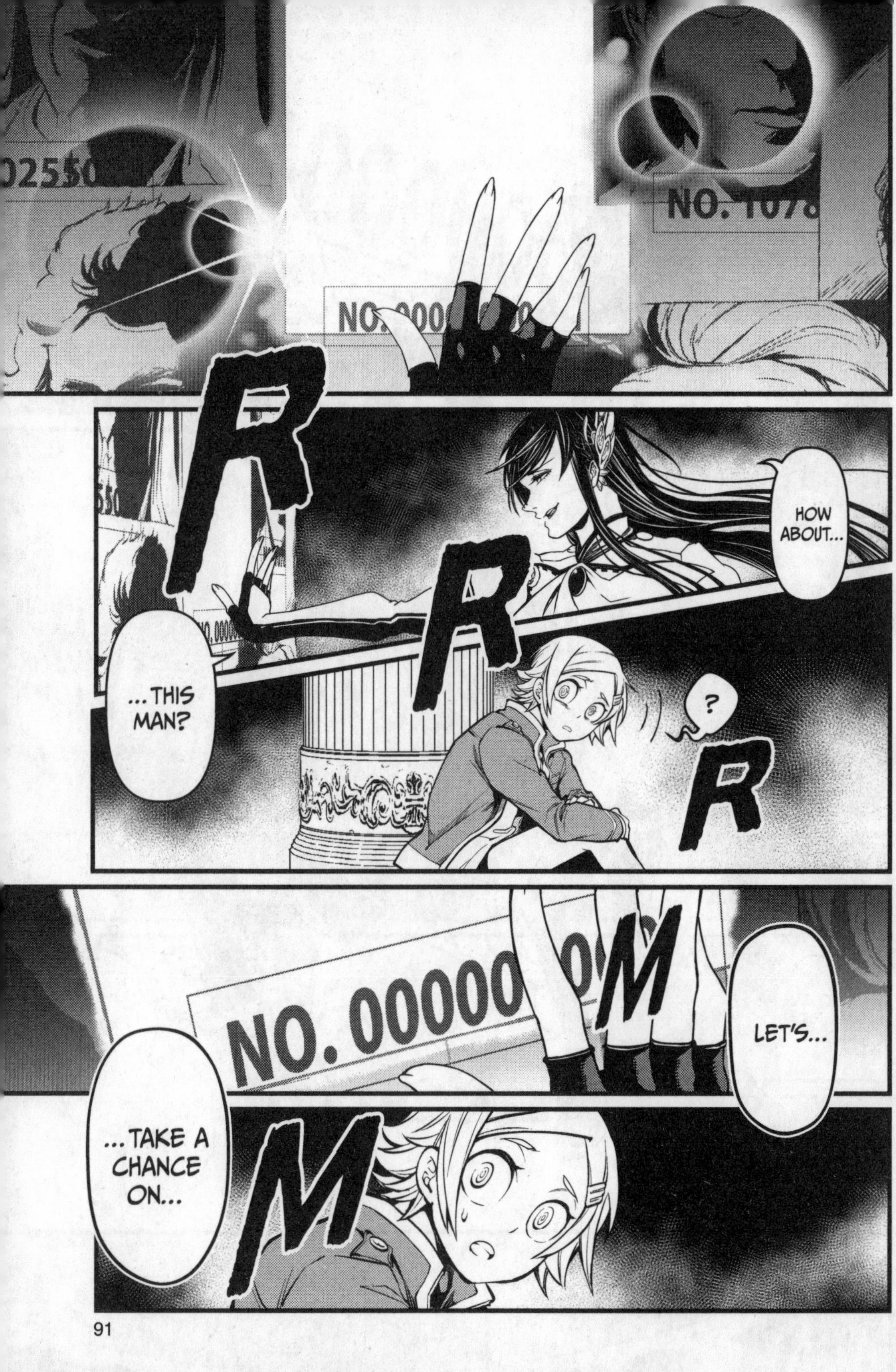
R
HOW ABOUT...
R
...THIS MAN?
?
R
M
LET'S...
NO. 00000
...TAKE A CHANCE ON...
M

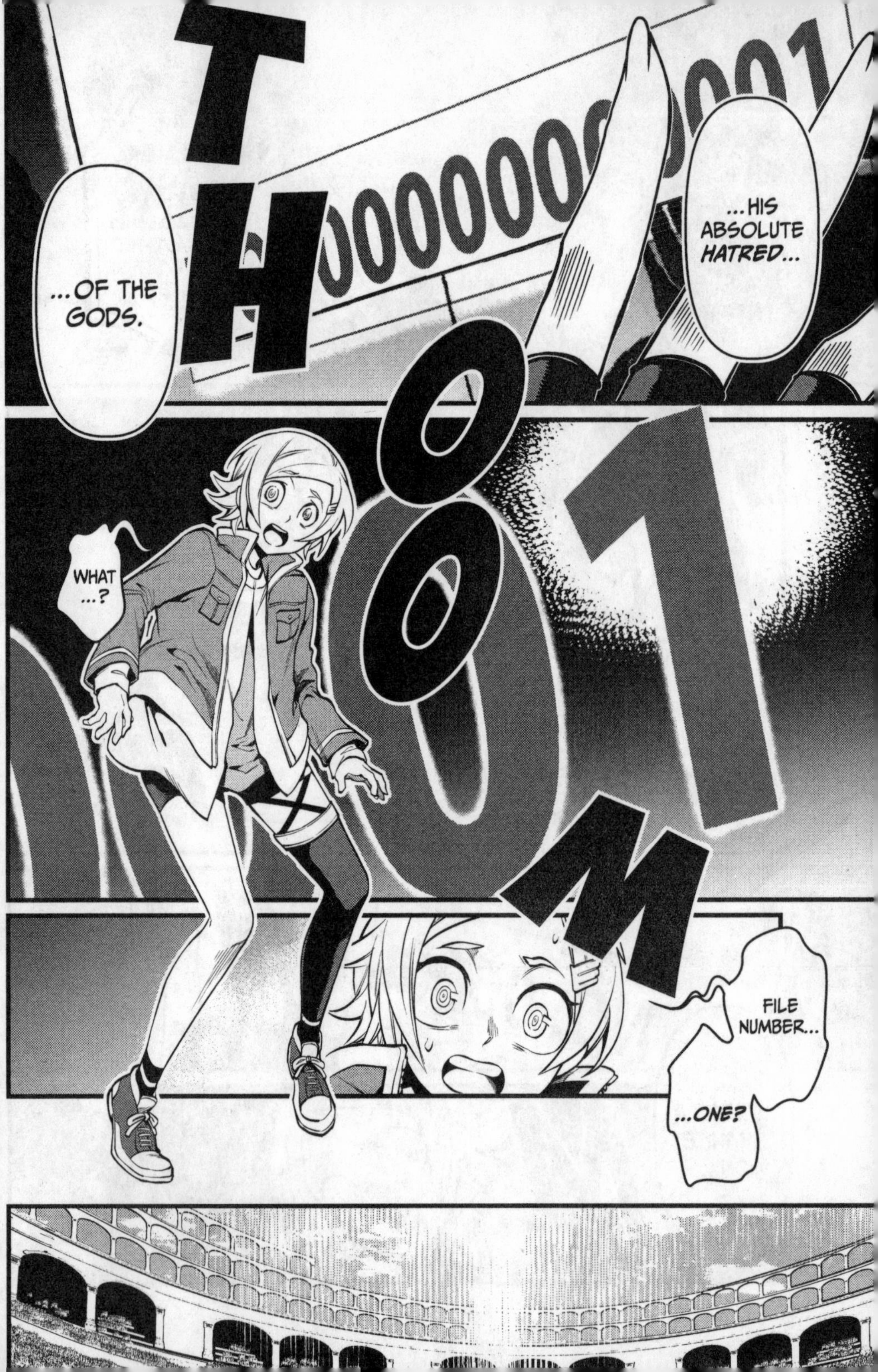
...HIS ABSOLUTE HATRED...
...OF THE GODS.
THOOM
WHAT...?
FILE NUMBER...
...ONE?

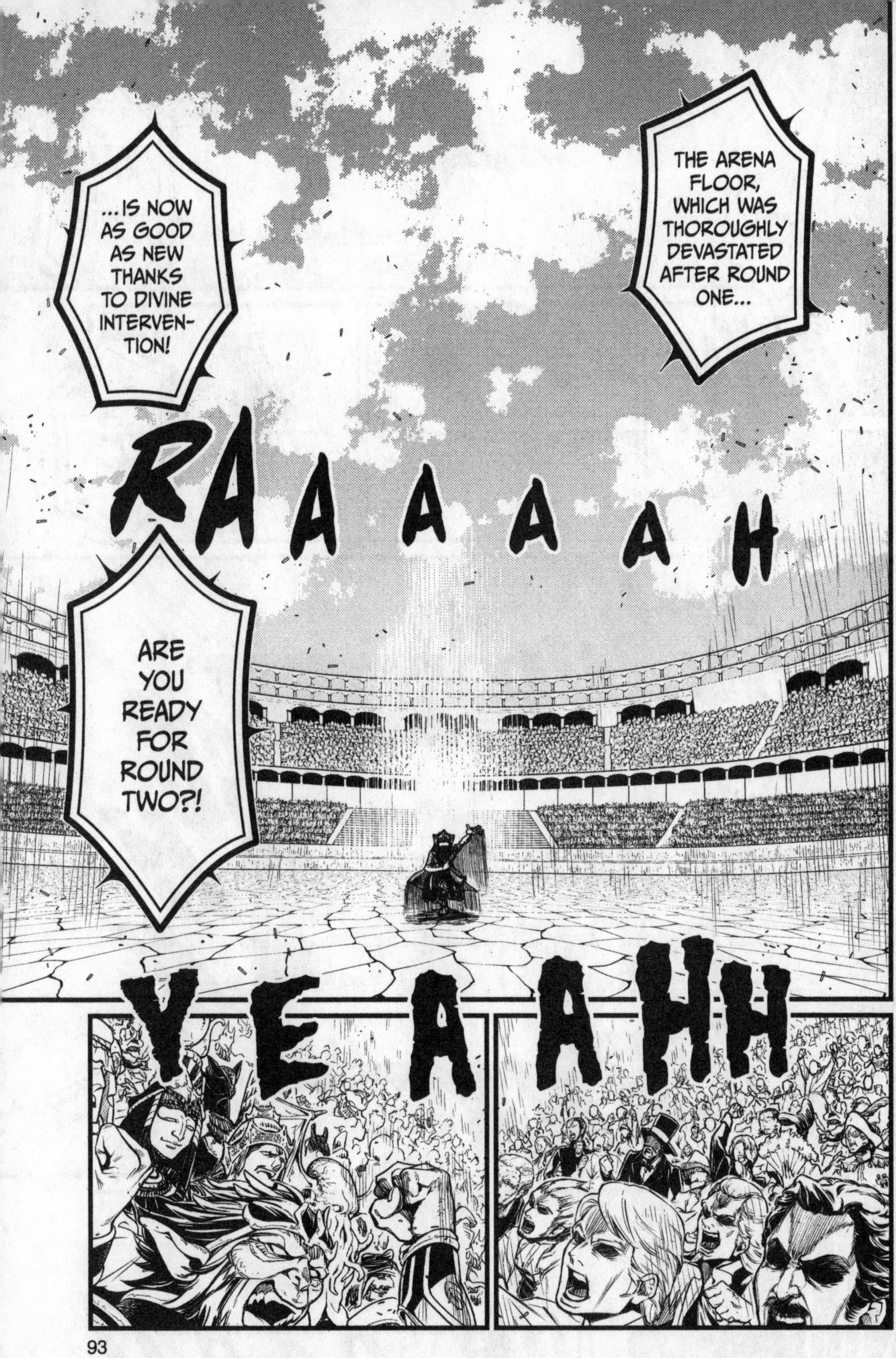
THE ARENA FLOOR, WHICH WAS THOROUGHLY DEVASTATED AFTER ROUND ONE...
...IS NOW AS GOOD AS NEW THANKS TO DIVINE INTERVENTION!
RAAAAAH
ARE YOU READY FOR ROUND TWO?!
YEAAHH

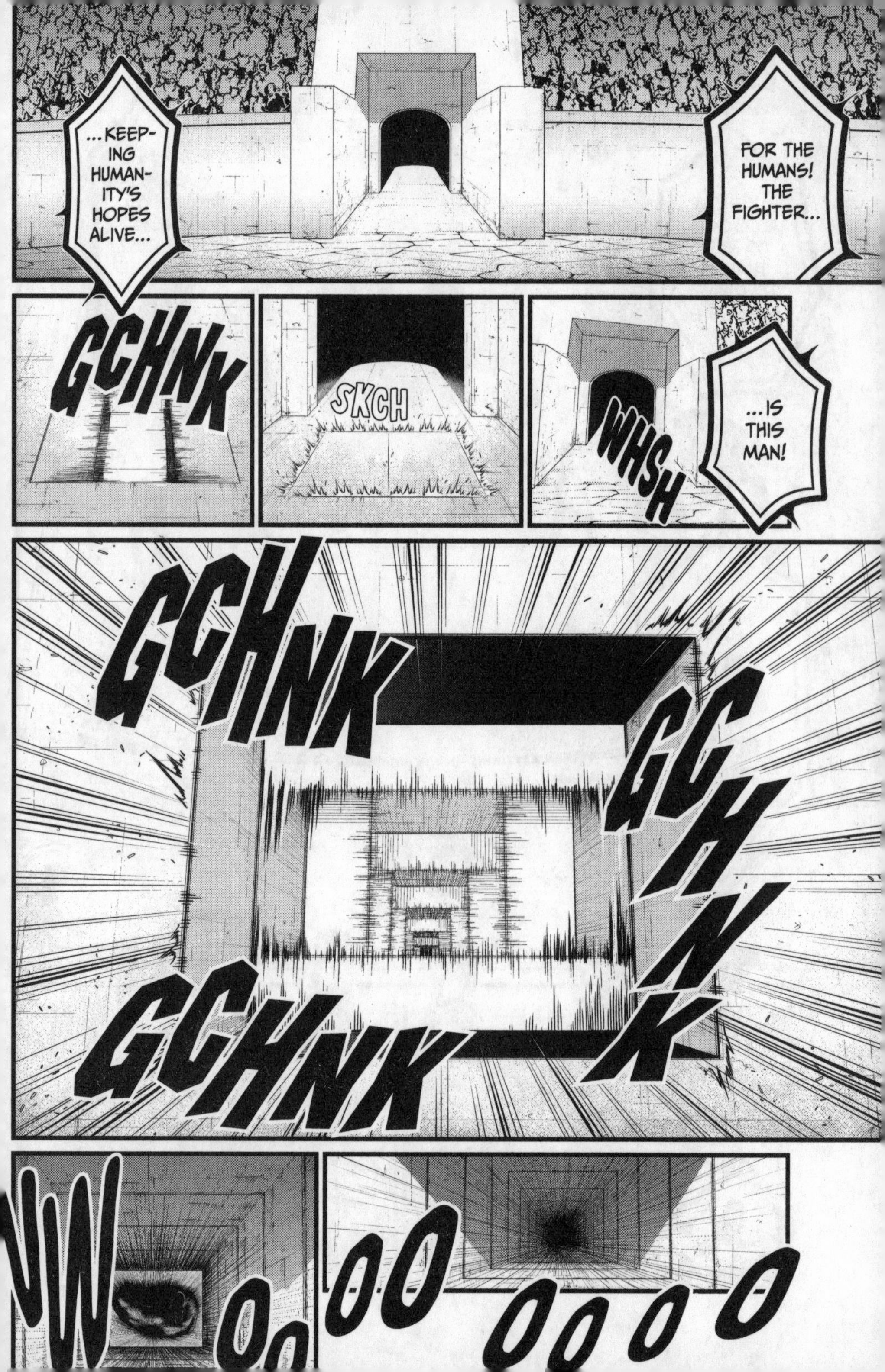
FOR THE HUMANS! THE FIGHTER...
...KEEPING HUMANITY'S HOPES ALIVE...
...IS THIS MAN!
WHSH
SKCH
GCHNK
GCHNK
GCHNK
GCHNK
WWOOOOOOOOO

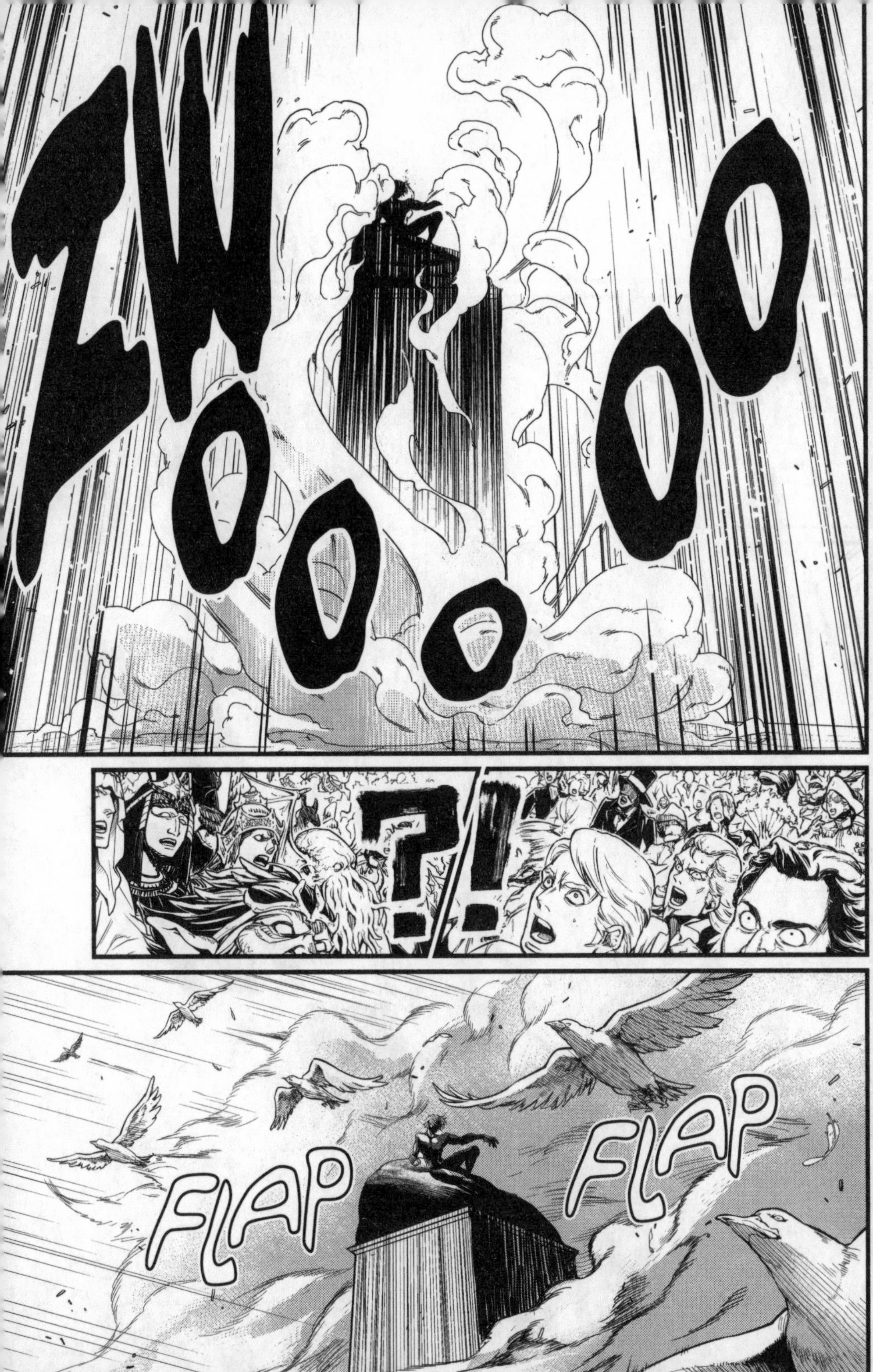
ZWOOOOOO
?!
FLAP
FLAP

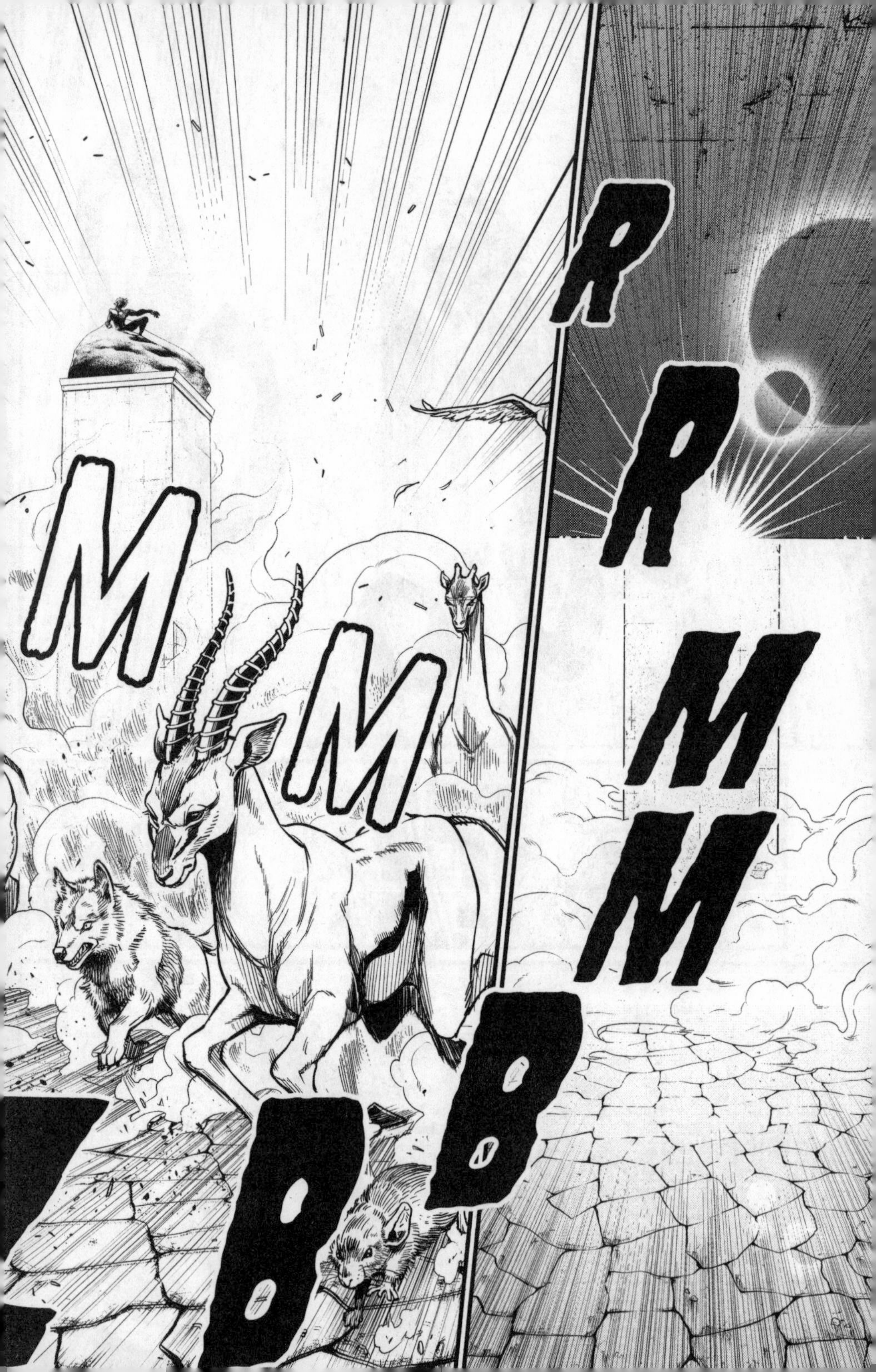
RRMM
MM
BBB

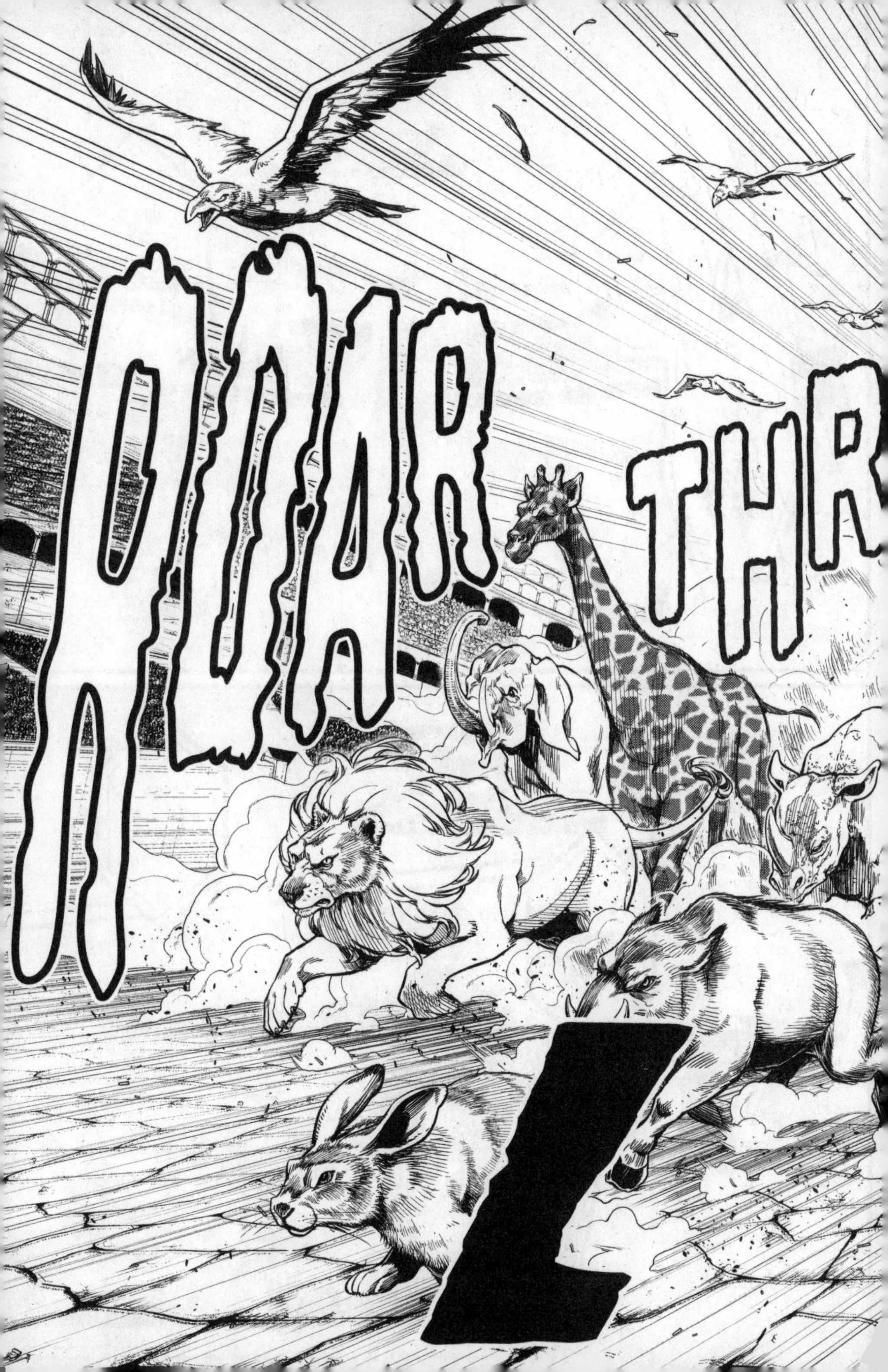
THR
ROAR

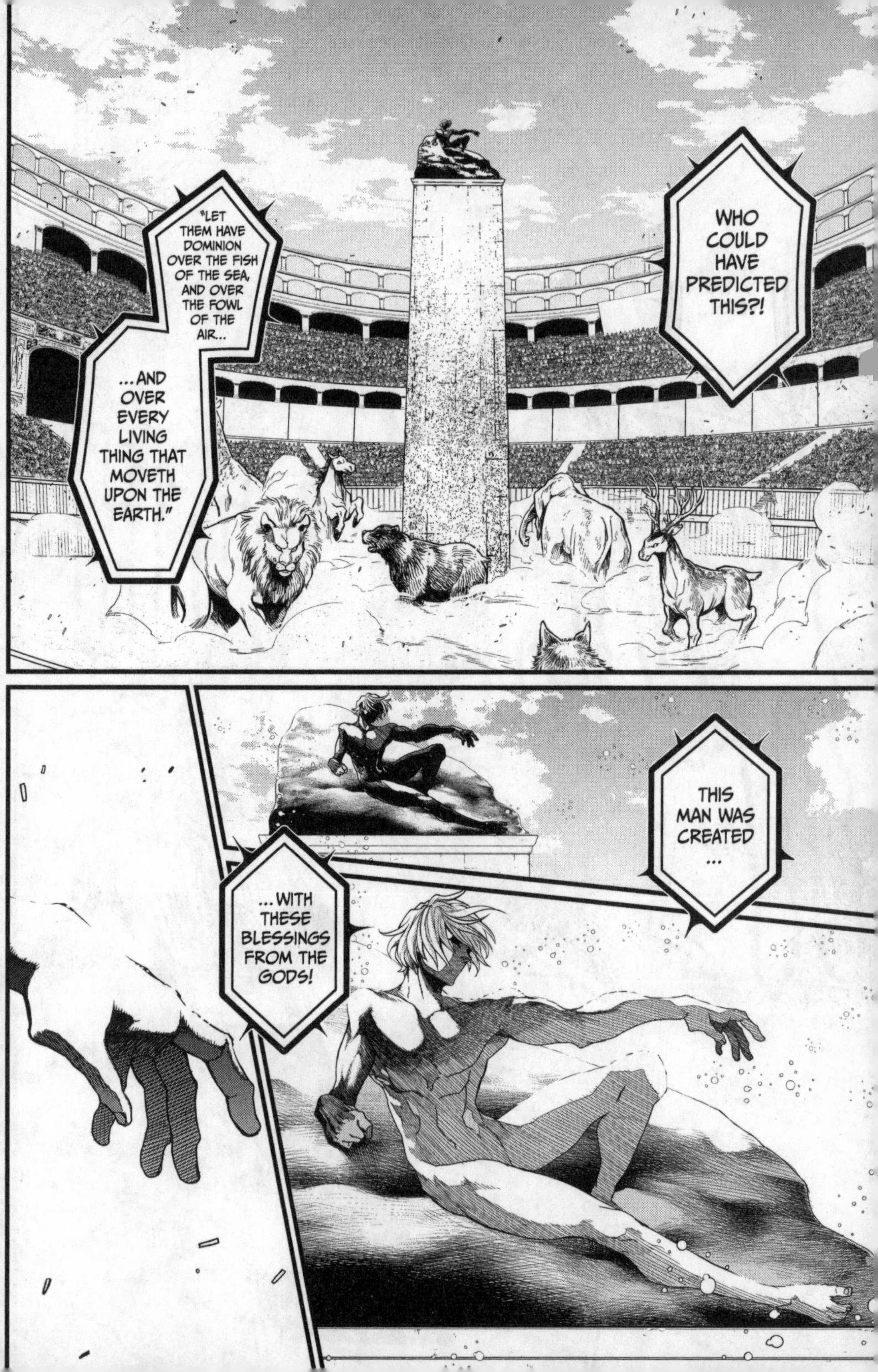
WHO COULD HAVE PREDICTED THIS?!
"LET THEM HAVE DOMINION OVER THE FISH OF THE SEA, AND OVER THE FOWL OF THE AIR...
...AND OVER EVERY LIVING THING THAT MOVETH UPON THE EARTH."
THIS MAN WAS CREATED ...
...WITH THESE BLESSINGS FROM THE GODS!

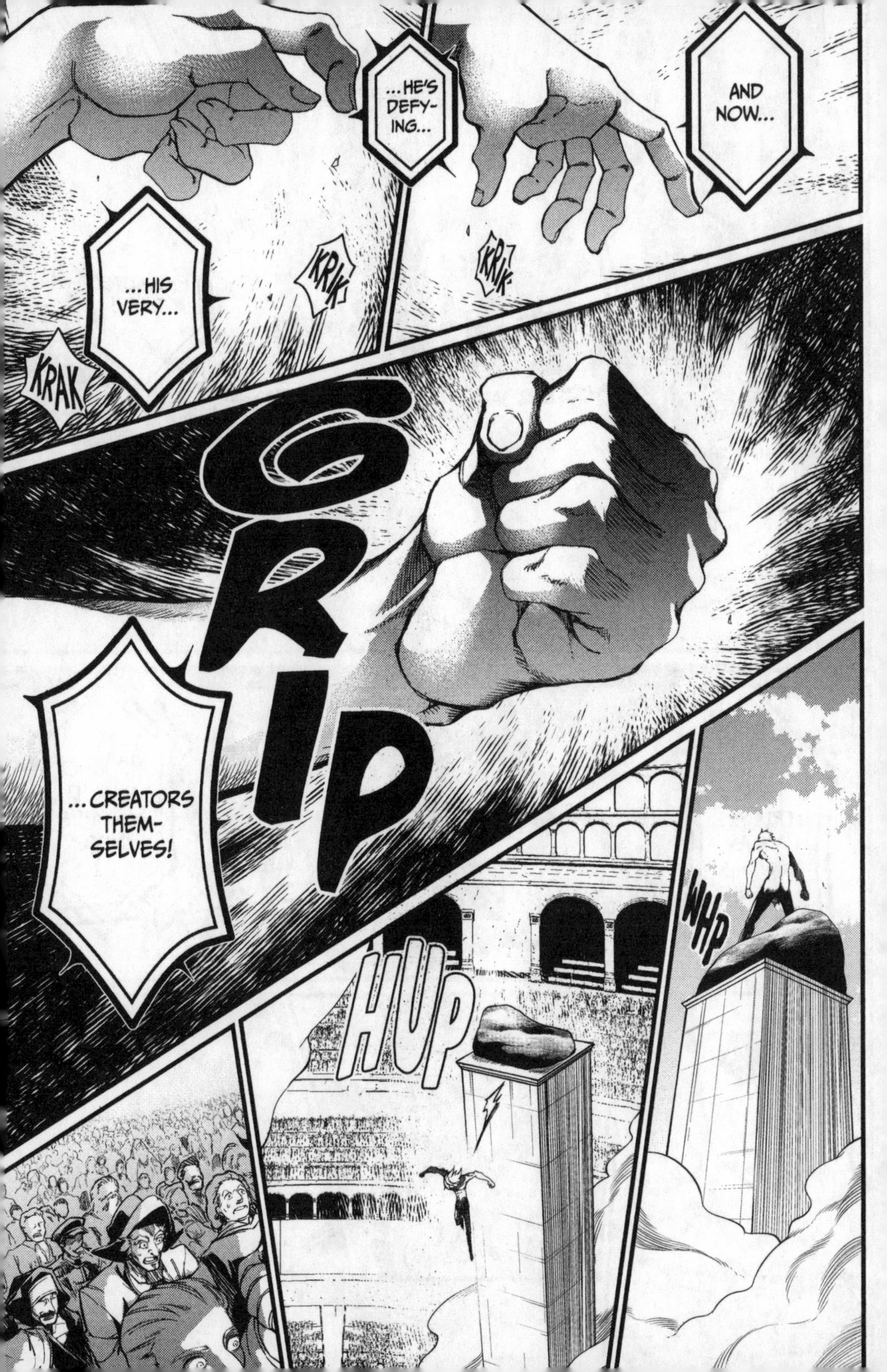
AND NOW...
...HE'S DEFYING...
KRIK
KRIK
...HIS VERY...
KRAK
GRIP
...CREATORS THEMSELVES!
WHP
HUP

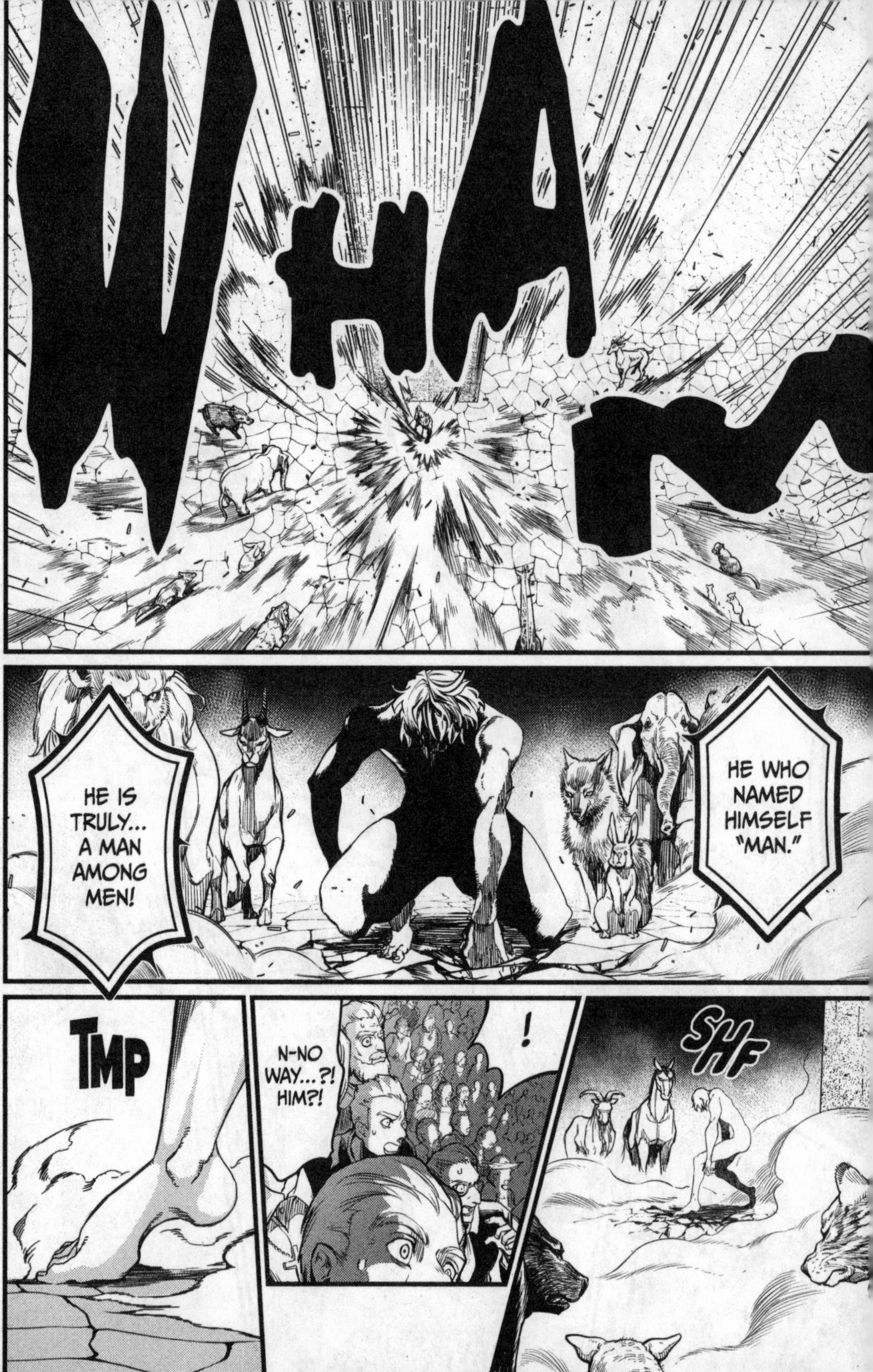
WHA
HE WHO NAMED HIMSELF "MAN."
HE IS TRULY... A MAN AMONG MEN!
SHF
!
N-NO WAY...?! HIM?!
TMP

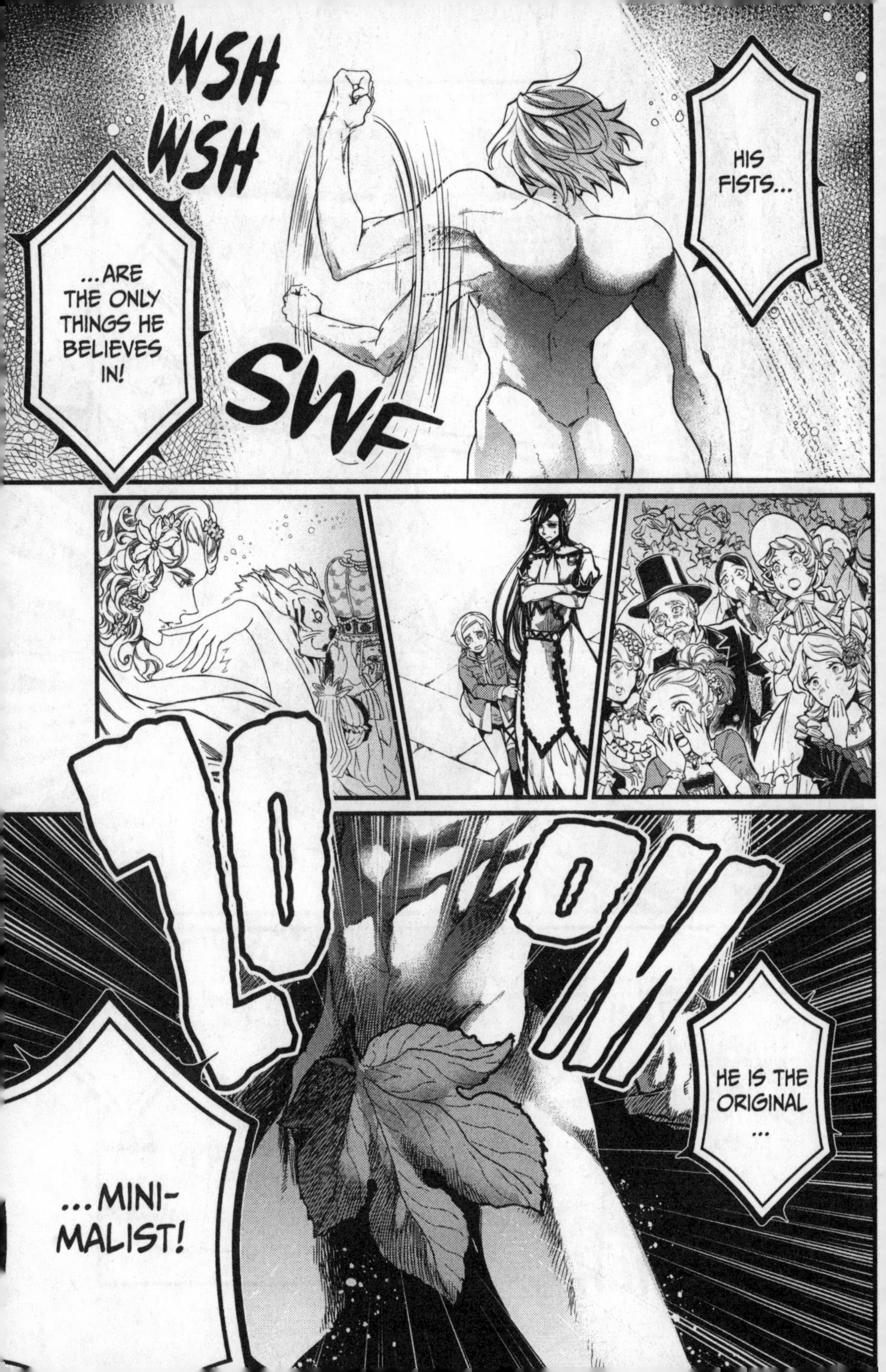
HIS FISTS...
WSH WSH
...ARE THE ONLY THINGS HE BELIEVES IN!
SWF
HE IS THE ORIGINAL ...
...MINI-MALIST!

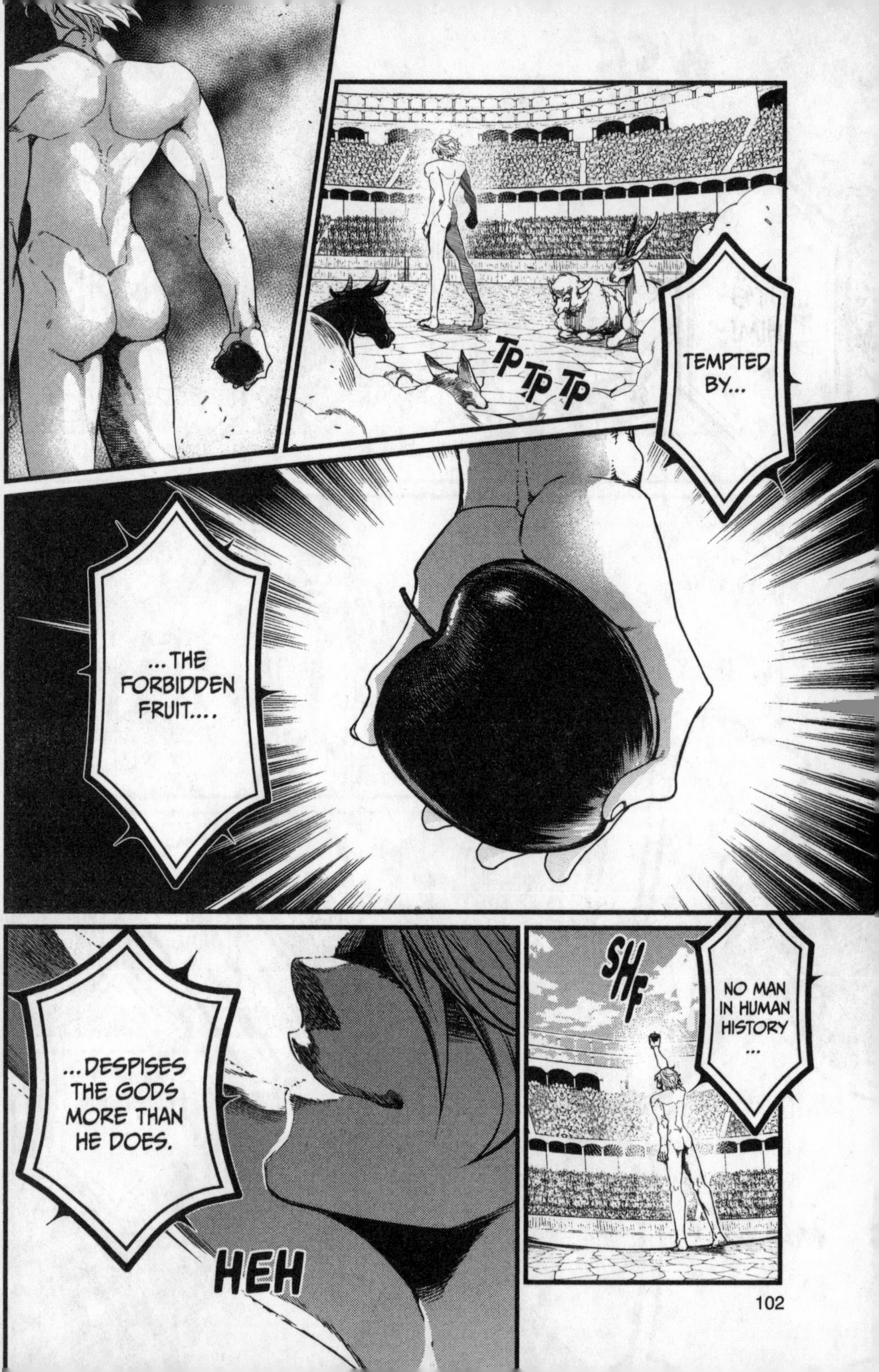
TP TP TP
TEMPTED BY...
...THE FORBIDDEN FRUIT....
SHF
NO MAN IN HUMAN HISTORY ...
...DESPISES THE GODS MORE THAN HE DOES.
HEH

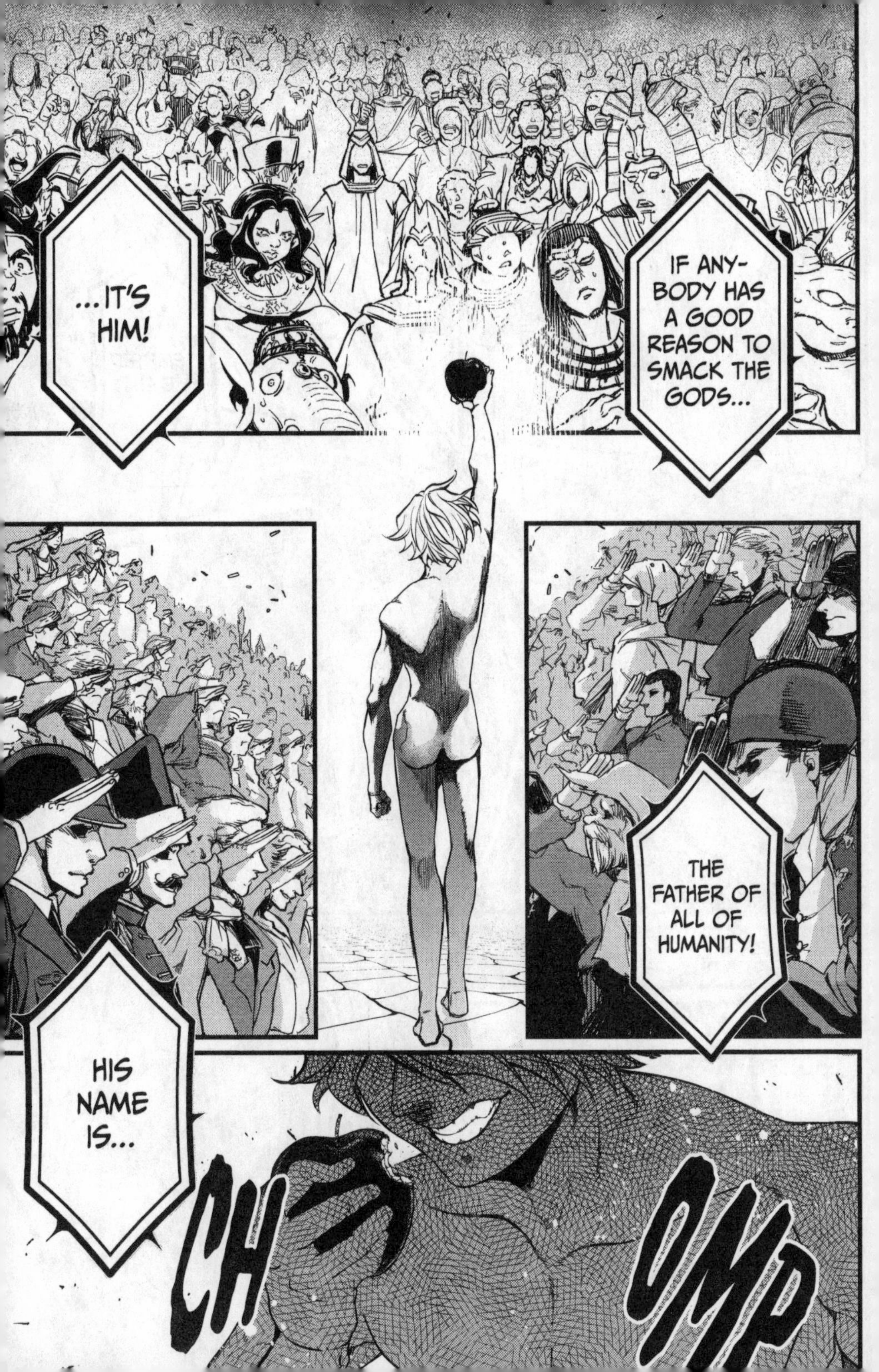
IF ANY-BODY HAS A GOOD REASON TO SMACK THE GODS...
...IT'S HIM!
THE FATHER OF ALL OF HUMANITY!
HIS NAME IS...
CHOMP

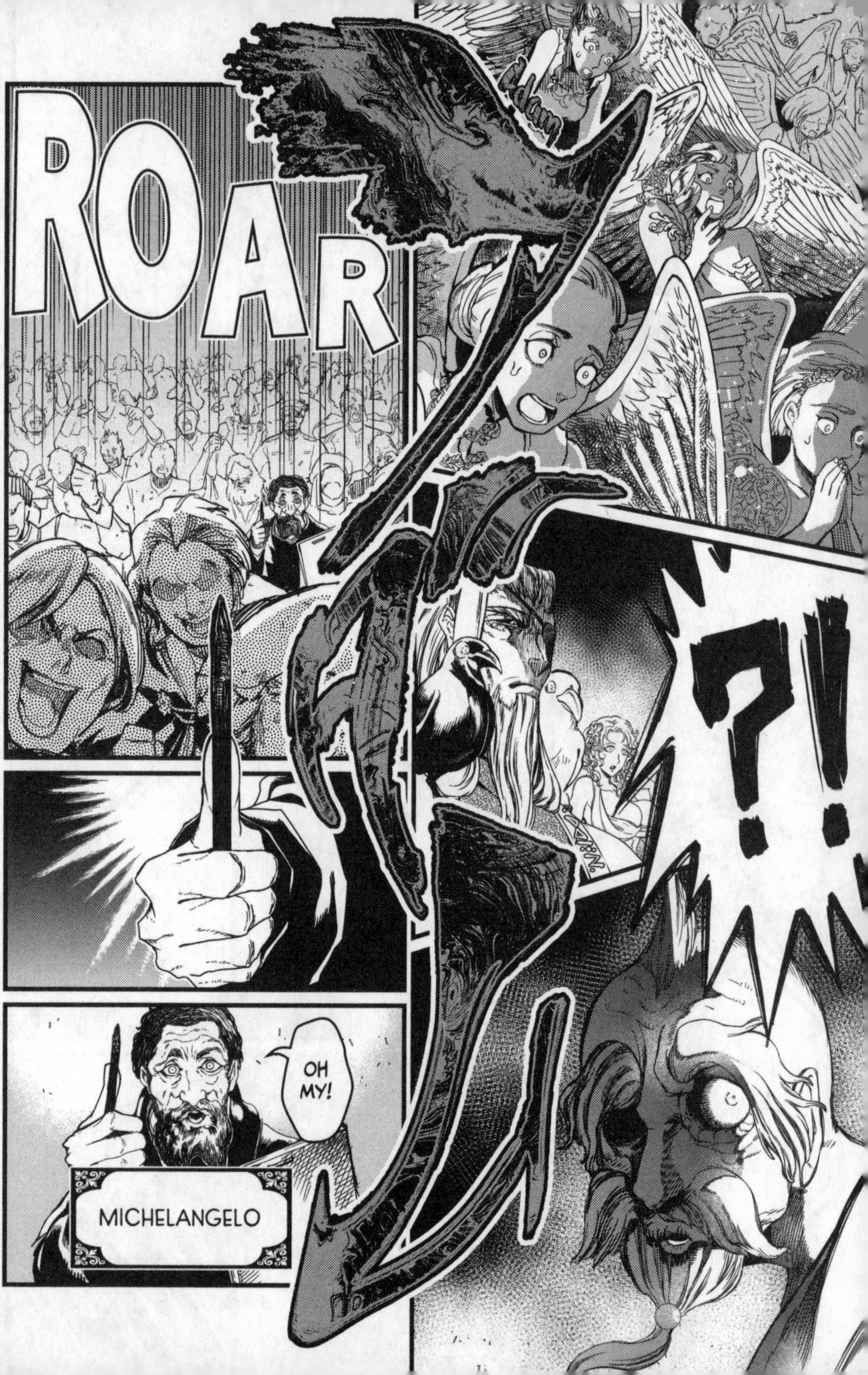
?!
ROAR
OH MY!
MICHELANGELO

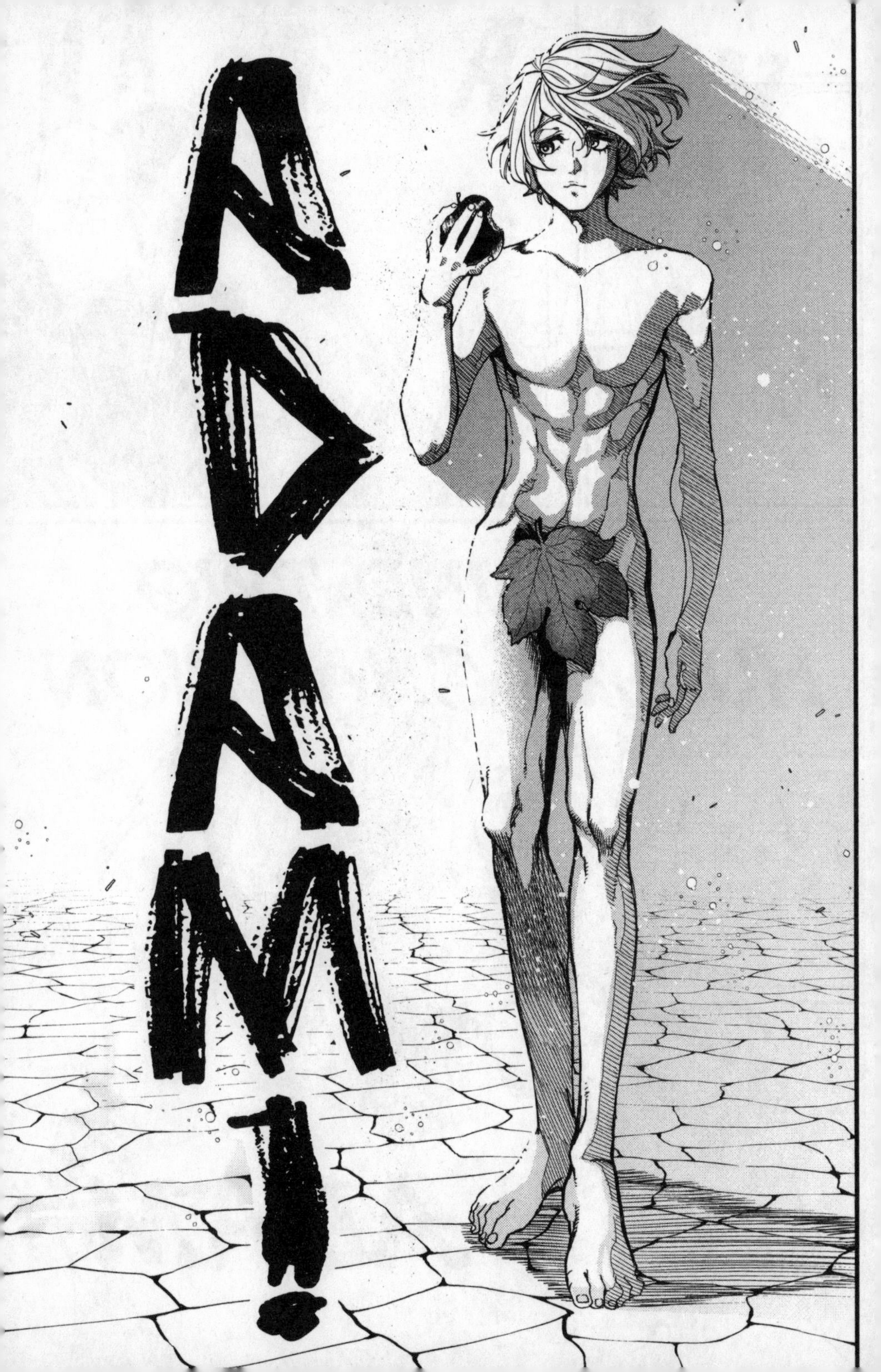
ADAM!

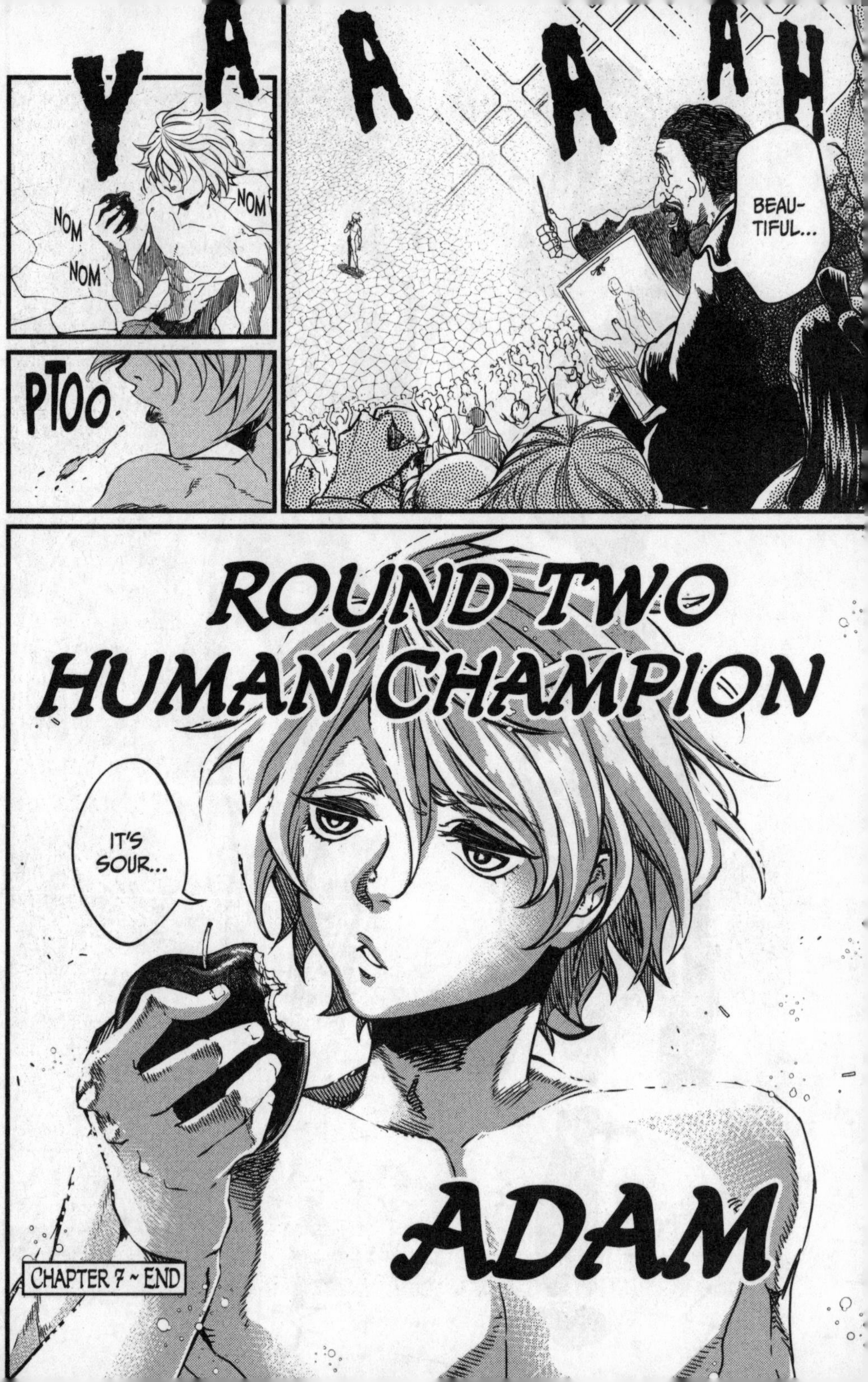
YAAAAH
BEAU-TIFUL...
NOM
NOM
NOM
PTOO
ROUND TWO HUMAN CHAMPION
IT'S SOUR...
ADAM
CHAPTER 7 ~ END

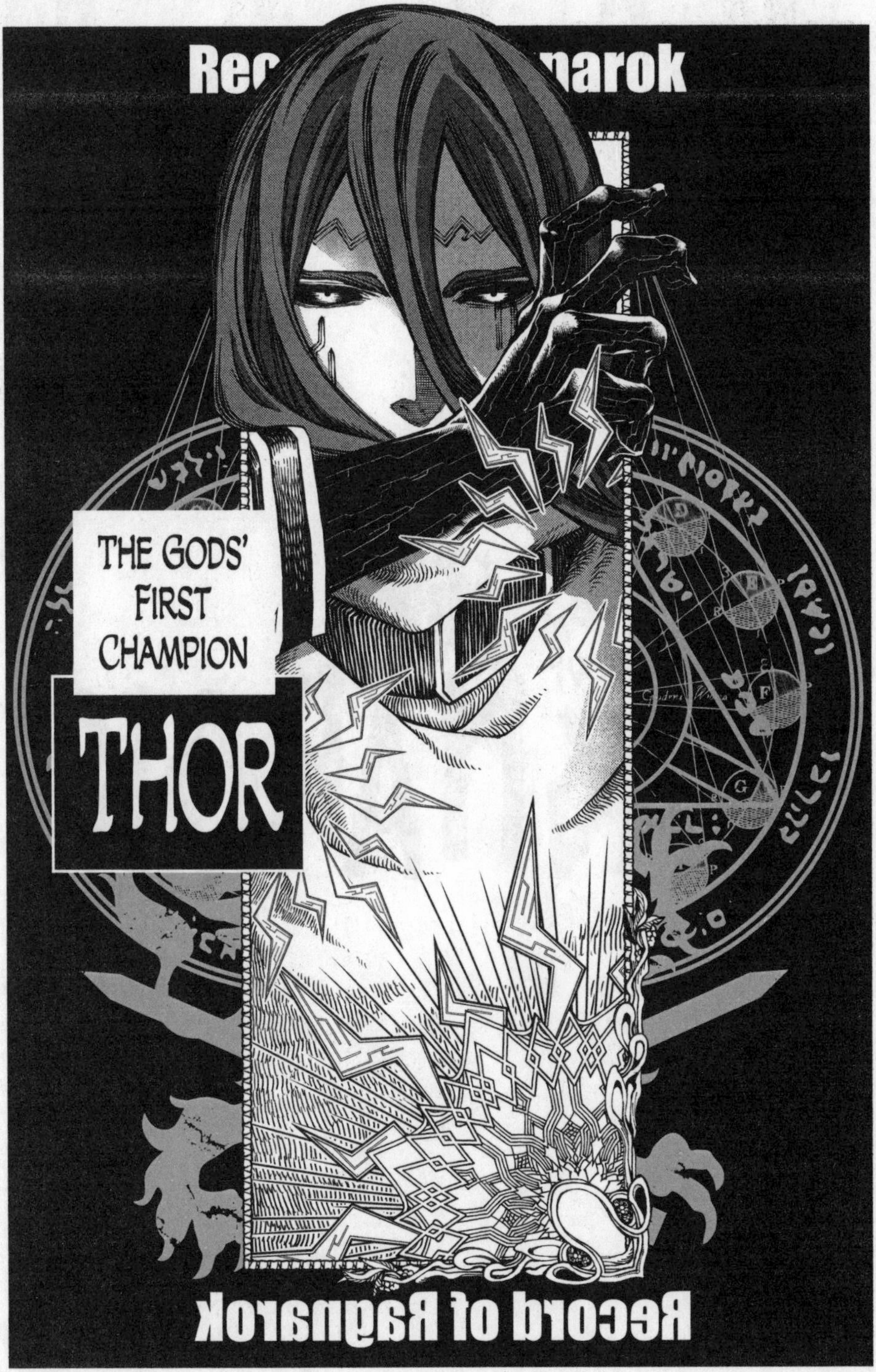
THE GODS' FIRST CHAMPION
THOR
Record of Ragnarok

RECORD OF
RAGNAROK

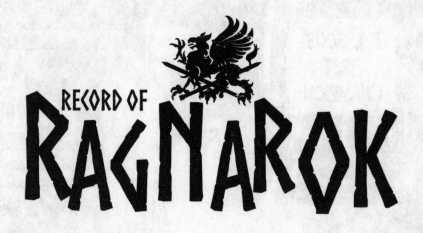

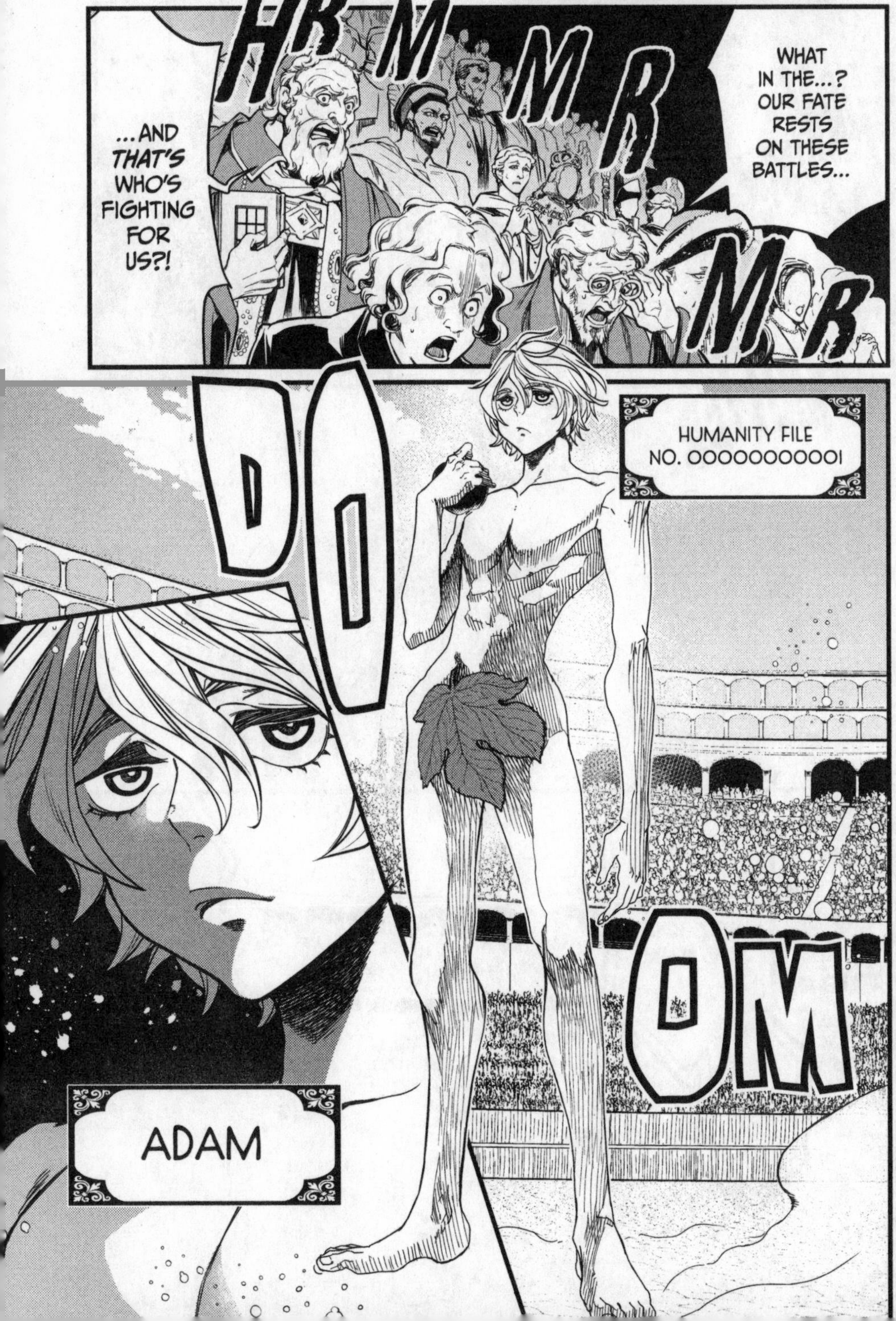
HBMMMR
WHAT IN THE...? OUR FATE RESTS ON THESE BATTLES...
...AND THAT'S WHO'S FIGHTING FOR US?!
MMR
DOOM
HUMANITY FILE NO. 0000000001
ADAM

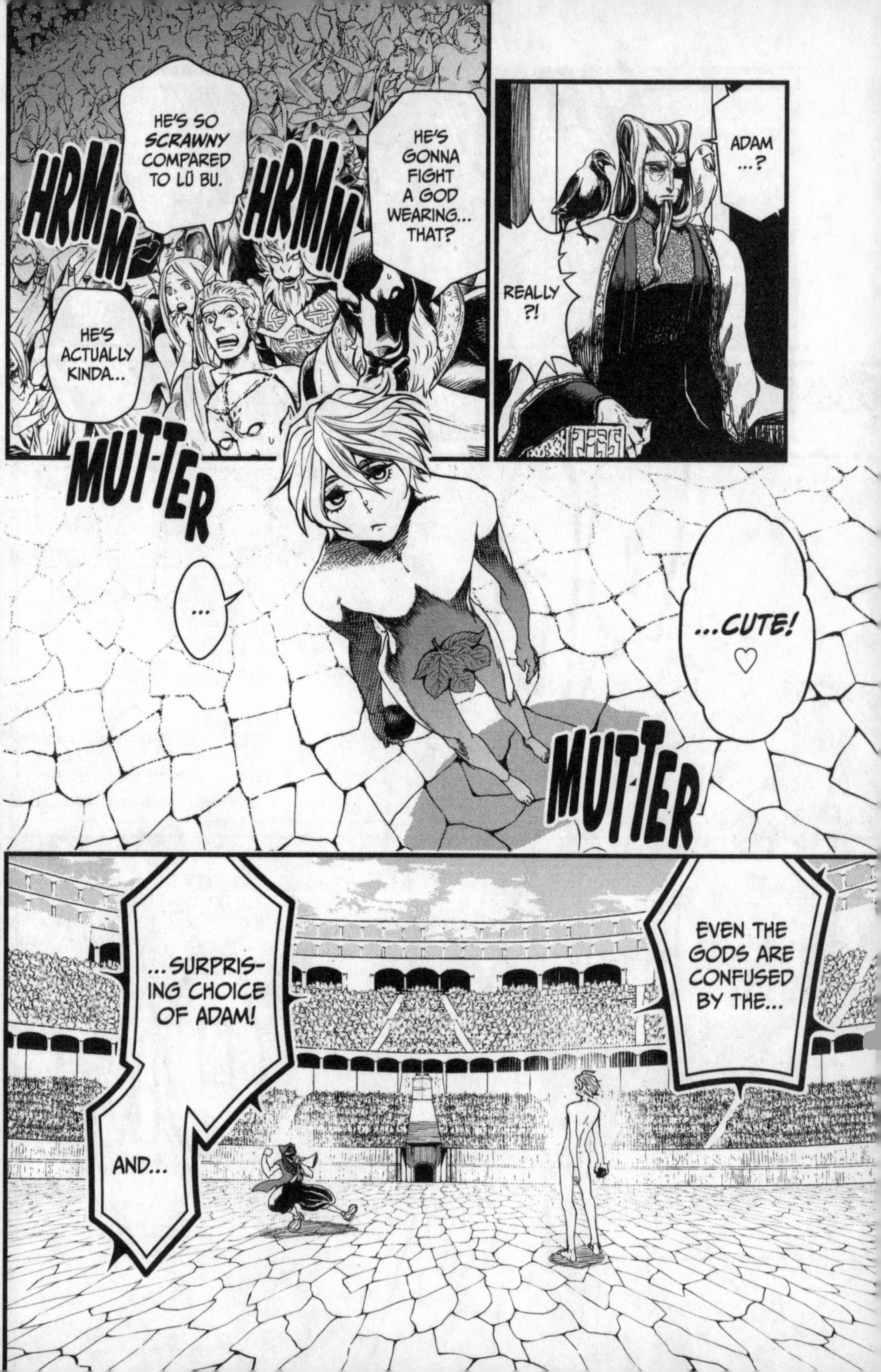
ADAM ...?
REALLY ?!
HE'S GONNA FIGHT A GOD WEARING... THAT?
HRMM
HE'S SO SCRAWNY COMPARED TO LÜ BU.
HRMM
HE'S ACTUALLY KINDA...
...CUTE! ♡
MUTTER
MUTTER
...
EVEN THE GODS ARE CONFUSED BY THE...
...SURPRIS-ING CHOICE OF ADAM!
AND...

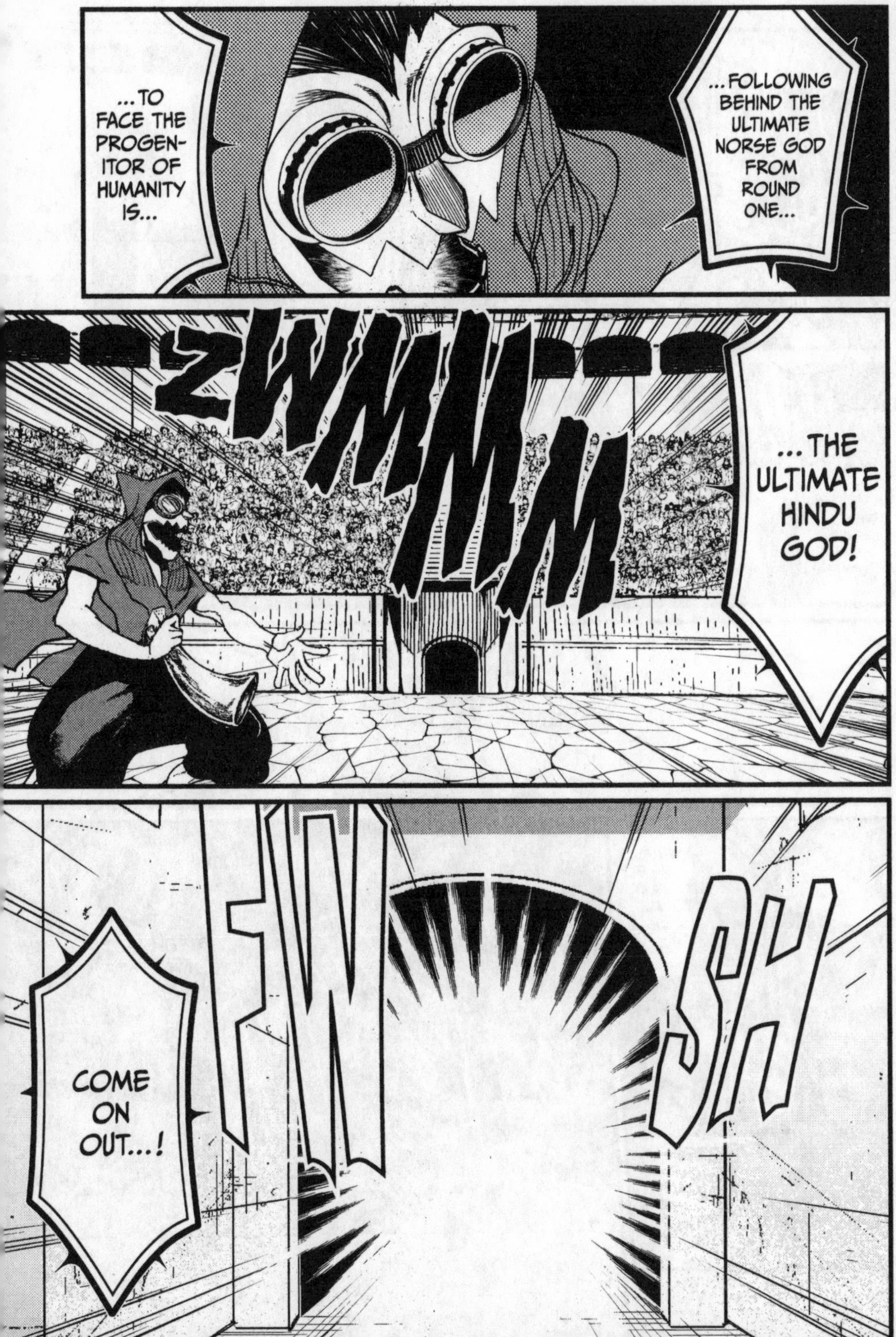
...FOLLOWING BEHIND THE ULTIMATE NORSE GOD FROM ROUND ONE...
...TO FACE THE PROGENITOR OF HUMANITY IS...
ZWMMM
...THE ULTIMATE HINDU GOD!
FWSH
COME ON OUT...!

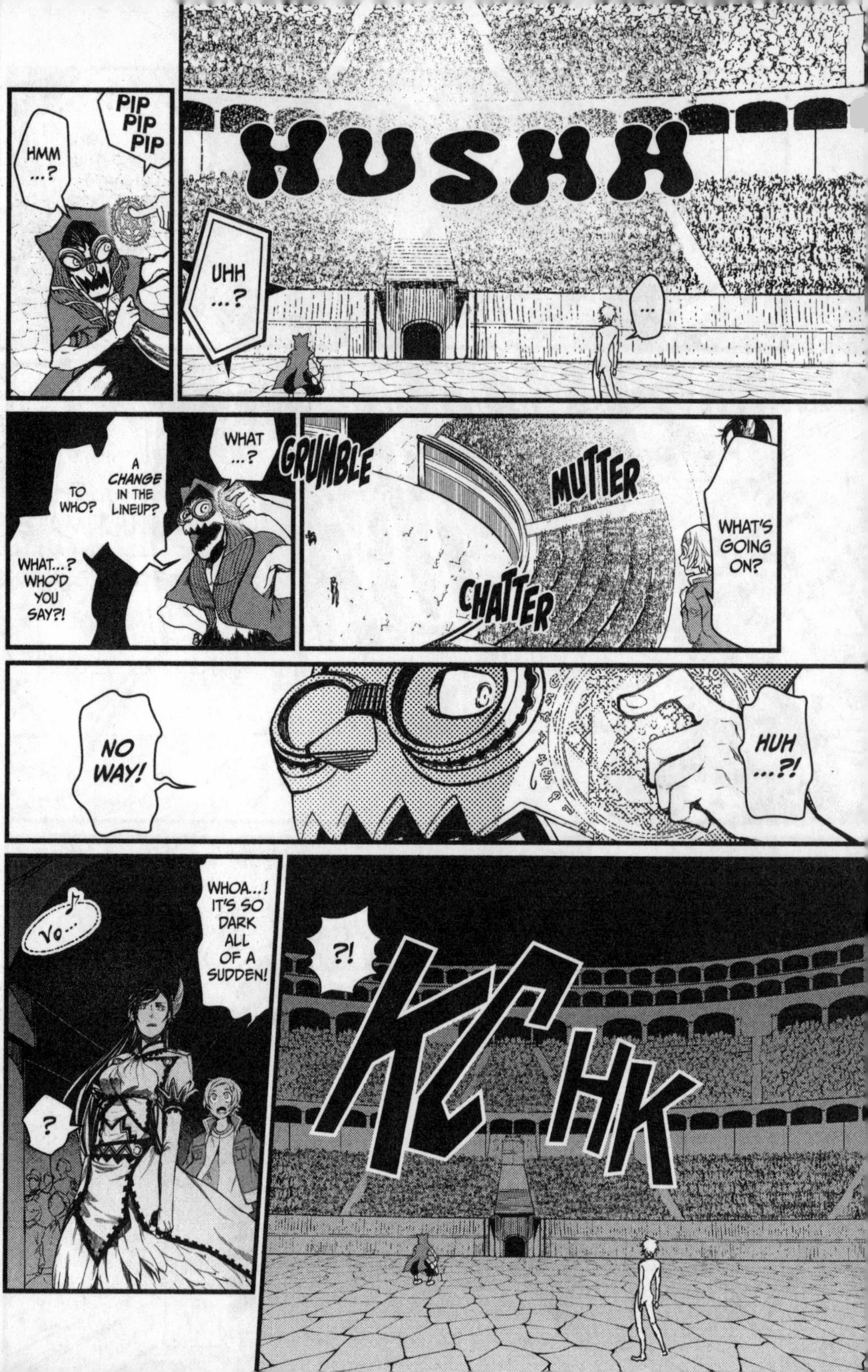
HUSHH
...
UHH ...?
PIP PIP PIP
HMM ...?
MUTTER
GRUMBLE
WHAT'S GOING ON?
CHATTER
WHAT ...?
A CHANGE IN THE LINEUP?
TO WHO?
WHAT...? WHO'D YOU SAY?!
HUH ...?!
NO WAY!
?!
KCHK
WHOA...! IT'S SO DARK ALL OF A SUDDEN!
Vo...
?

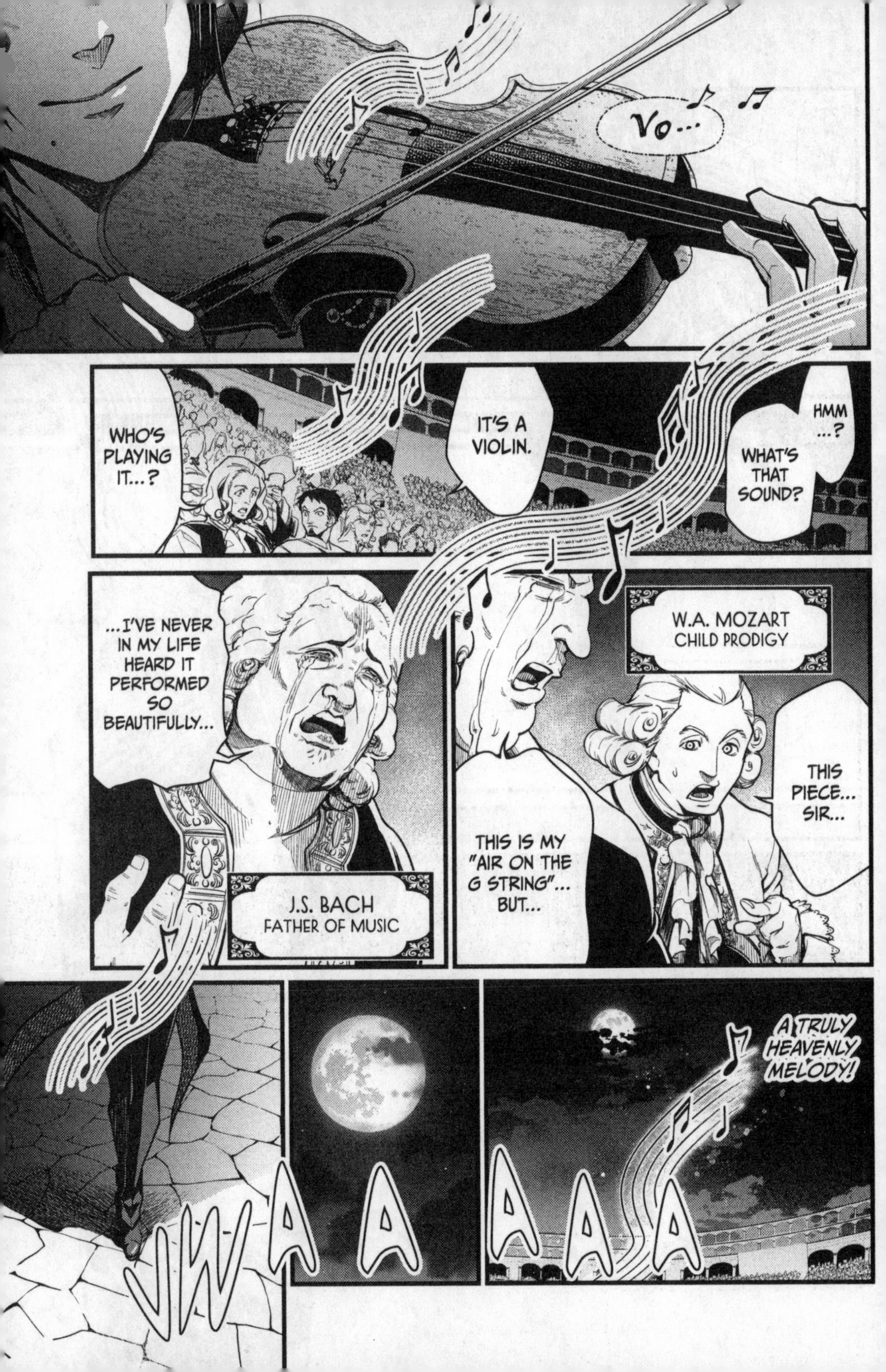
Vo...
HMM ...? WHAT'S THAT SOUND?
IT'S A VIOLIN.
WHO'S PLAYING IT...?
W.A. MOZART CHILD PRODIGY
THIS PIECE... SIR...
THIS IS MY "AIR ON THE G STRING"... BUT...
...I'VE NEVER IN MY LIFE HEARD IT PERFORMED SO BEAUTIFULLY...
J.S. BACH FATHER OF MUSIC
A TRULY HEAVENLY MELODY!
WAAAAA

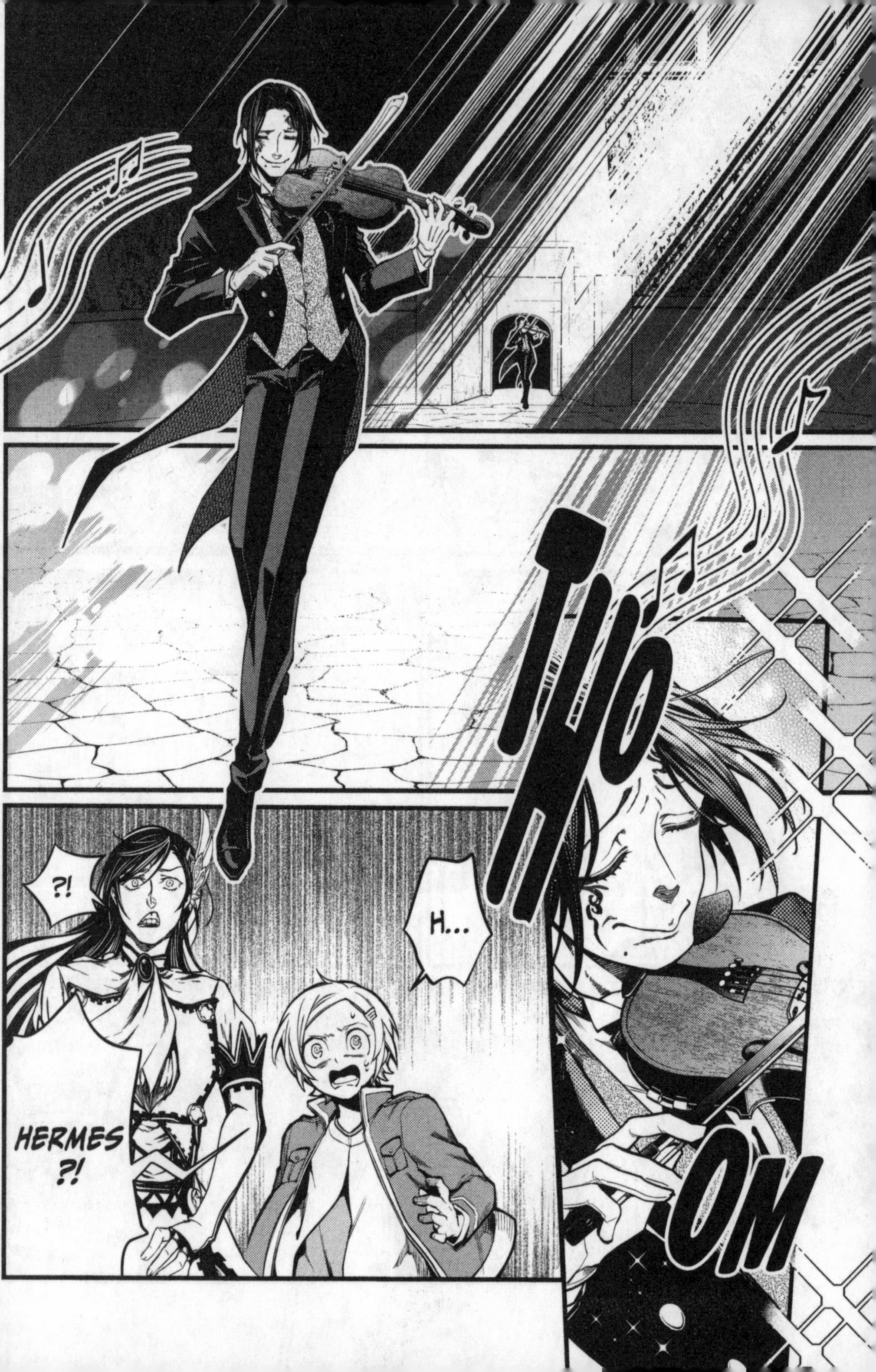
THO
OM
H...
?!
HERMES ?!

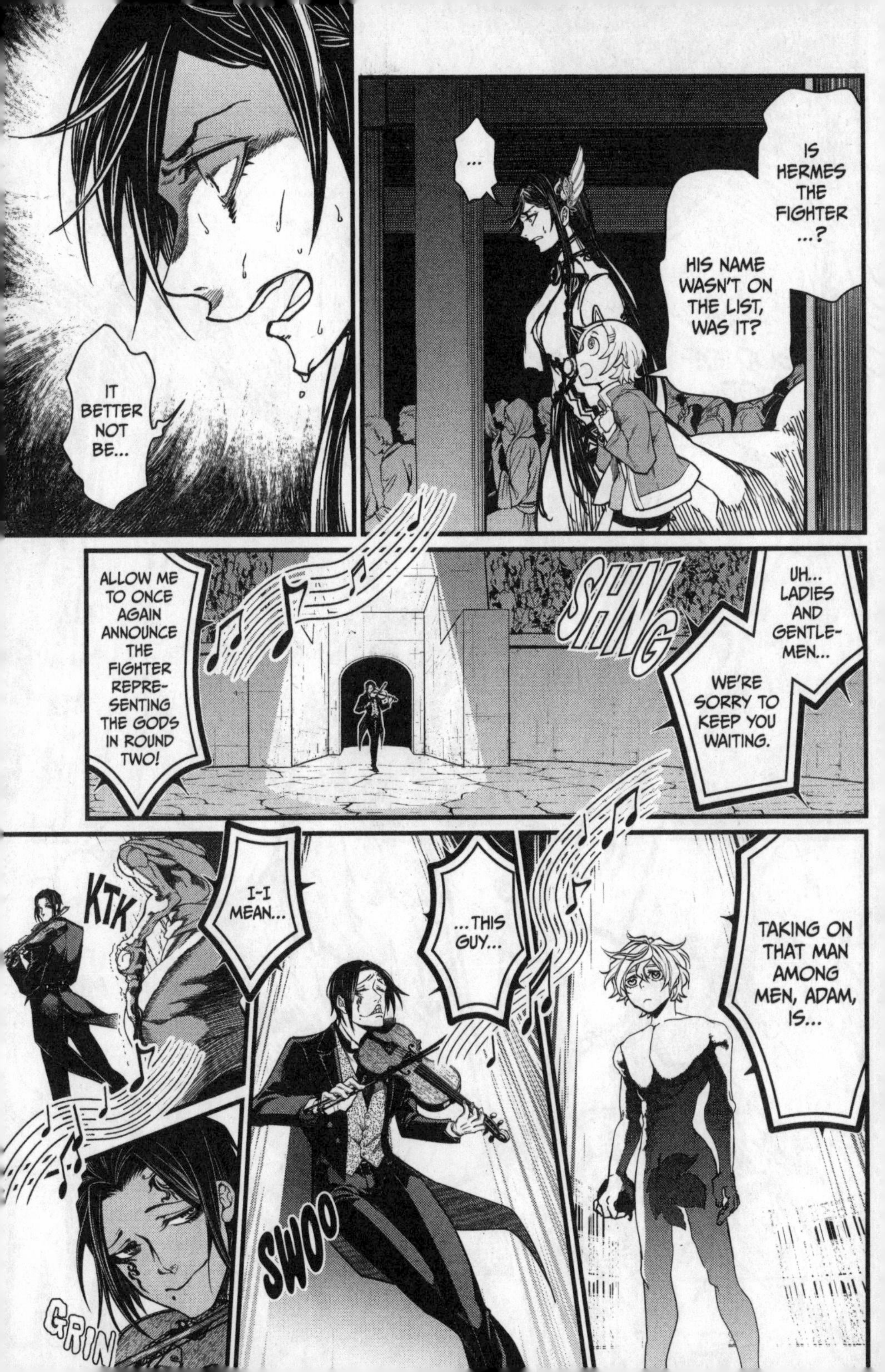
IS HERMES THE FIGHTER ...?
HIS NAME WASN'T ON THE LIST, WAS IT?
...
IT BETTER NOT BE...
UH... LADIES AND GENTLE-MEN...
WE'RE SORRY TO KEEP YOU WAITING.
SHNG
ALLOW ME TO ONCE AGAIN ANNOUNCE THE FIGHTER REPRE-SENTING THE GODS IN ROUND TWO!
TAKING ON THAT MAN AMONG MEN, ADAM, IS...
...THIS GUY...
I-I MEAN...
SWOO
KTK
GRIN

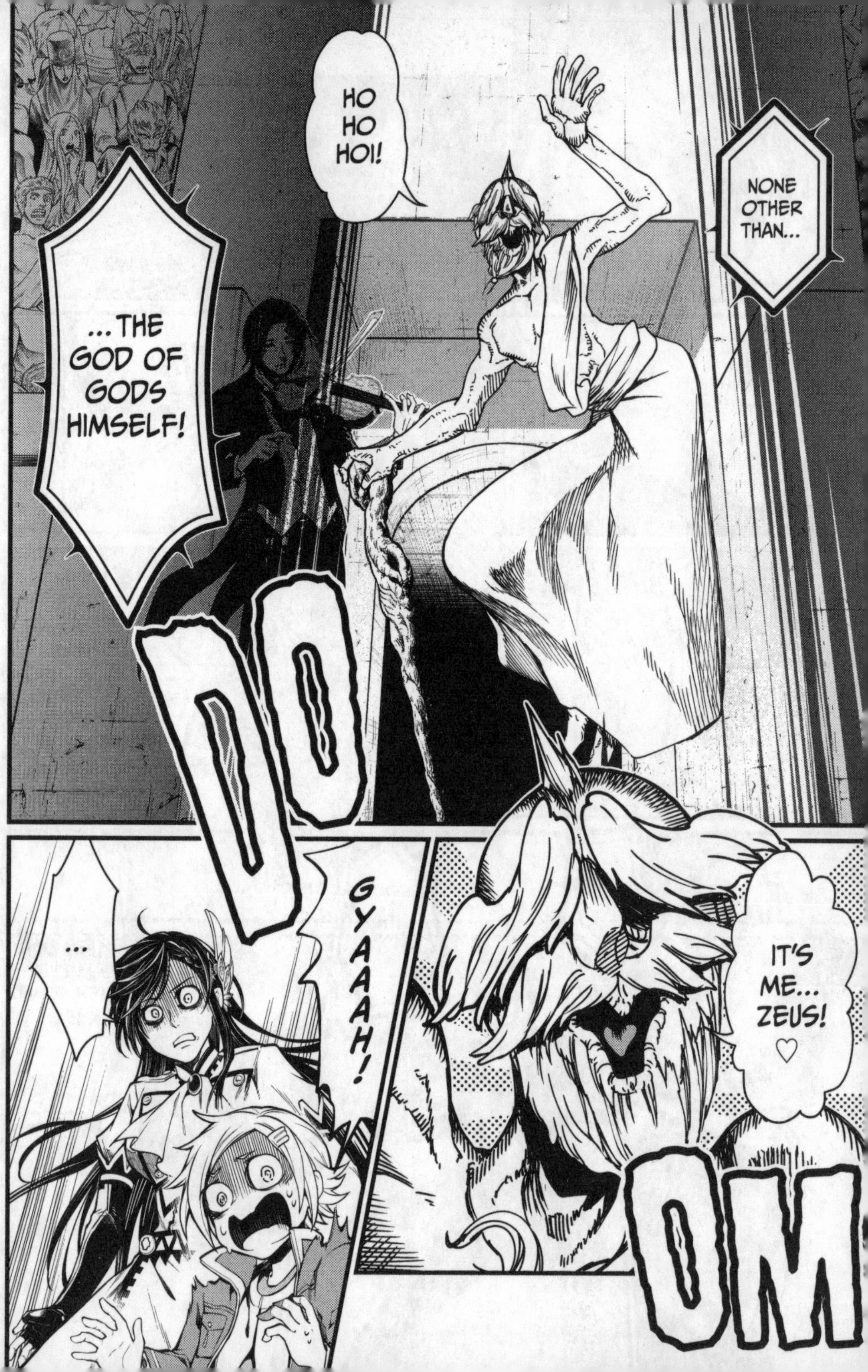
NONE OTHER THAN...
HO HO HOI!
...THE GOD OF GODS HIMSELF!
DO
IT'S ME... ZEUS! ♡
OM
GYAAAAH!
...

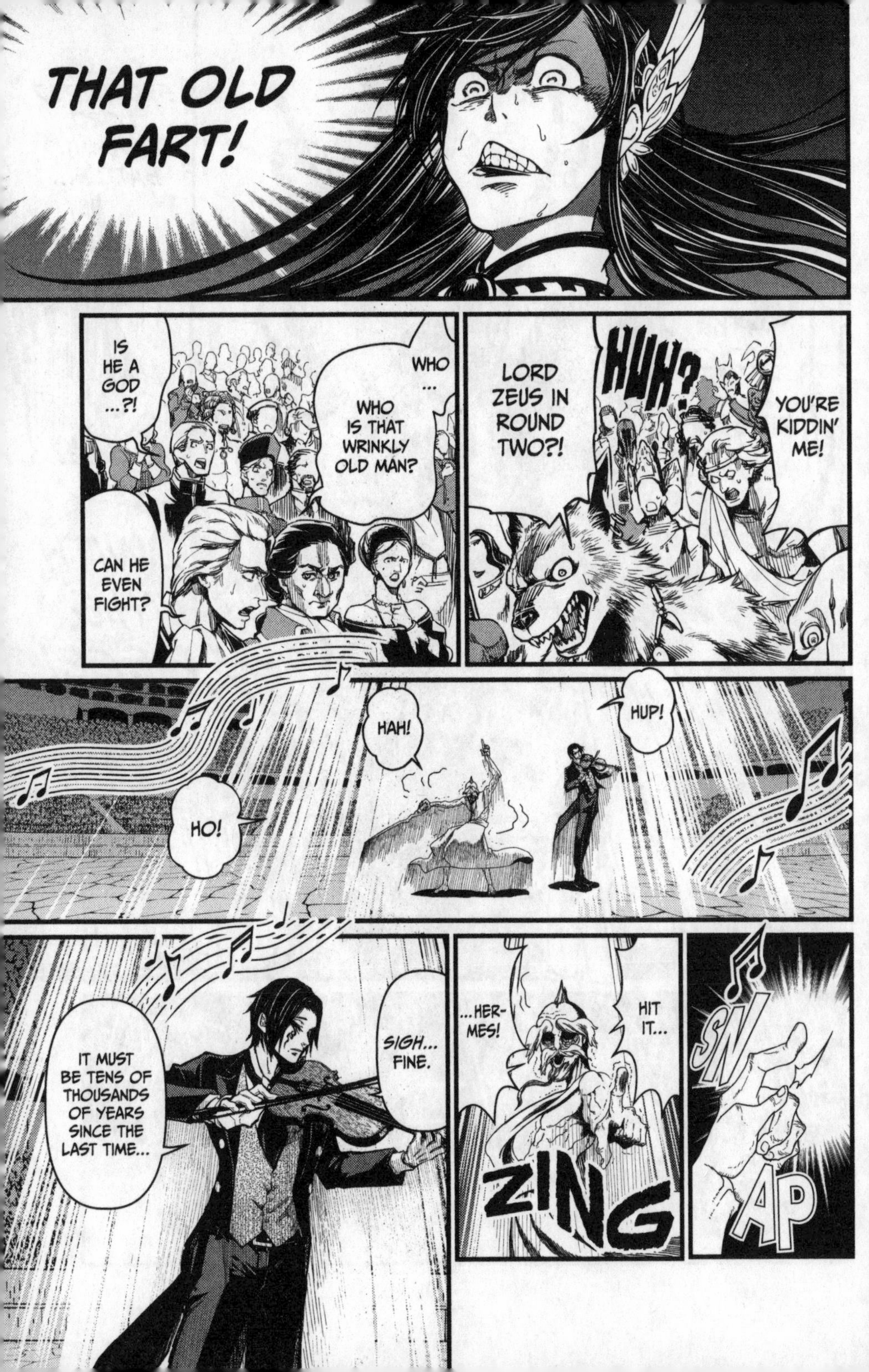
THAT OLD FART!
YOU'RE KIDDIN' ME!
HUH?
LORD ZEUS IN ROUND TWO?!
WHO ...
WHO IS THAT WRINKLY OLD MAN?
IS HE A GOD ...?!
CAN HE EVEN FIGHT?
HUP!
HAH!
HO!
SNAP
HIT IT...
...HER-MES!
ZING
SIGH... FINE.
IT MUST BE TENS OF THOUSANDS OF YEARS SINCE THE LAST TIME...

...I SERENADED LORD ZEUS INTO BATTLE...

FW

...WITH THIS PIECE!

JAA

JANG

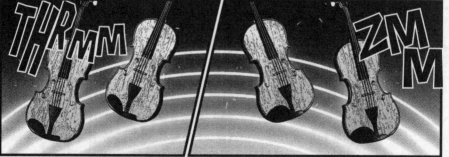

THRMM

ZMM

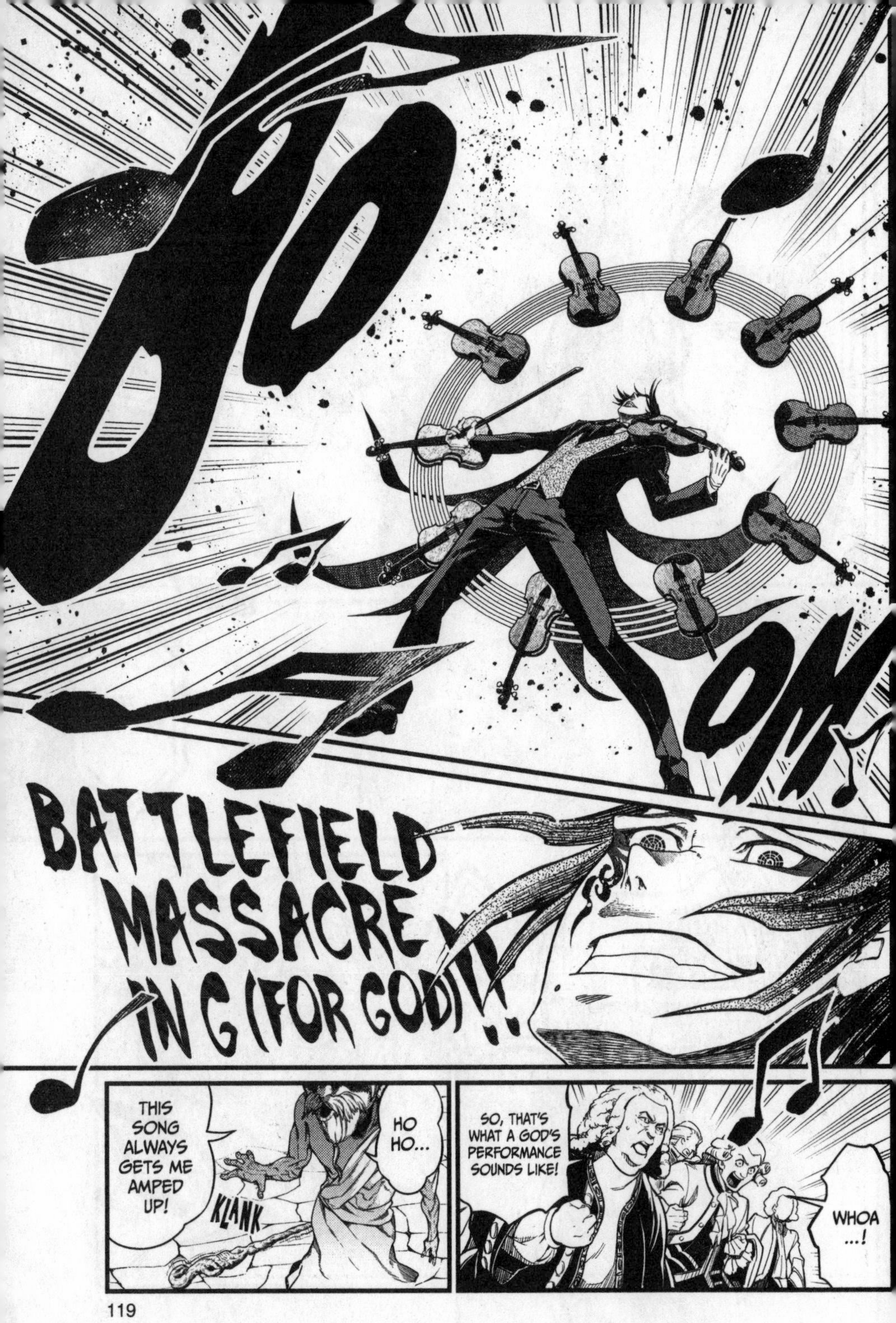
BATTLEFIELD MASSACRE IN G (FOR GOD)!!
SO, THAT'S WHAT A GOD'S PERFORMANCE SOUNDS LIKE!
WHOA ...!
HO HO...
THIS SONG ALWAYS GETS ME AMPED UP!
KLANK

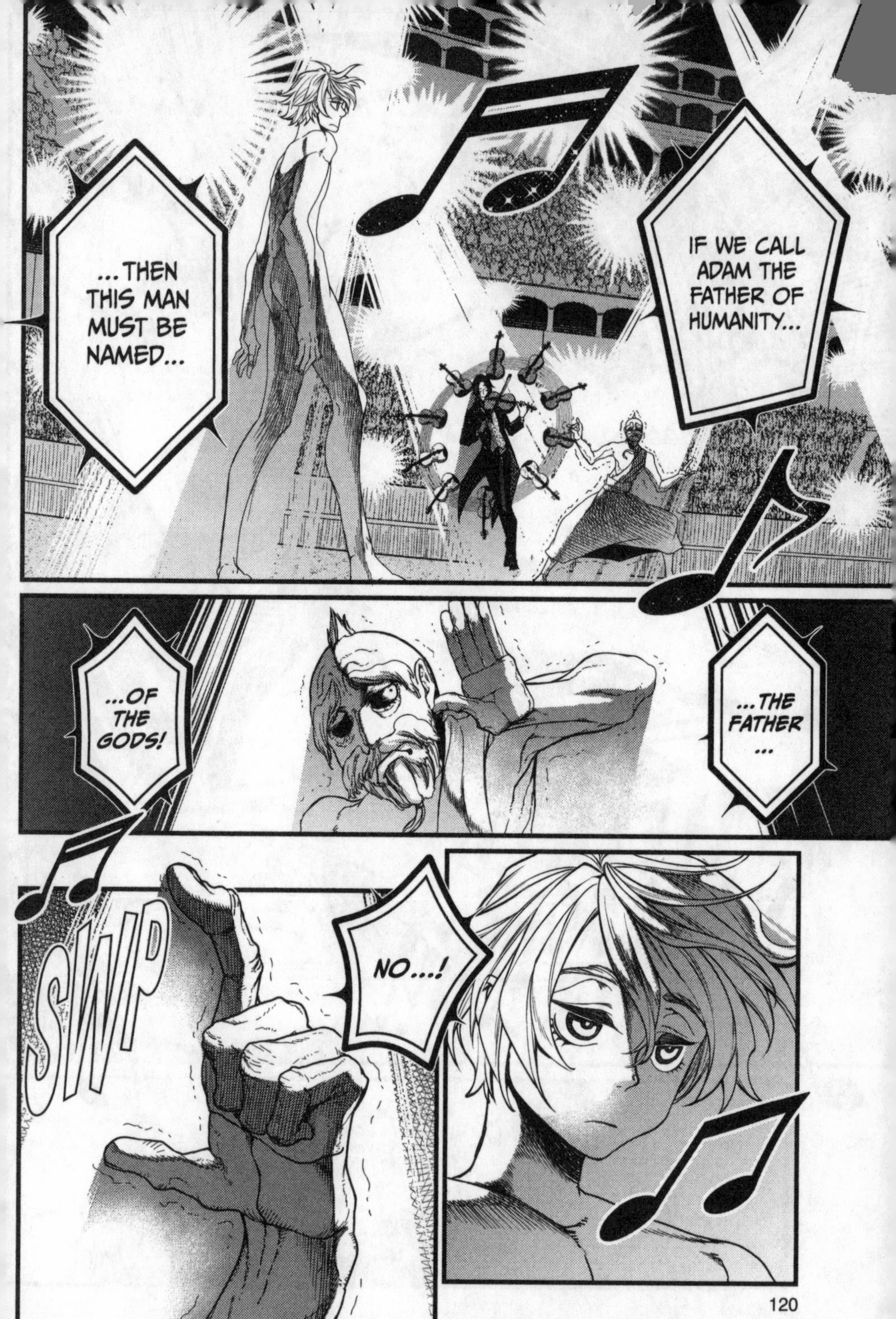
IF WE CALL ADAM THE FATHER OF HUMANITY...
...THEN THIS MAN MUST BE NAMED...
...THE FATHER...
...OF THE GODS!
NO...!
SWIP

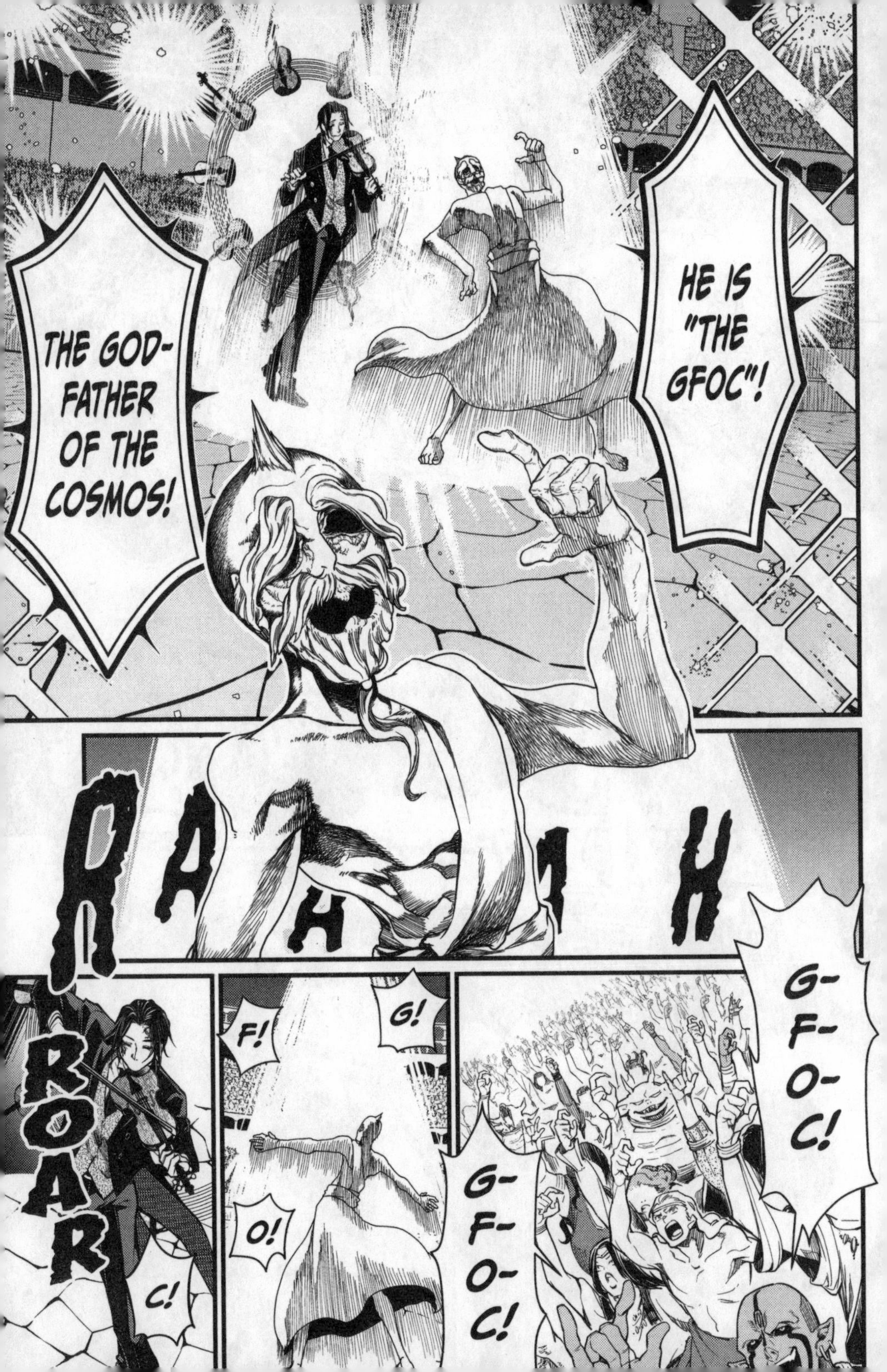

HE IS "THE GFOC"!
THE GOD-FATHER OF THE COSMOS!
RAHH
G-F-O-C!
G-F-O-C!
G!
F!
O!
C!
ROAR

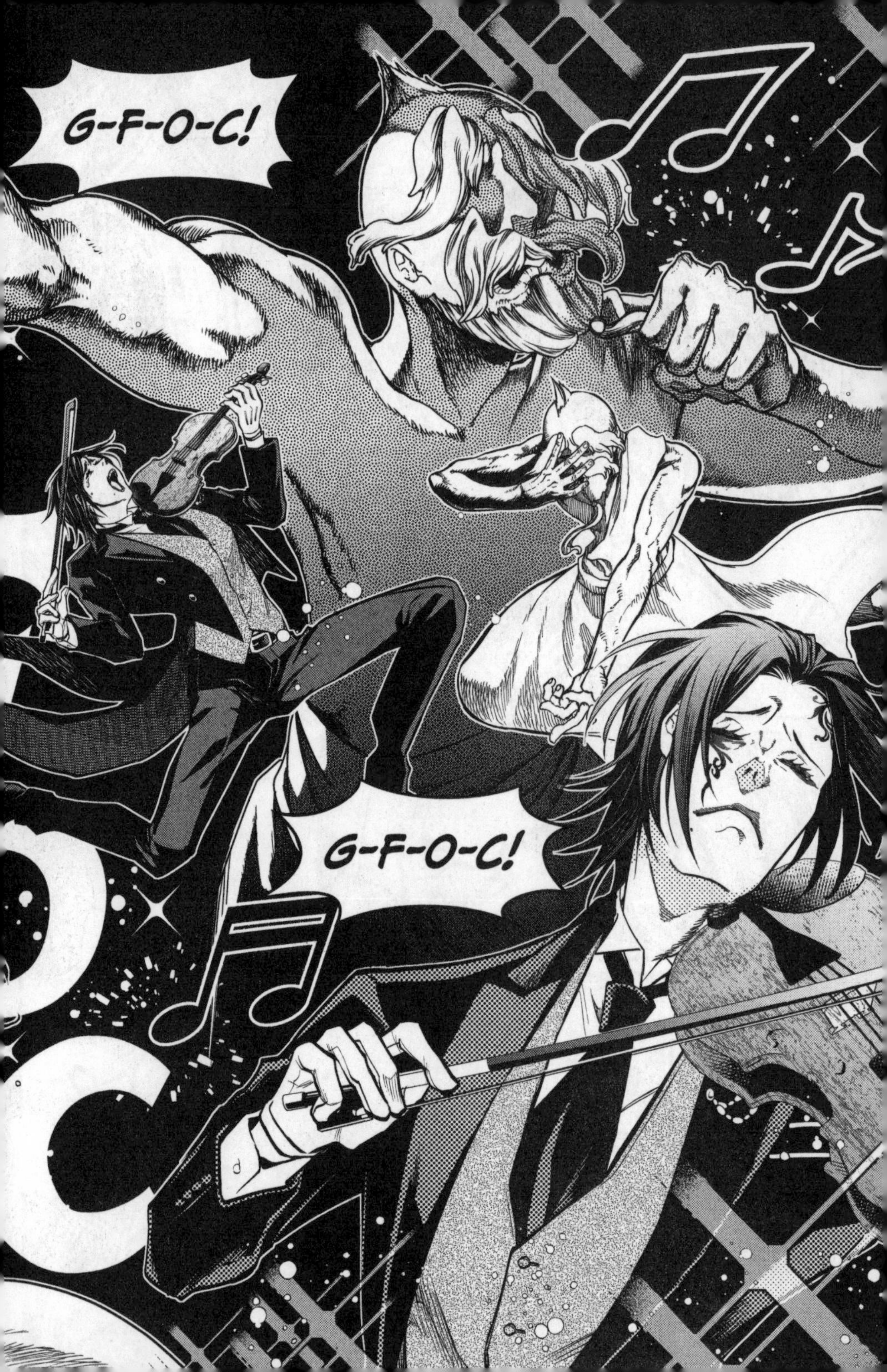
G-F-O-C!
G-F-O-C!

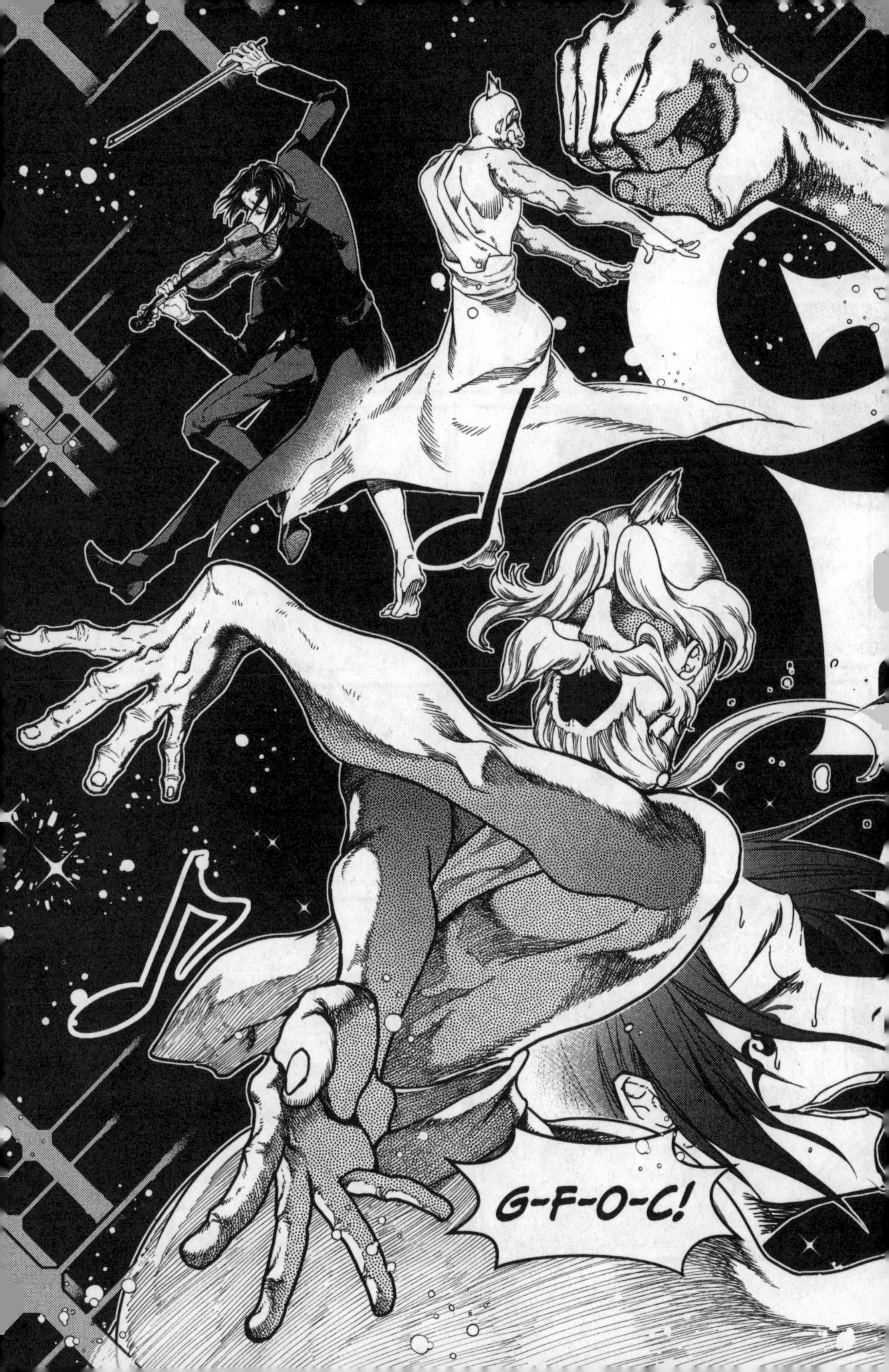
G-F-O-C!

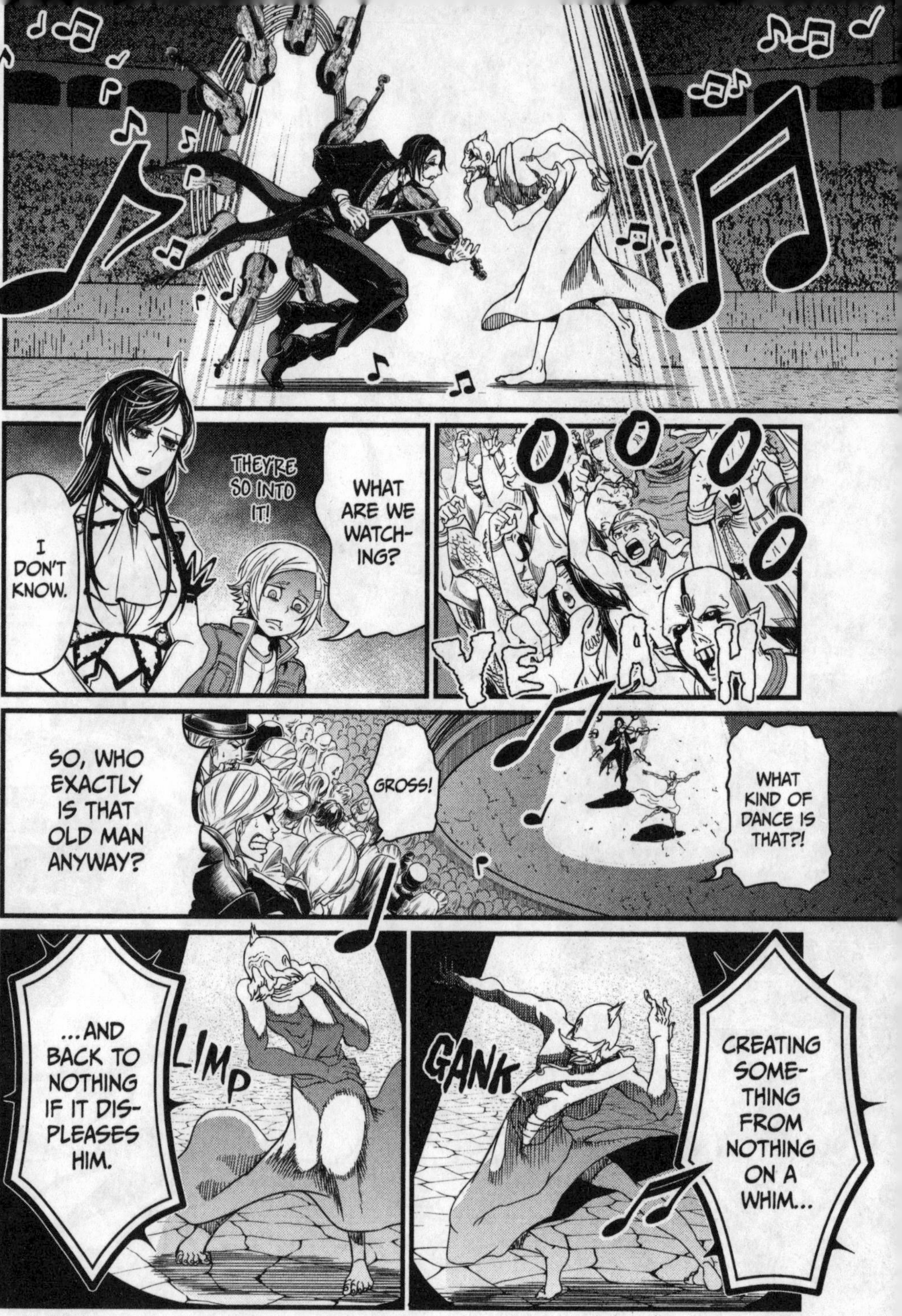
OOOO
YEAH
WHAT ARE WE WATCHING?
THEY'RE SO INTO IT!
I DON'T KNOW.
WHAT KIND OF DANCE IS THAT?!
GROSS!
SO, WHO EXACTLY IS THAT OLD MAN ANYWAY?
CREATING SOME-THING FROM NOTHING ON A WHIM...
GANK
...AND BACK TO NOTHING IF IT DIS-PLEASES HIM.
LIMP

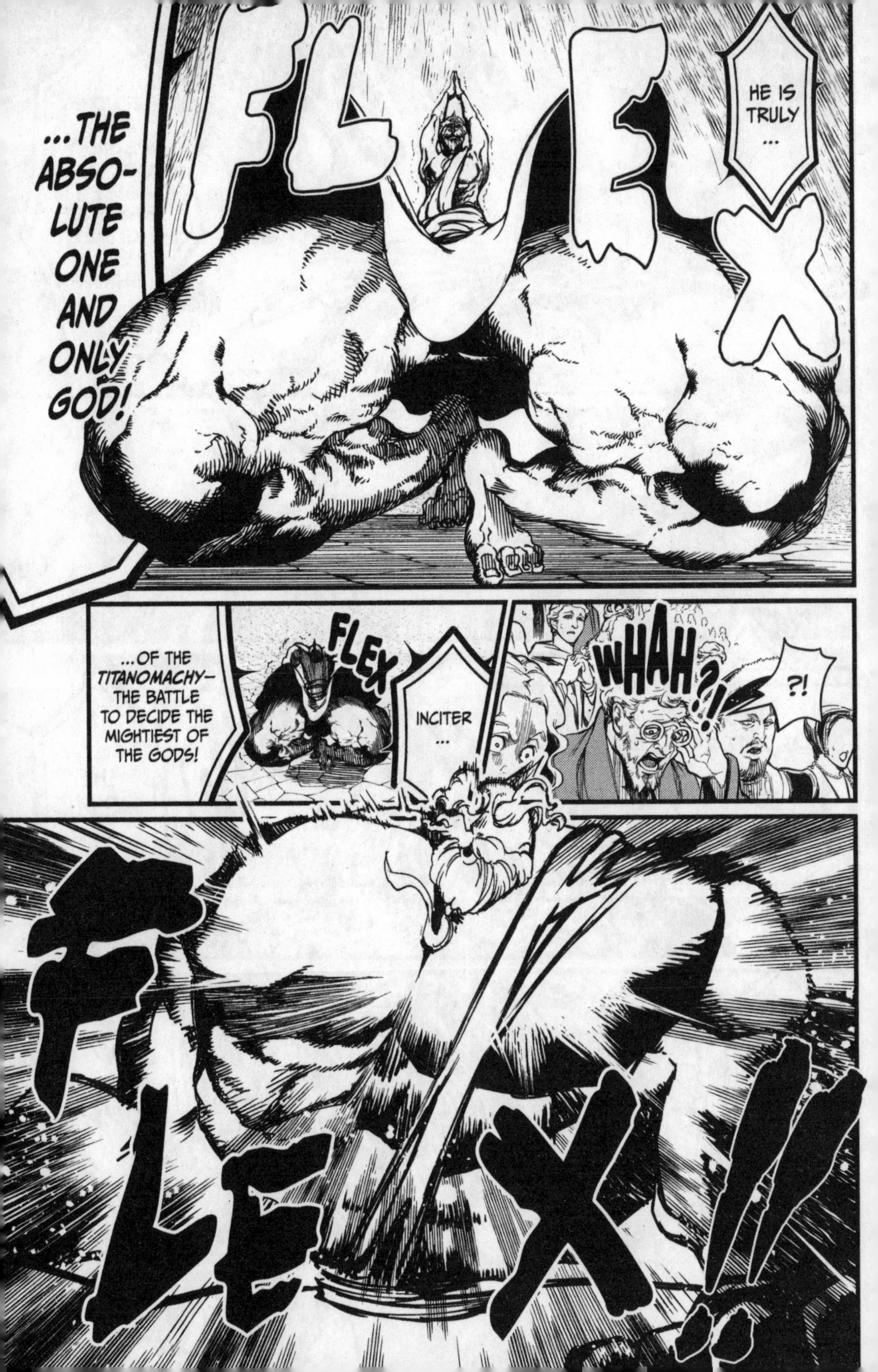
FLEX
HE IS TRULY ...
...THE ABSO-LUTE ONE AND ONLY GOD!
?!
WHAH?!
INCITER ...
FLEX
...OF THE TITANOMACHY—THE BATTLE TO DECIDE THE MIGHTIEST OF THE GODS!
FLEX!!

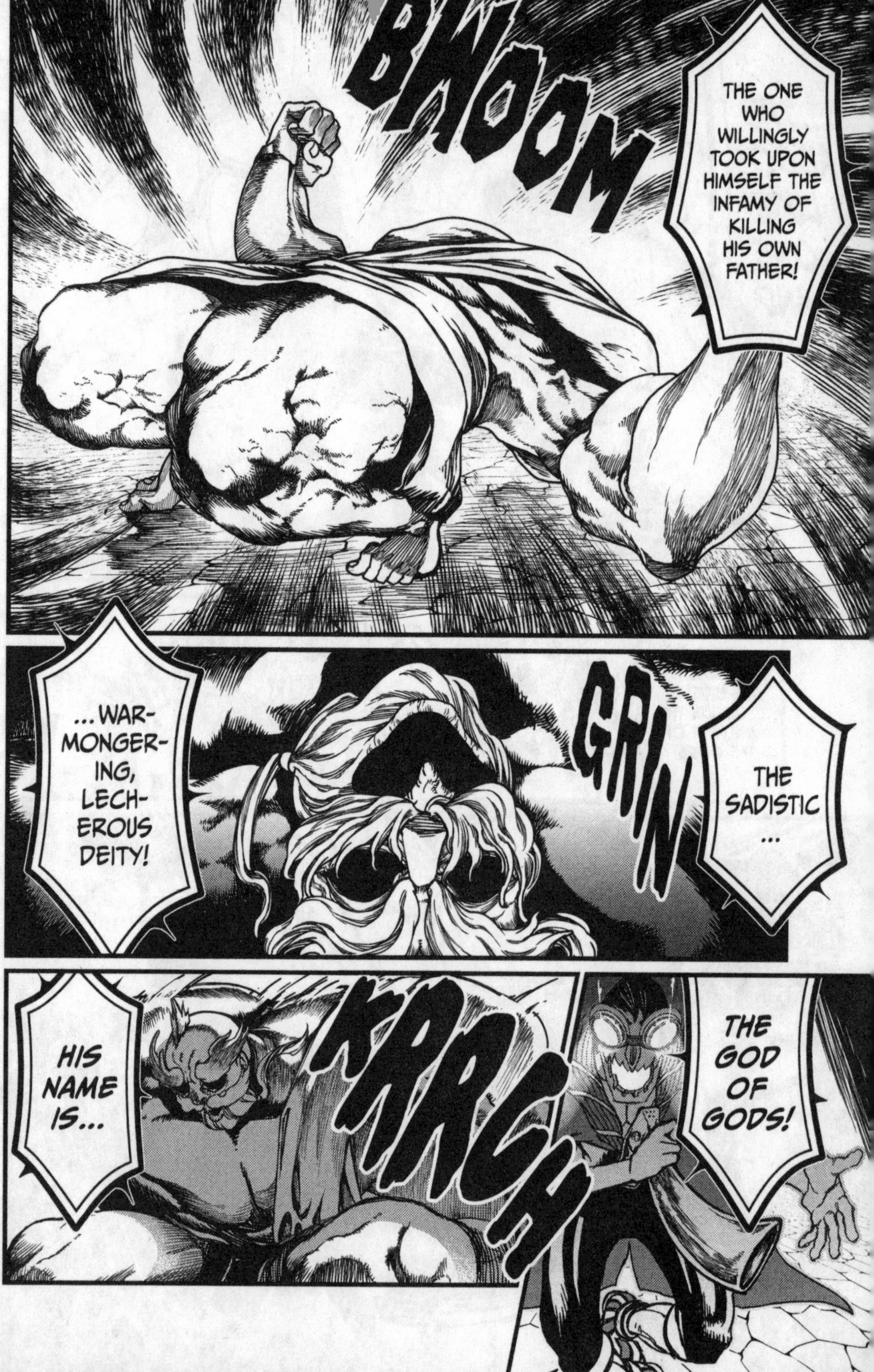
THE ONE WHO WILLINGLY TOOK UPON HIMSELF THE INFAMY OF KILLING HIS OWN FATHER!
BWOOM
THE SADISTIC ...
GRIN
...WAR-MONGER-ING, LECH-EROUS DEITY!
THE GOD OF GODS!
KRRCH
HIS NAME IS...

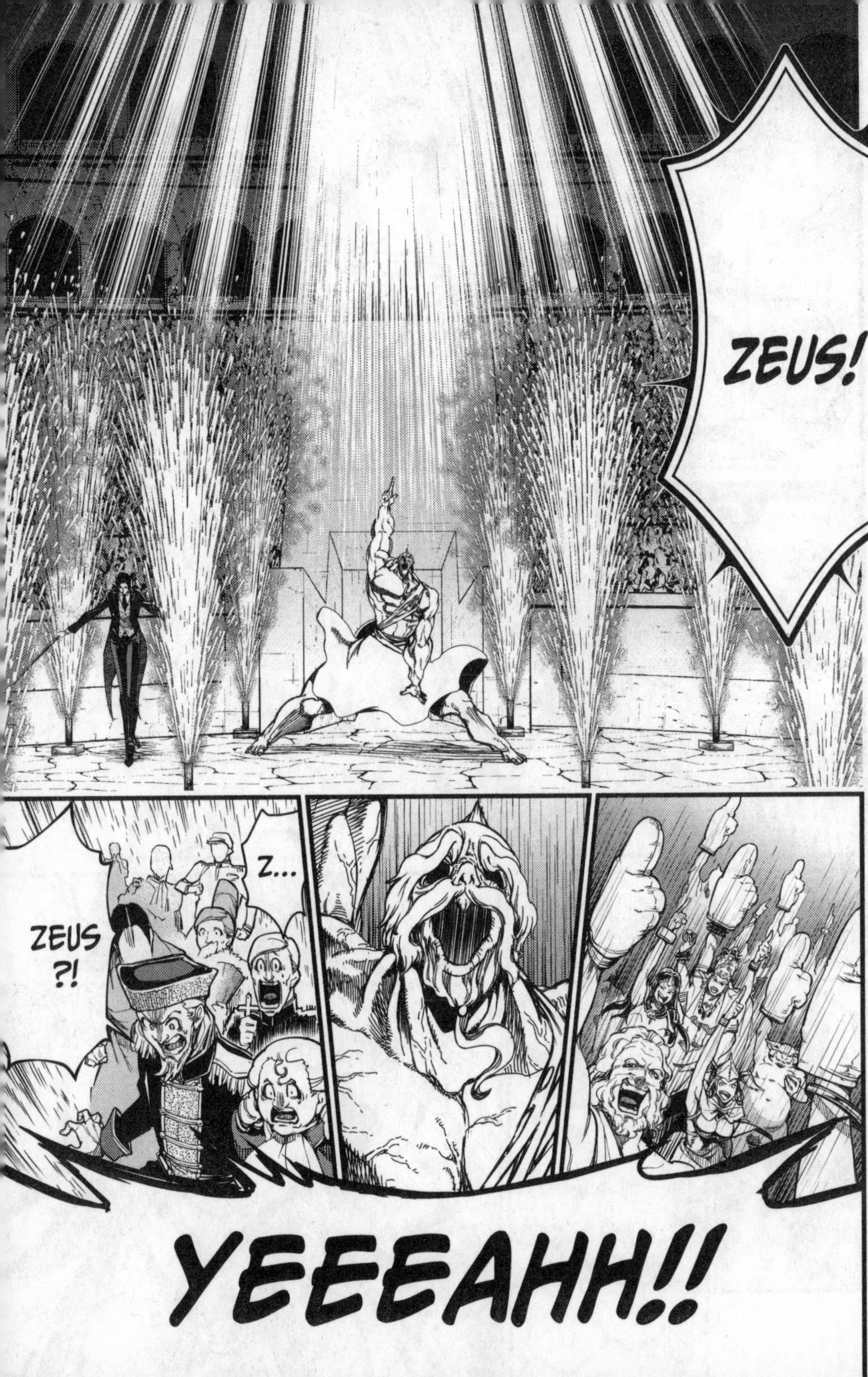
ZEUS!
Z...
ZEUS ?!
YEEEAHH!!

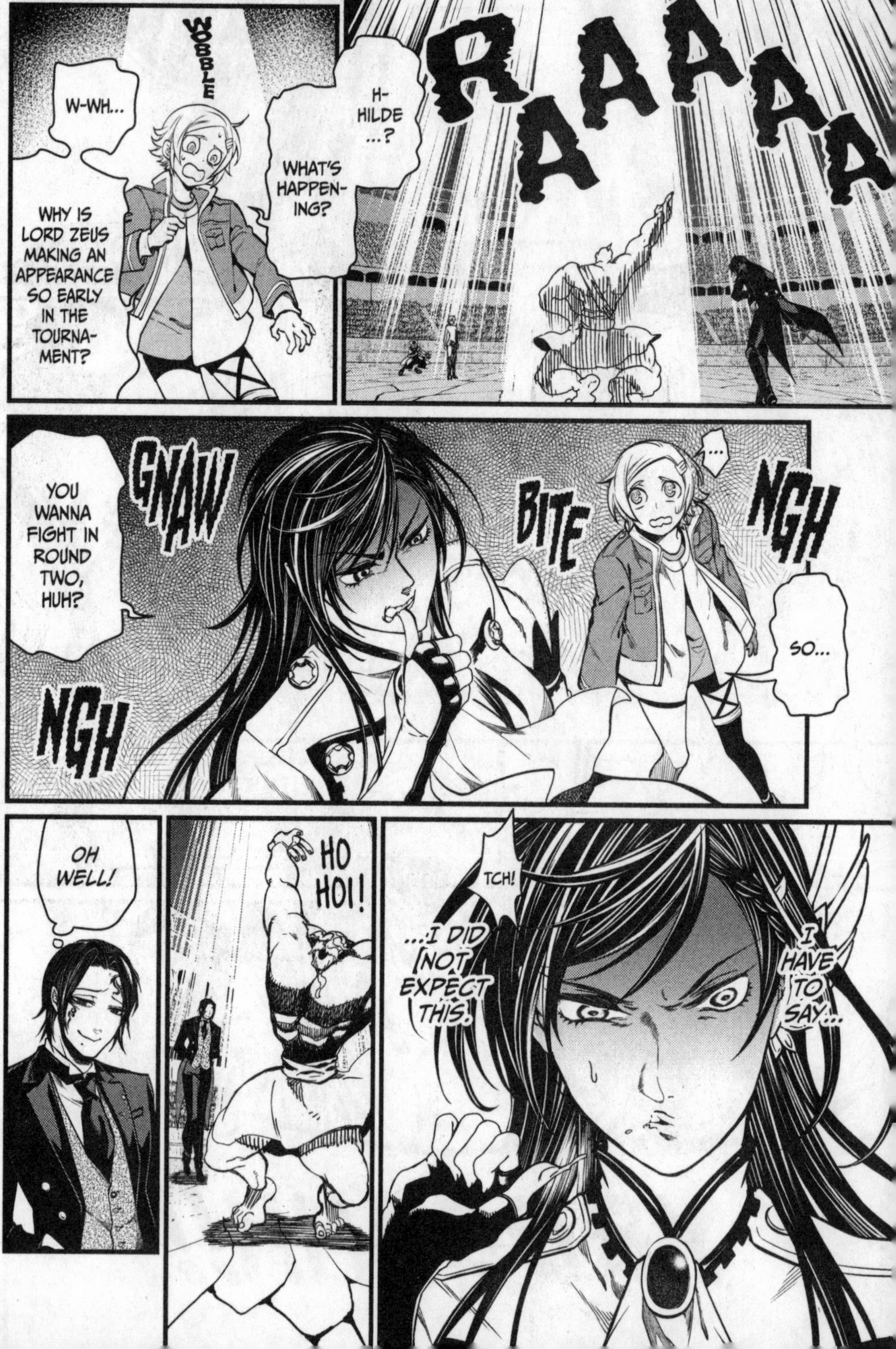
RAAAAAA
H-HILDE ...?
WHAT'S HAPPENING?
WOBBLE
W-WH...
WHY IS LORD ZEUS MAKING AN APPEARANCE SO EARLY IN THE TOURNAMENT?
...
NGH
SO...
BITE
GNAW
YOU WANNA FIGHT IN ROUND TWO, HUH?
NGH
TCH!
I HAVE TO SAY...
...I DID NOT EXPECT THIS.
HO HOI!
OH WELL!

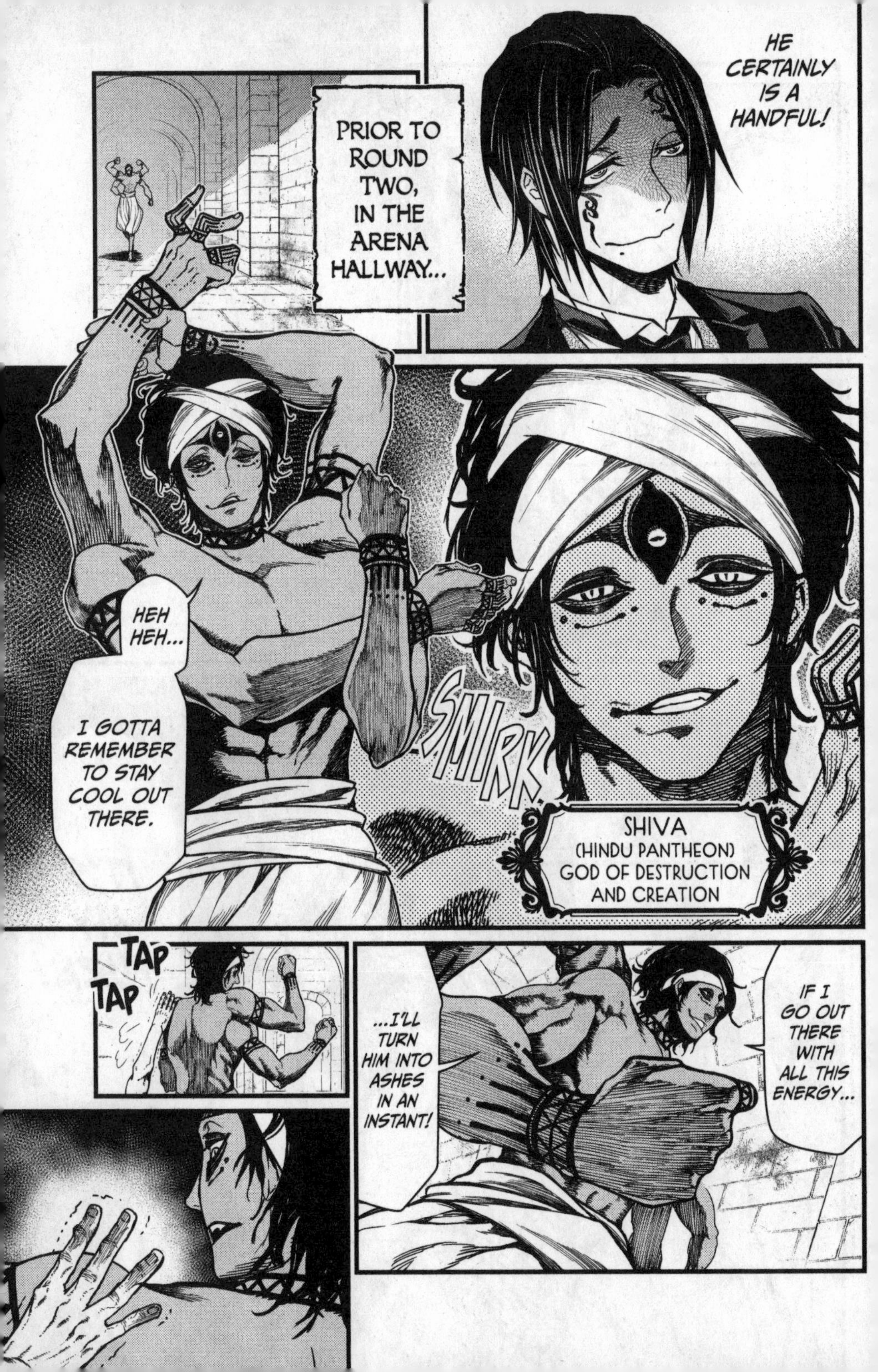
HE CERTAINLY IS A HANDFUL!
PRIOR TO ROUND TWO, IN THE ARENA HALLWAY...
SMIRK
SHIVA
(HINDU PANTHEON)
GOD OF DESTRUCTION AND CREATION
HEH HEH...
I GOTTA REMEMBER TO STAY COOL OUT THERE.
IF I GO OUT THERE WITH ALL THIS ENERGY...
...I'LL TURN HIM INTO ASHES IN AN INSTANT!
TAP
TAP

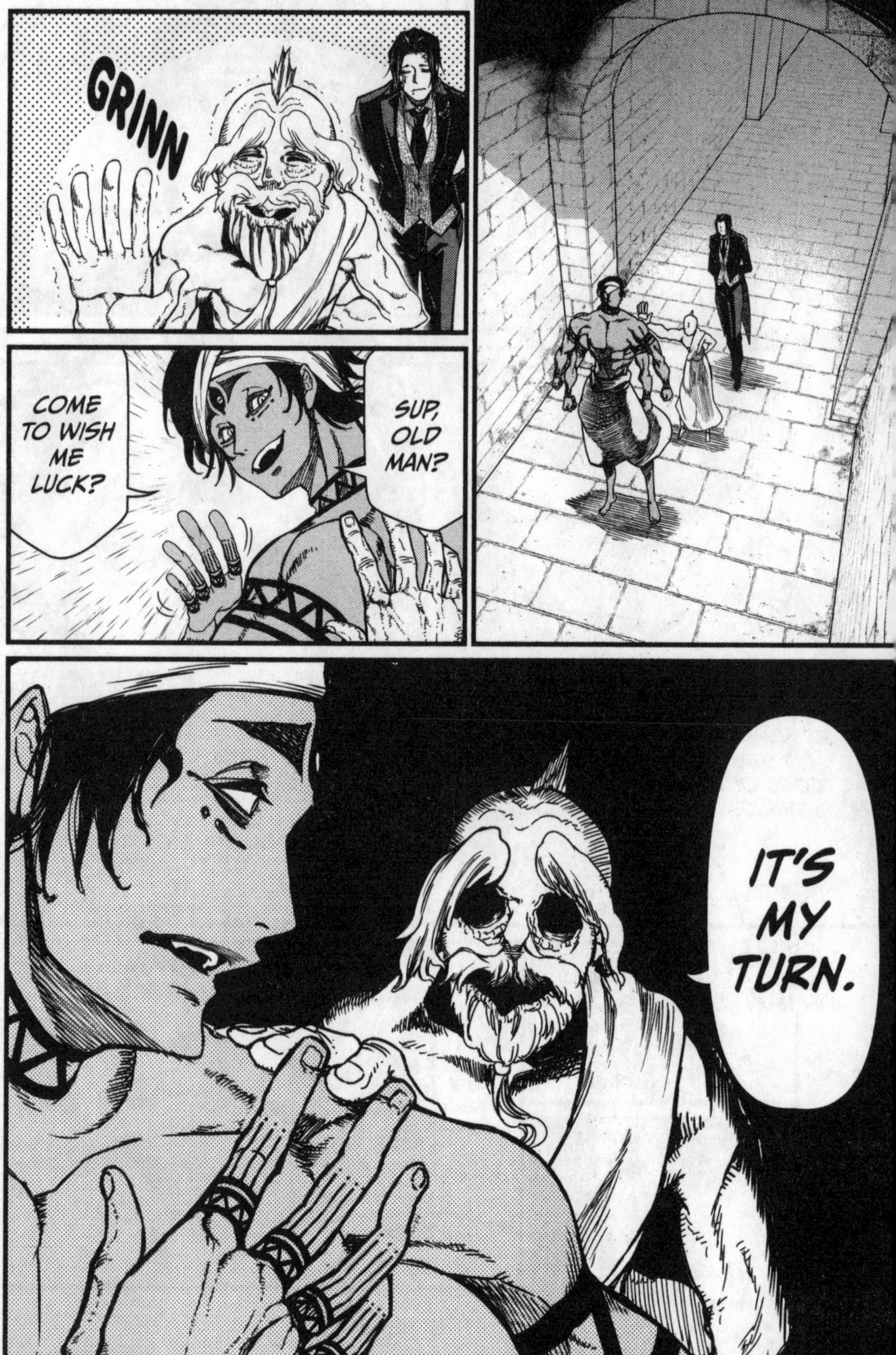
GRINN
SUP, OLD MAN?
COME TO WISH ME LUCK?
IT'S MY TURN.

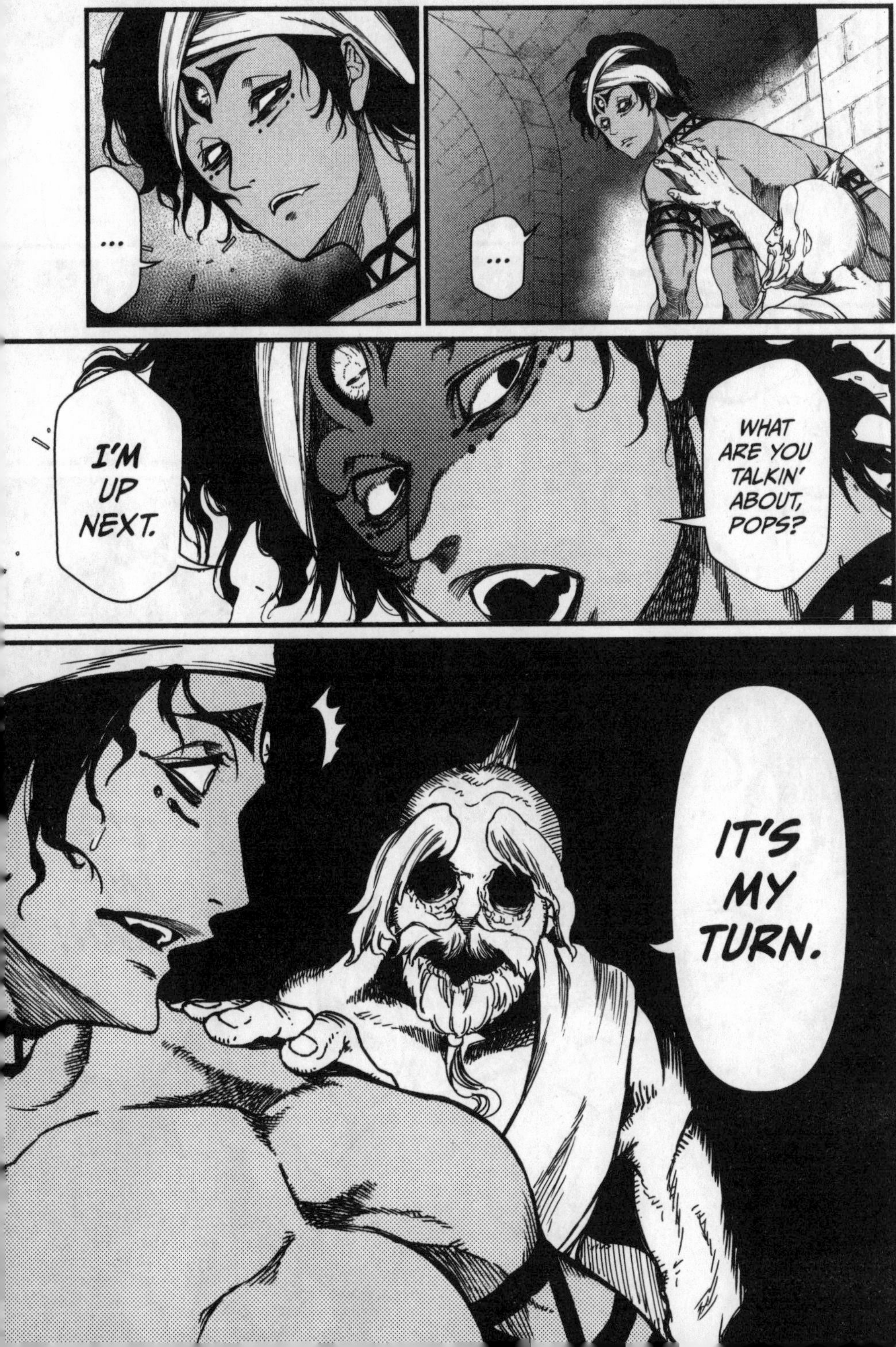
...
...
WHAT ARE YOU TALKIN' ABOUT, POPS?
I'M UP NEXT.
IT'S MY TURN.

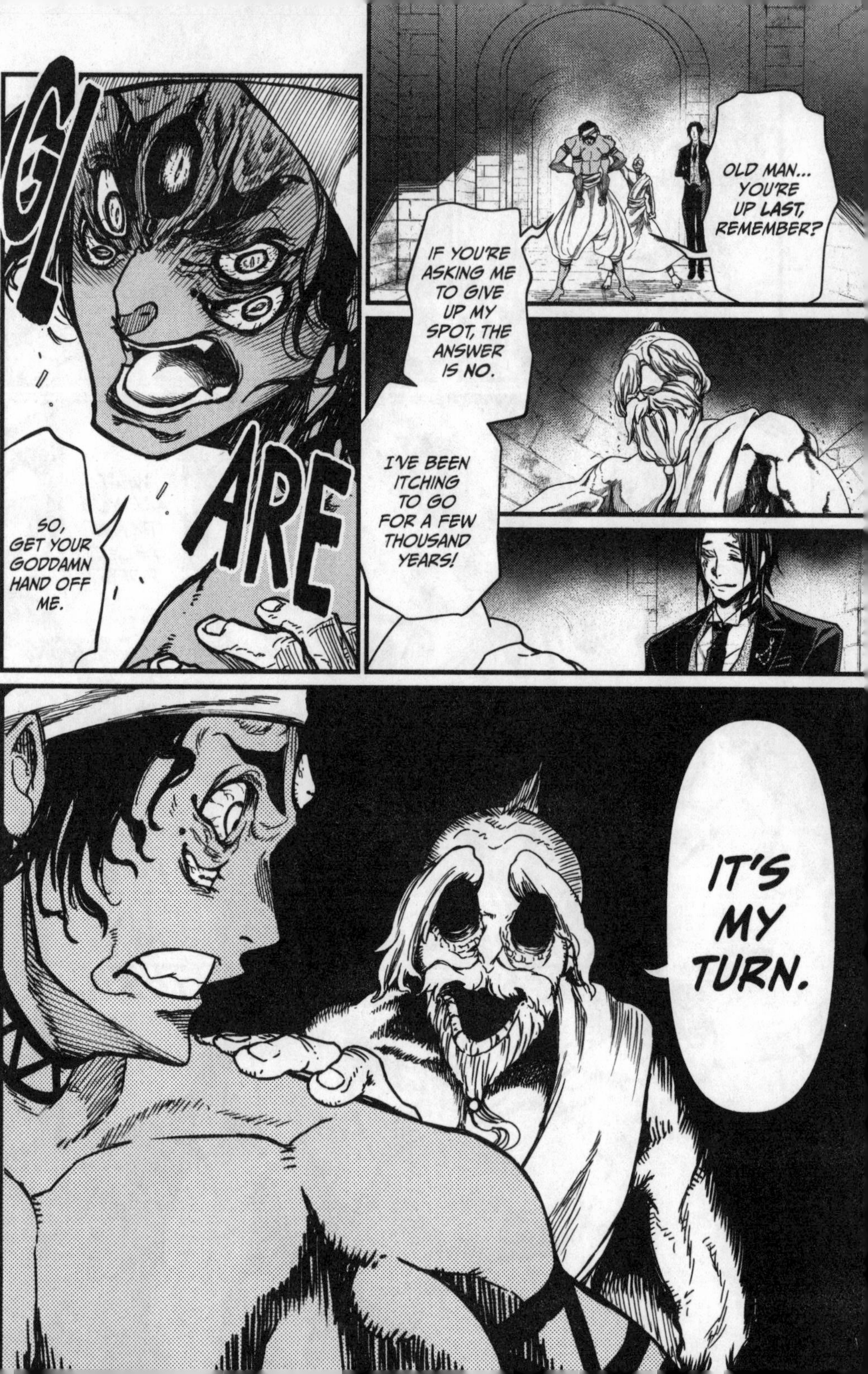
OLD MAN... YOU'RE UP LAST, REMEMBER?
IF YOU'RE ASKING ME TO GIVE UP MY SPOT, THE ANSWER IS NO.
I'VE BEEN ITCHING TO GO FOR A FEW THOUSAND YEARS!
GI
ARE
SO, GET YOUR GODDAMN HAND OFF ME.
IT'S MY TURN.

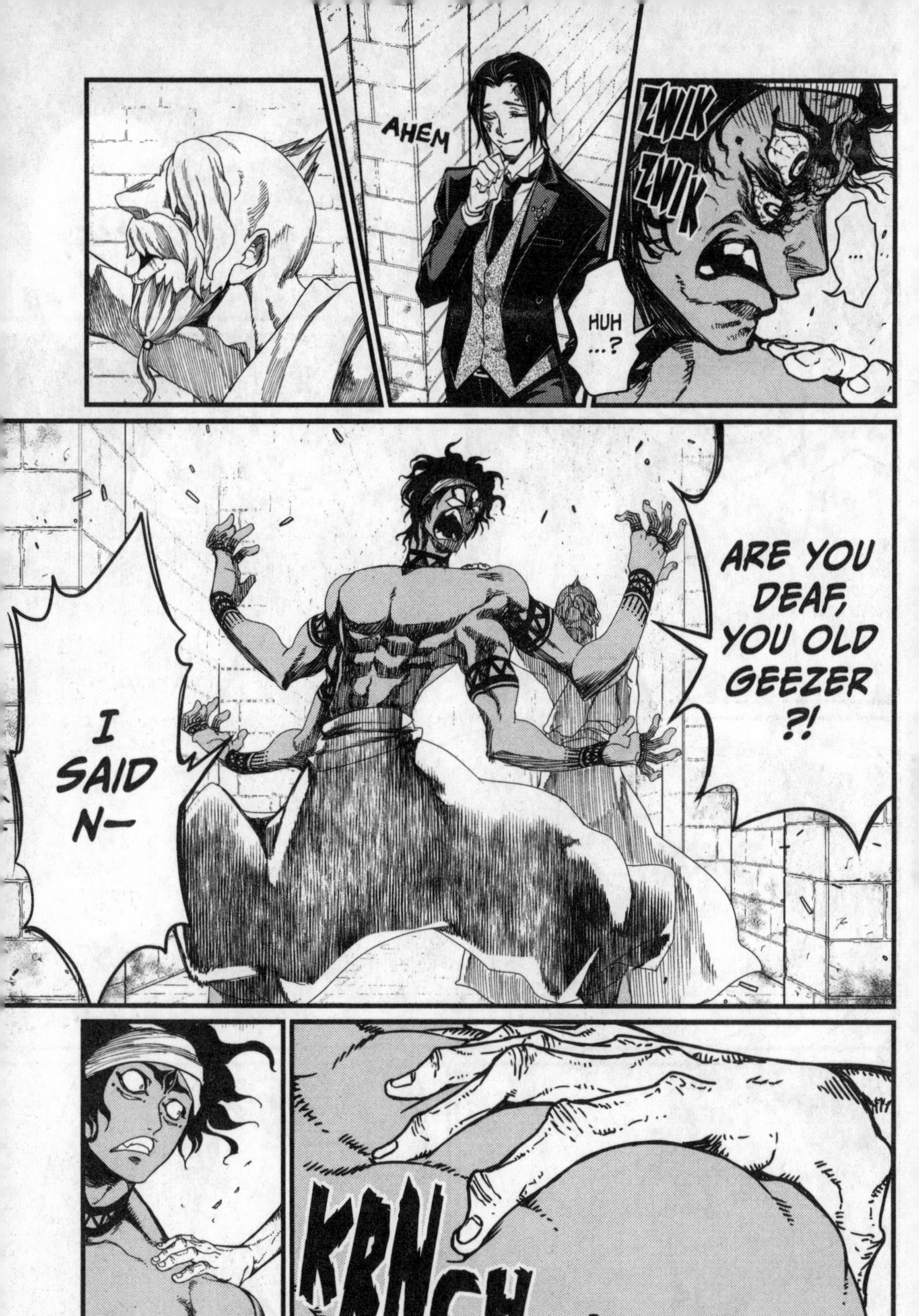
ZWIK ZWIK
...
HUH ...?
AHEM
ARE YOU DEAF, YOU OLD GEEZER ?!
I SAID N—
KRNCH

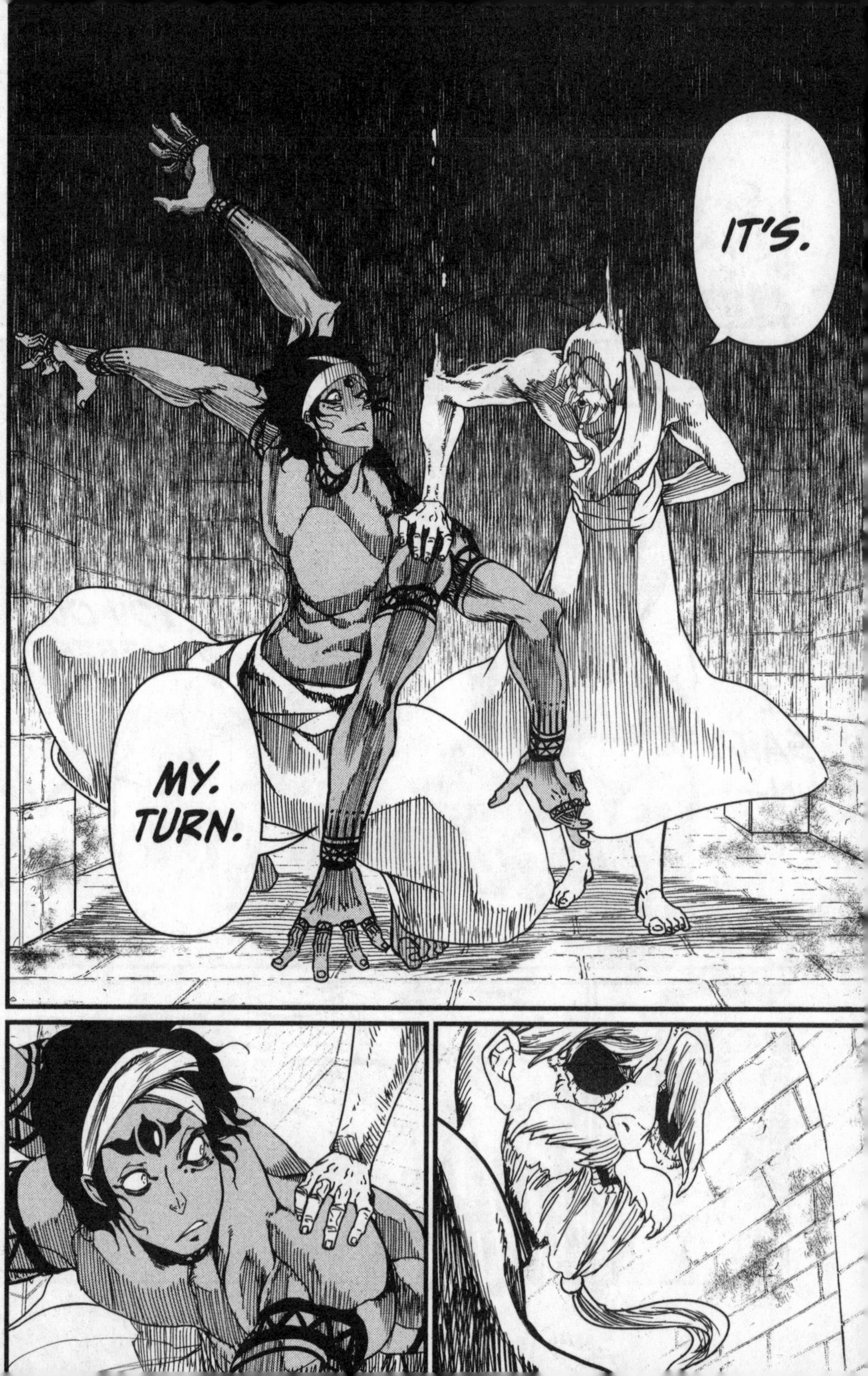
IT'S.
MY. TURN.

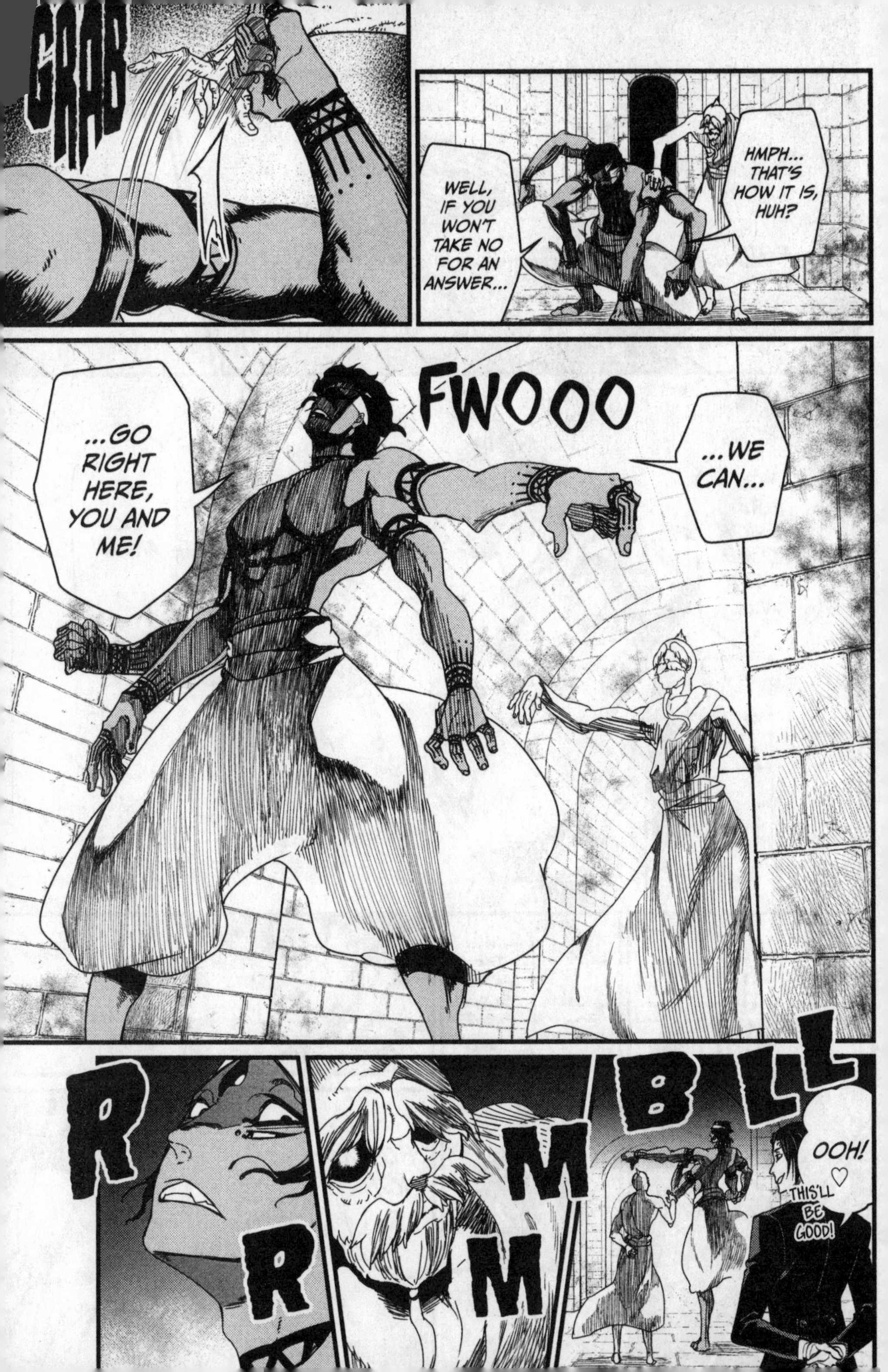
HMPH... THAT'S HOW IT IS, HUH?
WELL, IF YOU WON'T TAKE NO FOR AN ANSWER...
GRAB
...WE CAN...
FWOOO
...GO RIGHT HERE, YOU AND ME!
OOH! ♡
THIS'LL BE GOOD!
RRMMMBBLL

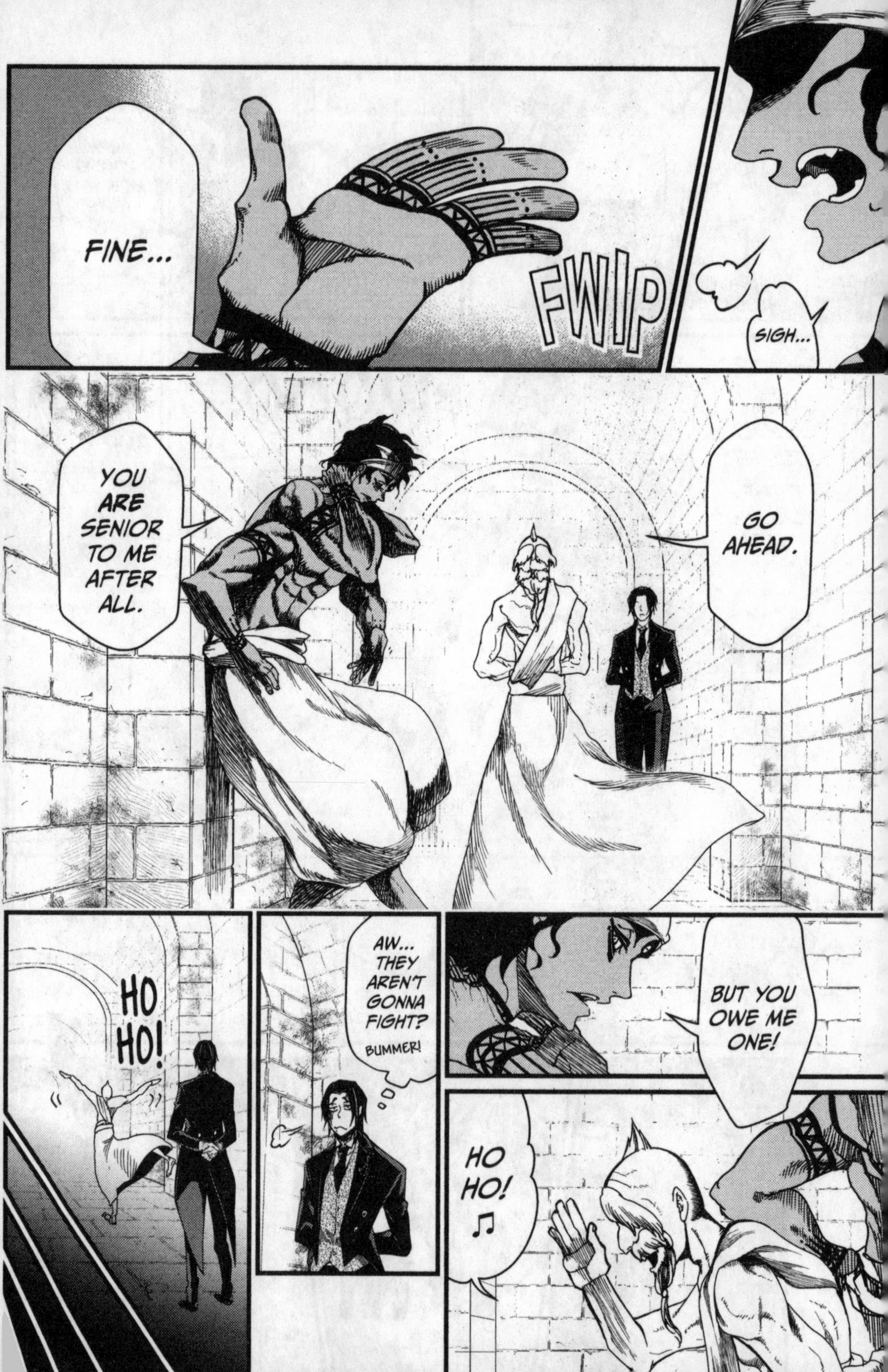
SIGH...
FWIP
FINE...
GO AHEAD.
YOU ARE SENIOR TO ME AFTER ALL.
BUT YOU OWE ME ONE!
HO HO! ♪
AW... THEY AREN'T GONNA FIGHT?
BUMMER!
HO HO!

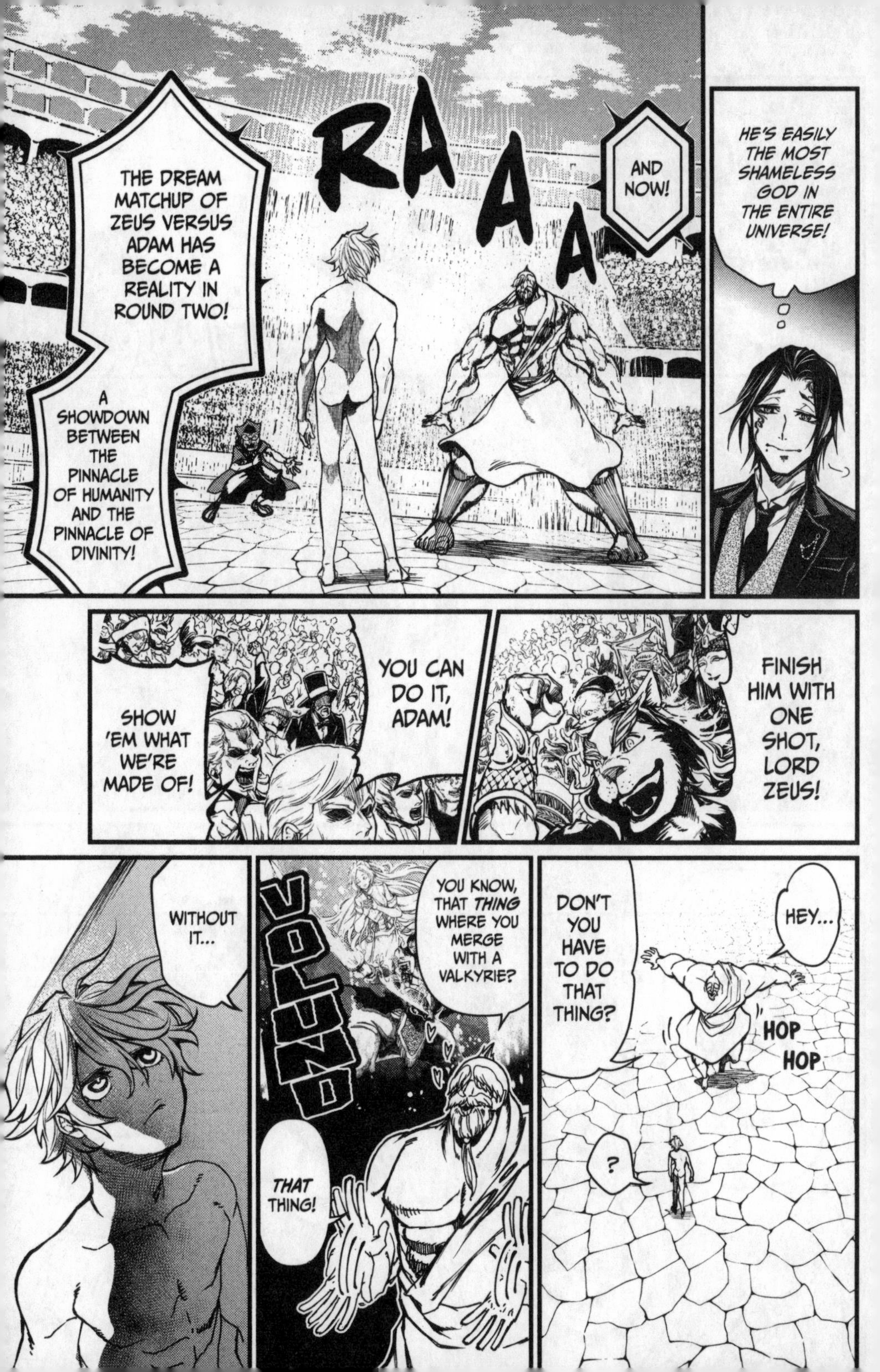
HE'S EASILY THE MOST SHAMELESS GOD IN THE ENTIRE UNIVERSE!
AND NOW!
RAAAA
THE DREAM MATCHUP OF ZEUS VERSUS ADAM HAS BECOME A REALITY IN ROUND TWO!
A SHOWDOWN BETWEEN THE PINNACLE OF HUMANITY AND THE PINNACLE OF DIVINITY!
FINISH HIM WITH ONE SHOT, LORD ZEUS!
YOU CAN DO IT, ADAM!
SHOW 'EM WHAT WE'RE MADE OF!
HEY...
HOP
HOP
DON'T YOU HAVE TO DO THAT THING?
?
YOU KNOW, THAT *THING* WHERE YOU MERGE WITH A VALKYRIE?
VOLUND
THAT THING!
WITHOUT IT...

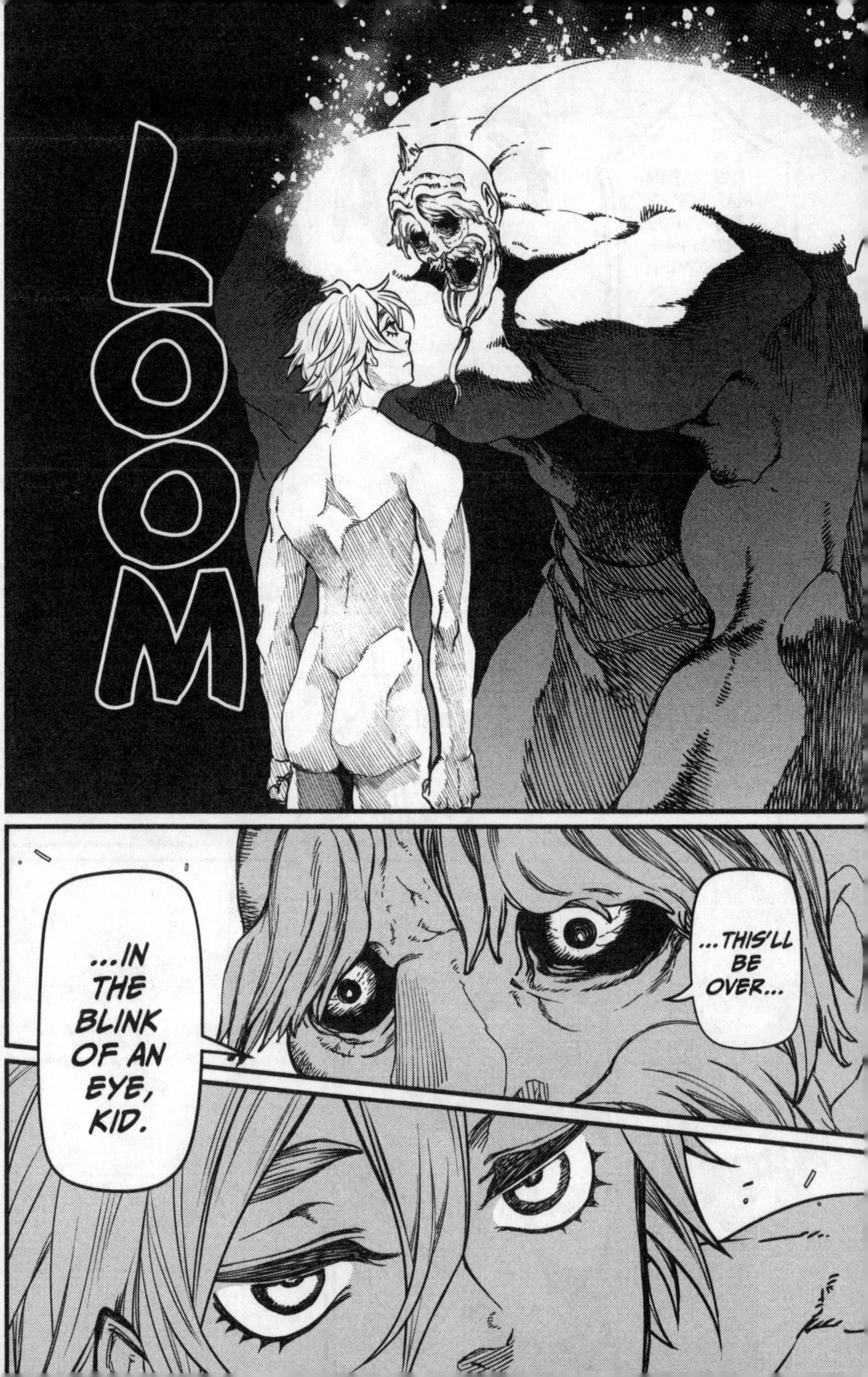
LOOM
...THIS'LL BE OVER...
...IN THE BLINK OF AN EYE, KID.

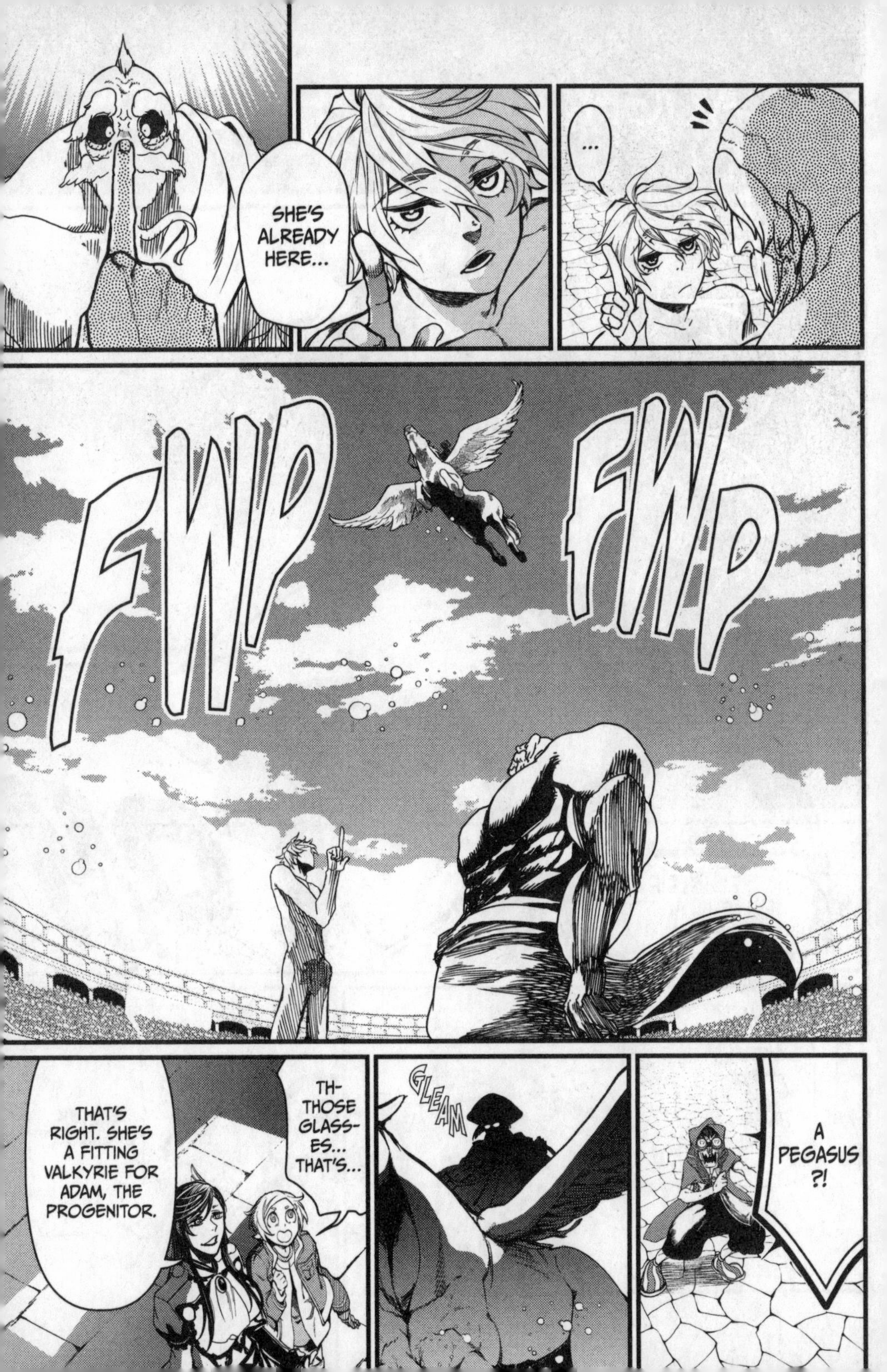
...
SHE'S ALREADY HERE...
FWP
FWP
A PEGASUS ?!
GLEAM
TH- THOSE GLASS- ES... THAT'S...
THAT'S RIGHT. SHE'S A FITTING VALKYRIE FOR ADAM, THE PROGENITOR.

DAUGHTER OF THE GODS

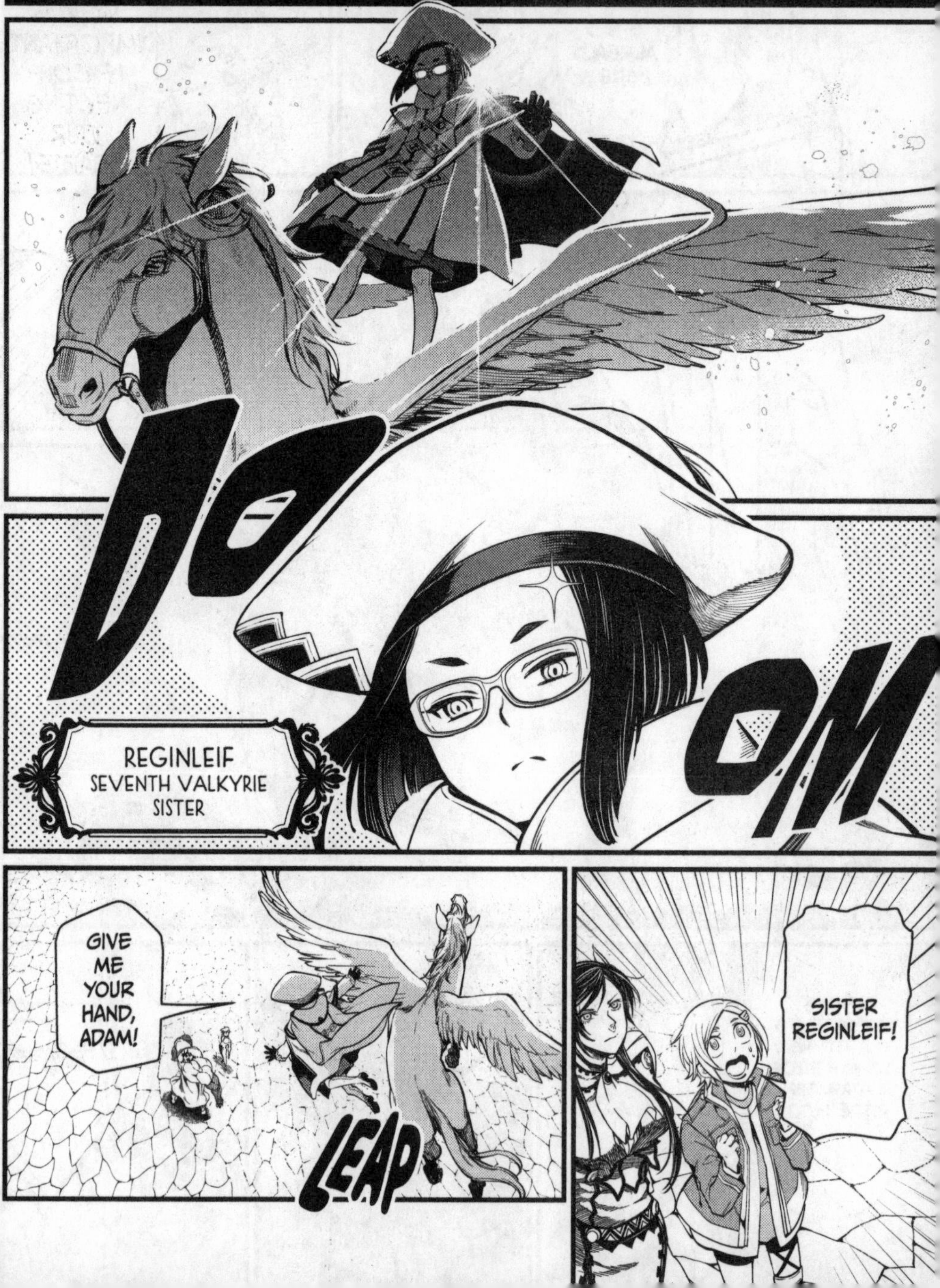
BOOM
REGINLEIF
SEVENTH VALKYRIE SISTER
SISTER REGINLEIF!
GIVE ME YOUR HAND, ADAM!
LEAP

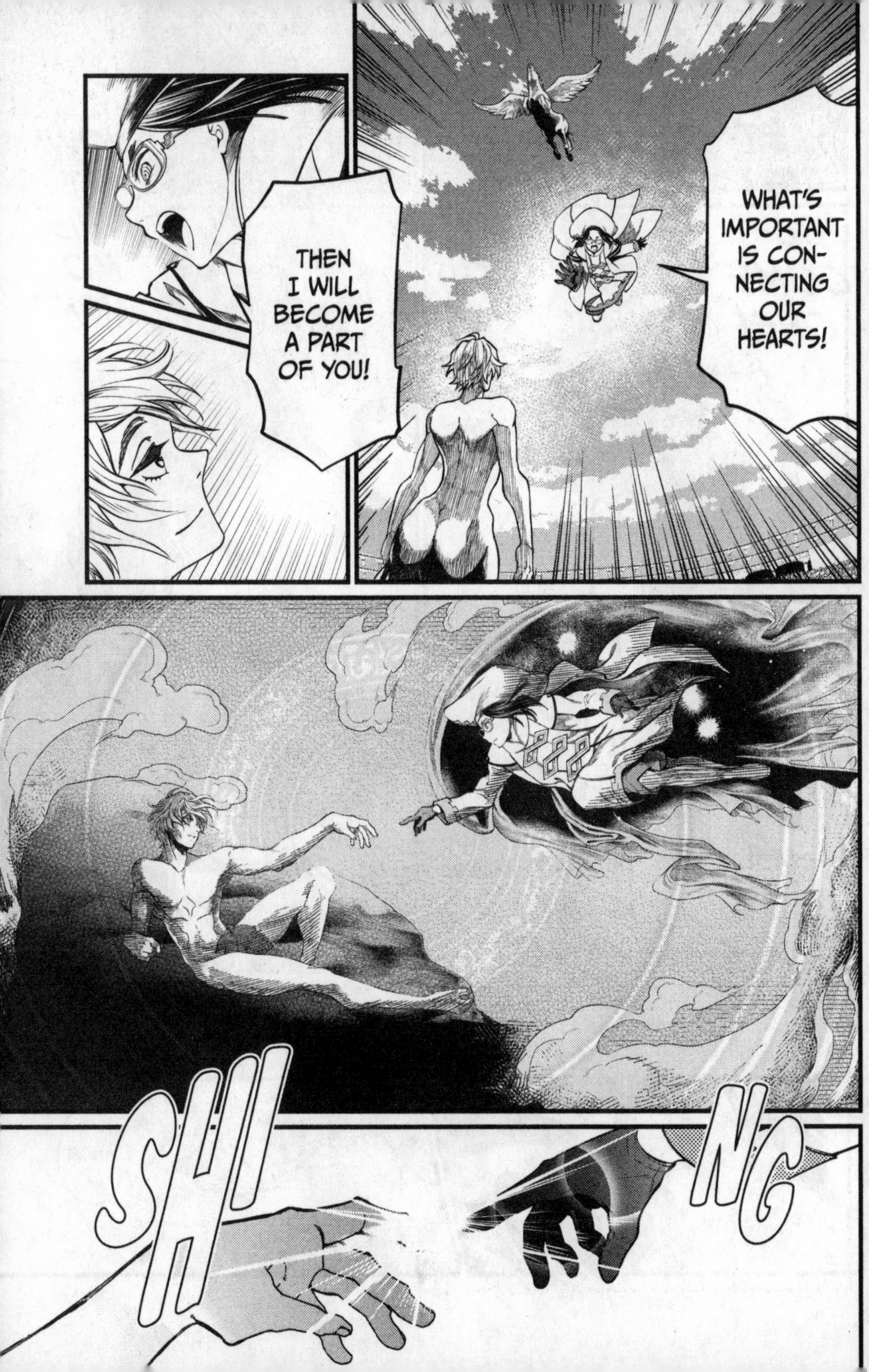
WHAT'S IMPORTANT IS CON-NECTING OUR HEARTS!
THEN I WILL BECOME A PART OF YOU!
SHING

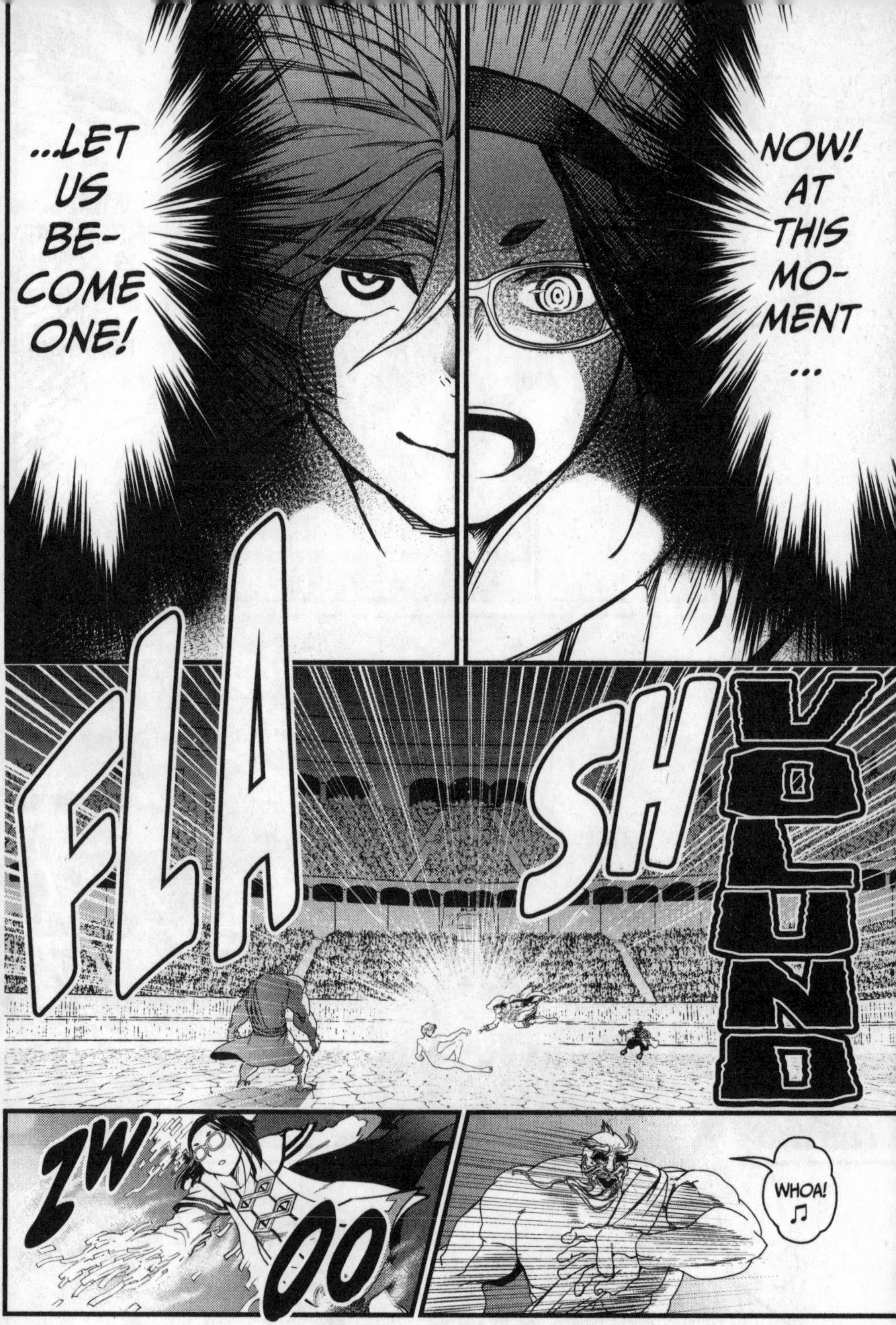
NOW! AT THIS MOMENT ...
...LET US BECOME ONE!
FLASH
VOLUND
WHOA! ♫
ZWOO

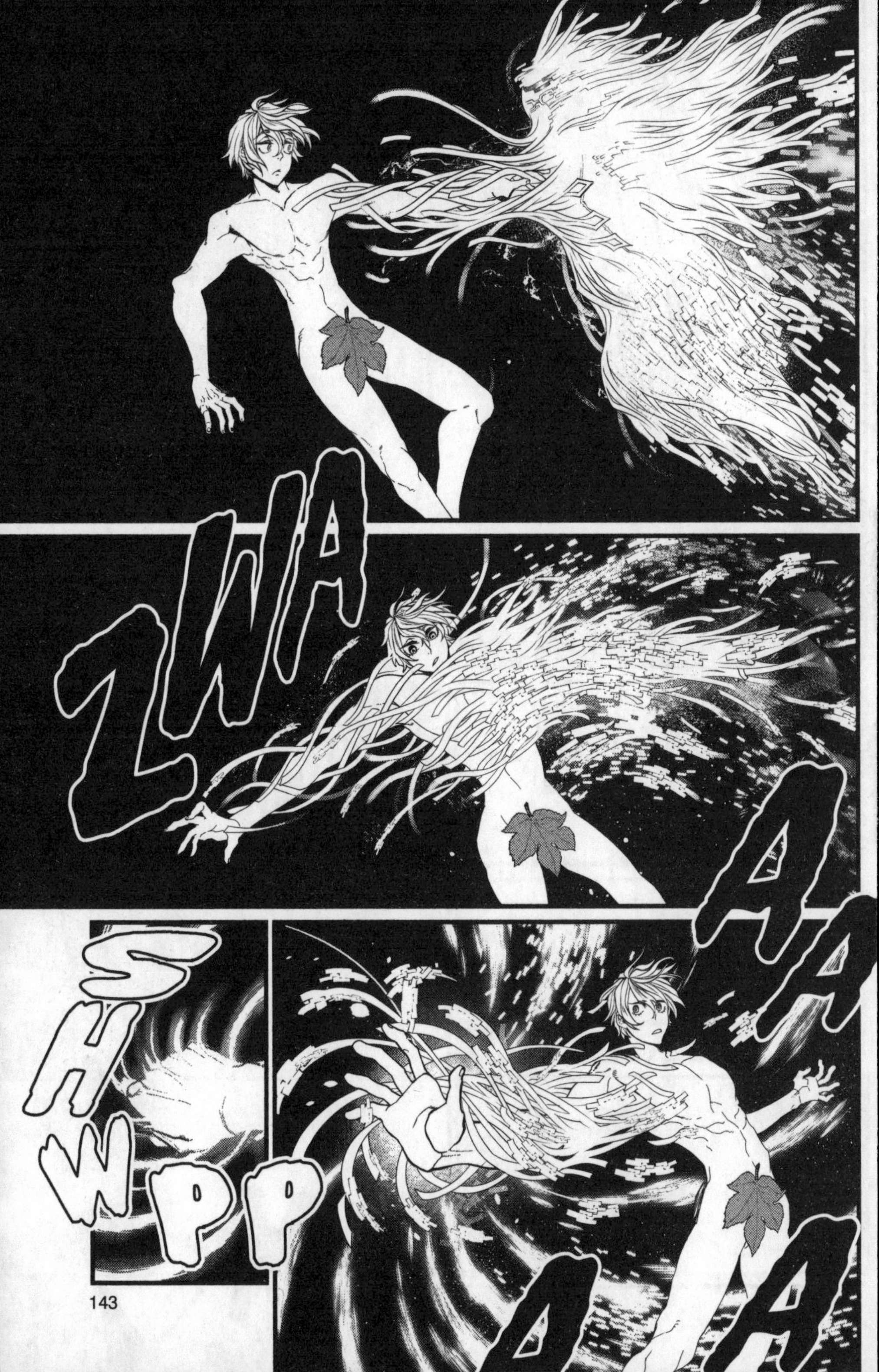
ZWA
AAAA
SHWPP

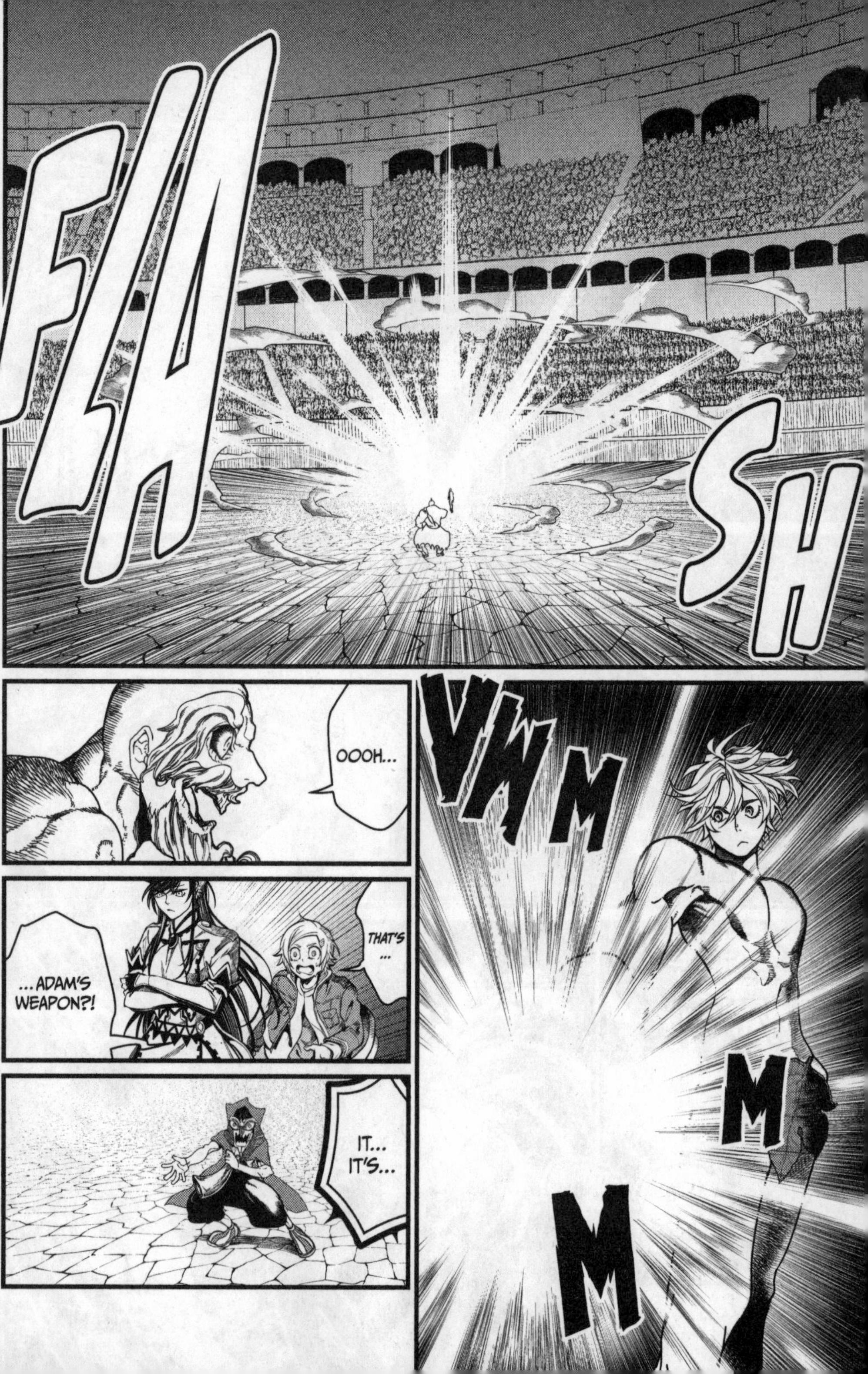
FLASH
VWMMM
OOOH...
THAT'S...
...ADAM'S WEAPON?!
IT... IT'S...

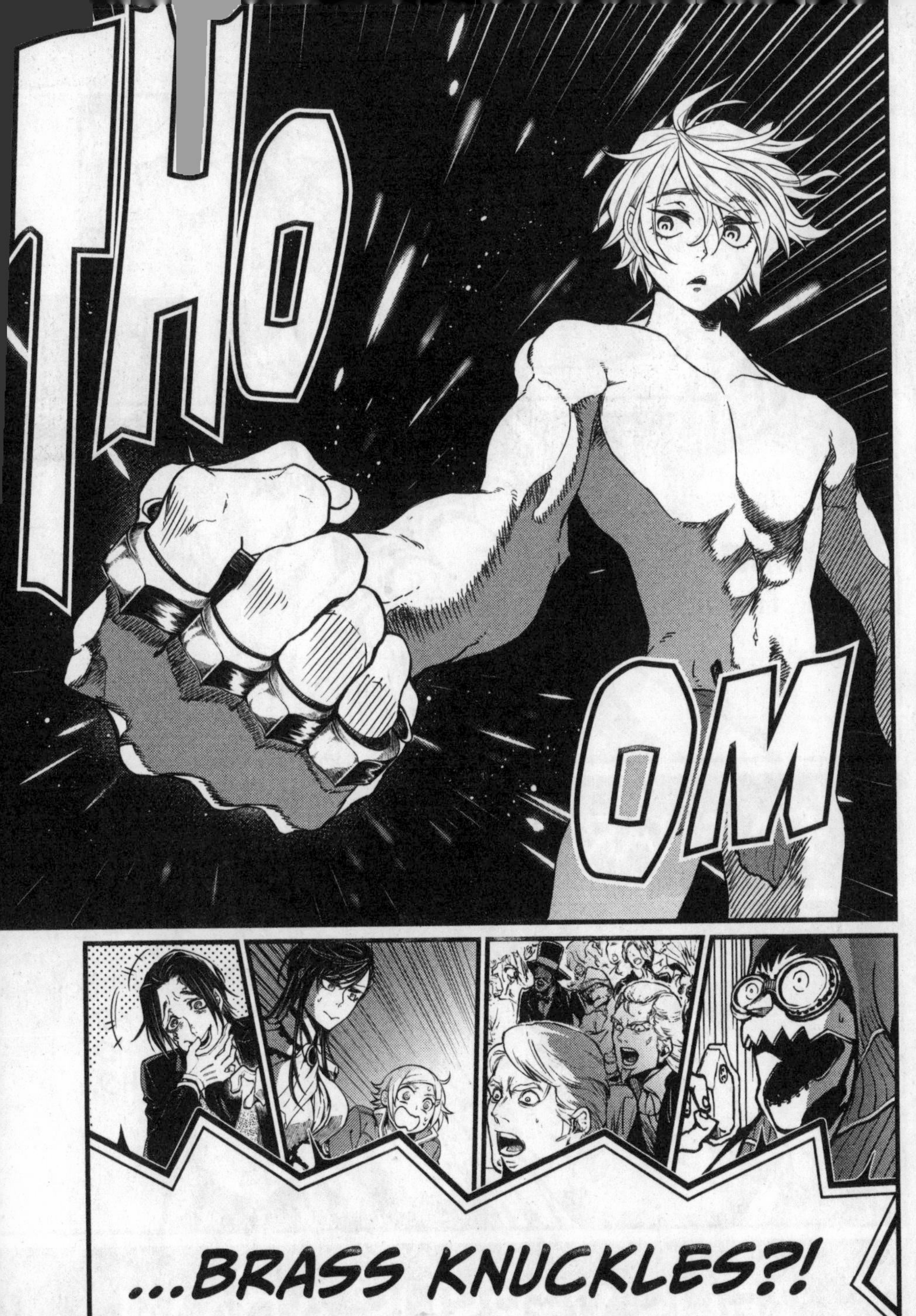
THOOM
...BRASS KNUCKLES?!

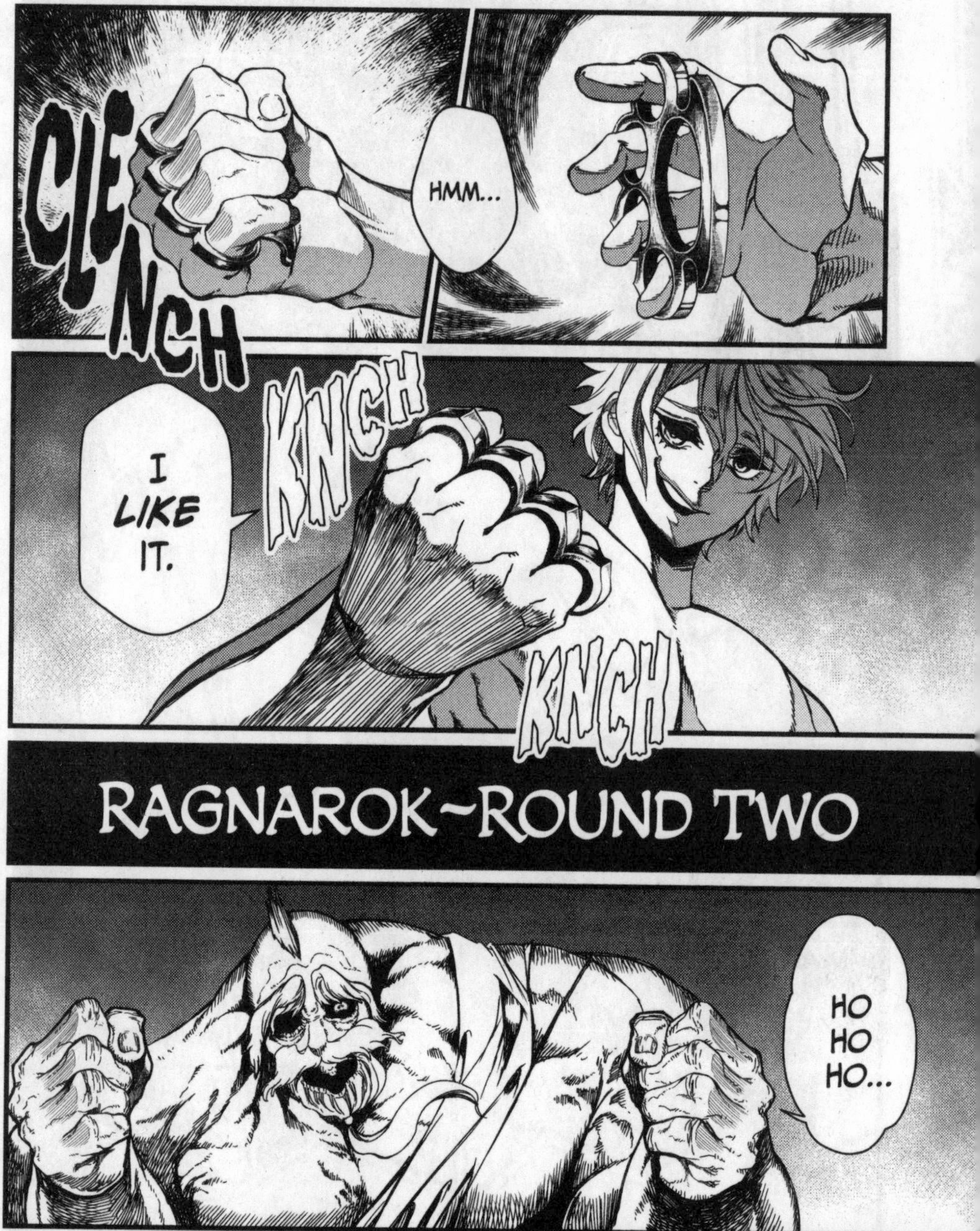
HMM...
CLENCH
KNCH
I LIKE IT.
KNCH
RAGNAROK~ROUND TWO
HO HO HO...

Record of Ragnarok
HUMANITY'S SECOND CHAMPION
ADAM
Record of Ragnarok

RECORD OF
RAGNAROK

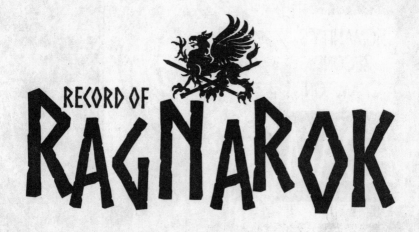

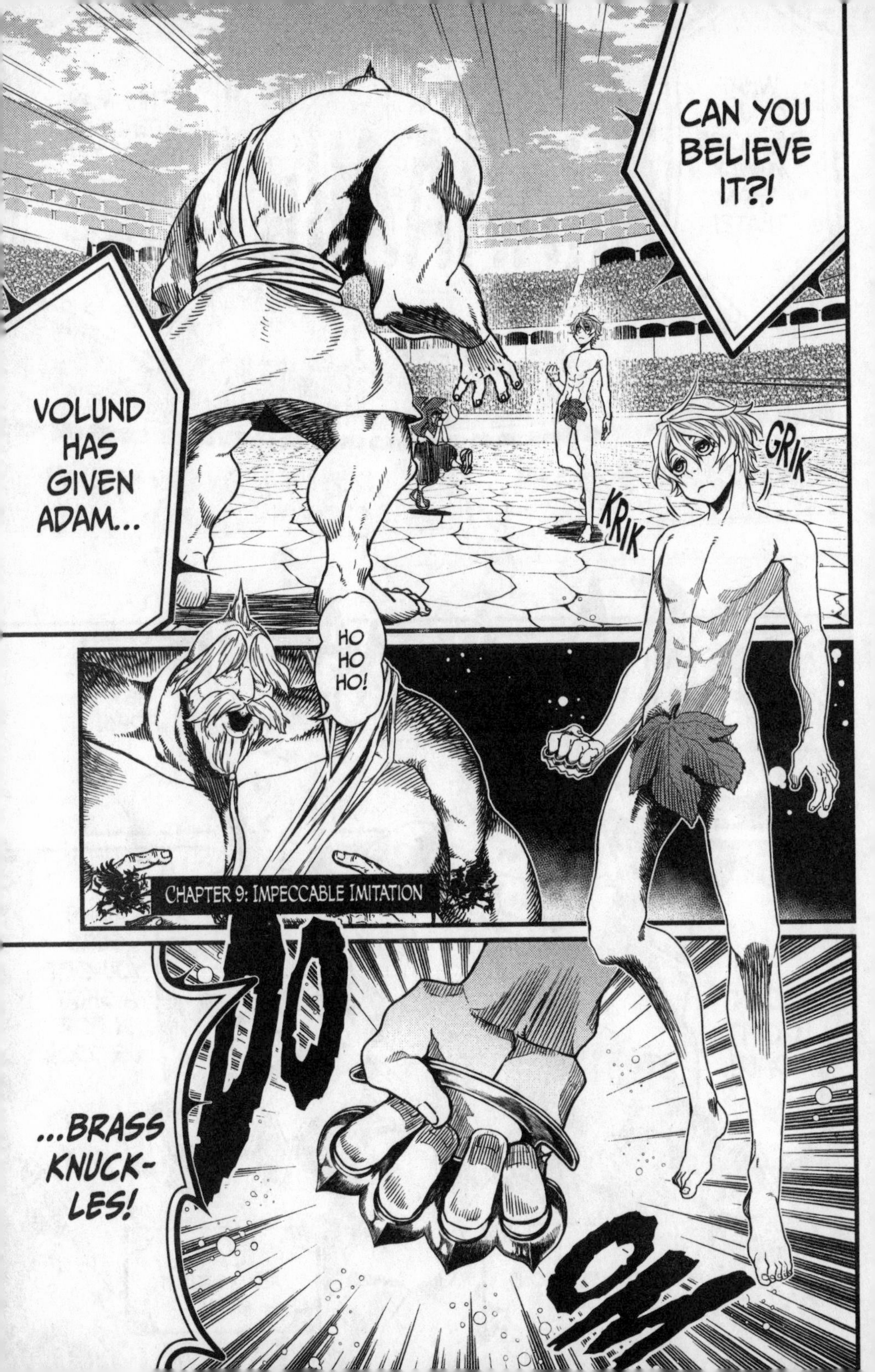
CAN YOU BELIEVE IT?!
VOLUND HAS GIVEN ADAM...
GRIK
KRIK
HO HO HO!
CHAPTER 9: IMPECCABLE IMITATION
...BRASS KNUCK-LES!

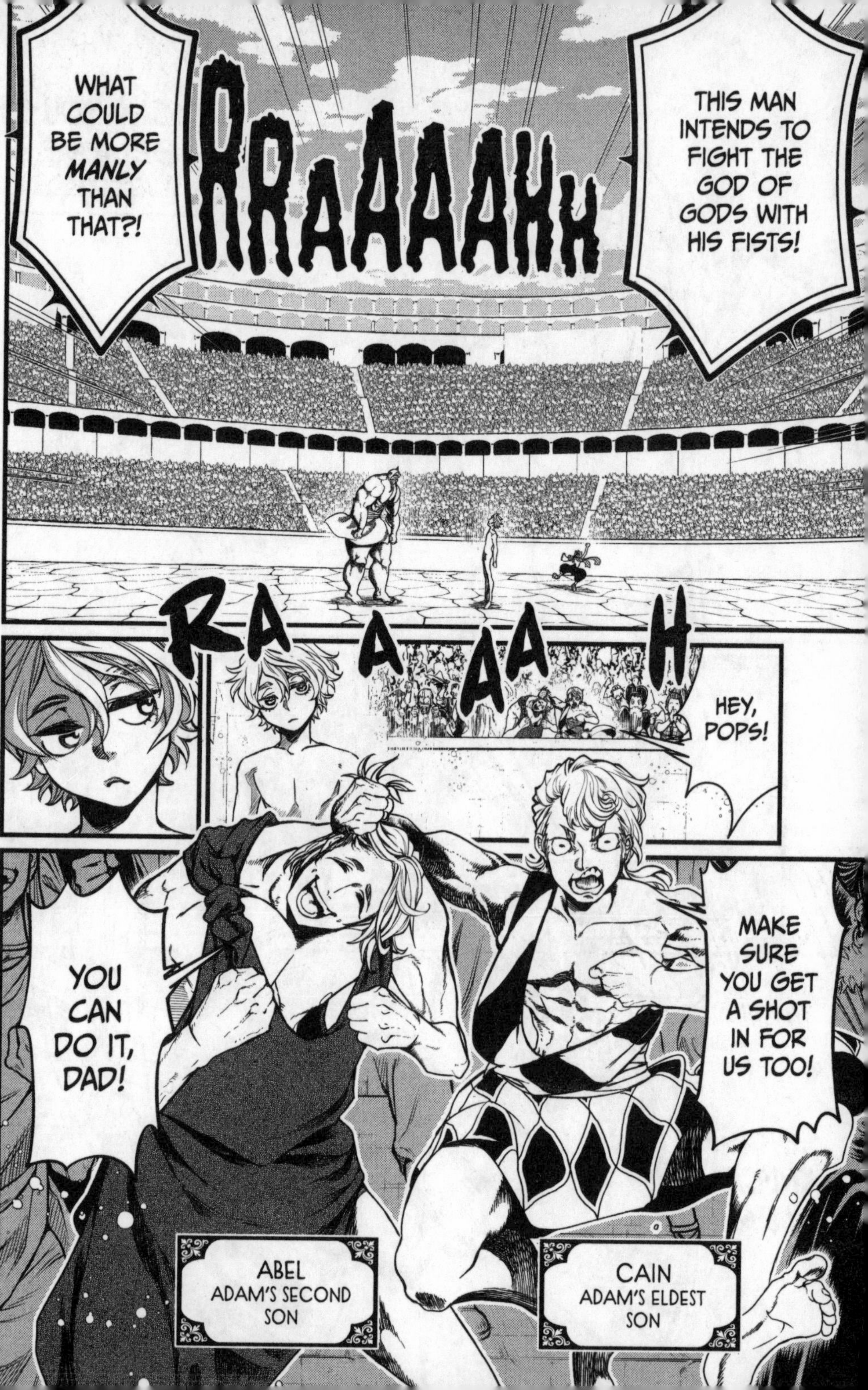
THIS MAN INTENDS TO FIGHT THE GOD OF GODS WITH HIS FISTS!
WHAT COULD BE MORE *MANLY* THAN THAT?!
RRAAAAHH
RAAAAH
HEY, POPS!
MAKE SURE YOU GET A SHOT IN FOR US TOO!
CAIN ADAM'S ELDEST SON
YOU CAN DO IT, DAD!
ABEL ADAM'S SECOND SON

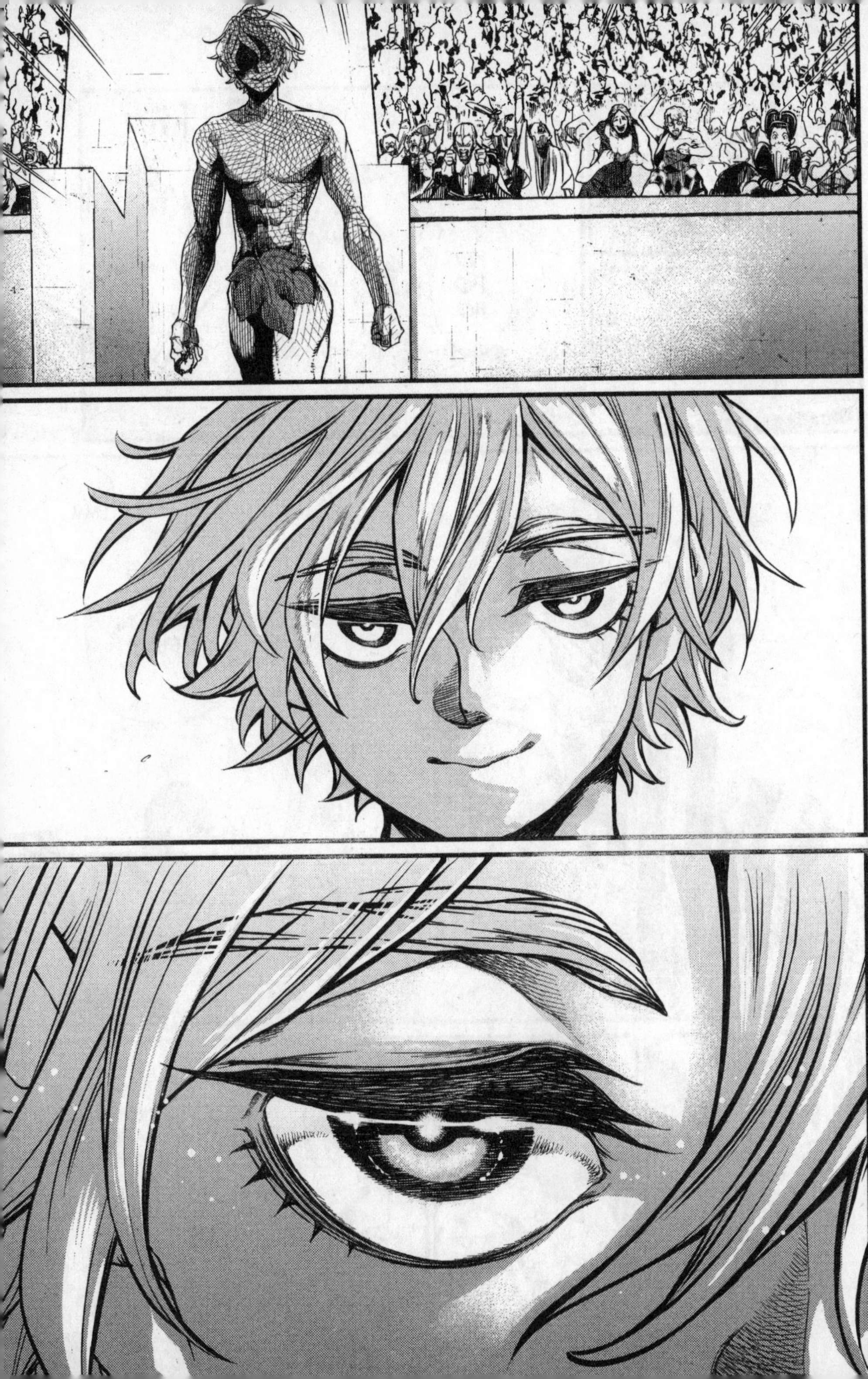

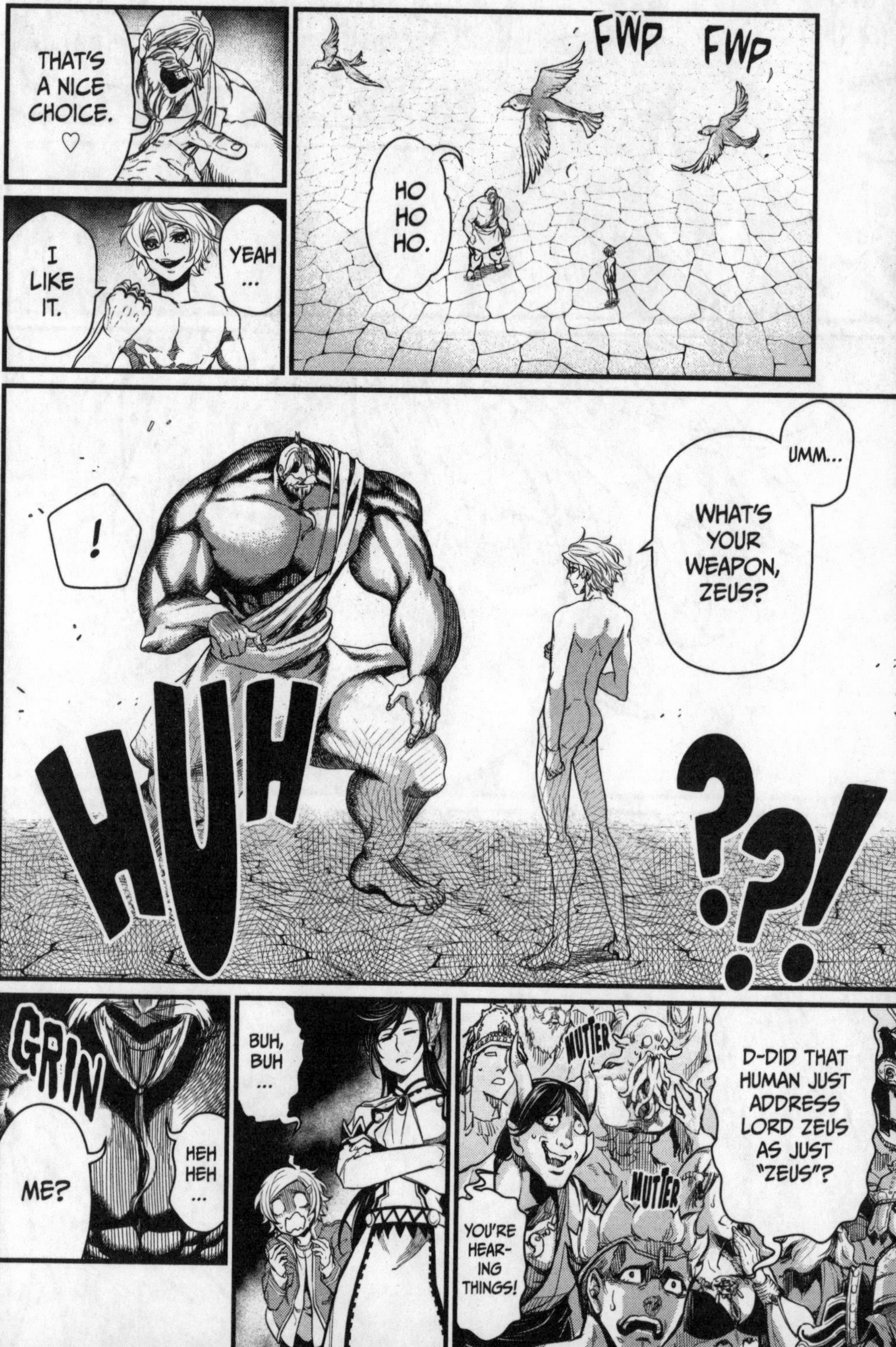
FWP
FWP
HO HO HO.
THAT'S A NICE CHOICE. ♡
YEAH ...
I LIKE IT.
UMM...
WHAT'S YOUR WEAPON, ZEUS?
!
HUH
??!
MUTTER
D-DID THAT HUMAN JUST ADDRESS LORD ZEUS AS JUST "ZEUS"?
MUTTER
YOU'RE HEAR-ING THINGS!
BUH, BUH ...
GRIN
HEH HEH ...
ME?

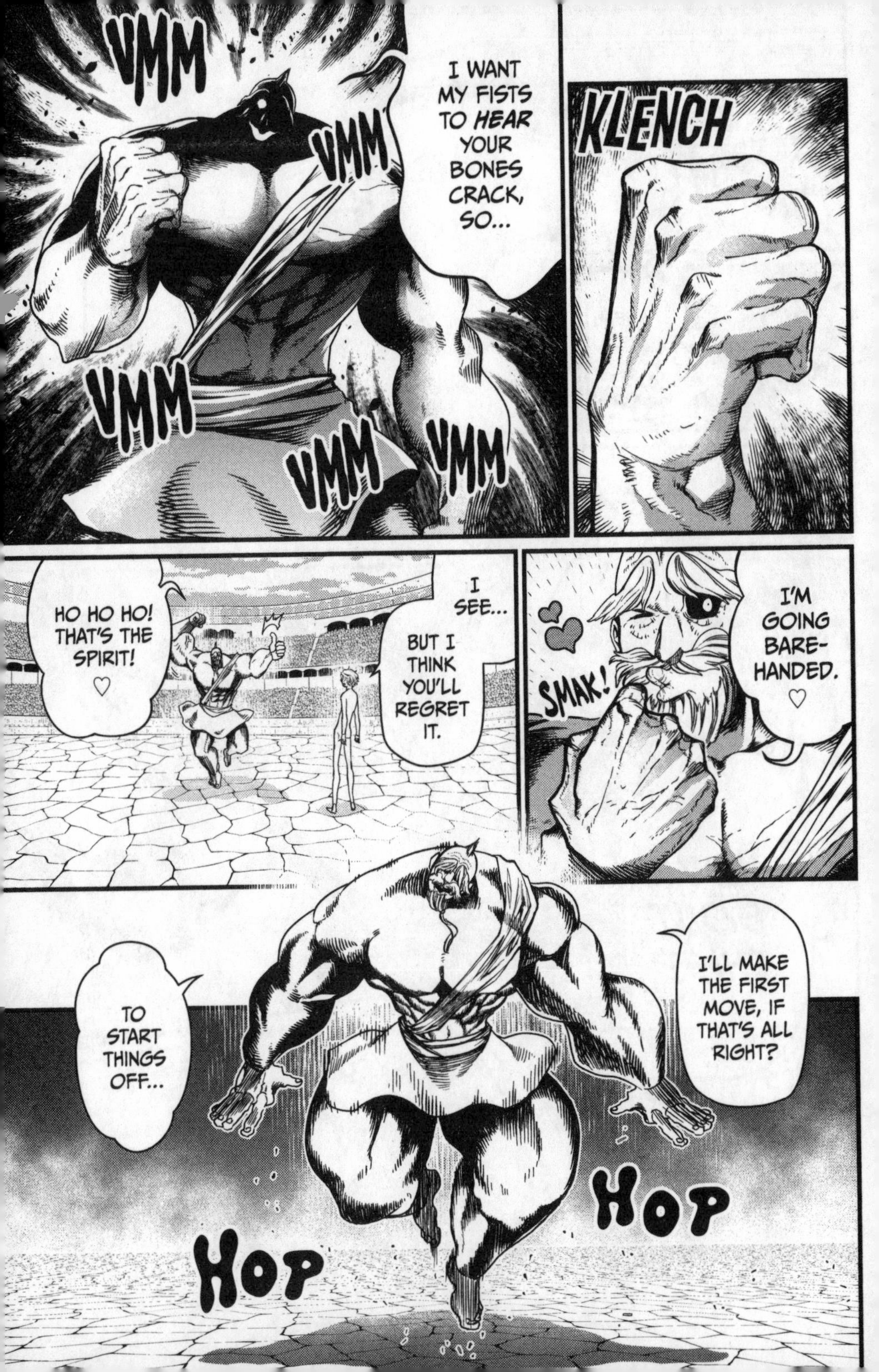
KLENCH
I WANT MY FISTS TO *HEAR* YOUR BONES CRACK, SO...
VMM
VMM
VMM
VMM
VMM
I'M GOING BARE-HANDED. ♡
SMAK!
I SEE...
BUT I THINK YOU'LL REGRET IT.
HO HO HO! THAT'S THE SPIRIT! ♡
I'LL MAKE THE FIRST MOVE, IF THAT'S ALL RIGHT?
TO START THINGS OFF...
HOP
HOP

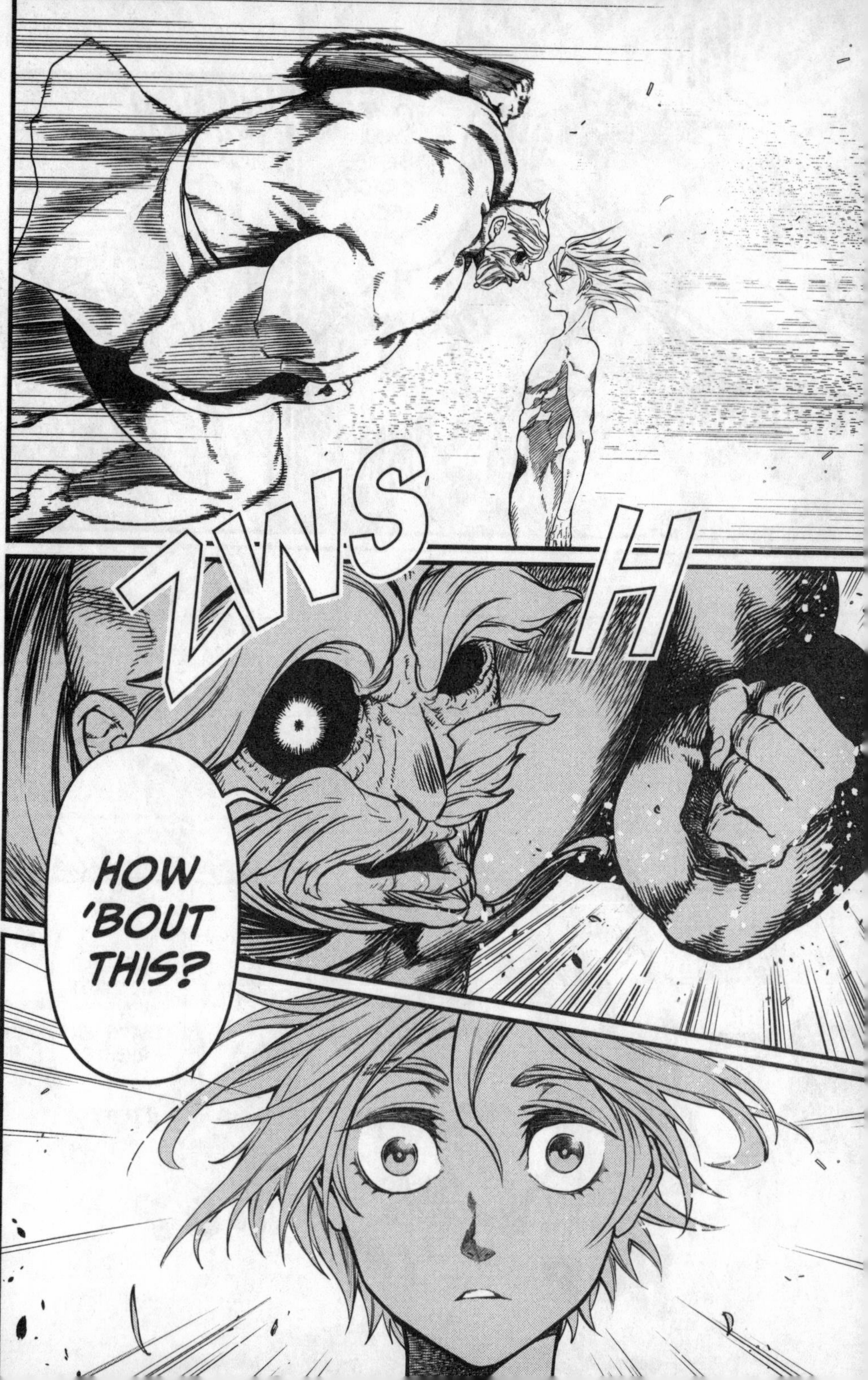
ZWSH
HOW 'BOUT THIS?

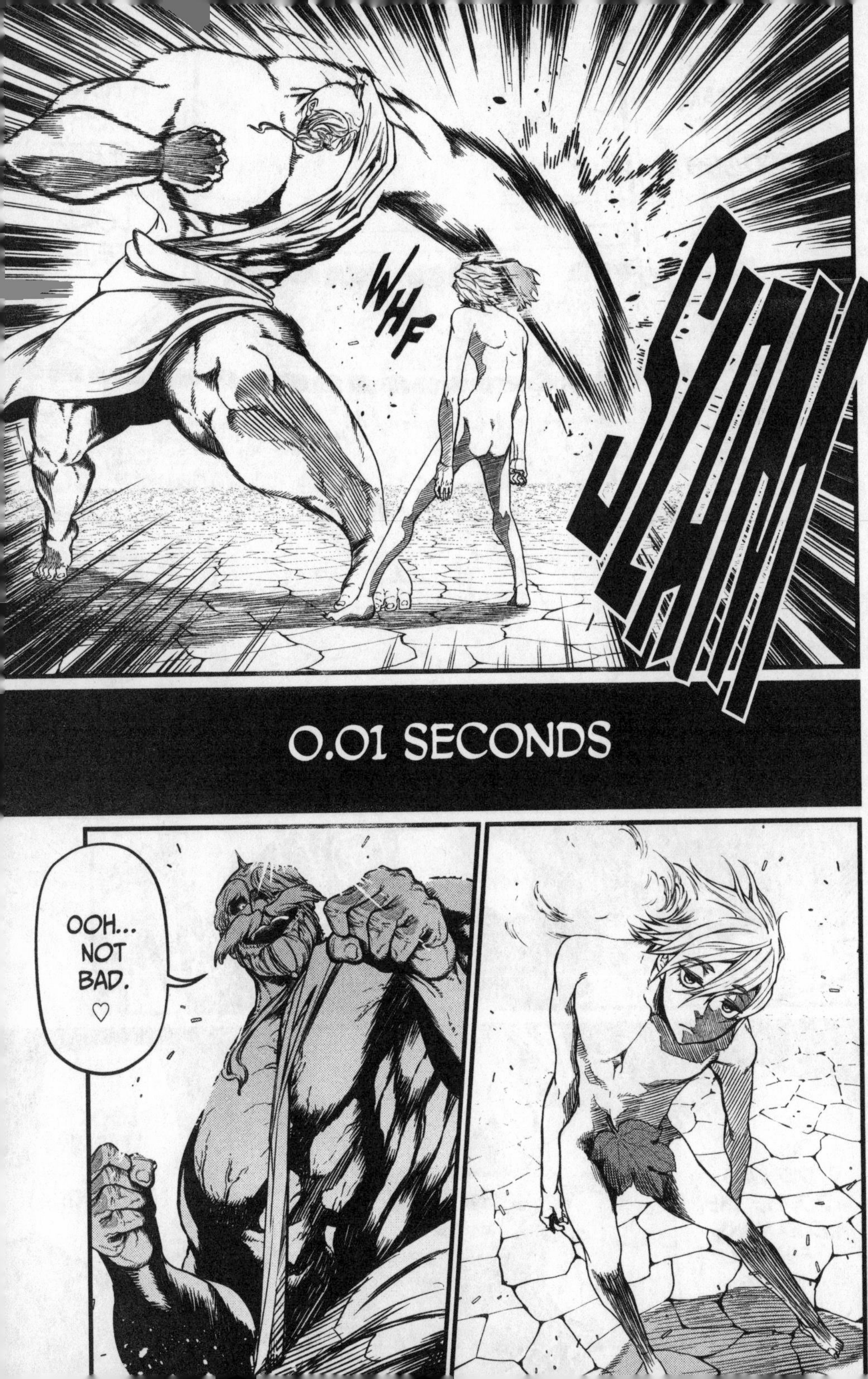
WHF
0.01 SECONDS
OOH... NOT BAD. ♡

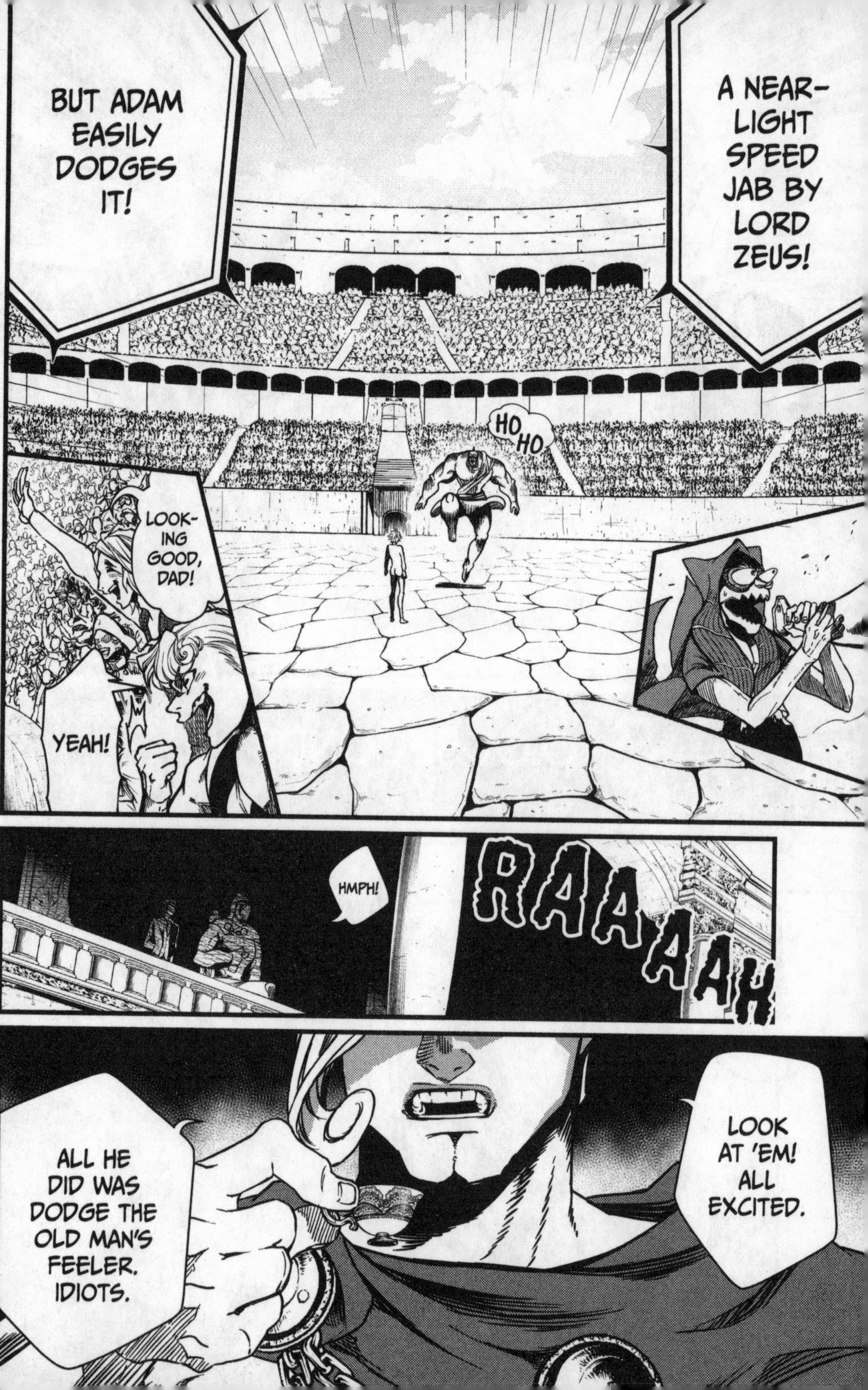
A NEAR-LIGHT SPEED JAB BY LORD ZEUS!
BUT ADAM EASILY DODGES IT!
HO HO
LOOKING GOOD, DAD!
YEAH!
RAAAAH
HMPH!
LOOK AT 'EM! ALL EXCITED.
ALL HE DID WAS DODGE THE OLD MAN'S FEELER. IDIOTS.

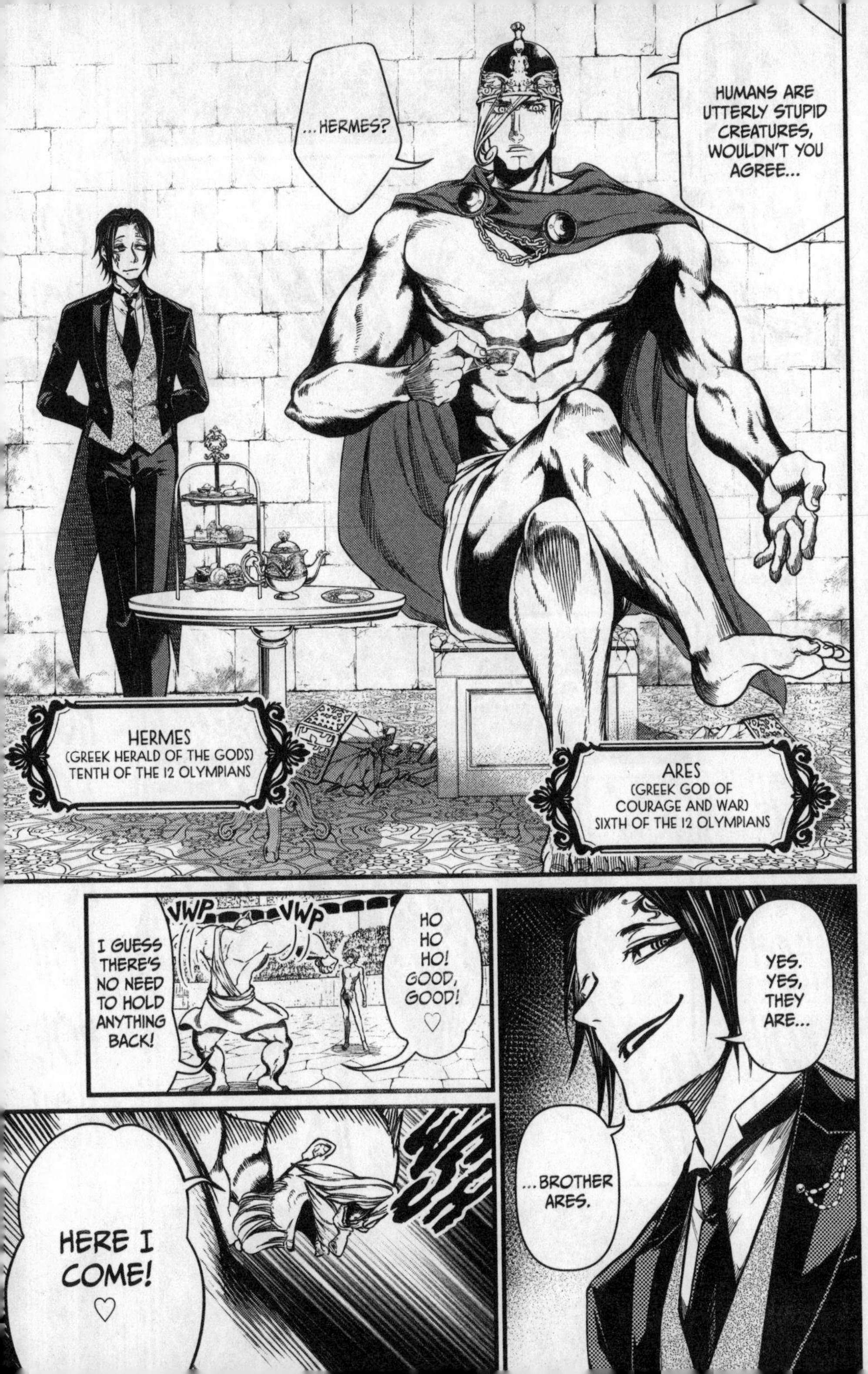
HUMANS ARE UTTERLY STUPID CREATURES, WOULDN'T YOU AGREE...
...HERMES?
ARES (GREEK GOD OF COURAGE AND WAR) SIXTH OF THE 12 OLYMPIANS
HERMES (GREEK HERALD OF THE GODS) TENTH OF THE 12 OLYMPIANS
YES. YES, THEY ARE...
...BROTHER ARES.
VWP VWP
HO HO HO! GOOD, GOOD! ♡
I GUESS THERE'S NO NEED TO HOLD ANYTHING BACK!
HERE I COME! ♡

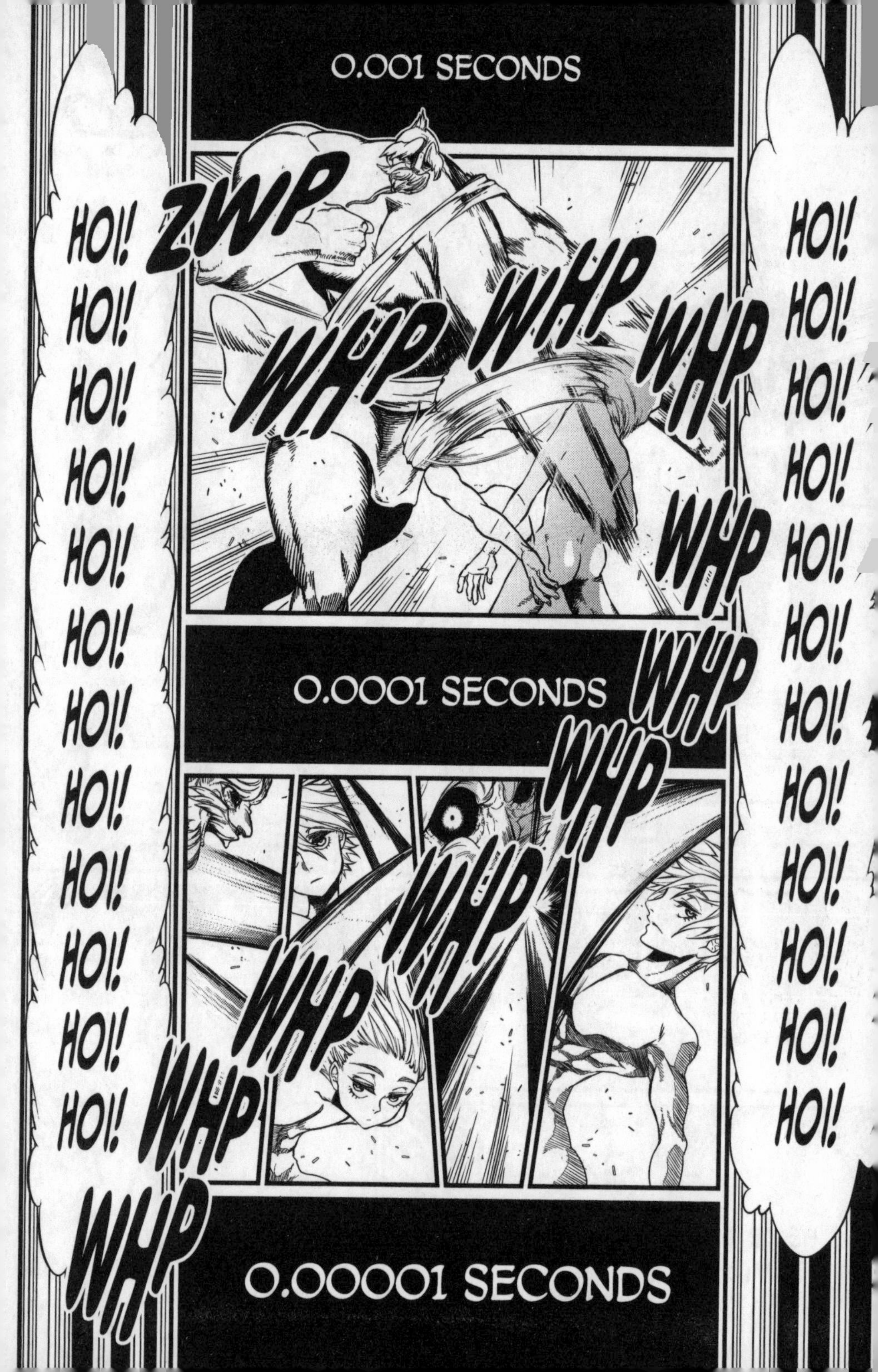
HOI! HOI! HOI! HOI! HOI! HOI! HOI! HOI! HOI! HOI! HOI! HOI! HOI! HOI!
0.001 SECONDS
WHP
WHP
WHP
ZWIP
WHP
WHP
0.0001 SECONDS
WHP
WHP
WHP
WHP
WHP
0.00001 SECONDS
HOI! HOI! HOI! HOI! HOI! HOI! HOI! HOI! HOI! HOI! HOI! HOI! HOI! HOI!

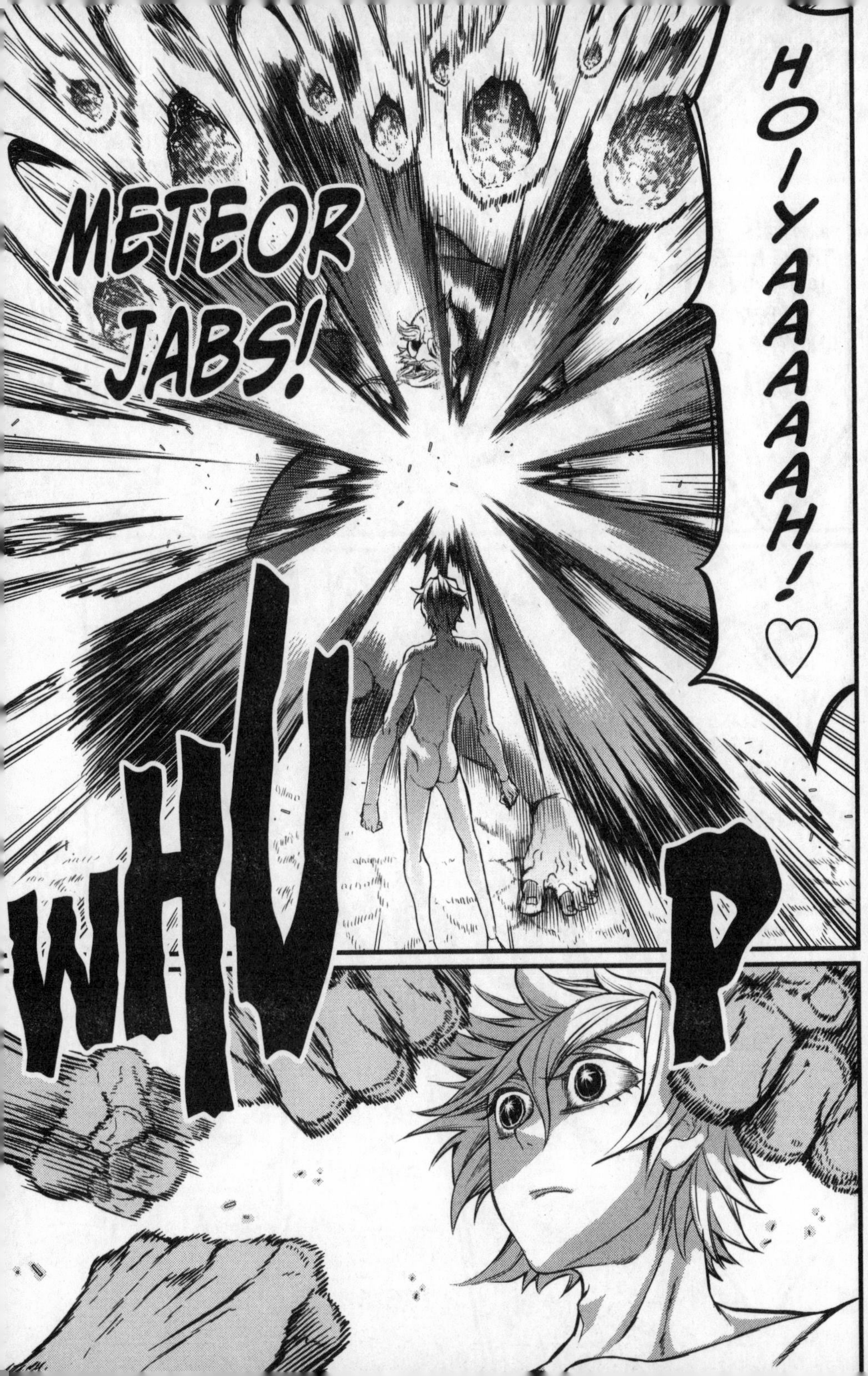
HOIYAAAAAAH! ♥
METEOR JABS!
WHUP

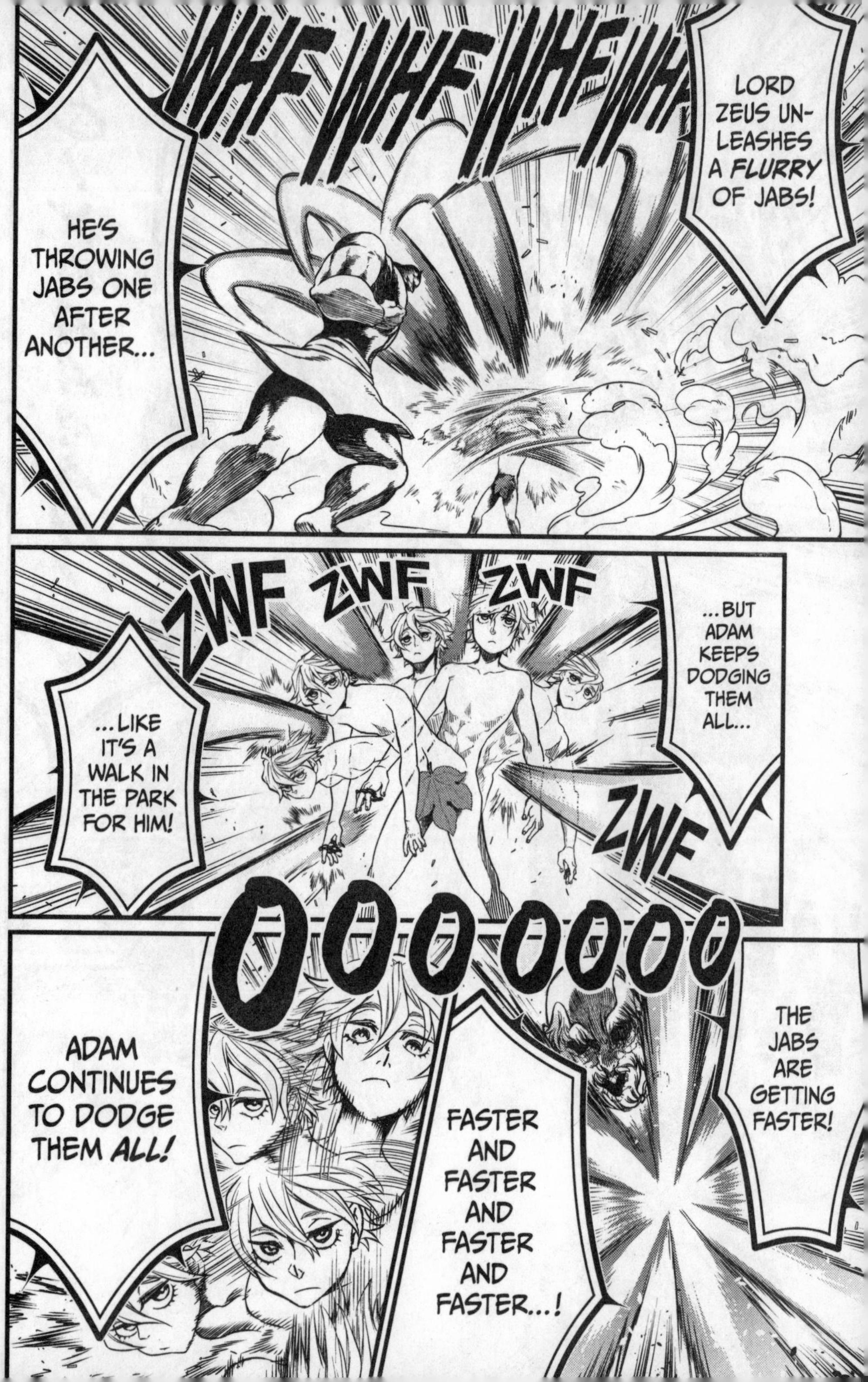
LORD ZEUS UN-LEASHES A *FLURRY* OF JABS!
WHF WHF WHF WHF
HE'S THROWING JABS ONE AFTER ANOTHER...
...BUT ADAM KEEPS DODGING THEM ALL...
ZWF ZWF ZWF
...LIKE IT'S A WALK IN THE PARK FOR HIM!
ZWF
OOOOOOO
THE JABS ARE GETTING FASTER!
FASTER AND FASTER AND FASTER AND FASTER...!
ADAM CONTINUES TO DODGE THEM *ALL!*

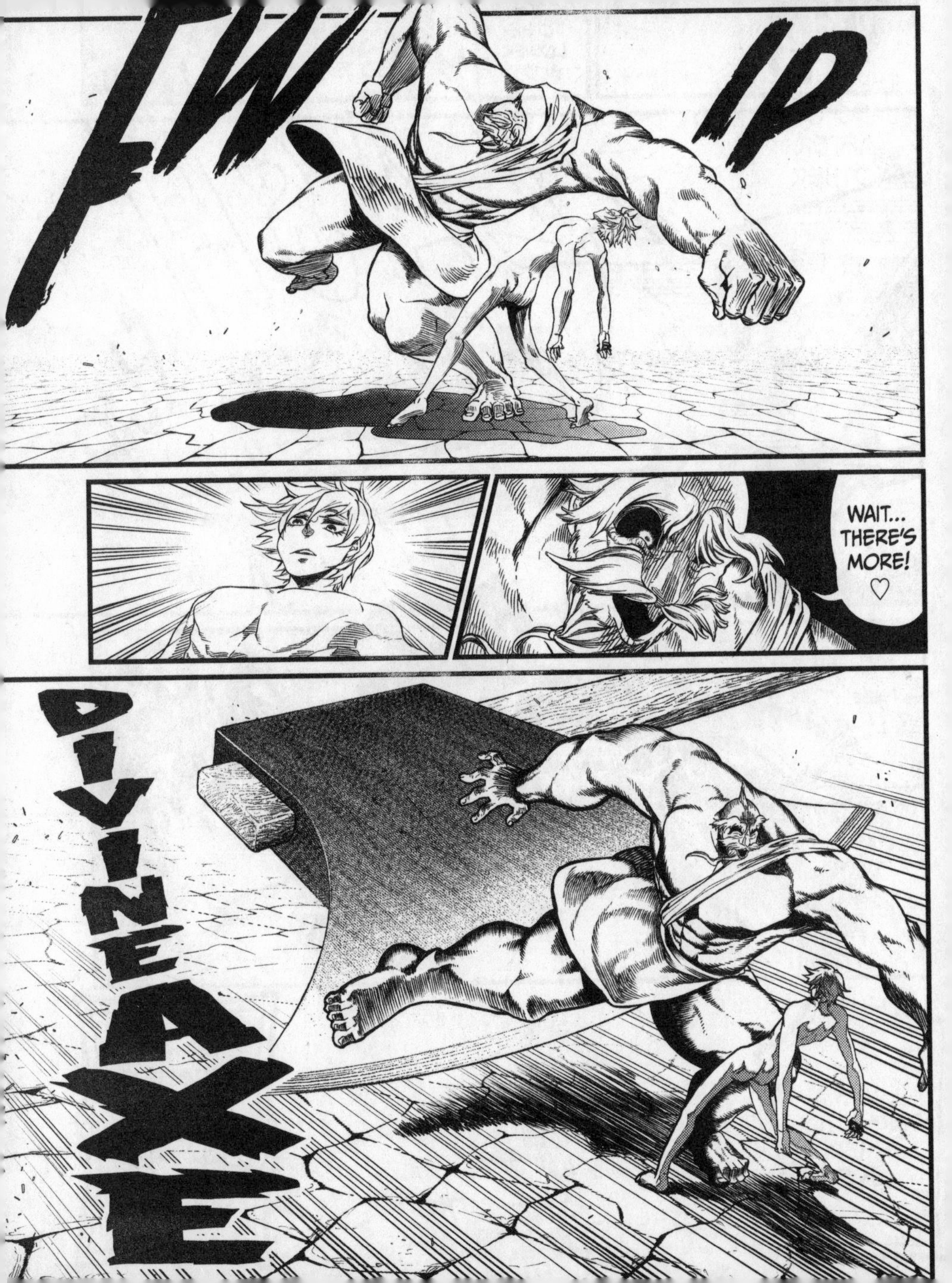
FWIP
WAIT... THERE'S MORE! ♡
DIVINE AXE

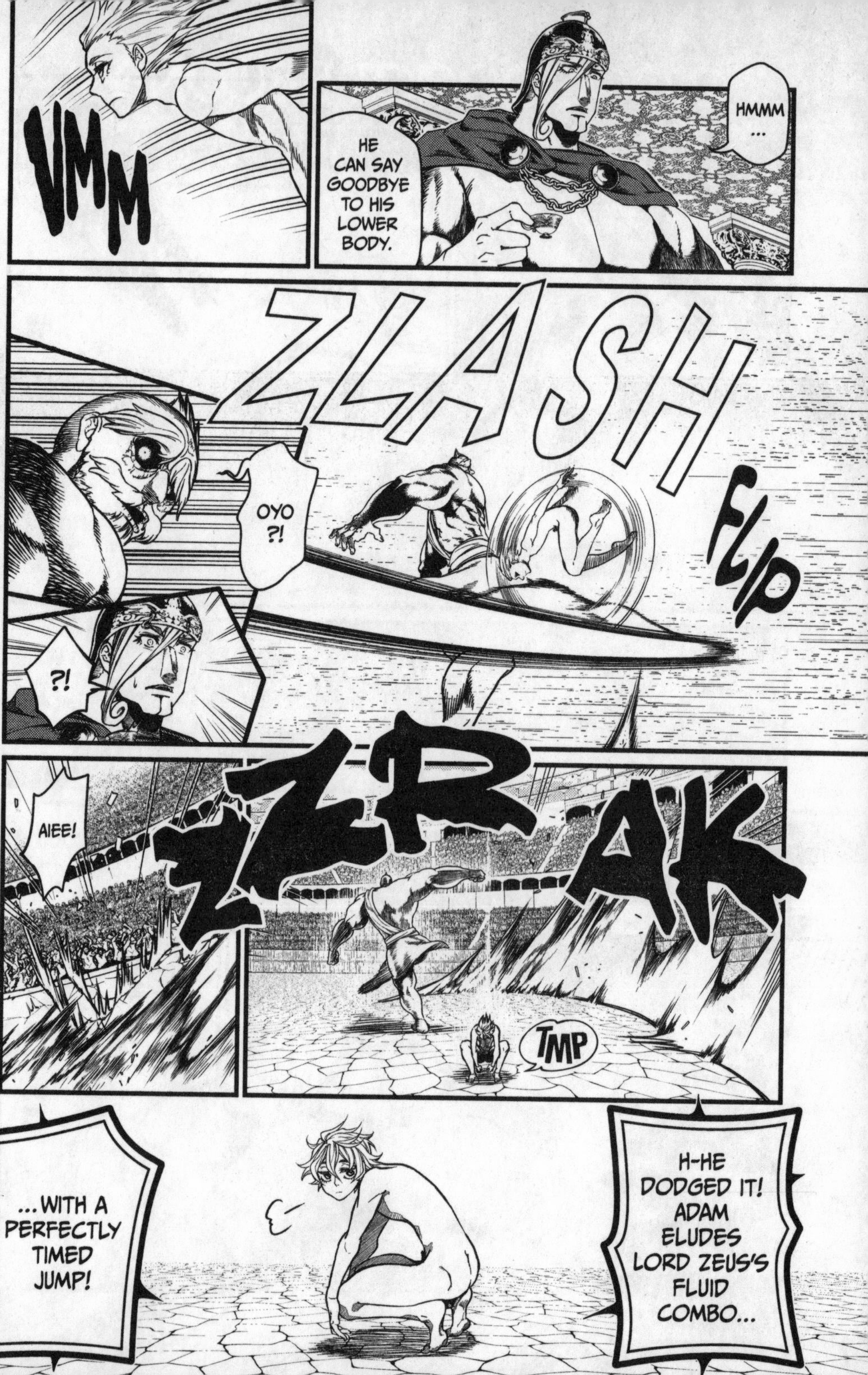
HMMM ...
HE CAN SAY GOODBYE TO HIS LOWER BODY.
VMM
ZLASH
FLIP
OYO ?!
?!
ZRAK
TMP
AIEE!
H-HE DODGED IT! ADAM ELUDES LORD ZEUS'S FLUID COMBO...
...WITH A PERFECTLY TIMED JUMP!

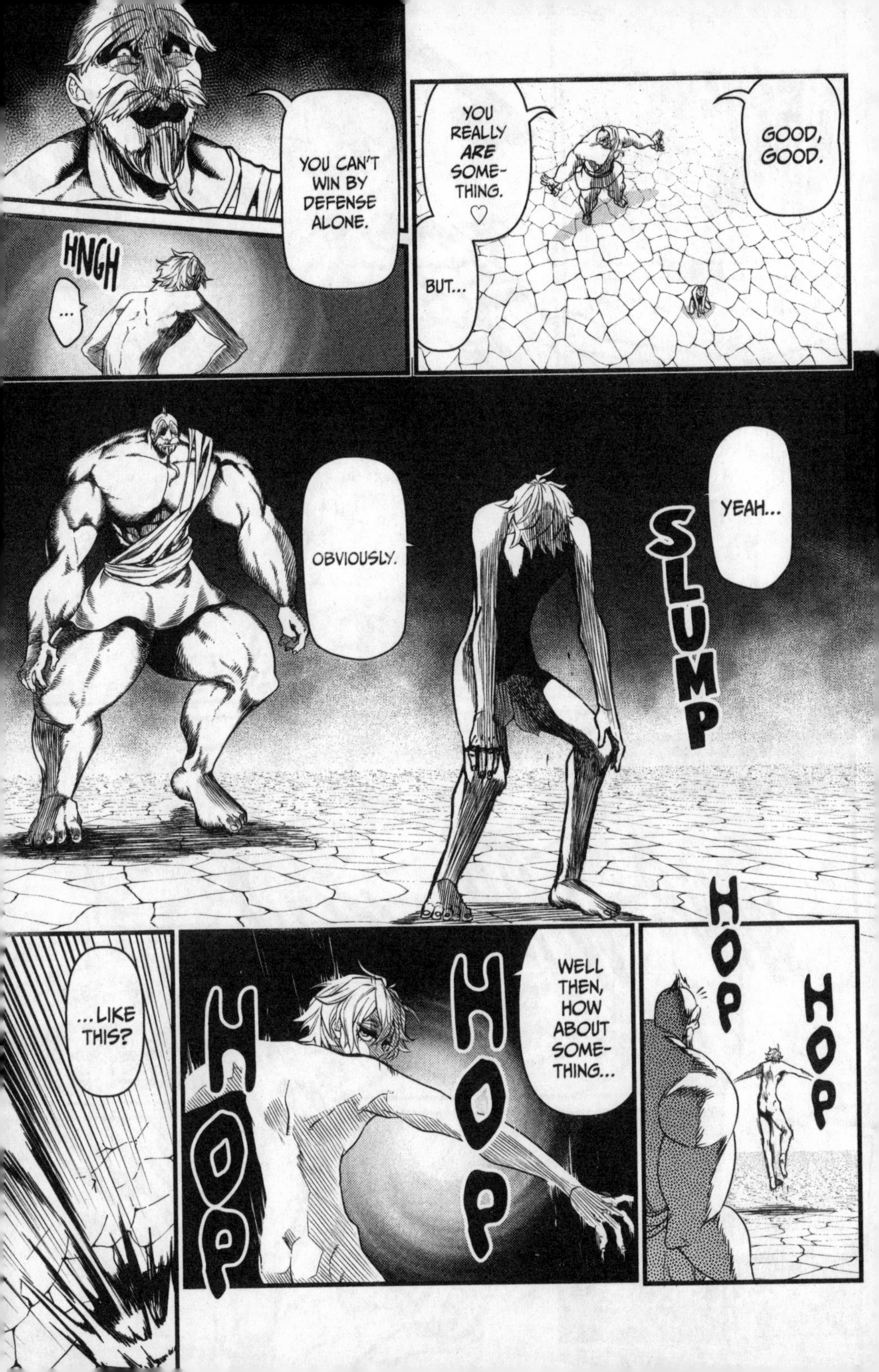
GOOD, GOOD.
YOU REALLY ARE SOMETHING. ♡
BUT...
YOU CAN'T WIN BY DEFENSE ALONE.
HNGH
...
YEAH...
SLUMP
OBVIOUSLY.
HOP
HOP
WELL THEN, HOW ABOUT SOMETHING...
HOP
HOP
...LIKE THIS?

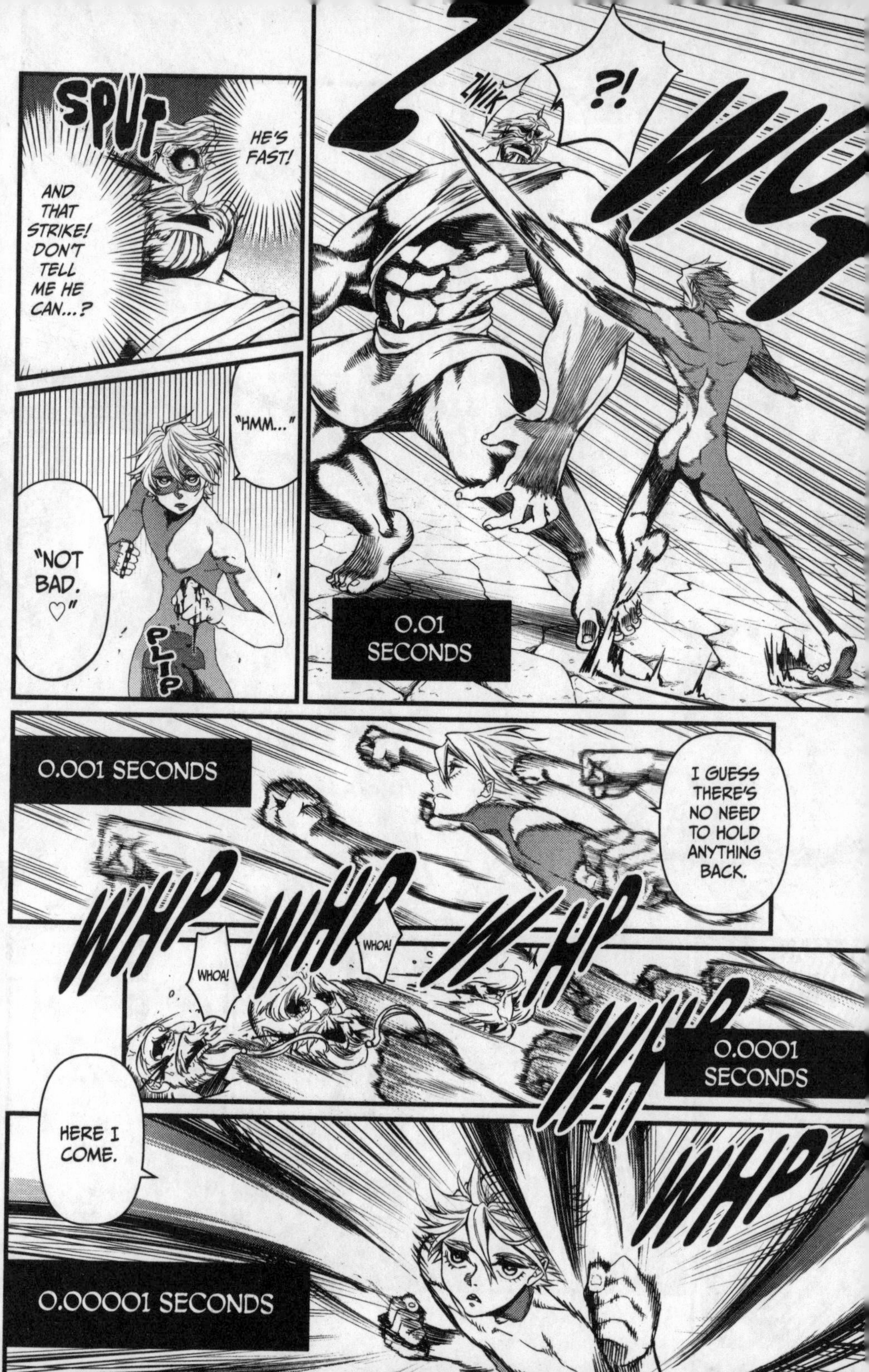
ZWIK
?!
0.01 SECONDS
SPUT
HE'S FAST!
AND THAT STRIKE! DON'T TELL ME HE CAN...?
"HMM..."
"NOT BAD. ♡"
PLIP
I GUESS THERE'S NO NEED TO HOLD ANYTHING BACK.
0.001 SECONDS
WHP
WHP
WHP
0.0001 SECONDS
WHOA!
WHOA!
WHP
WHP
HERE I COME.
0.00001 SECONDS

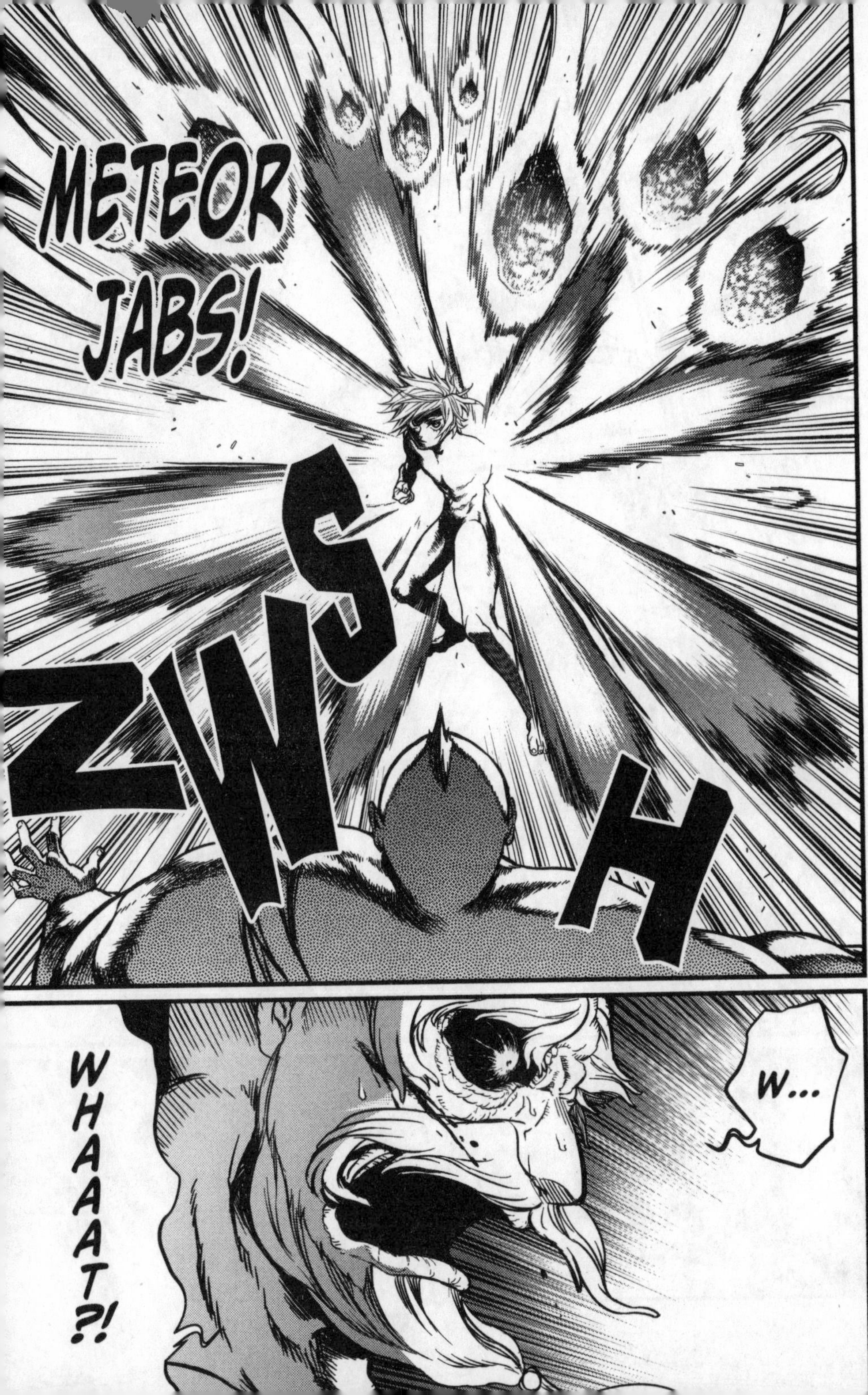
METEOR JABS!
ZWSH
W...
WHAAAT?!

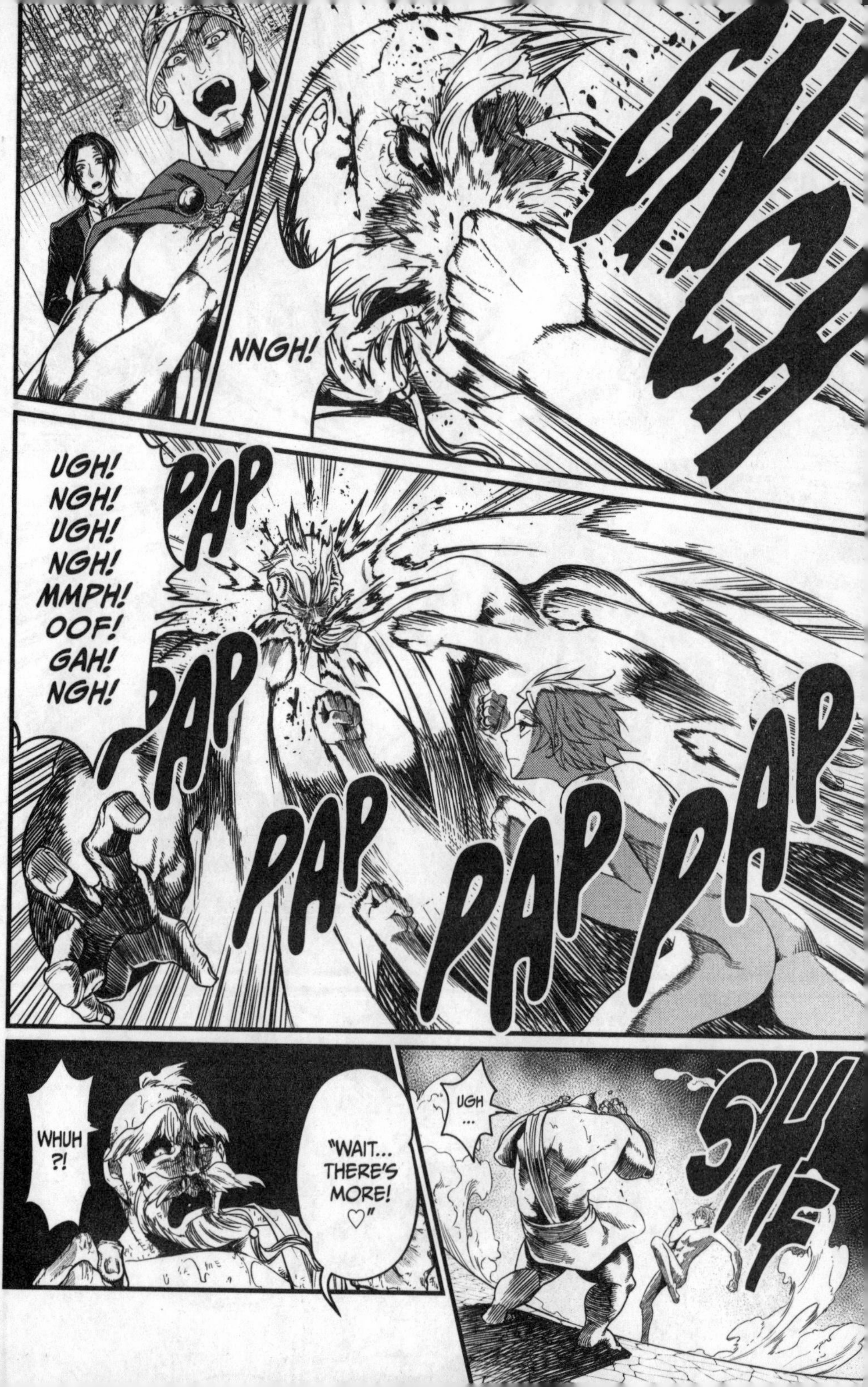
NNGH!
PAP PAP PAP PAP PAP
UGH! NGH! UGH! NGH! MMPH! OOF! GAH! NGH!
UGH...
"WAIT... THERE'S MORE! ♡"
WHUH?!

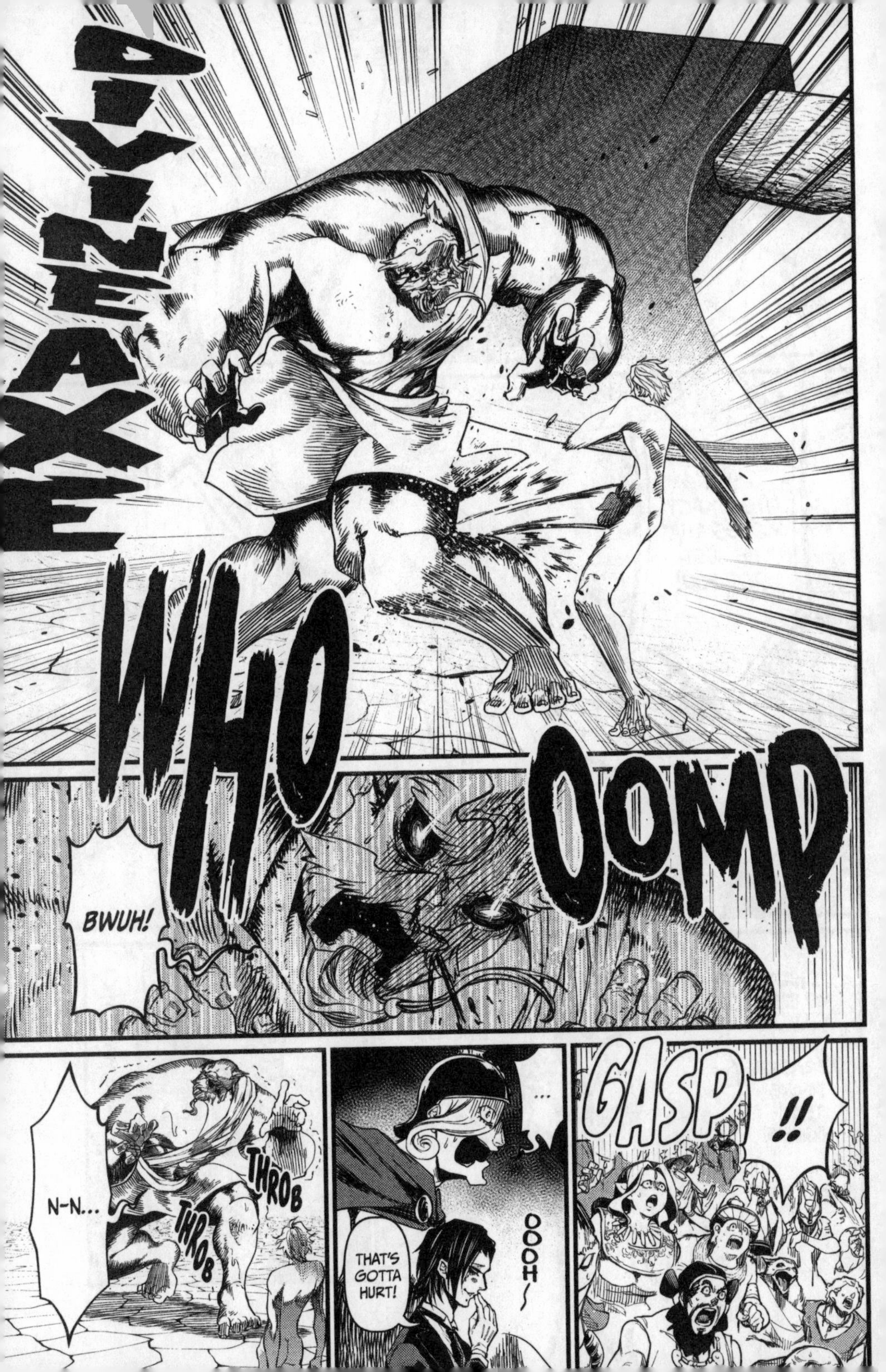
DIVINE AXE
WHO
OOMP
BWUH!
GASP!!
...
OOOH~
THAT'S GOTTA HURT!
THROB
THROB
N-N...

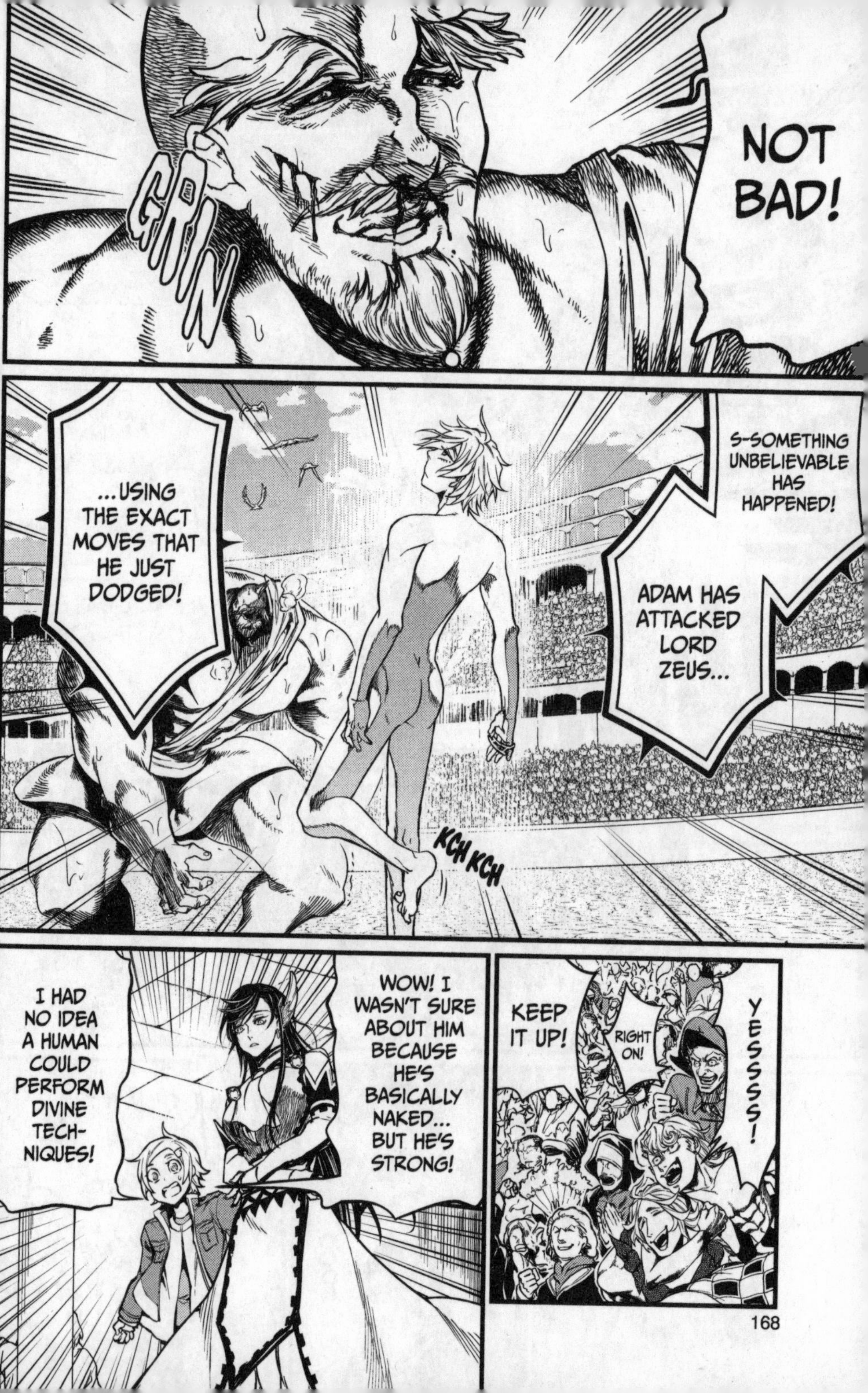
NOT BAD!
GRIN
S-SOMETHING UNBELIEVABLE HAS HAPPENED!
ADAM HAS ATTACKED LORD ZEUS...
...USING THE EXACT MOVES THAT HE JUST DODGED!
KCH KCH
YESSSS!
RIGHT ON!
KEEP IT UP!
WOW! I WASN'T SURE ABOUT HIM BECAUSE HE'S BASICALLY NAKED... BUT HE'S STRONG!
I HAD NO IDEA A HUMAN COULD PERFORM DIVINE TECH-NIQUES!

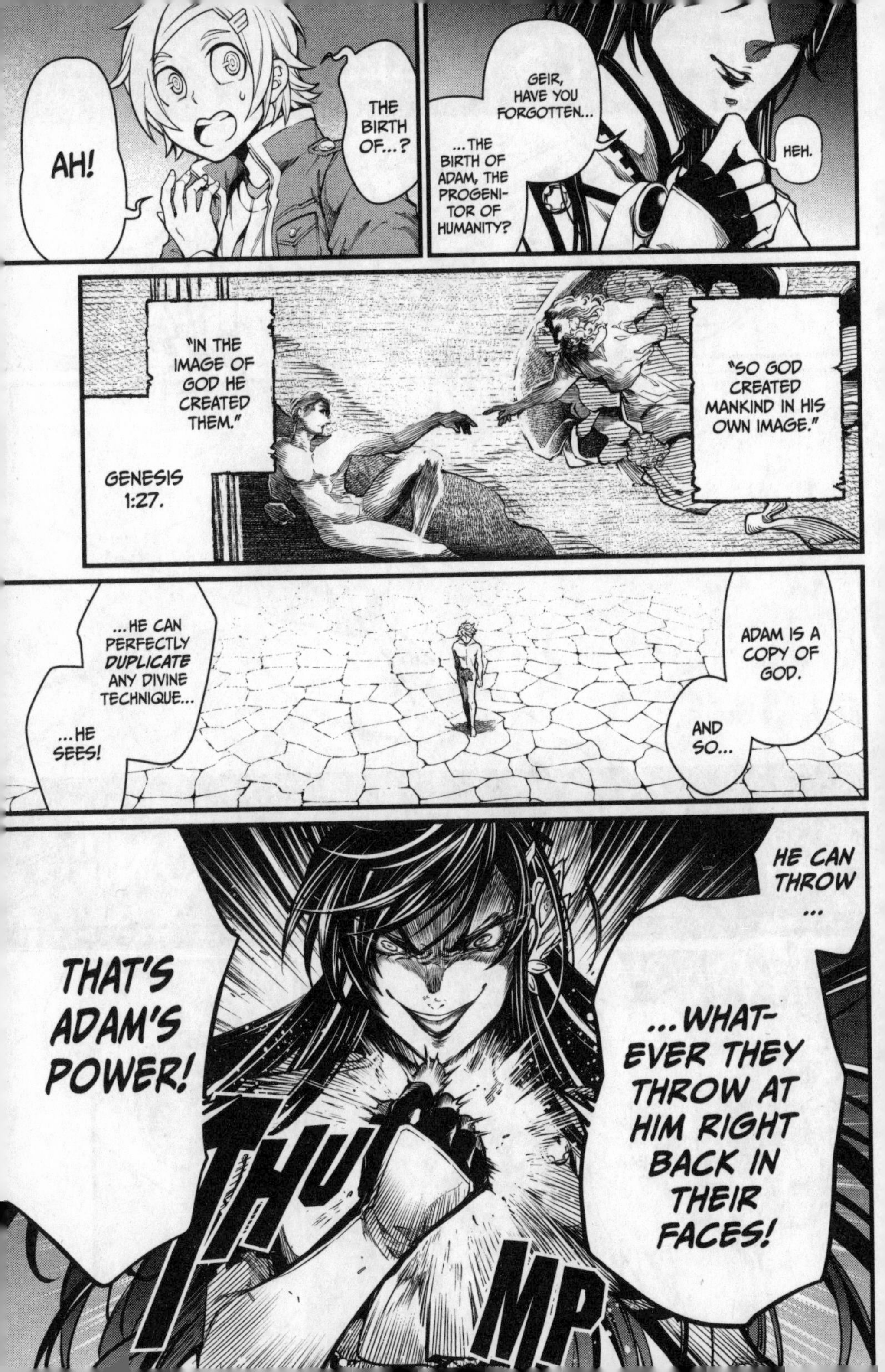
HEH.
GEIR, HAVE YOU FORGOTTEN...
...THE BIRTH OF ADAM, THE PROGENITOR OF HUMANITY?
THE BIRTH OF...?
AH!
"SO GOD CREATED MANKIND IN HIS OWN IMAGE."
"IN THE IMAGE OF GOD HE CREATED THEM."
GENESIS 1:27.
ADAM IS A COPY OF GOD.
AND SO...
...HE CAN PERFECTLY DUPLICATE ANY DIVINE TECHNIQUE...
...HE SEES!
HE CAN THROW ...
...WHAT-EVER THEY THROW AT HIM RIGHT BACK IN THEIR FACES!
THAT'S ADAM'S POWER!
THUMP

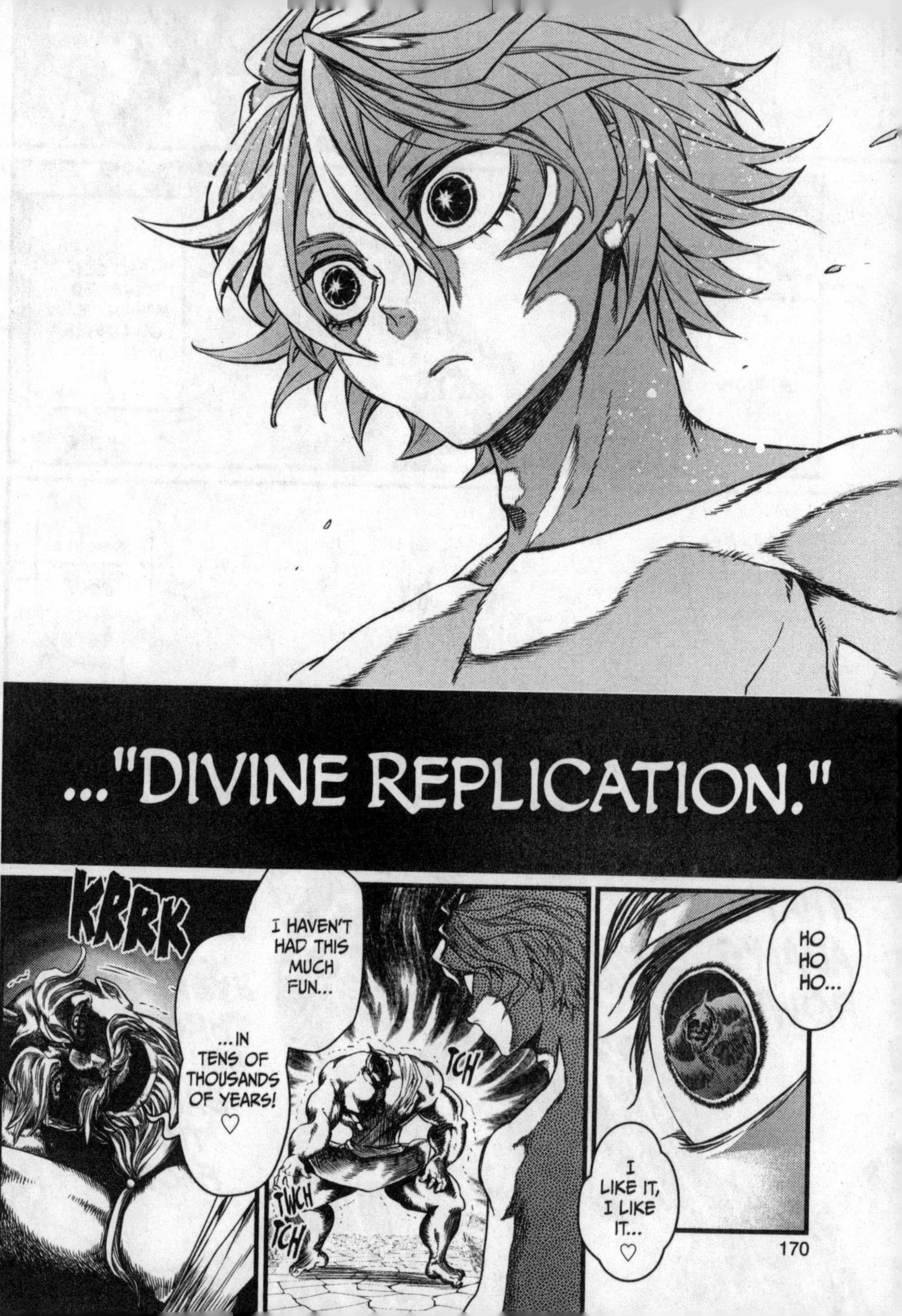
..."DIVINE REPLICATION."
HO HO HO...
I LIKE IT, I LIKE IT... ♡
TCH
I HAVEN'T HAD THIS MUCH FUN...
...IN TENS OF THOUSANDS OF YEARS! ♡
TWCH TCH
KRRK

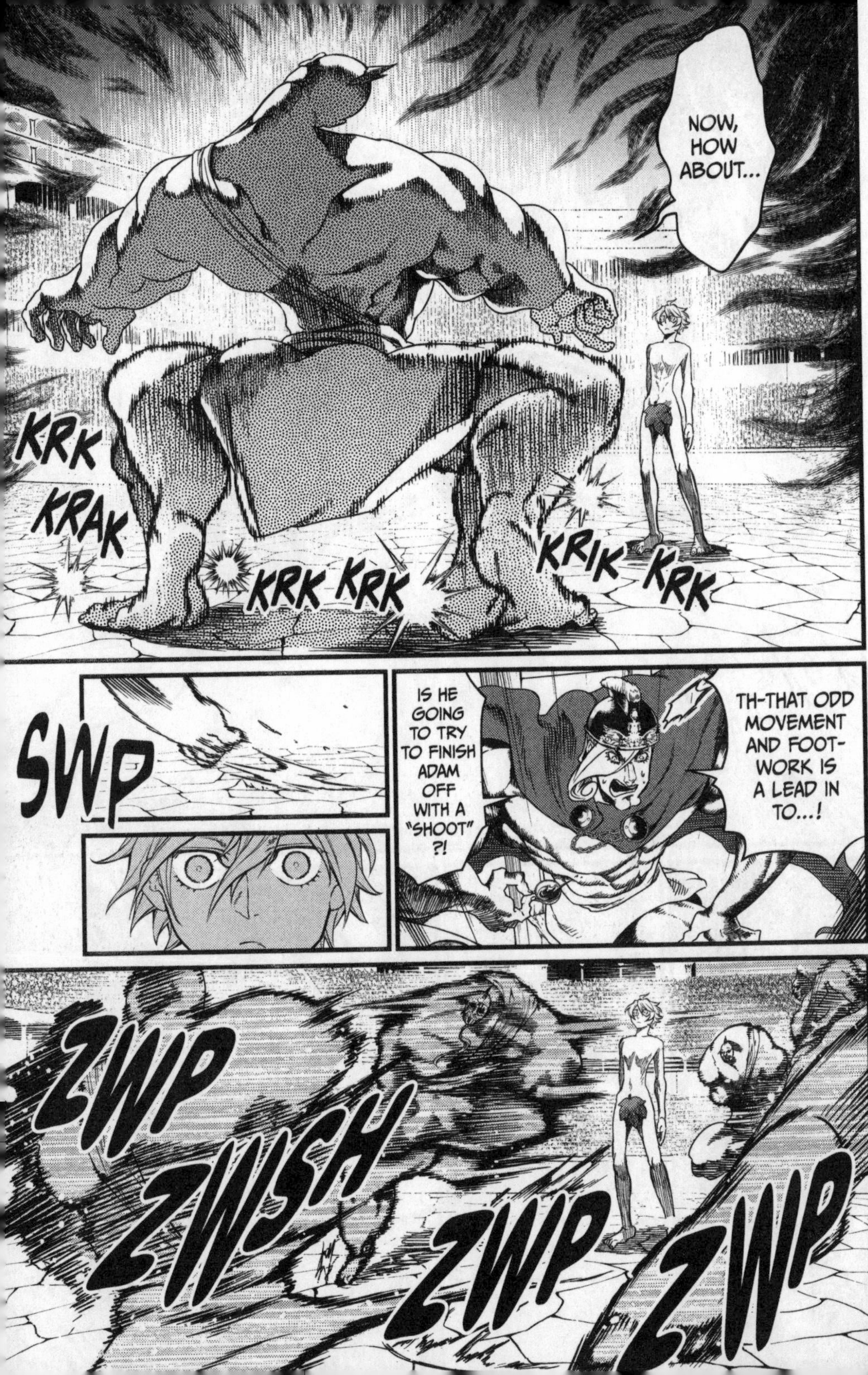
NOW, HOW ABOUT...
KRIK KRK
KRK KRK
KRK
KRAK
TH-THAT ODD MOVEMENT AND FOOT-WORK IS A LEAD IN TO...!
IS HE GOING TO TRY TO FINISH ADAM OFF WITH A "SHOOT" ?!
SWP
ZWP
ZWP
ZWISH
ZWP

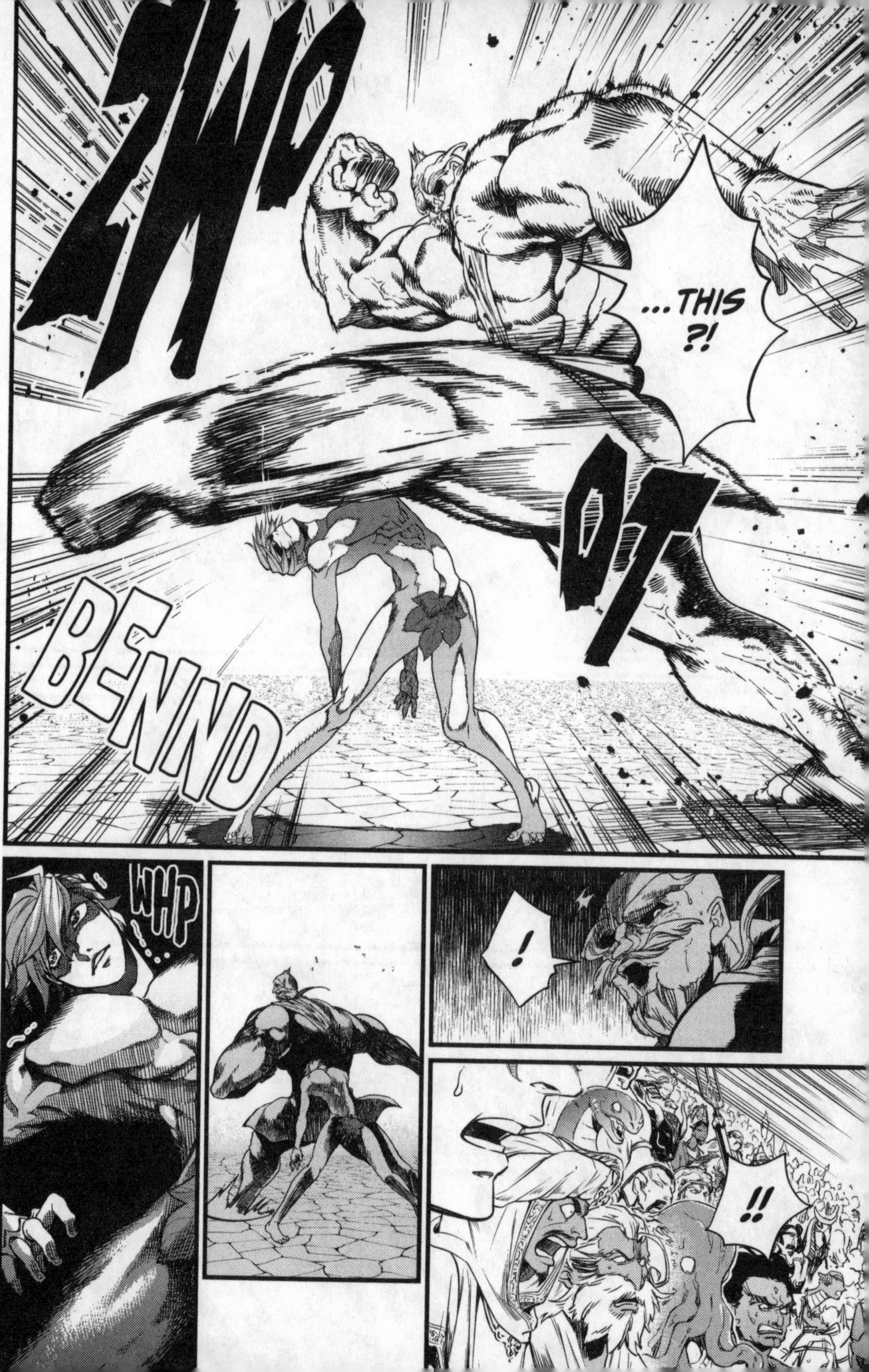
...THIS ?!
BENNND
!
!!
WHP

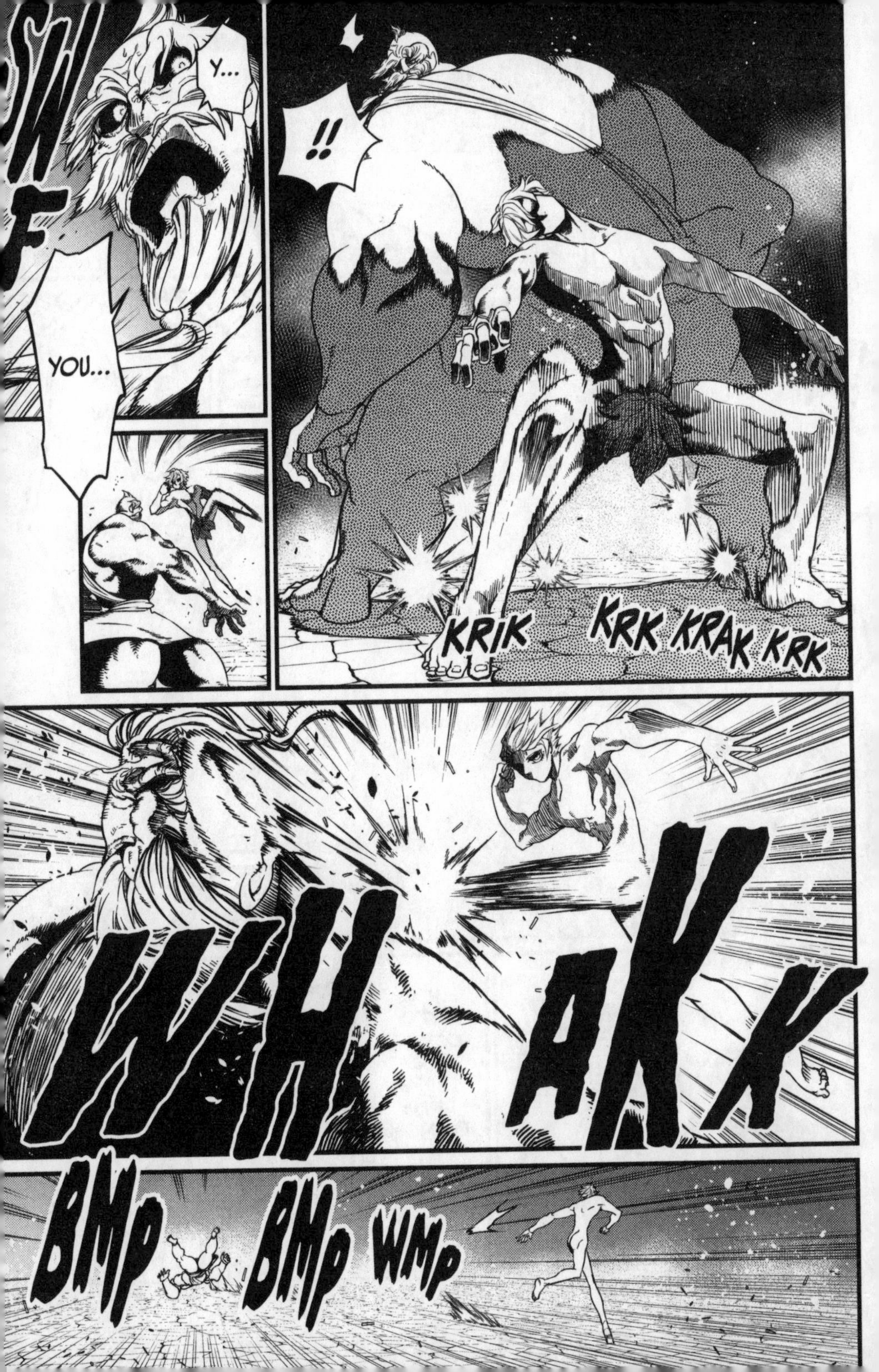
!!
KRIK
KRK KRAK KRK
Y...
SWF
YOU...
WHAKK
BMP
BMP
WMP

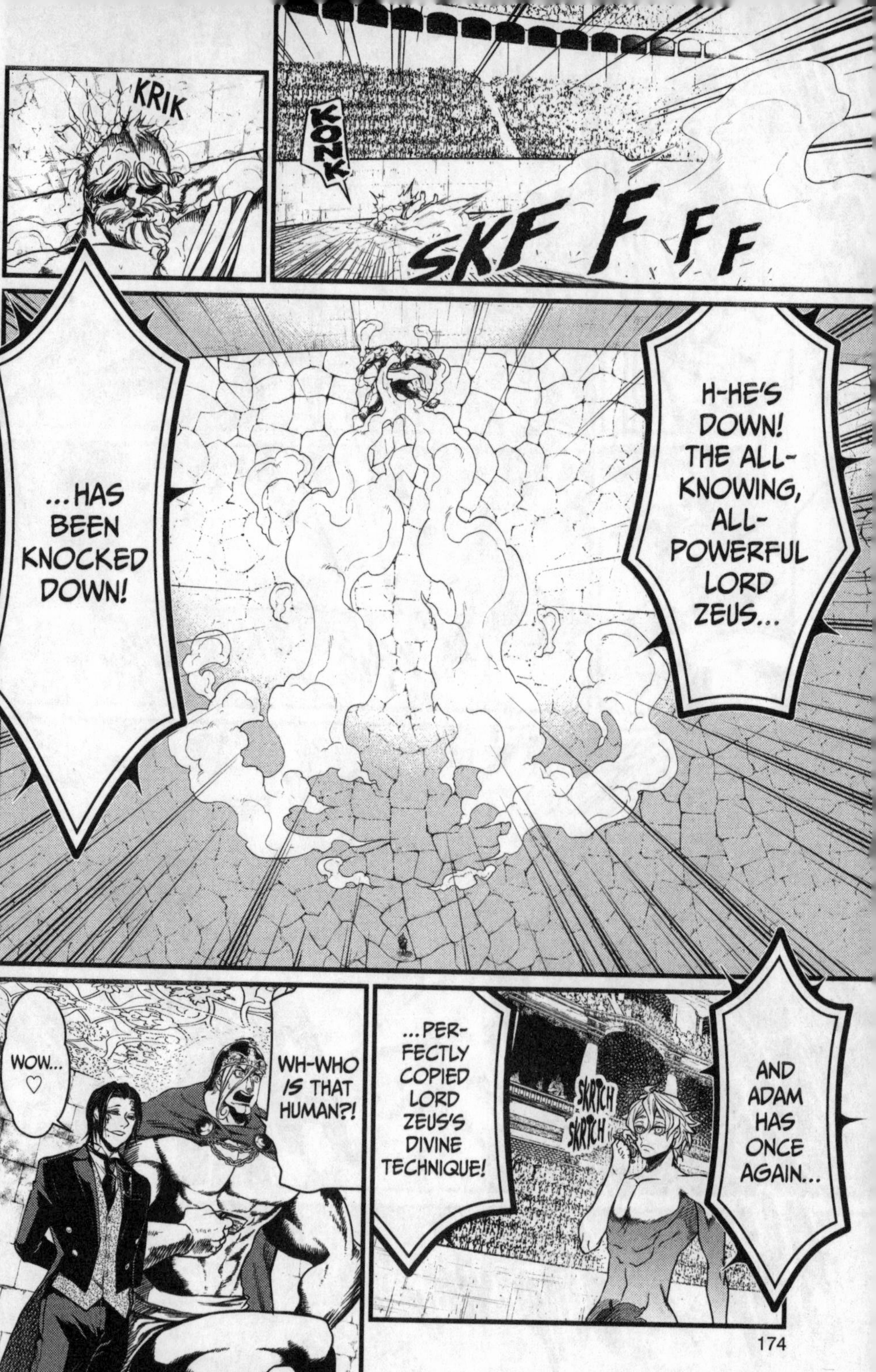
KONK
SKF FFF
KRIK
H-HE'S DOWN! THE ALL-KNOWING, ALL-POWERFUL LORD ZEUS...
...HAS BEEN KNOCKED DOWN!
AND ADAM HAS ONCE AGAIN...
SKRTCH SKRTCH
...PER-FECTLY COPIED LORD ZEUS'S DIVINE TECHNIQUE!
WH-WHO *IS* THAT HUMAN?!
WOW... ♡

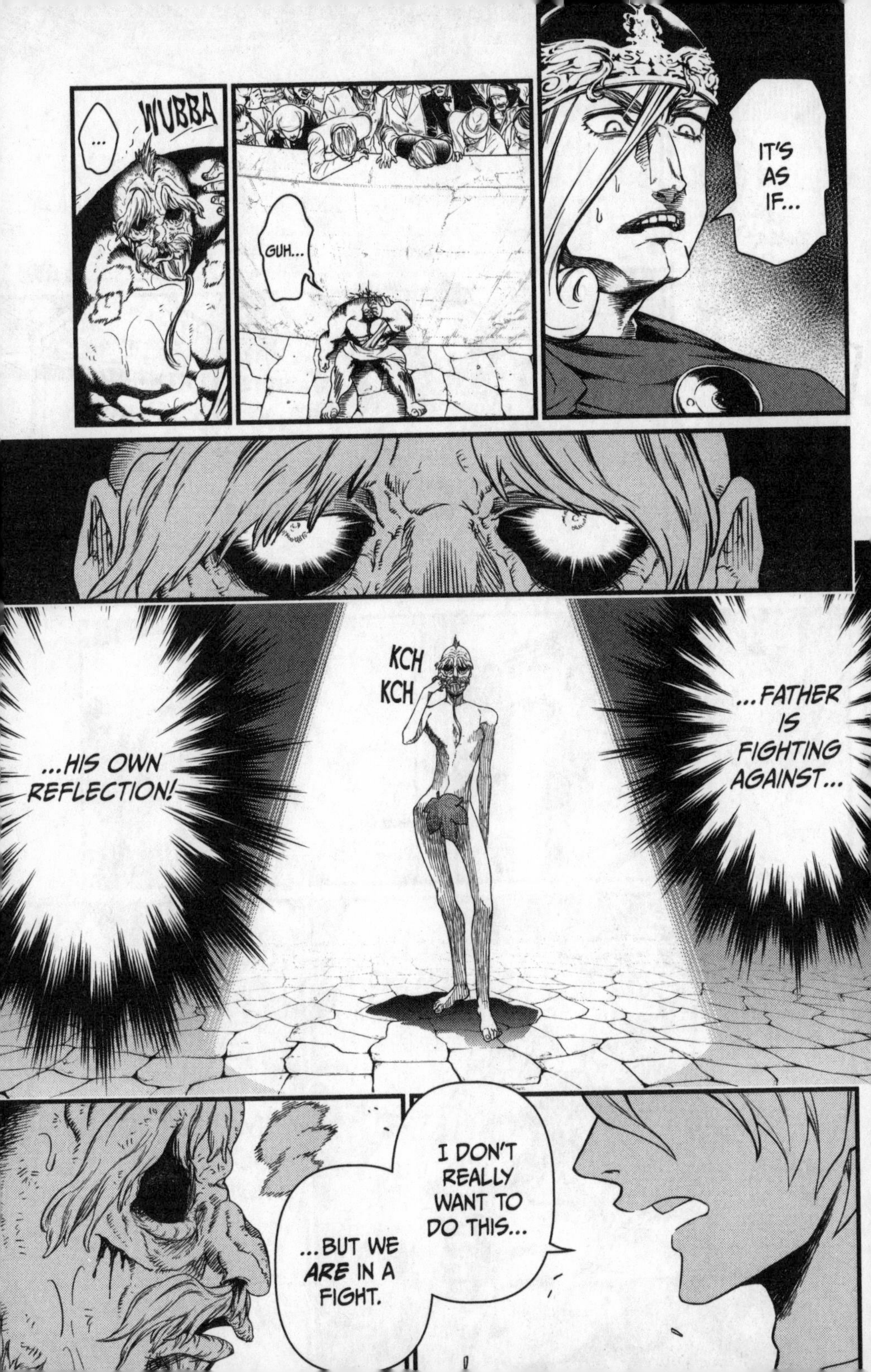
IT'S AS IF...
GUH...
...
WUBBA
...FATHER IS FIGHTING AGAINST...
KCH KCH
...HIS OWN REFLECTION!
I DON'T REALLY WANT TO DO THIS...
...BUT WE ARE IN A FIGHT.

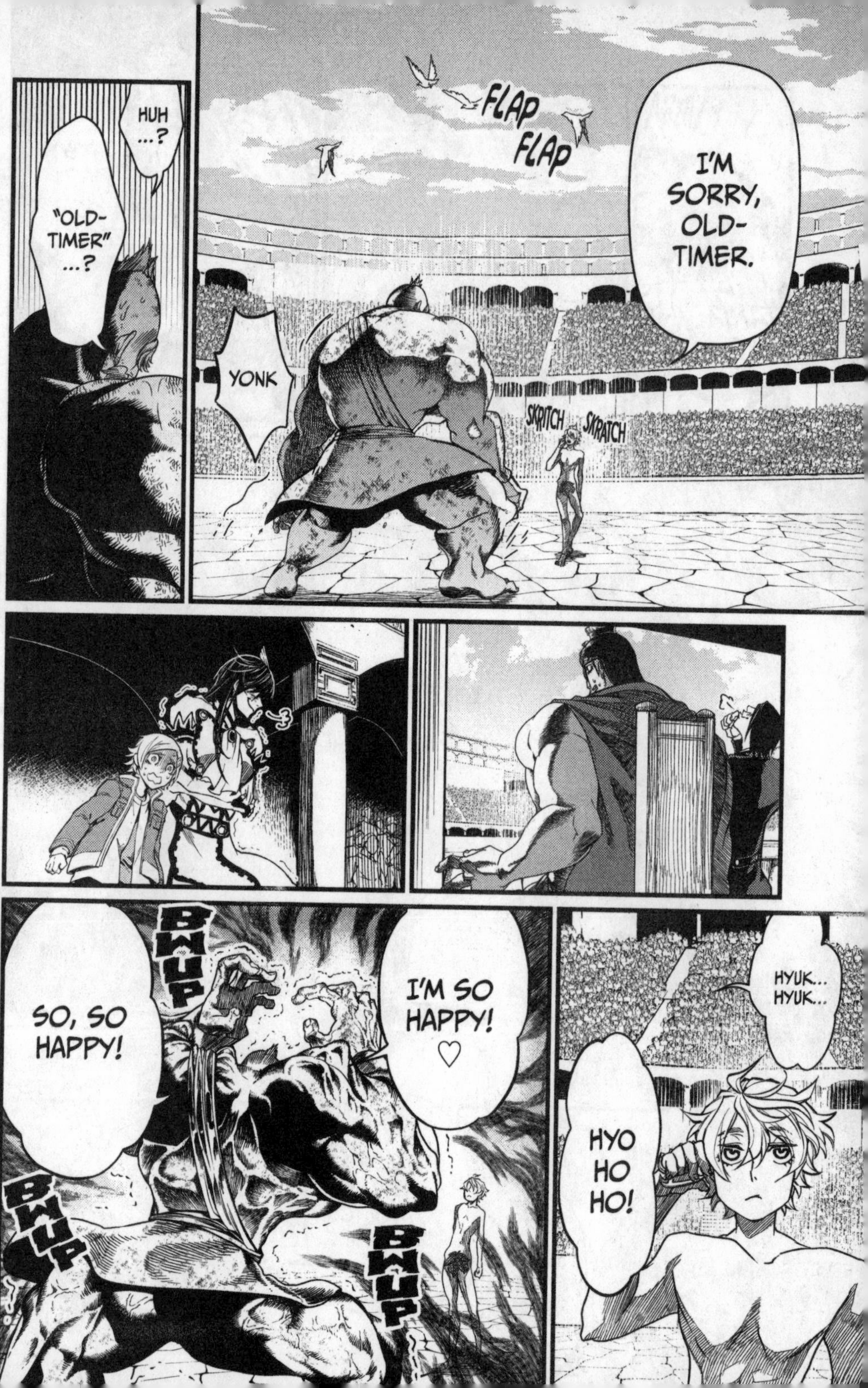
I'M SORRY, OLD-TIMER.
FLAP
FLAP
YONK
SKRITCH
SKRATCH
HUH ...?
"OLD-TIMER" ...?
HYUK... HYUK...
HYO HO HO!
I'M SO HAPPY! ♡
BWUP
SO, SO HAPPY!
BWUP
BWUP

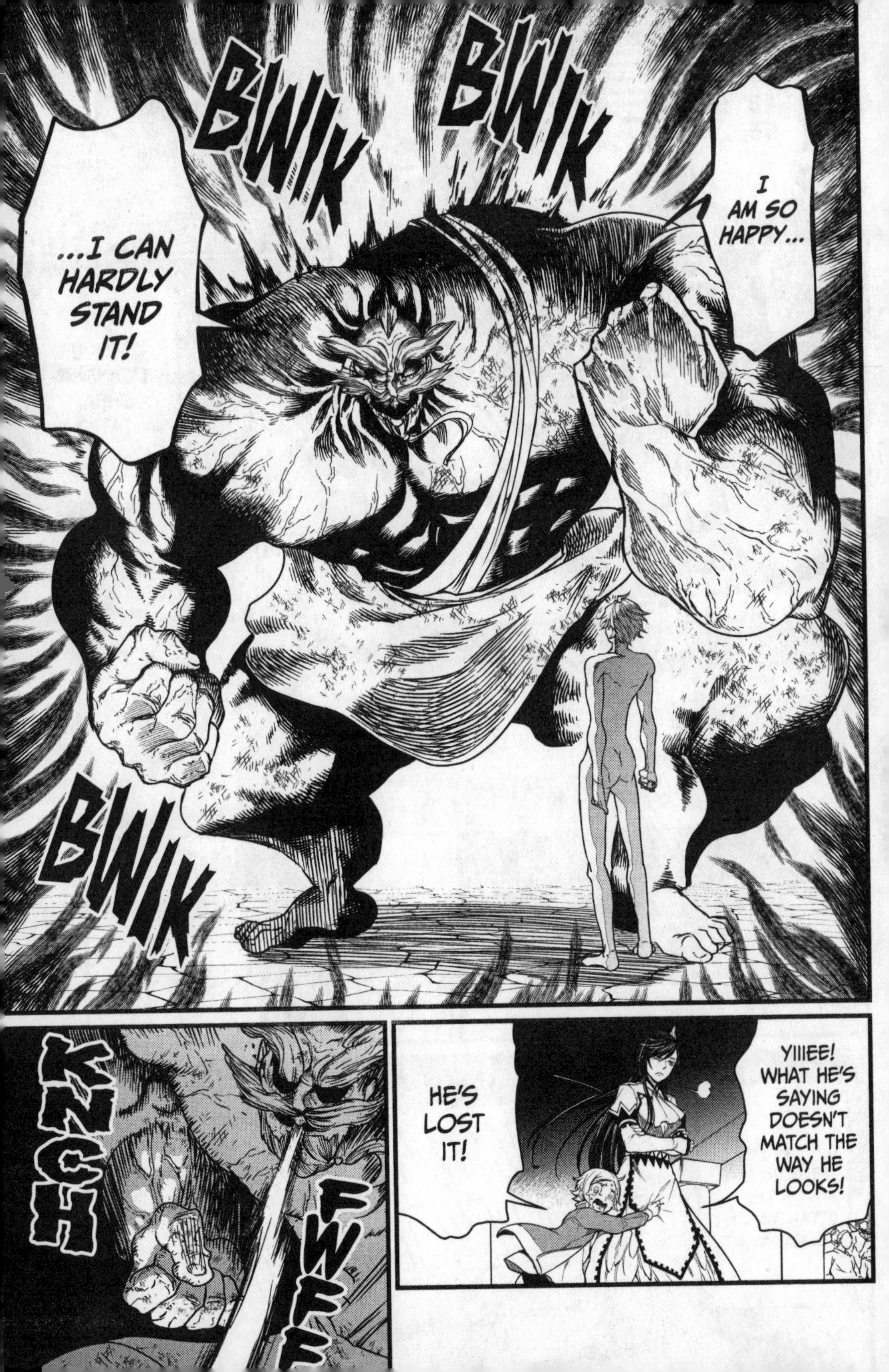
BWIK
BWIK
I AM SO HAPPY...
...I CAN HARDLY STAND IT!
BWIK
YIIIEE! WHAT HE'S SAYING DOESN'T MATCH THE WAY HE LOOKS!
HE'S LOST IT!
KNCH
FWFF

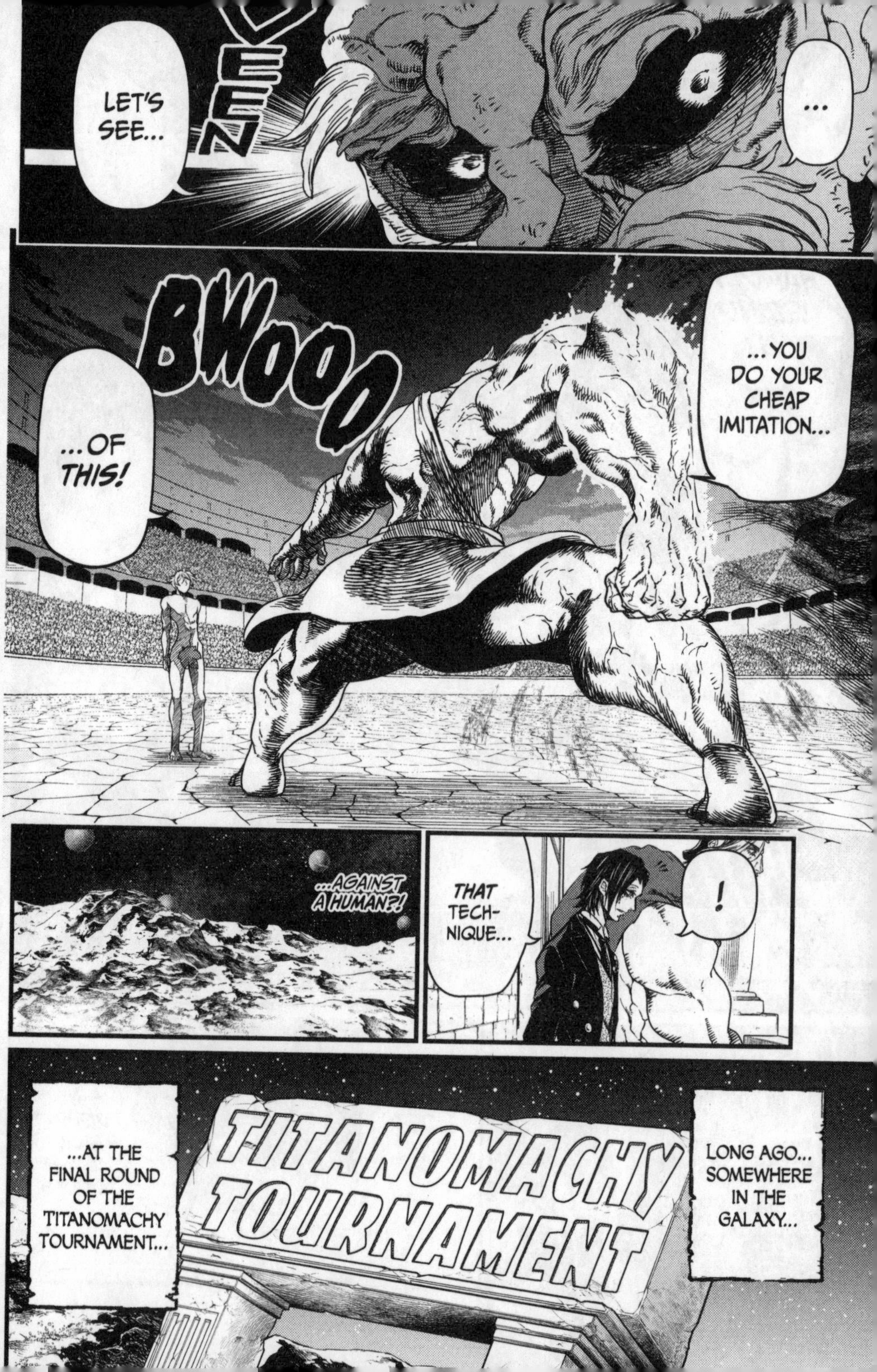
...
LET'S SEE...
...YOU DO YOUR CHEAP IMITATION...
BWOOO
...OF THIS!
!
THAT TECH-NIQUE...
...AGAINST A HUMAN?!
LONG AGO... SOMEWHERE IN THE GALAXY...
TITANOMACHY TOURNAMENT
...AT THE FINAL ROUND OF THE TITANOMACHY TOURNAMENT...

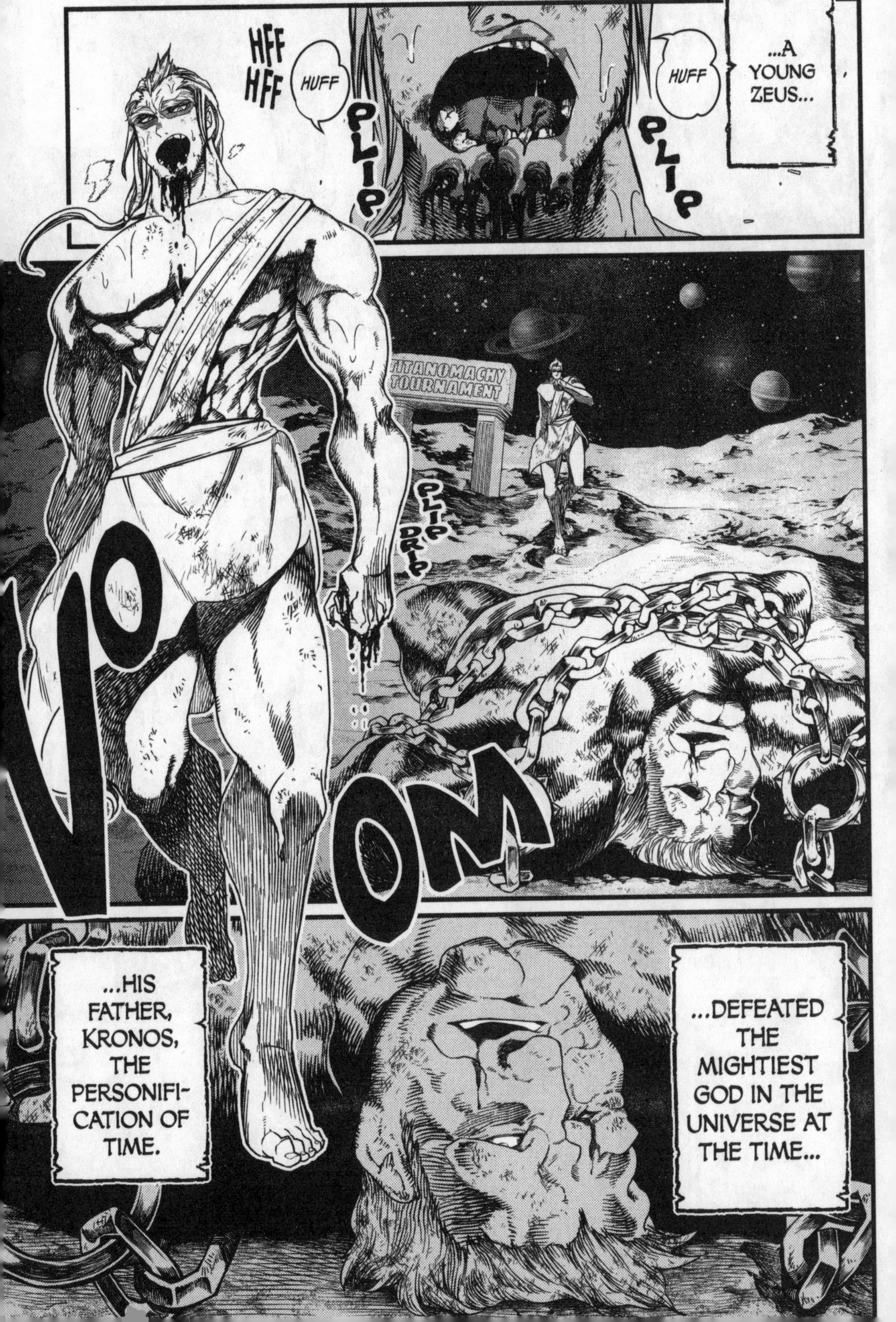
...A YOUNG ZEUS...
HUFF
PLIP
PLIP
HUFF
HFF HFF
TITANOMACHY TOURNAMENT
PLIP
DRIP DRIP
VOOM
...DEFEATED THE MIGHTIEST GOD IN THE UNIVERSE AT THE TIME...
...HIS FATHER, KRONOS, THE PERSONIFICATION OF TIME.

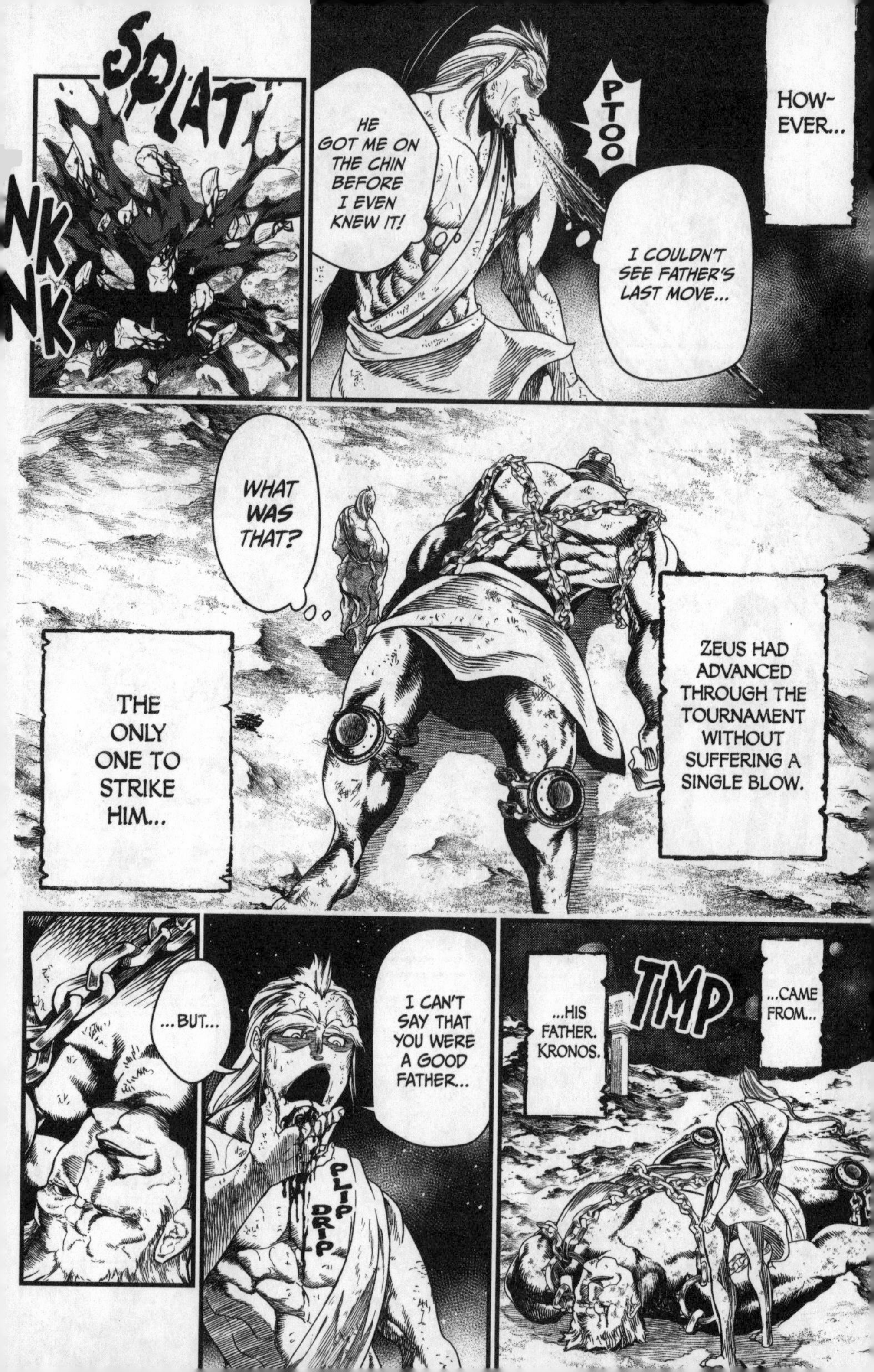
HOW-EVER...
PTOO
HE GOT ME ON THE CHIN BEFORE I EVEN KNEW IT!
I COULDN'T SEE FATHER'S LAST MOVE...
SPLAT
NK
NK
ZEUS HAD ADVANCED THROUGH THE TOURNAMENT WITHOUT SUFFERING A SINGLE BLOW.
WHAT WAS THAT?
THE ONLY ONE TO STRIKE HIM...
...CAME FROM...
TMP
...HIS FATHER. KRONOS.
I CAN'T SAY THAT YOU WERE A GOOD FATHER...
PLIP
DRIP
...BUT...

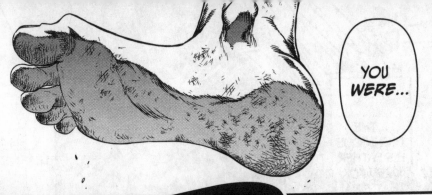

YOU WERE...

...A GREAT WARRIOR!

STOMP

LATER...

DRII

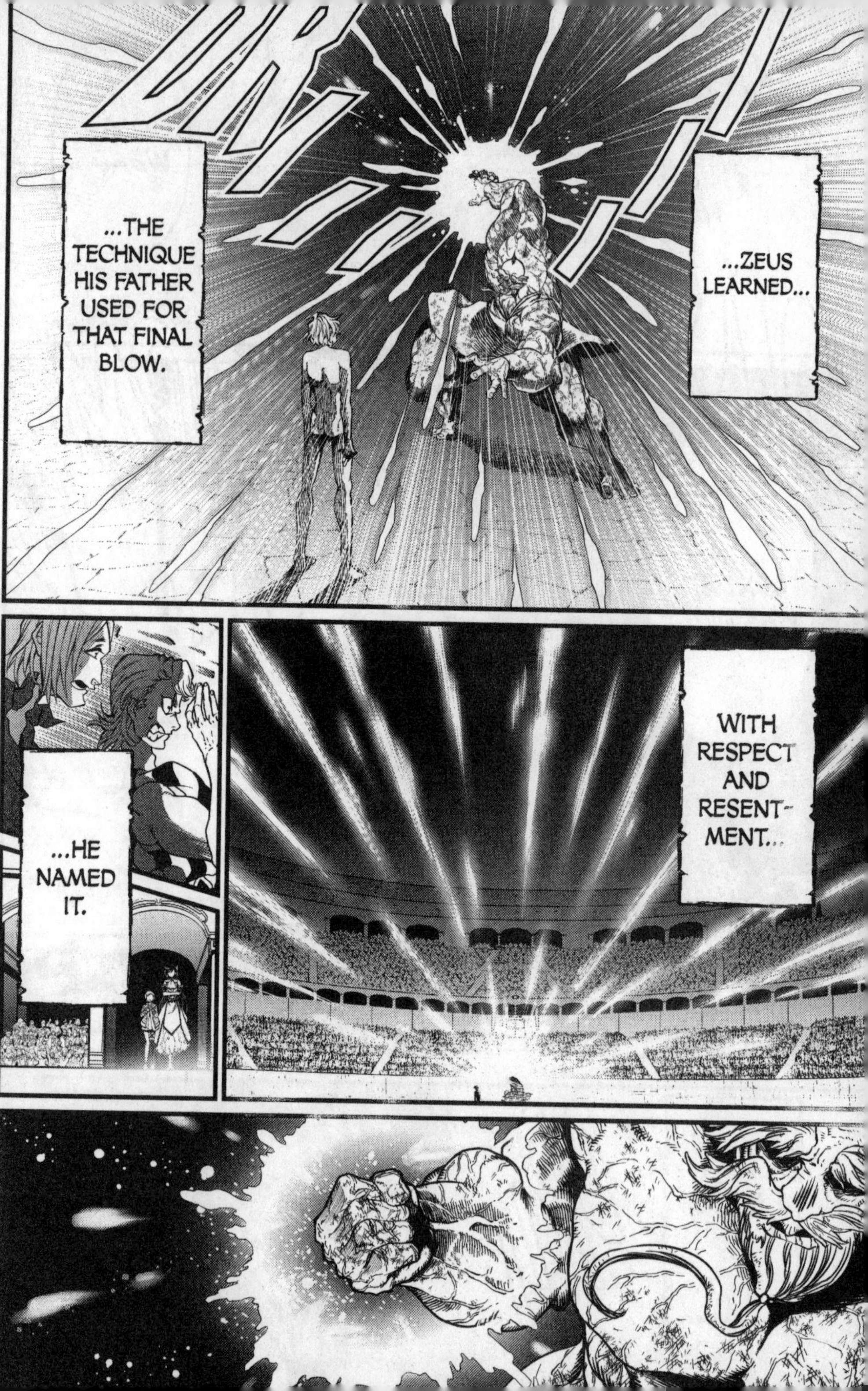
...ZEUS LEARNED...
...THE TECHNIQUE HIS FATHER USED FOR THAT FINAL BLOW.
WITH RESPECT AND RESENT-MENT...
...HE NAMED IT.

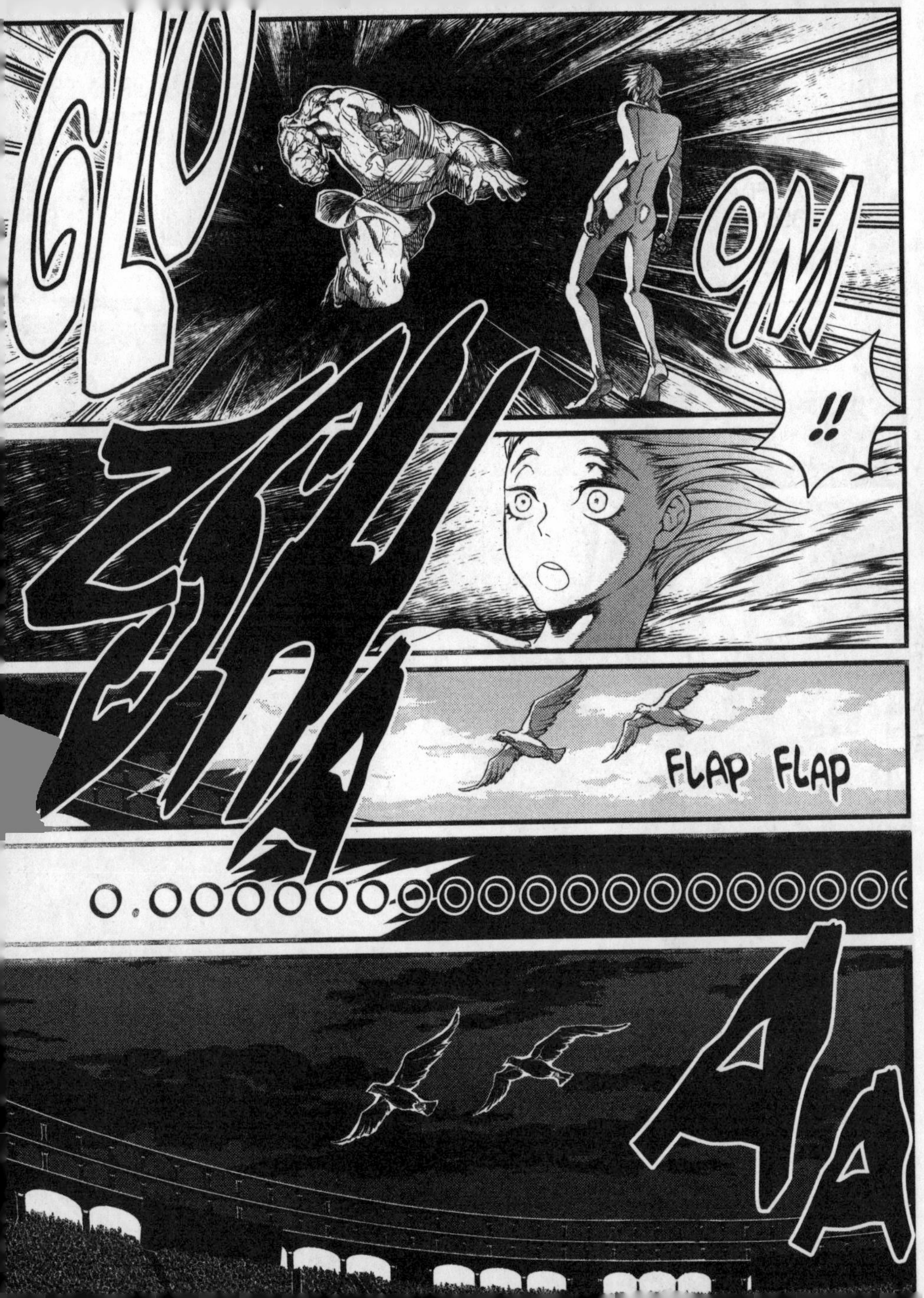
GLO
OM
!!
FLAP FLAP
O.OOOOOOOOOOOOOOOOOOOOOOO
AA

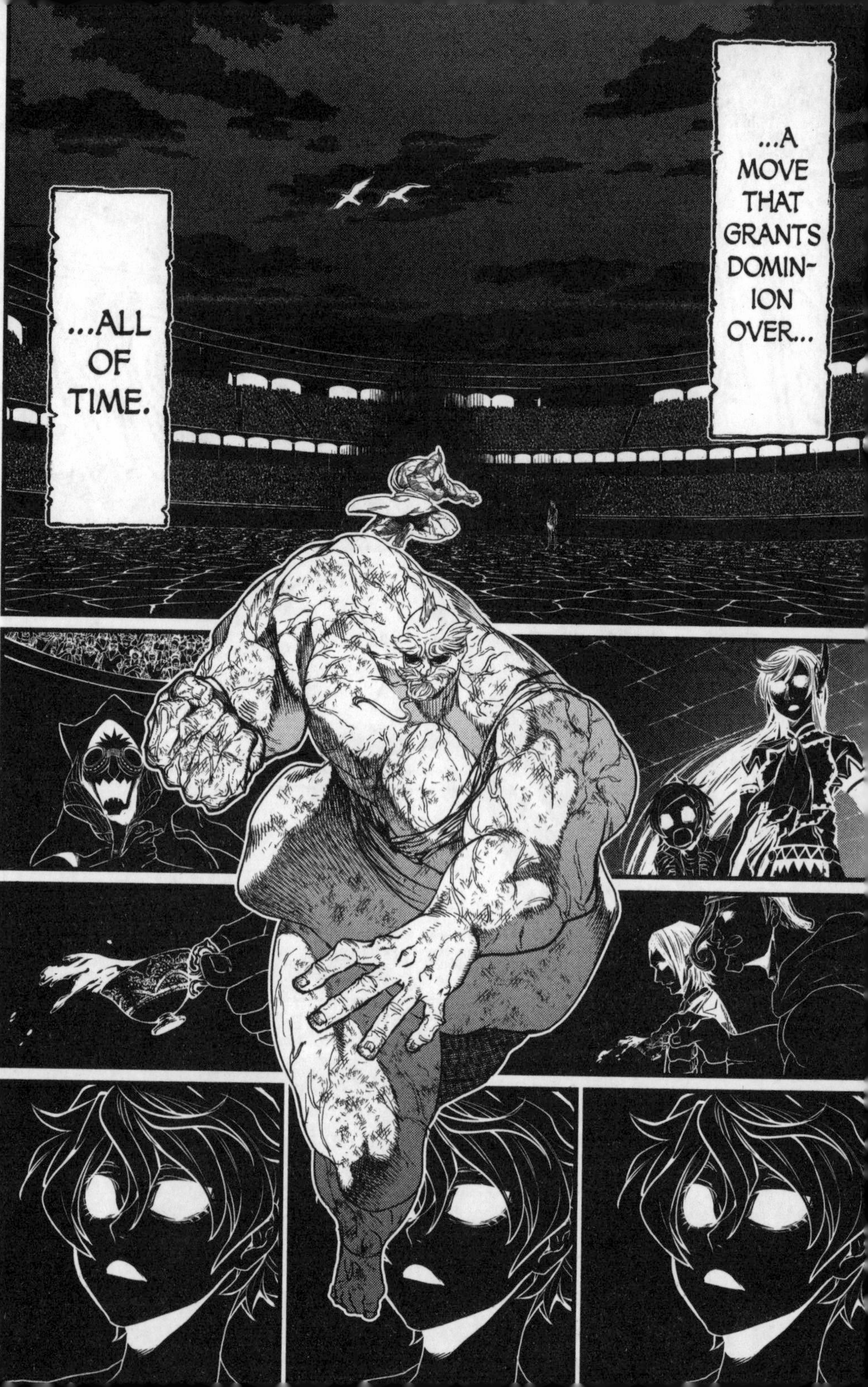
...A MOVE THAT GRANTS DOMIN- ION OVER...
...ALL OF TIME.

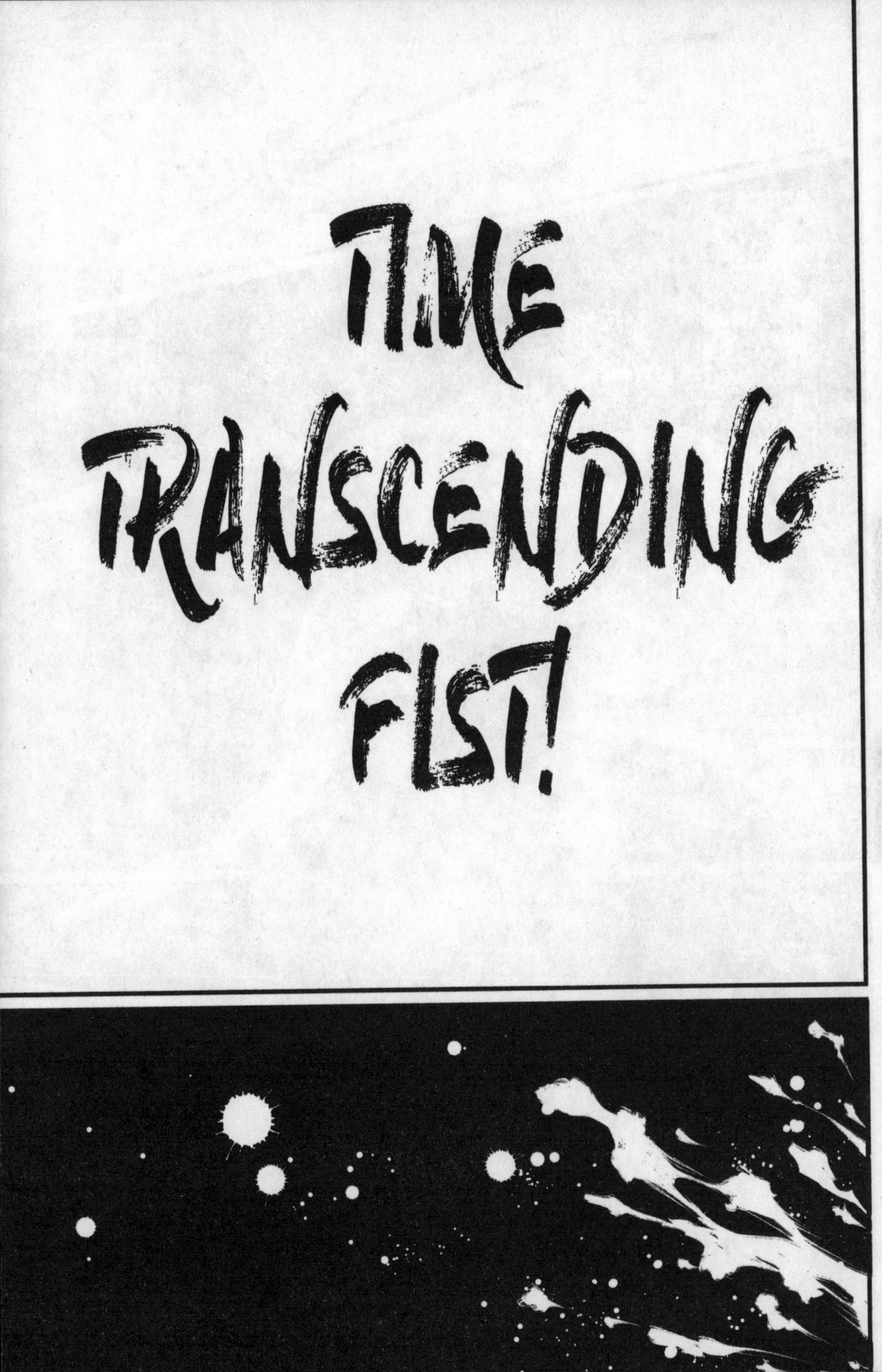

TIME TRANSCENDING FIST!

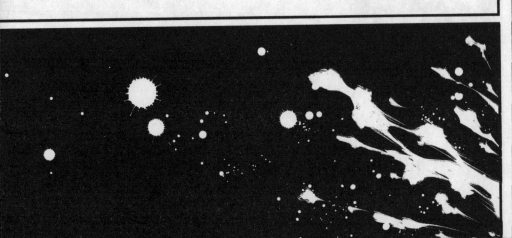

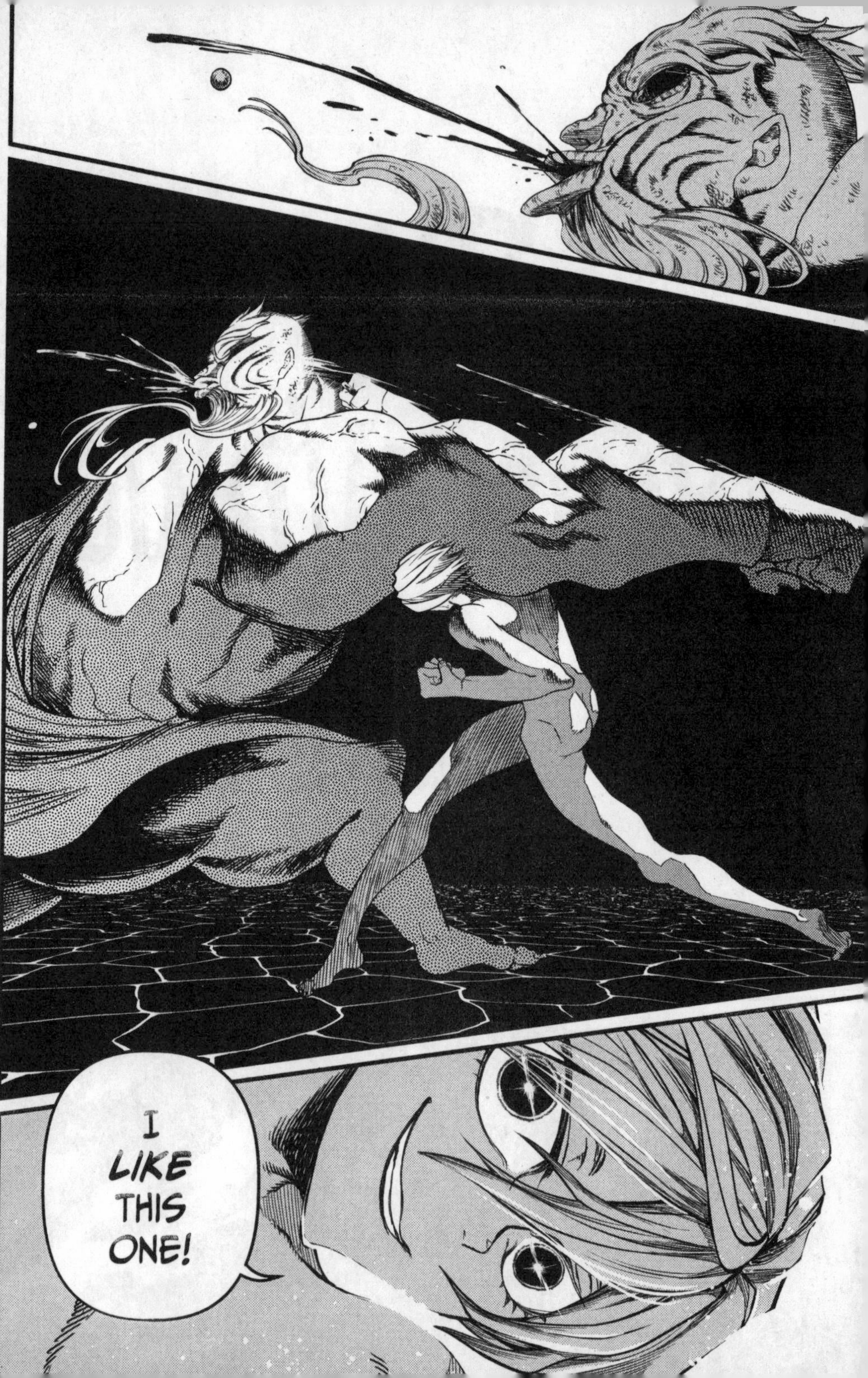
I LIKE THIS ONE!

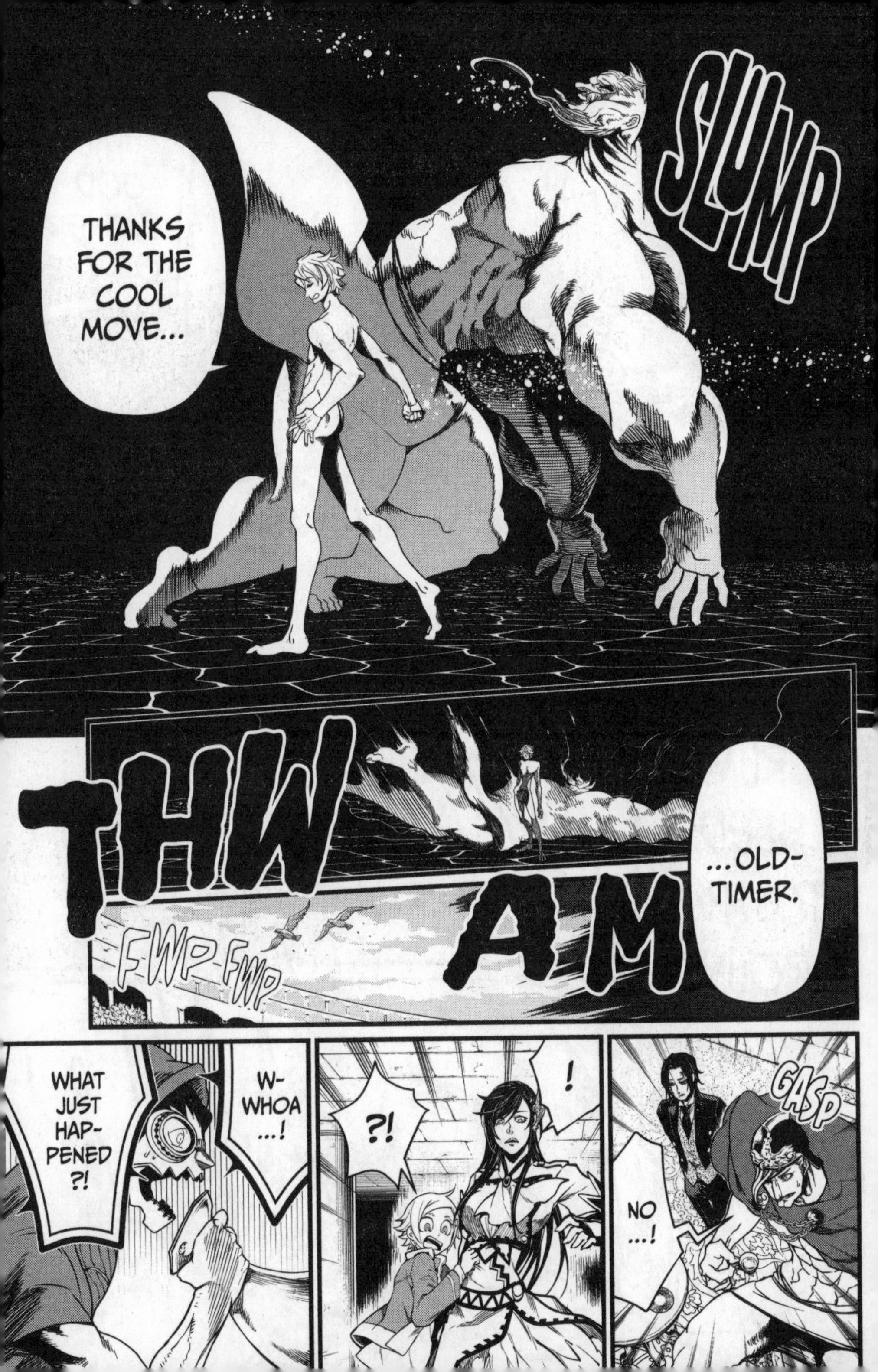
SLUMP
THANKS FOR THE COOL MOVE...
...OLD-TIMER.
THWAM
F-WP-FWP
GASP
NO ...!
!
?!
W-WHOA ...!
WHAT JUST HAP-PENED ?!

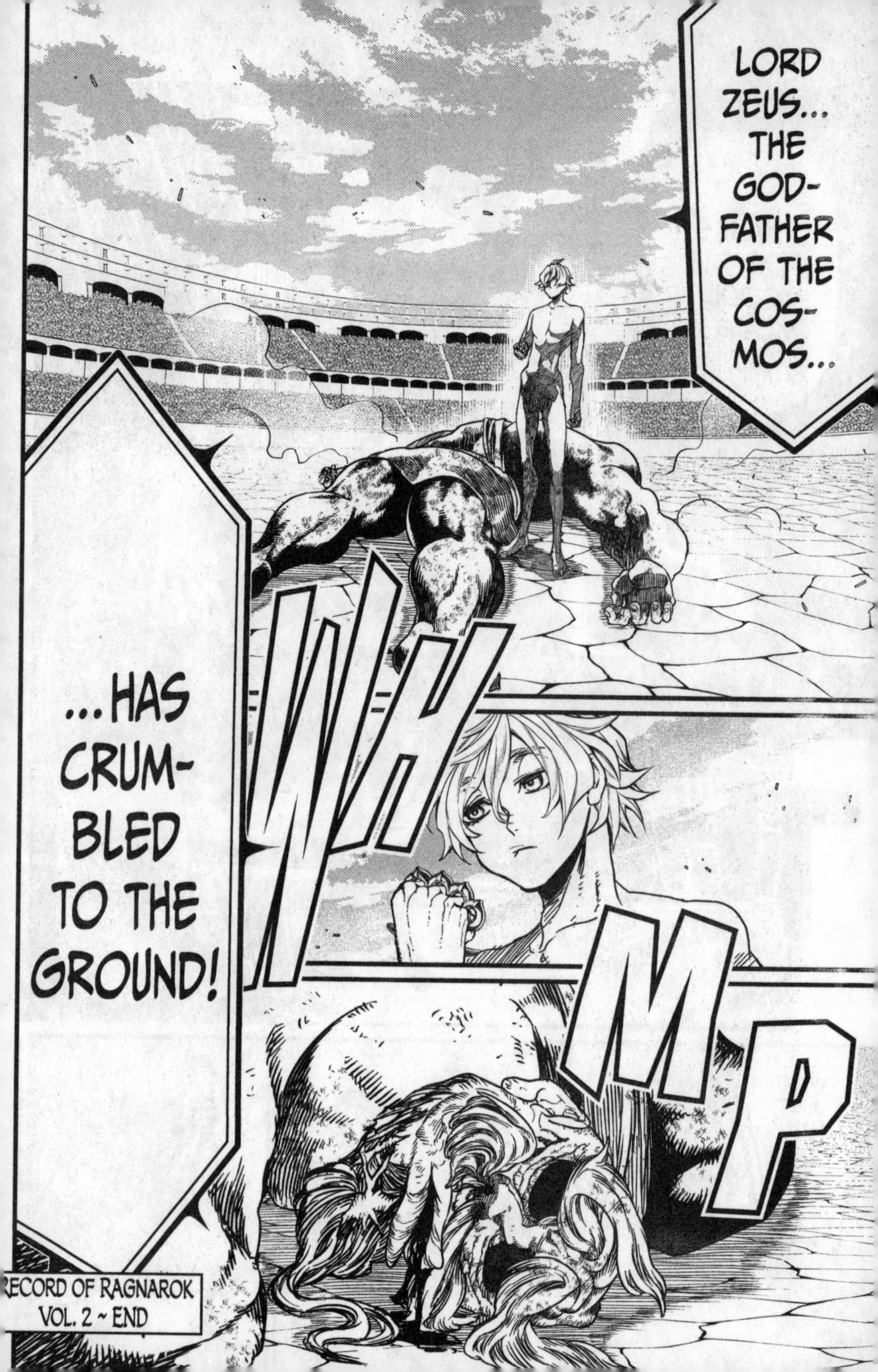
LORD ZEUS... THE GOD-FATHER OF THE COS-MOS...
...HAS CRUM-BLED TO THE GROUND!
WHMP
RECORD OF RAGNAROK VOL. 2 ~ END

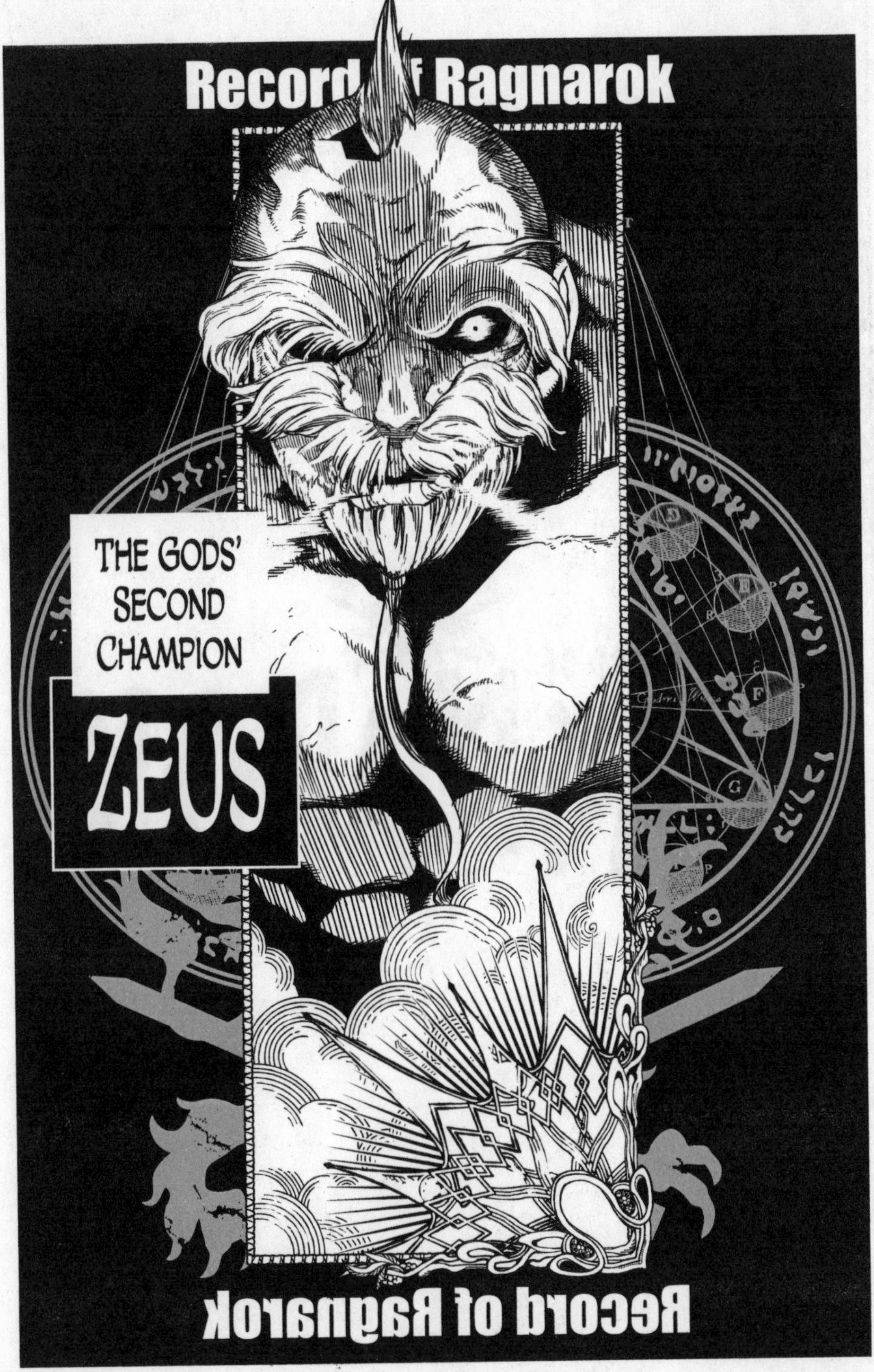
Record of Ragnarok
THE GODS' SECOND CHAMPION
ZEUS
Record of Ragnarok

RECORD OF

RAGNAROK

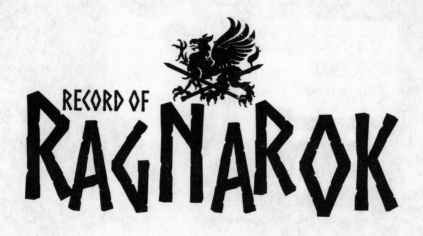

RECORD OF RAGNAROK

VOLUME 2
VIZ Signature Edition

Art by **Azychika**

Story by **Shinya Umemura**

Script by **Takumi Fukui**

Translation / Joe Yamazaki
Touch-Up Art & Lettering / Mark McMurray
Design / Julian (JR) Robinson
Editor / Mike Montesa

Shumatsu no Walkure
©2017 by AZYCHIKA AND SHINYA UMEMURA AND TAKUMI FUKUI/COAMIX
Approved No. ZCW-123W
First Published in Japan in Monthly Comic ZENON by COAMIX, Inc.
English translation rights arranged with COAMIX Inc., Tokyo
through Tuttle-Mori Agency, Inc., Tokyo

Printed in Canada

Published by VIZ Media, LLC
P.O. Box 77010
San Francisco, CA 94107

10 9 8 7 6 5 4 3 2 1
First printing, April 2022

viz.com

vizsignature.com

YOU'RE READING IT
WRONG!

RECORD OF
RAGNAROK

reads right to left starting in the upper-right corner. Japanese is read from right to left, meaning that action, sound effects, and word-balloon order are completely reversed from English order.

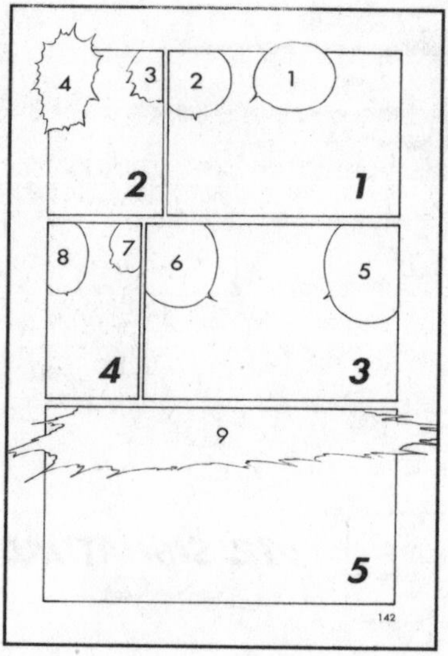
1
2
3
4
1
2
5
6
7
8
3
4
9
5
142

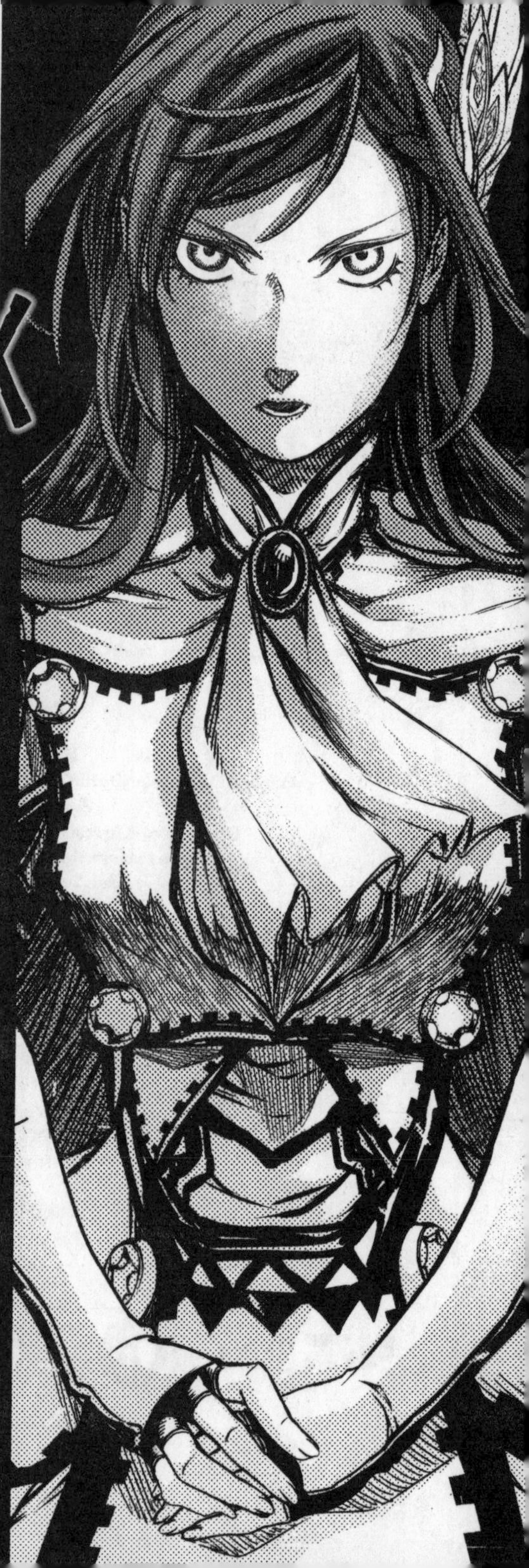